VARNISHED LEAVES

THIS BOOK IS THE PROPERTY OF
MANDER BROTHERS
AND FORMS PART OF THEIR
WORKPEOPLE'S LIBRARY

THE WORKPEOPLE EMPLOYED IN OUR VARIOUS
FACTORIES ARE AT LIBERTY TO TAKE OUT
BOOKS, ONLY ONE BOOK CAN BE WITHDRAWN
AT ONCE AND MAY BE KEPT A REASONABLE
TIME, BUT MUST BE RETURNED, IN ANY CASE,
IMMEDIATELY ON REQUEST OF THE LIBRARIAN

Mander Brothers' bookplate by Robert Anning Bell, 1896

VARNISHED LEAVES

A Biography of the Mander Family of Wolverhampton, 1750-1950

by

Charles Nicholas Mander

The OWLPEN PRESS

MMIV

First published in Great Britain by:
The Owlpen Press
Owlpen Manor, Dursley,
Gloucestershire GL11 5BZ

www.owlpen.com

British Library Cataloguing in Publication Data.
A catalogue record for this book is available from the British Library.

This edition typeset CNM in 11-point Garamond
and printed on acid-free paper
and bound in Great Britain by
J.W. Arrowsmith Ltd., Bristol

ISBN 0-9546056-0-8

IN PATRIS MEMORIAM

VIVE BENE VIVE HODIE MOX TOLLVIT

The Leaves fresh varnisht lively green,
The Blossoms various to be seen.

Joshua Sylvester, *Spectacles*, xxxiii, 1618

As is the generation of leaves, so is that of men.
The wind scatters the leaves on the ground,
but the live wood
Swells with leaves again when spring returns.
So one generation of men will grow
while another passes away.

Iliad, vi, 146

Through all the wood ... the leaves are full of voices.

Ezra Pound, *Cantos*, III

CONTENTS

Preface and Acknowledgements

The Mander papers throw a rich seam which has been quarried and hacked at by several others in the last century or so, with increasing interest as the micro-histories and themes they illustrate have attracted wider analysis, understanding and popularity. They include eighteenth- and nineteenth-century social and company history, the rise of Midland industry, nonconformity, Victorian architecture and philanthropy, liberal ideals and reform, education, imperial wars, country house life. It is an arbitrary slice of life, perhaps, but one revealing vividly the formation of a recognisably modern world.

The first family historian was Gerald Mander, my great uncle, an antiquarian and professional Midland historian who had 'gathered together all that was then known' by 1906. Unfortunately, his working habits could be untidy and he never produced a systematic study, rather a series of sporadic articles in the company journal, *The Green Can*—itself a typically 'Mander' progressive project. These were collected, edited and worthily produced by Sir Geoffrey Mander after his death as *The History of Mander Brothers 1773-1955* (1955), with a few obituary notices and topical items tacked on, so that the result falls short of Gerald's own high standards of scholarship, order and readability. From a vantage point nearly a century ahead of us, he saved and sorted much; in the early chapters I have quoted liberally from his writings, if only to avoid going over the old ground, because they have become scarce, and his prose echoes his inimitable, donnish humour, so disarming on first acquaintance, which is remembered by all who knew him.

In 1972 Philip Mander, Gerald's son, had the good sense to commission a company history in readiness to celebrate the bicentenary of Manders Holdings Limited, as it then was, the following year. Sadly, cousin Philip died that year, aged 57, as the only Mander left on the Board, when the company was by default taken over by a management with little time for history, ideals, or all that the paternalist company had stood for, so it never saw the light of day. I was unaware of this history, an essay rather than a full-scale study, until alerted to it by St. John Brooke-Johnston—officiating rather quaintly as the Lord Mayor of London's Sword-Bearer—who introduced me to its author, Hugh Barty-King. With the author's kind permission, I have again made free use of his text, which is definitive in many respects, bringing the story up to 1972.

But Hugh Barty-King's remains a *company* history, and my own fortune was to find myself sitting on the original archive, as the head of the family apparent and the owner of a largish house where family things tended to accumulate, continuing in a crescendo to the present day. As such, I met the Wightwick archivist, Mark Weaver, who was putting the papers in order there for the National Trust after the death of Rosalie, Lady Mander, in 1988. The Wightwick archive has enriched the interpretation of a great Victorian domestic building, fleshing it out as a sharper, more incisive human story, with its record of upper-middle class life 'giving clues' (writes Anthea Coles) 'to numerous personal human betrayals and abandonments'. They have given rise triumphantly to the book by Patricia Pegg, *A Very Rich Heritage: the Family Papers of Samuel Theodore Mander* (1996), which has spared me the trouble of dwelling on his own short and fruitful life, immortalized vividly a century after his death in the house he built, visited by thousands of curious seekers every year.

My own study began as a collection of lives and letters, with their anecdotes and stories telling of moments of success and failure, or merely recording the passing of seasons, maturing of infants, inevitable sorrows. It has grown as a result of being invited to talk on the family to a number of societies, and being asked constant questions by visitors to Owlpen, whose curiosity may be aroused by seeing the family portraits and clutter of possessions, giving me confidence that All is not Vanity as a futilitarian project, but that there is some enduring interest in aspects of the family story. The section on the architecture of Wightwick is based on one of these talks, forming part of a symposium on *Architecture 1900* held at the Institute of Advanced Architectural Studies at the University of York in May 1997, at which nineteen nationalities were represented. It was published under the editorship of Peter Burman in book form in 1998.

A number of specialist studies have been indispensable. I thank their authors: Stella Blazier on 'The Wolverhampton Chapel Case' (1985); Jane Cooksey on CBM's project for the establishment of the Wolverhampton School of Art in the 1850s; Yvonne Jones on the Midland japanning industry (partly published by the Wolverhampton Art Gallery as a catalogue); and John Ward, on *Blood Money: an incident in Wolverhampton with national consequences* (Wolverhampton Public Libraries, 1988). Other unpublished histories of Manders which I have never seen have apparently been researched by Dr F.W. Stoyle of Bognor, co. Down, and Noel Currier-Briggs, commissioned by Hutchinson Benham in 1969.

I give special gratitude to many friends and members of the wider family who have helped, including particularly: Anthea Coles, Richard Hanbury Tenison, Hilary Jarrey, Daphne Mander, Alan Neame, Peter Nevile, John Osborne, Pippa Thorneycroft and Jill Wallis; also to John Farmer (former

Company Secretary of Manders Holdings Plc), David German (of the Museum of the Staffordshire Yeomanry and the Staffordshire Shievralty Association), Peter Hickman (formerly of Manders), Bev Parker (of the Wolverhampton History and Heritage Society), Stephen Ponder and Monty Smith (both formerly of Wightwick), J.D. Pickles (of the Cambridge University Registry), Sarah Howard (of the Mount Hotel), and Joy Woodall (historian of Lapworth); and to the staffs of the Wolverhampton Central Library and Archives and Local Studies collection, the London Library, the Cambridge University Library, the National Library of Ireland, the Public Records Office, the Dr Williams Library and the William Salt Library, Stafford. In Canada, I am indebted to the patience of Lorena Forbrigger (of the Royal Nova Scotia Historical Society), and Garry Shutlak and Rosemary Barbour (of Nova Scotia Archives and Records Management, Halifax).

To all these, to many predecessors, and above all to my mother, Maria Dolores, with her firm grasp of family history and relationships, to my father, Charles 'the Fifth' Marcus, for allowing me to rummage through and borrow bundles of dusty papers, and to my wife, Karin, for indulgence in her despair as they spilled out of drawers and trunks and boxes, I owe my heartfelt thanks.

FOUNDED IN 1803 BY CHARLES MANDER

MESSRS MANDER BROTHERS request the pleasure of the company of *Miss Mau*

to Dinner at the Drill Hall, on Friday, 18th inst. at 7 p.m. to commemorate the Centenary of the establishment of their House.

WOLVERHAMPTON
DECEMBER 1903.

INTRODUCTION

This study attempts to narrate anecdotes in the public—and, less avidly, the private—lives of the Mander family in the context primarily of their House, the famous firm of Mander Brothers established in 1773, and their altars and homes. The places they lived—or live—in assume a continuity of their own. John Street, resurrected as Mander Square and the Mander Centre, dominates the commercial heart of the Midland city of Wolverhampton; the Perton housing estate ramifies as a full-blown village on the family's farmland outside it; family houses at The Mount, Wightwick (and now Owlpen) are open to the public in one way or another, and all are more or less well known.

The Mander family, from sturdy origins as farmers on the Warwickshire/Worcestershire borders, where they had settled as prosperous yeomen without achieving fame or distinction since the thirteenth century, entered the vanguard of the early industrial expansion of Wolverhampton, as entrepreneurs, city fathers and philanthropists. Thomas Mander, a younger son, had migrated to Wolverhampton, then a market town of 7,500 people, in about 1742. He inherited property in John Street which became, just over two hundred years later, the Mander Centre.

Already by the early 1770s, Benjamin and John, his sons, were active as industrialists, setting up a cluster of loosely-integrated businesses, including a large chemical manufacturing works mainly supplying chemicals and pigments for the local metal-bashing, pottery and japanning industries, and later a varnish works. They also had interests in widely-ranging businesses from baking, japanning and tin-plate working, to canals and gas manufacture. The japanning works was sold in 1840, but the more industrial varnish side of the business expanded, to be formed as a partnership known as Mander Brothers in 1845.

This was to prosper through the nineteenth century as a progressive company, establishing a paint and colour works by 1865 and then a printing ink division, with branches first in London, and soon in Paris, Florence, Vienna and Berlin, and agencies throughout the 'enlightened countries of the world'. By late Victorian/Edwardian times, as the applications of their products multiplied with the industrial revolution, Mander Brothers was established a household word, the subject of *Punch* cartoons, and the Number One producer of paints and varnishes, when a few microns of their coatings gave a gloss to a fair share of the vast range of products that were being churned out by the biggest Empire and industrial power in the world. A myriad surfaces every day left their factories enamelled in an opaque and glossy leaf of Manders 'black japan'.

From the outset, as successful trades people, the family espoused many local causes. They were noted nonconformists, grave and earnest, but always progressive and public spirited, and became champions in their small way of the religious and social reforms of the early nineteenth century. They financed prolonged litigation personally—one Chancery suit dragged on for 32 years—lobbied for reform in the criminal code, campaigned against the slave trade, involved themselves wholeheartedly in philanthropic initiatives and civic affairs, four of them standing at the same time among the first commissioners of the Georgian borough, and helped to found free libraries, chapels and schools. As they prospered, they joined the leisured and estated county gentry, and served as mayors and aldermen, high sheriffs, deputy lieutenants and magistrates, as officers in the yeomanry and eventually in national government.

It was an age of confident and powerful city governments in the heyday of the industrial city, when public life was a fashionable pursuit, and England's great new trading cities, businesses—and by definition families—were seen as the dynamos which powered the Empire to international pre-eminence. They had fingers in many pies, becoming involved in a wide variety of charities and in the manifold affairs of the wider county; also one of the biggest employers in a thriving manufacturing town. They became typical examples of the high-minded liberal, with a strong belief in public service and sense of social duty. As such, they were at the centre of a network of connections by marriage and association with a small group of local families who formed, for 150 years, the patriciate of Wolverhampton. At times they must have seemed to contemporaries like the puissant satraps of Xerxes, only more benign. Charles Tertius (the third) Mander was made a baronet for his public services in the Coronation honours of George V in 1911. An older correspondent, visiting Owlpen, recalls at the moment of writing: 'the name Mander meant so much to the Midlands—they were great benefactors'.

From the late nineteenth century, they married increasingly outside the local nexus, from British North America to Imperial India. Apart from two maharajah's daughters, 'descended from a god by a maiden', they intermarried with half a dozen other titled families; several were baronetcies similarly deriving from newer industrial and commercial wealth, as such families came to define their settled stratum in Victorian society.[1] This is a

[1] From the late nineteenth century, Miss Manders married into the families of Hickman (Staffordshire baronetcy from Midlands ironworking); Phillips (baronetcy from South African diamonds); Guinness (baronetcy from Irish banking); Loder (baronetcy, and later peerage, from the Russian trade); Vaughan of Trawscoed (Lisburne barony from Welsh politics); and Hoare (baronetcy from City banking). On the 'brewer' Neame side, are Wrightson (baronetcy from co. Durham engineering) and Broughton (Fairhaven barony, and baronetcy from American railways). On the Hargreaves side, are the Wolseleys (another Staffordshire baronetcy). Some of these were of earnest, low church background in the early nineteenth century. Many in due course acquired notable houses or gardens, including: Hale Park (Hickman), Tylney Hall (Phillips), High Beeches and Wakehurst (Loder), Stourhead (Hoare) and Anglesey Abbey (Broughton).

biography of their varnished lives, not a technical genealogical study sustained by the patient antiquarian delving of a Gerald Mander. The genealogy is confined largely to the footnotes and appendices, and little documentary research outside such family books and papers as have rather randomly come down to me has been attempted.

Living in the same large houses for successive generations, the family were remarkable for never throwing anything (much) away, and so accumulating a rich and haphazard archive. Mander papers, including diaries, letters, notes and publications (some 150 items are listed), as well as watercolour sketches, well-kept press-cuttings books of their public lives, photographs and ephemera, give a well-documented history of their careers as pioneer manufacturers, merchant industrialists and public figures with wide-ranging interests and social contacts over seven or eight generations, against the background of the emergence of modern Britain.

They contributed not only to stolid industry and public life: they produced a modest quota of soldiers, antiquarian scholars, artists and writers of distinction, gentleman farmers, a suffragist and Irish nationalist, even a stray Hollywood actor who married an Indian princess—whose tales are briefly touched on here. Invariably, they were cultivated and well read, with opportunities for foreign travel, friendships and marriages; and art patronage.

The family were responsible for building two great Victorian houses. Wightwick Manor was built by the architect Edward Ould for Theodore Mander in 1889-93. In a sixteenth-century picturesque, half-timbered style of exquisite workmanship and detailing, and with its richly-textured surfaces of stained glass, tiles, plaster and metalwork, and William Morris furnishings and textiles, it is the ideal of the 'Ould English' house. The collections were extended by his son, the radical MP Sir Geoffrey Mander, to include pre-Raphaelite and late Romantic paintings and literary manuscripts. It is now preserved as one of England's most representative late Victorian houses, given by the family to the National Trust in 1937 as the first country house presented during the lifetime of its donor.

The Mount was also completed by Ould in two phases, but most successfully in the more splendid 'English Renaissance' style of 1909. It was a lighter, more visible house, visited by many public figures of the day. It is today a hotel with 56 bedrooms. Many of its collections survive at Owlpen, described in the projected second volume, a romantic Tudor manor house open to the public, which was saved from ruin in 1926. Today it contains collections of works by the Cotswold Group of artist-craftsmen, including Ernest Gimson, Ernest and Sidney Barnsley, Norman Jewson and their followers. The stories of the three contrasting houses illustrate successive themes of the Arts and Crafts movement, and their patrons' interaction with the industry which made such houses possible.

Manders Plc remained based in Wolverhampton, the town—at the millennium raised to the rank of a city—where it was established, into its third century, with interests in paint (or 'coatings'), property and printing inks. The successful mini-conglomerate was broken up in the 1990s by a career management no longer involved with the family or the town. First the paint and property businesses were stripped out in 1994. Finally, after 225 years, the core business, by then an international company developing the higher-technology activities of 'speciality chemicals', with particular emphasis on printing inks, was sold for £100 million in 1997 to Flint Ink of Detroit, in the United States, so ending a long chapter in the British chemicals industry. The Mander brands survived a little longer as dominant players in the global coatings and decorative paints industries, when Manders Premier established itself in the late 1990s as one of the world's largest suppliers of coatings and inks.

It will become clear that 'Charles Mander', the author of the title, refers to seven generations in successive metempsychoses. I have often let my forebears speak for themselves, quoting verbatim and seriatim from the fragments they have left. The succession of Charleses is distinguished with a kingly pretension by numbers, of whom I would be Sixtus, the sixth of the name; and the seventh, Charles Septimus, is an heir more real than apparent.

This book ramified in the telling, as I found myself adding something of the living generations of Charleses, and then sideways connections into the distaff side of the family. The result became increasingly unwieldy for a single book, so it sees the light as the first of two volumes, taking the story up to about 1951-3. It was a natural break, when the house at The Mount was sold, and the deaths of four family members occurred: Charles Arthur, Gerald Poynton, Howard Vivian and, aged 92, of Mary le Mesurier.

Although the foundation year of the business has long been taken as 1773, the year 2003 marks exactly 200 years since Charles Mander the First began his varnish-making operations in John Street which were to prove so successful and durable. Gunmetal medals, with the openwork monogram 'MB' for Mander Brothers, were struck in 1903 as part of the celebrations to mark the centenary. A century later, it is likely that this book will be the only commemoration.

Owlpen
Christmas 2003

EARLY YEARS

1

EARLY YEARS
in Shakespeare's Warwickshire

The family of Mander (or Maunder) was settled at Tredington, Warwickshire,[1] a Cotswold village of rich ochre stone in the English Midlands, by the end of the thirteenth century. Johannes Maundwer was a villein who held half a virgate of land there (say, 17 acres) in the time of Pope Nicholas IV (*circa* 1291).[2] The early record[3] is confusing, and the trail goes to ground in a thicket of recurrent Christian names and migrations around a group of villages on the Warwickshire and Worcestershire borders.

We know that William and Matilda Mander, of the hamlet of Armscote in the same parish, married in 1494/5, when they paid one mark for their marriage licence to the Guild of the Holy Cross in Stratford-upon-Avon.[4] A line of three further generations, probably deriving from them, were prosperous yeomen at farms around Tredington: John of Blackwell (1518-1587), William (1543-1622) and Richard (1575/6-1629), whose will was proved at £384 4*d.*[5]

The Guild House at Aston Cantlow, needlework by Daisy Mander, 1922

The Staffordshire branch of the family traces its descent from one Henry Mander (1601-1672), Richard's eldest son. Henry married Anne Wheigham of Aston Cantlow, on the edge of the Forest of Arden, seven miles northwest of Stratford-upon-Avon, in 1636. The wedding was in the same church where, according to tradition, Shakespeare's parents had been married some 80 years before. The poet's mother, Anne, daughter of Robert Arden, came from the hamlet of Wilmcote, on a ridge of grassy land above Aston Cantlow. The Manders were part of a network of connected yeoman families in this heart of Shakespeare's Warwickshire. The genealogists tell us that Anne Wheigham was related to George Gibbes, son-in-law of Katherine Arden Edkins, who owned in the 1590s the house now known as 'Mary Arden's House', where Shakespeare's mother was born about 1540.[6]

Henry soon moved from Tredington to his wife's village of Aston Cantlow, where he became a responsible citizen as constable and churchwarden. They left eight sons, as well as a sizeable estate,[7] and their descendants remained in the village till 1828, farming and running a water-powered paper mill. A descendant, Charles Tertius Mander, by then a munificent industrialist, became lord of the manor in 1918, when he bought and restored the old half-timbered guild hall for the use of the villagers; it is probably that of the Guild of St Mary first recorded in 1442.

By 1675 Henry and Anne's fifth son, Samuel (1648-1716), had moved to settle at Ireland's Farm,[8] Lapworth, near Henley-in-Arden, six miles north. The farm, at 150 acres, was one of the biggest in the parish, set in the heart of the Forest of Arden, on the edge of the old enclosed hunting park of the manor of Lapworth. The house stood on the site of the old fourteenth-century manor house of Sir John de Bishopsdon.[9] In the sixteenth century it is still referred to as 'Lapworth Hall, commonly called Ireland's Farm', after the tenant Robert Ireland (*d.* 1590) who rebuilt it at that time. But by Samuel's time the house was reduced to a farmhouse. The Mander family was to occupy Ireland's Farm 'from father to son for fully 200 years'.

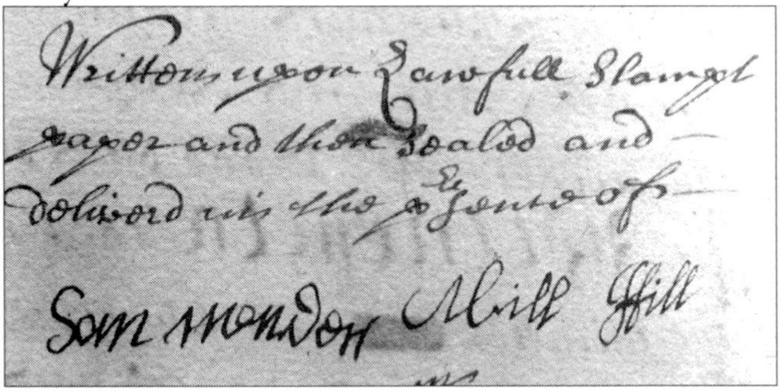

Samuel Mander's signature [detail], circa 1690

Ireland's Farm, sketch by George Busby, showing front (?)rebuilt 1820 and the older back premises with kitchen, dairy and service rooms of Samuel and then Robert Mander. Ireland's was the original manor house of Lapworth.

Samuel married Mary, daughter of Thomas Shakespeare of the next door parish of Rowington, at the epicentre of the Shakespeare surname in sixteenth- and seventeenth-century Warwickshire.[10] The early records are famously sparse, but Thomas almost certainly sprang not many generations back from the same stock as the Bard, and it would be appealing to fancy that a few common genes filtered through to give literary animus to his successors.[11] We know William Shakespeare the poet was keen to preserve connections with Rowington, twelve miles north of Stratford, acquiring a copyhold with a cottage and garden there in 1602.

Samuel and Mary's son, Robert (1681-1749), married Catherine, daughter of John Cotterell of Bushwood Hall, the next door farm. In due course, the Manders took over the tenancy of this farm as well. It was a moated farmstead, in early times forming a separate manor of the Bishops of Worcester (hence the name, 'Bishop's Wood'). It was the Lapworth seat of the Catesbys on an estate which they had acquired in the 1480s. As such, it was thought of by the historian Sir William Dugdale as the manor house of Lapworth. He describes Sir William Catesby as 'residing much at Bushwood'. His house substantially survives, with timber framing.

The Catesby family was one of a tight-knit group of South Warwickshire gentry families who struggled to retain the old religion.

Under Sir William Catesby, Bushwood was a hotbed of Catholicism, where the brilliant Jesuit martyr Edmund Campion had preached in 1581, resulting in Catesby's imprisonment. William Shakespeare—'the papist', as the antiquary Aubrey called him—may have been among his listeners. For recent scholarship suggests that this was the circle from which he left Stratford to join a cultivated household at Hoghton in Lancashire.[12] And it was reputedly at Bushwood Hall that Sir William's son, Robert Catesby, the instigator of the Gunpowder Plot, was born in 1573.[13] From then on the Catesbys were beggared by recusancy fines which had forced the sale of Lapworth by about 1602 (together with their Oxfordshire estate at Chastleton).

Robert and Catherine Mander had a large family, and evidently not enough land to set up all their growing tribe of sons. They were tenants of Sir Lister Holte, of Aston Hall, near Birmingham, and were falling into arrears with their rents (£104 per year for Ireland's) in the 1730s and '40s, with the decline in corn prices. By 1753 the family had repaid the arrears, and their second son, also Robert, was a large farmer, tenant of the three farms adjoining in Lapworth: Ireland's, Bushwood Hall and Mill Farm.

It was their fifth son, Thomas Mander (1720-1764), who, in about 1742 emigrated north again, to Wolverhampton, then a prosperous market and manufacturing town of 7,454 inhabitants and 1,440 houses (according to Isaac Taylor). Leafy with gardens, he could not have known that it was poised to enter the industrial revolution and to become the chief town of the 'Black Country', and the thirteenth largest town in Britain.

Haymaking outside Wolverhampton by T. Pitt, 1796, with St John's to right

In due course Thomas set up in trade as a merchant, and we hear of him as a baker and maltster, on the fringes of the brewing trade.[14] He married Elizabeth, daughter of one Samuel Clemson (1683-1741), a currier from Bridgnorth. When Samuel died, he left to Thomas family property at 48 John's Lane (later John Street), Wolverhampton, which had been in the Clemson family since the seventeenth century. The property gives a backbone of continuity to this story: in all, as we shall see, six generations of the family were born there.

The John Street house had been looted by a Tory mob of Jacobite rioters—described as 'a Gang of Ragamuffins, Pick-Pockets and Gaol Birds' —in June 1715, when they ransacked the Presbyterian chapel—known as the old meeting-house—next door. The damage to the chapel was assessed by a government commission at £254 16*s.* 2*d.*; while that to Samuel Clemson's house was also considerable:

> Samuel Clemson, of [Wolverhampton], currier, aged 33, deposed that on 11 July, 1715, a great number of rioters attacked his house, being his inheritance, broke the windows, flung great stones and pieces of timber into the house, threw down the pewter from the shelves, wounded and bruised the deponent and his wife, and threatened his life so that he was forced to keep a number of armed men in the house for a fortnight. Damages were estimated at £20.[15]

Gerald Mander, historian of the family, the company and the town, remarks: 'Why Samuel Clemson should have been singled out for special treatment is a matter for conjecture: perhaps he was particularly odious, perhaps less able to command protection. His property suffered depreciation; but his sentiments lived again in his descendants, who (if truth be told) have vexed the town not a little and continue unto the present day.'[16]

The meeting house had been built in 1701 'for the worship and service of God, without any restriction as to points of doctrine'. Gerald writes of it:[17]

> It did not stand unscarred and in peace and quiet, but rather became a centre of storm and resistance... Nonconformity as expressed by the Independents was still represented by a tiny body of people who worshipped in the small chapel in John's Lane; they bore the brunt of the attack by the mob in 1715 and, although much damaged, survived it. The authorities were faced with a very heavy bill for restitution and it was to prevent disturbances of this kind in future that the Riot Act was passed into law.
>
> Only the body of the Meeting House seems to have survived and in due course it was restored to something of its former glory at the expense of the taxpayer. At this time the congregation numbered about 400 and the cause flourished. In 1720 John Scott gave an acre of land towards the endowment, and the Presbyterian Fund in London gave about five or six pounds a year towards the stipend of the minister.

In due course, the site of the meeting-house was added to other John Street land owned by the family to become the nucleus of landholdings in Wolverhampton which form the Mander Shopping Centre today, a Wolverhampton landmark. Thomas died on 3 October 1774 and is buried in the family vault in the churchyard of St Peter's Collegiate Church in Wolverhampton, the first of a score or so of Manders to be buried there.[18]

The Thomas Manders had two sons, Benjamin, born in 1752, and John, in 1754. They both became industrialists in different, but related, trades.

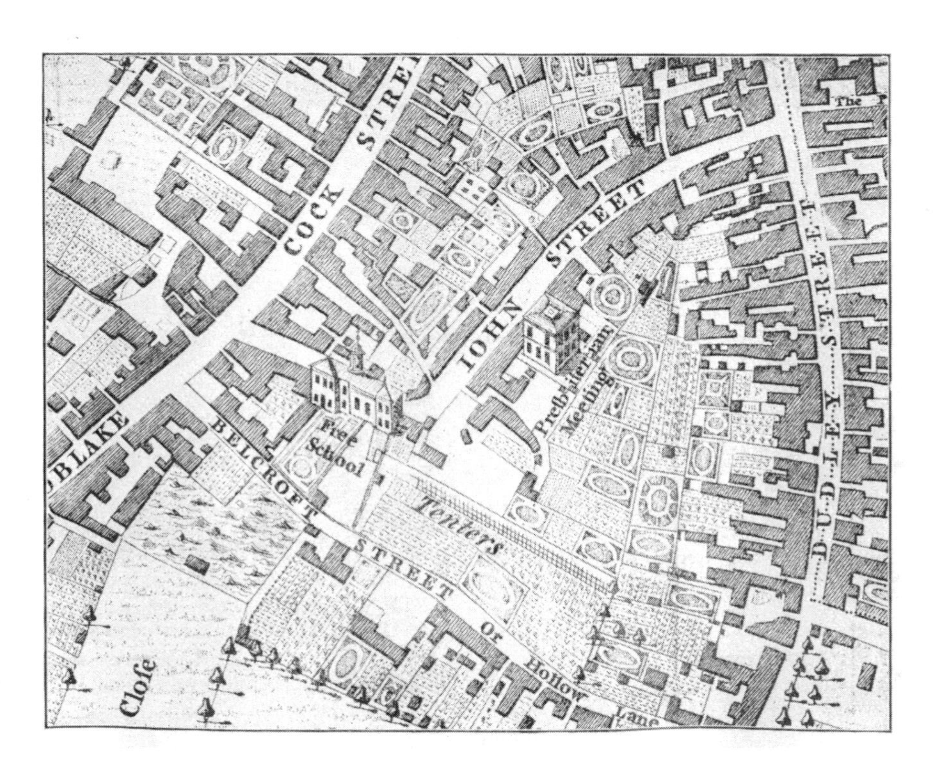

The land around John Street, with meeting house, from Isaac Taylor's map of Wolverhampton, 1750

[1] Traditionally a detached parish of Worcestershire, although in the Warwickshire deanery of Kineton, it was transferred by the Gloucestershire and Worcestershire to Warwickshire Transfer Order 1931. A Jone Mander, widow, was still residing in Tredington in 1881.
[2] '*Johannes Maundwer tenet dimidium virgatem per servitum ijs. ivd. per annum ad predictos iiij terminus, et debet per omnia sicut predictos Nicholas*' (*The Red Book of the Bishopric of Worcester, transcribed from a lost volume by Dr W. Thomas in the eighteenth century* [PRO], ed. Marjory Hollings, Worcs. Historical Society, London, 1934-50, vol 3, p. 284.) The virgate would have been composed of a bundle of acre and half-acre strips scattered about the common fields. A half virgate would have been held typically by tenants of the rank of villein, who comprised about a third of the rural population, below the freemen and above cottars, crofters, 'pytel-holders' and lesser serfs (see F. Seebohm, *The English Village Community*, 1883; H.S. Bennett, *Life on the English Manor*, 1937 [Sutton, 1987]).

The name. The earlier origins of the patronymic remain obscure. The name may originate from the French place-name *Mandres*, signifying in Old French a 'small house', 'outhouse', 'stable', 'hovel', 'cottage'; 'byres, shippons, hoggots and out-barns', etc. It occurs, eg., *Mandrae*, Eure, 1301; *villa Mandris*, Haute-Marne, 1160; *Mandrae*, Meuse, 1033. (See A. Dauzet and C. Rostaing, *Dictionnaire étymologique des noms de lieux de France*, 1962.) The Normandy Eure (Verneuil-sur-Avre, Calvados) connection has a logic here; it may not be a coincidence that three early rectors of Tredington (John 1295, Thomas 1296 and John again in 1301) were 'd' Evreux'.

Alternatively, C.W. Bardsey in his *Dictionary of English and Welsh Surnames* (1901) suggests the derivation from the Old English substantive *maund*, a '[wicker] basket'; hence 'basket-maker'. (See W.G. Hoskins, *Local History in England*, 1972, p. 189.) Others suggest it is a nickname for a beggar, from an agent derivative of the same word (probably from Old French *mendrier*, Late Latin *mendicare*, although this word is not attested before the sixteenth century). Finally, there is a suggestion it indicates someone in a position of authority, from the aphetic form of Middle English *com[a]under* (from *coma[u]nden*, to command).

The pronouncing dictionaries (G.E. Pointon [ed.], *BBC Pronouncing Dictionary of British Names*, 1983) state that the name is commonly pronounced with a short 'a' in Staffordshire: 'mænder. The long 'a' variant is also used by this branch: mah-nder.

[3] **Early Ma[u]nders.** John Mander (Maundour, Mandour, Maundore, Maundouer, Mawndour). He was a fellow of Merton College, Oxford, in 1360; still in 1372; 2nd bursar 1367-8 (Mert. Coll. Rec. 2117. 3694-8, 3700-1, 3705, 4164b, c; Mert. Coll. Cat. Vetus, p. 11; *Mem. Mert. Coll.* (O.H.S.) p. 210; *Alumni Oxoniensis*, Oxford, 1888-91). He is recorded as M.A.; B.C.L. by 1371; D. Th.; *nuntius* of the University to the Roman Curia for the presentation of its roll for papal graces 1371 (Vatican Arch., Reg. Avin. 174, fos. 118v-119v, ex inform. Dr D. E. R. Watt.; Ord. pr. 23 Sept 1385, Reg. Braybroke, London); he was included in University Roll for papal graces and granted reservation of a benefice in the gift of Ramsay Abbey, Hunts., 24 March 1366 (*C. Pap. Pet.* i. 516, 520); canon of St Paul's London, with exception of prebend, by papal provision 28 Jan 1371 (Vatican Arch., Reg. Avin. 174, fos. 118v-119v); prebendary of Chiswick, in St Paul's London, coll. 24 Mar 1373; vac. by 1377 (*C.P.R. 1370-74*, p. 262; ibid. *1374-7*, p. 385; Hennessy, p. 21); treasurer of St Paul's London in April 1378; still in 1380-81 (loc. cit.; P.R.O., E 179/62/4; E 179/62/5); canon and prebendary of Norton, Dur., coll. 31 Oct 1379 (ibid., fo, 166v); vicar of Pelham Furneaux, Herts., in 1384; still in 1386 (*C.P.R. 1381-5*, p. 406; 1385-9, p. 282); archdcn. of Durham, estate ratified 11 August 1387; revoked 21 August 1389; appointment subject to the appeal to the Roman Curia 1393 (ibid. *1385-9*, p. 349; *1388-92*, p. 109; *C. Pap. L.* iv. 479); canon of Wells and prebendary of Easton-in-Gordano, estate ratified 28 Sept 1391; till death (*C.P.R. 1388-92*, p. 485; *C. Pap. L.* iv. 431; v. 431; *Cal. MSS.* 11. 33, 34, 483); rector of Fairsted, Essex, coll. 8 Feb 1397; till death (Reg Braybroke. fo. 149; Newcourt, ii, 249); Chancellor of the bishop of

Durham, app. 25 Nov 1375; still in 1379 (Reg. Hatfield, Dur., fos. 80, 166v); co-feoffee of Batt's Inn in Oxford, in 1380; the pardon granted to him after outlaw for contempt on account of his attempt to expel the King's presentee to the treasurership of St Paul's, 11 Feb 1397, may indicate that he has endeavoured to retain the treasurership after his appointment as archdeacon of Durham (*C.P.R. 1396-9,* p. 83); died in Rome at the end of 1399 [*C. Pap. L.* v. 340]. (See J. Foster, *Alumni Oxoniensis,* Oxford, 1888-91.)

Roger Mander (1649-1704) is another Oxford Mander who achieved some distinction (but was no antecedent). He matriculated at Balliol College, Oxford, on 30 March 1666, son of Roger Mander, 'plebeian', of Bicknoller, Withycombe, Somerset. He was a fellow, then Master, of Balliol, and while Master was Vice-Chancellor of the University. As such, his imprimatur is found in books of that period published by the University Press. He was buried in the Antechapel, but his marker stone did not survive the Victorian rebuilding.

Branches. John F. Osborne of Peterborough has compiled an exhaustive genealogy of the Tredington/Aston Cantlow branch, indexing some 200 Mander families from the sixteenth century (to June 1994). Other (apparently agnate) branches of the Mander family include that settled at Todenham, NE Gloucestershire (recorded ante 1584 and still residing at the 1851 census). The Church of St Thomas à Becket has a monument with finely anatomized skull-and-crossbones and crest to John Mander, 'sometime since of Blackwell', d. 1723/8, aet. 30, on the external south wall of the chancel, and a ledger stone (1747) in the chancel with the arms of Mander impaling Taylor. Arms: ermine, three annulets interlaced gules. Crest: a demi lion holding in the dexter paw a sword erect. See F. Were, 'Index to the Heraldry in Bigland's *History of Gloucestershire*', *Trans. Bristol & Glos. Arch. Soc.*, xxviii, Pt. 2, 300. He writes: 'The histories do not give the Mander family. Papworth [see John W. Papworth, *Ordinary of British Armorials,* 1874; Bath: Five Barrows, 1977] gives the arms and names them Mandere... Fairburn says "a swallow volant sa."'. (Thomas Mander married 14 June 1709 Elizabeth Taylor of Todenham.)

The Bakewell, Derbyshire, branch descends from John (son of Thomas, possibly 4th son of Henry and Anne of Aston Cantlow, by Judith Clarkson), who settled there c. 1744. His son James Mander of Bakewell, land agent/solicitor to the Dukes of Devonshire, published *The Derbyshire Miners' Glossary; or an explanation of the Technical Terms of the Miners* (Bakewell: Minerva Press, 1824, 131p). Other Manders of this line include a Bedford branch, giving Sir Frederick Mander (b. 1883), gen. sec. NUT and Liberal chm Beds. C.C.; and a London branch, men of law, giving successive clerks to the Cordwainers' Company, of whom C.H.W. Mander was author of *A Descriptive and Historical Account of the Guild of Cordwainers of the City of London* (London, 1931). A descendant of this line, Col. d'Arcy Mander (1909-2001), was author of *Mander's March on Rome* (Sutton, 1987), describing his escape from a POW train in Italy in 1943, when he set up an espionage network in occupied Rome and discovered the details of the German plans for Anzio.

The noted New Zealand novelist, Jane Mander, descends from Henry the Younger, eldest son of Henry and Anne of Aston Cantlow.

Other families. Numerous Ma[u]nder families occur in Midland England and the West Country whose connection is as yet unknown. (The name also occurs in many countries on the Continent. The best known representative in the Low Countries is Karel van Mander [1548-1606], the 'Dutch Vasari', author of the *Schilder-boeck* [trans. *Lives of the Illustrious Netherlandish and German Painters,* ed. Hessel Miedema, Doornspijk, 1995], the standard historiography of the artists of the Netherlandish school. In the autobiographical section, he gives an account of his descent from a 'prominent' family settled at Meulebeecke in Courtrai, by the Mandel river, claiming descent from one Walter van Mander, bishop of Tournai from 1219.) The Devon family were settled in that county by the early sixteenth century. See W.G. Hoskins, *Devon and its People,* Exeter: A. Wheaton & Co. [n.d.] for

Henry Maunder, merchant (born Shobrooke, Devon, 1515—died Exeter 24 Feb. 1564). Noel Mander founded the St Peter's Organ works at Bethnal Green, London, in 1936.

John Osborne and others are (27 April 1998) building up genealogical databases for the Mander/Manders surnames in Great Britain, extending to Mander lines in New Zealand and the USA. He writes:

Although there are genuine records for MANDERS, in some cases the genitival 's' is a mistranscription of a flourish after the 'r'. There is also confusion with MAUNDER (my own line has cases of parish clerks writing MAUNDER when the family write MANDER).

[There are] about 8900 entries in the Baptism/Birth database, of which about 2850 are for MANDER and about 600 for MANDERS; the marriages database now has 5370 entries, of which 984 are for MANDER husbands, 846 for MANDER brides, 246 for MANDERS husbands and 256 for MANDERS brides; the burial/death database now has 2956 entries, of which 1206 are for MANDER and 218 entries are for MANDERS. I am still extracting names from the General Register Office Indexes but have looked at births to 1856 and marriages to 1890 and have included IGI entries to the 1997 Addendum in the LDS Family Search program.

Other internet sites were by 2002 building up large databases for MANDER and MAUNDER.

[4] J. Harvey Bloom, MA, *The Register of the Gild of the Holy Cross, The Blessed Mary and St John the Baptist*, Phillimore and Co., 1907

[5] He married Elizabeth, née Teale, in Tredington, 13 June 1598, by whom he had two sons and two daughters. She was buried at Tredington 4 Feb. 1631/2.

[6] But the identity of the house changed in 2000, after Dr N. Alcock demonstrated by documentary research and confirmed by dendrochronology that the house long shown as 'Mary Arden's House' did not exist at the time of her birth (the oldest part dates to c. 1569). Instead, the true house was proven to be Glebe Farm (built c. 1514) next door, which indeed belonged to Mary's stepmother, Agnes. The Shakespeare Birthplace Trust (owner of both properties) has renamed the old 'Mary Arden's House' as 'Palmer's Farm', while the old Glebe Farm has been renamed 'Mary Arden's House'. (See N.W. Alcock, 'Topography and Land Ownership in Wilmcote' [2000] and Bob Meeson 'Glebe Farm, Wilmcote, Warwickshire' [2000], unpublished reports for the Shakespeare Birthplace Trust.)

[7] Will proved at £257 17*s.* 6*d* (which puts him in the top quartile of estates at the time).

[8] According to Mander family information (ref. Mark Weaver), Samuel was tenant of Lapworth Park Farm, in the old enclosed hunting park of the manor. But according to Joy Woodall (*Portrait of Lapworth*, 1986, p. 14), the tenants there 'from at least the 1660s' were the Edkins family. Robert Hudson writes that from the time of Samuel, 'the family occupied the above-named Ireland's Farm, Bushwood, from father to son for fully two hundred years' (*Memorials of a Warwickshire Parish, Being Papers Mainly Descriptive of the Records and Registers of Lapworth*, Methuen, 1904, p. 170).

[9] John de Bishopsdon contracted to build the manor, 40 ft long by 18 ft wide, at a cost of 25 marks in 1313. The four-roomed house (hall, parlour, chamber and kitchen) was occupied in the sixteenth century by John Ireland and is described in Robert Ireland's will of 1559/60. Ireland's Farm was refronted in the early nineteenth century, replacing an earlier block, 'for it seems unlikely that the Mander family, who occupied the house for 200 years and were people of consequence in the parish, would have been prepared to live in only the old part of the present house.' (Joy Woodall, *Portrait of Lapworth*, 1986, pp. 22-4.

[10] For the Shakesepeare surname in sixteenth- and seventeenth-century Warwickshire, where it is recorded in 34 parishes, see Sir Sydney Lee's *Life of William Shakespeare*, 1915. The first Shakespeares and Manders are both recorded in Lapworth registers in the 1560s, and the first Cotterell, 'Pernela Coterel' of Henley, in 1319 (Hudson, p. 275).

[11] Oliver Baker (*In Shakespeare's Warwickshire and the Unknown Years*, 1937), 'steering through a bewildering maze of Warwickshire Shakespeares', states the first recorded was Adam de Oldediche of Temple Balsall, near Baddesley Clinton, in 1389 (see H. Norris, *Notes & Queries*, 8th series, vol. vii, 501). (A William Shakespeare served on a coroner's jury

there in 1385.) He adds: 'these Warwickshire Shakespeares (including the poet William) were all more or less related to one another, because they were all descended from [him]' (p. 61). A John and Alice Shakespeare are settled in Rowington by 1460. The first Thomas Shakespeare and Christian his consort of Rowington are recorded in the Register of the Guild of St Anne of Knowle in 1486: '*Thomas Chacsper Et xpian cons sue de Rownton*' (p. 70). Baker proposes a descent through one Thomas of Temple Balsall (*d.* 1511) to Richard (*d.* 1561) of Snitterfield (often referred to as 'Shakstaff' there), grandfather of the Bard. For Shakespeare genealogy, see G.R. French, *Shakespeare Genealogica*, 1869, 1977 (reptd).

[12] For Shakespeare the Catholic and his possible connections with Campion at Lapworth, see C. Richard Desper, 'Allusions to Edmund Campion in Twelfth Night', *Elizabethan Review*, Spring/Summer, 1995; Anthony Holden, *William Shakespeare: the Man behind the Genius*, 1999; E. Honigmann, *Shakespeare: the Lost Years*, 1985; and R. Wilson, 'Shakespeare and the Jesuits: new connections supporting the theory of the lost Catholic years in Lancashire': www.lancs.ac.uk/users/english/research/shakespeare/jesuits.html. For recusancy at Rowington, see 'Recusant Rowington', *Worcestershire Recusant*, no. 31, June 1978.

[13] Sir William was descended from the 'Cat', councillor of Richard III, who bought the Lapworth estate. Robert Catesby (1573-1605) the conspirator was his son by Anne Throckmorton of Coughton.

[14] A centre of the malting trade was Stratford. For his baking, see: Wolverhampton Archives and Local Studies: Deeds relating to lands in Dudley Road, Wolverhampton: Assignment of mortgage (copy), ref. DX91/36, 30 Jan. 1758, 'Thomas Mander of the same place, baker'; DX91/35, 25 Dec. 1761, 'Thomas Mander of Wolverhampton, baker'.

[15] *Commons Journals*, XVIII, 227; A.G. Matthews, *Trans. Congregationalist History Society*, XII, no. 1, 9.

[16] *The Wolverhampton Antiquary*, vol. I, no. 1, 30.

[17] *History of Wolverhampton*, pp. 111, 130.

[18] His will, signed 12 December 176[4] 'being in a state of bad health but of sound and disposing Mind, Memory and Understanding', is in the William Salt Library, Stafford.

BENJAMIN AND JOHN

2

BENJAMIN AND JOHN

Miniature, aged 67, by Mrs Morris, 1818

Benjamin Mander
1752-1819

Benjamin Mander was a pioneer manufacturer and entrepreneur, and a public figure in the Wolverhampton of the early industrial revolution. His upbringing was distinctly pious: 'He was brought up under the sound of the Gospel ... even in his youth he sought the company of the most serious and experienced christians'. But his father died when he was twelve, so he must have taken over the family businesses early under the supervision of his stepfather, a dour Scottish Presbyterian called Charles Hunter, who was also responsible for turning the family from Anglicanism to strong nonconformity.

Benjamin Mander & Son, Japanners, 1792

Benjamin continued for a while in the old family business as a baker and maltster. But in 1792, when he was 40, he changed direction and we find him setting up in one of the new industries becoming established in the town as a manufacturer of japanned ware and tin-plate work.[1] The japanning trade was always connected, particularly in the Midlands, with the varnish trade. His eldest son, Charles Mander, was making varnish to supply the growing japanning business by 1803 and it was the symbiosis of these trades which led to the development of the famous manufacturing business in the nineteenth century.

The earliest formal account of the industry, J. Stalker and G. Parker's *A Treatise of Japanning and Varnishing*, published in Oxford in 1688, already links the two trades. As a strict neo-classical account, it traces japanning back to the time of Alexander the Great: 'True, genuine Japan, like the salamander, lives in the flames, and stands unalterable, when the wood which was imprisoned in it, is utterly consumed'. The japanned ware trade grew up to provide goods in imitation of the fashionable and exotic 'lackwork' which had begun to be imported by the English East India Company in the early seventeenth century, but in quantity after 1660.

Japan 'state' furniture was produced in trading cities from Venice[2] (where it was called *mobili laguna*, prepared in dust-free conditions on the islands) to London. In its industrial form, the techniques and processes of japanning on surfaces of iron plated with tin were pioneered on the estate of Major John Hanbury (1664-1734) at Pontypool Park in South Wales.[3] Here, during the last years of the seventeenth century, his manager Thomas Allgood, from Northamptonshire, made advances in iron making, with adjustable rolling machinery capable of producing thin iron sheets of uniform thickness.[4] Soon Thomas Allgood had set up a successful tin-plate works where his famous 'Pontypool ware' was made for three generations, up to 1790, and in Usk up to 1820.

This japanned or 'Pontypool' ware trade perpetrated a deliberate fake, imitating the effect and 'tiger patterns' of the costly resin lacquers of the Far East by coating tin, or a tin-plated sheet iron, called *tôle* in French—or other materials like wood, slate (for architectural items), iron, copper and leather—with numerous layers of varnish. Each coat is separately dried and hardened in stoves or hot chambers in successive 'stovings' and then polished until it builds up the characteristic lustrous surface. The tinned plate was a contraction of 'tinned iron plate', involving the coating of iron with a thin layer of tin, as in galvanising (where zinc is the coating), to preserve the iron from rust, 'while the tin itself is the most wholesome and cleanly of metals'.[5] The lacquer formed a protection and decoration, a brilliant and durable polished surface, less easily affected by heat, moisture or other corrosive influences than a plain painted or varnished finish.

At first oriental 'japan' lacquers (the 'true' sumac lacquer prepared from *rhus vernicifera*) had been imitated with ordinary gum-lac, seed-lac and shell-lac (all preparations of a substance deposited on trees by an insect, *coccus laca*), dissolved in alcohol, 'spirits of wine'. But with Pontypool ware a stronger English varnish evolved based on by-products of coal, the 'asphaltum' or tar varnishes, which hardened when applied to metal tinwares with heat. For the typical black japan, the pure, natural asphaltum is mixed with gum animé dissolved in linseed oil and thinned with turpentine. Other colours were used; 'sealing wax red', greens and blues.

By the 1720s the japanned ware trade had started to find its way to the Midlands. We find records of it in Bilston, where Joseph Allen and Samuel Stone are mentioned as japanners in 1719. Imports of German, notably Saxon, tinplate were still contributing well over a million plates a year in the years up to 1738, when the War of the Austrian Succession put a stop to it. English manufacturers seized their opportunity.[6] John Baskerville (1706-75) was one of the first. Best known today as a typefounder and printer, he had followed the same pattern as also a varnish maker and pioneer japanned ware manufacturer, setting up the first Birmingham japanning works in 1740, which produced mostly 'cheap tin trays'.

The Midlands trade developed quickly. In 1740, the Shropshire ironmasters, Edward and Ralph Knight of Stourport, were engaged in early industrial espionage, sending John Cooke (grandson of Thomas Cooke, right-hand man to Major John Hanbury) to Pontypool to gather what trade secrets he could, paying him £36 15*s.* for 'information on tinning'. Japanning became a fashionable amateur pursuit: *The Ladies' Amusement, or The Whole Art of Japanning Made Easy* (1760) was a best seller. By 1798, we hear that the Pontypool trade is falling off. Richard Colt Hoare writes (25 August): 'Formerly a brisk trade was carried on in Japan goods, called Pontypoole Ware but is now reduced to a very low ebb, only eight hands being employed in it'.[7]

The japanning trade had reached Wolverhampton by the 1760s, where it fitted in well with the existing pattern of the local metalwork trades, and others like vitreous enamelling established in Bilston, so that Wolverhampton gradually became the centre of manufacture.[8] Trades established there included locksmithing, ornamental iron and brass casting, 'toy' making (which of course meant manufacturing small articles and trinkets, such as snuff boxes, étuis, needlecases), and the manufacture of fine steel goods. Sword hilts, steel buttons and buckles, chatelaines, chains, fob seals and jewellery were made of polished and 'cut' steel, faceted like pyrites. The trade was already described by Dr Robert Plot, Staffordshire's first county historian, in 1686; thirty 'toy' makers are listed in 1770. One John Warralow became 'steel jeweller' to George III at the height of the trade in

1782. A large export trade developed to markets in France and Spain, where before the events of the Revolution and the tariffs that followed on, their merchants bought the fashionable steel goods of Wolverhampton for their weight in gold, 'Spanish doubloons in one scale, steel goods in the other'. A good deal of the talent which was no longer engaged in the fine steel ware trade was diverted into the rising japan ware trade 'and the sons and grandsons of the best workmen in steel became ... the best japanners in England'.[9]

A major innovation came in 1772, when Baskerville's one-time apprentice, Henry Clay, took out a patent for making papier mâché out of pressed paper, producing an alternative material which was tough, stable and heat-resistant.[10] Importantly, it was cheaper and lighter than tin plate, and soon goods of japanned 'paper' ware, as he termed it, became more sought after.

Theodore Mander notes the traditional method of manufacturing papier mâché trays when he visits the works of Fred Walton & Co., as a young man aged 19 studying business in August 1872:

> 12 to 36 layers of paper pasted together on a block. Edges torn to prevent creases. Dried in a hot room. Saturated with hot linseed to harden. When dried in oven can be worked like wood. Japanned about 12 times, each coat being dried and rubbed with pumice stone.
>
> *Ornamentation.*—Gold leaf laid onto with water. Pattern painted over gold with 'asphaltum'. Uncovered gold taken off with wet rag. Asphaltum removed by turpentine. Other painted added by hand. Handed up with 'rotten stone'.

Items such as the 'paper' tray, usually oval, the more elaborate ones often sold in a set with matching smaller 'waiters'; the paper bottle stand (as we would term it, 'coaster'); the decanter frame; and the cruet and 'soy' stand; dish covers; tobacco boxes, became part of the standard paraphernalia of the late Georgian dining room. The product range extended rapidly to highly-varnished panels for carriages, as well as firescreens, wine coolers and then ink stands, work boxes, folio cases, card cases, cake baskets, tea caddies, jewellery boxes, and finally items of furniture.

The Midlands trade gradually developed traditions in increasingly industrial techniques and decoration all of its own. Midland trays and coasters became phenomenally popular, produced on a large scale. Sketchley & Adams' *True Guide* of 1770 lists eight japanners in Wolverhampton, including two women and the famous Taylor and Jones who occupied the Old Hall, then Turton Hall, which is described as 'the cradle of the Midlands japanning industry'. Successful Wolverhampton japanners included Edward Bird, son of a carpenter who trained at the Old Hall and became a Royal Academician; George Wallis, the art theorist and Deputy Commissioner of the Great Exhibition in 1851, who was apprenticed at the Old Hall and worked for Manders; and Junius Brutus Booth (1796-1852), the eccentric actor, who started life as a skilled decorator at the Old Hall and went on to found one of the most distinguished acting dynasties of nineteenth-century America.[11]

In the tin trade, were tea and coffee pots, kettles; the later ones with stamped decoration. In 1825 a Birmingham firm took out patents for reproducing the effect of mother-of-pearl decoration. Then there were techniques for 'snigging' or delineating details such as feathers or flower petals. Decoration became bizarre and garish, and objects evolved into impracticable and elaborate forms. In the end, the mass production of silver plate after Henry Elkington's patents of the 1840s sealed the fate of much of the japanned trade.[12]

Benjamin Mander established his japan shop in the family works in John's Lane, while continuing his bakery and malthouse on the same premises and living in the old family house next door. He took into partnership a Thomas Shepherd, introduced to him by his brother, John. They quickly advertised for more staff:

> Wanted immediately. Several Tinmen. Good workmen will meet with every encouragement from Mander & Shepherd, Tin-plate workers and Japanners in general, John Street, Wolverhampton.[13]

His japanning works was never large. 'Because the nature of the work demanded manual dexterity rather than capital', writes the *Victoria County History of Staffordshire*, 'most of the firms were small, consisting of the master craftsman and a handful of workers...' By 1802, there were eleven tinplate workers in Wolverhampton recorded in the rate book, including 'Mander—, 48 John Street'. In 1805, he is still described on a deed as 'baker and japanner'.

Examples of early 'paper' wares produced by their workshop turn up in the antiques' trade from time to time. Pieces are not usually signed, but a rare documented example recorded in the authorities is a 'rectangular papier mâché tray with canted corners and a deep chinoiserie border in tinted gold of figures in a landscape'.[14] A fire screen is listed in The Mount probate inventory of 1930 as a 'Mander heirloom': 'Mahogany pole fire screen with square base and papier mâché oblong banner with Nubian figures in coloured lacquer'. Six plaques with landscape scenes (possibly painted by Benjamin himself) were lent by the family to Mander Brothers in 1952, but have since become carelessly lost. Other items at The Mount included oval plaques of 'Lord Nelson', or of 'two children and a dog', or 'a girl with a basket'; also water cans, snuffer stands and, most impressively, 'a Regency black japanned and gilt cane-panelled couch with scroll end and back'. A music stand with bulbous support of about 1840 (at Owlpen) is said to be made by Manders, as are various items of late Georgian japan work extant in the family.

The firm became known as 'Benjamin Mander & Son', and was supplying a paper waiter and other japanned wares in April and July 1811 to Chamberlains of Worcester, a well-known porcelain manufacturer who purchased goods for resale in their retail shop: 'one 22 inch waiter No. 4. 10/6'. A letter sent to the firm in 1815 states that export was being considered by then:

> Mr. J. Shore called yesterday; he admires the winecoolers very much, also the plate-warmer, which he thought very elegant and quite suitable for the American market... He says his friend (an American) will want some trays for the spring trade, and hopes he will be able to do something with us.

The business seems to have been successful in late Georgian times, and its wares highly regarded. Benjamin became established by it as an early entrepreneur, active in public life as 'one of the leading and most public-spirited men of the town'.

He was appointed one of the original Town Commissioners. These were the forerunners of the town councillors, created under the Wolverhampton Town Improvement Act of 1777 which first established local government in the growing town. The Commissioners were responsible for levying rates for improving the streets, street lighting and drainage, and 'removing nuisances and encroachments'. They undertook a wide variety of work, including the regulation of markets and inspection of hazardous foodstuffs, the prevention of the slaughtering of live animals in the streets and punishing bear baiting by imposing fines of £5.

Commissioners were all people with property worth more than £12 a year and owning lands or goods worth more than £1,000, meeting at The Red Lion inn, where they were expected to pay sixpence 'to be spent in drink for the good of the house'. By 1814 four Manders are recorded among the sixty Commissioners of the borough at the same time. They were already setting the tradition for public service for which succeeding generations of Manders became distinguished.

Benjamin, like many japan masters, is described as a 'Liberal' in politics, distinctly on the side of reform. And, like many early industrialists, he was prominent as a local dissenter in religion, standing in opposition to the laxities and corruptions of established Georgian Anglicanism. As such he became a radical suspect at the time of the French Revolution. Nonconformists like Benjamin, who espoused the spirit of political decency and freedom, were marked down by those who supported the church and the king as 'Jacobins', sympathetic to the ideals of the French revolutionaries.

One story about him relates his stalwart defence of his house and property with a drawn sword against a rabble of rioters at the time of the so-called 'Church and the King riots', one of the famous events of eighteenth-century social history. On Thursday 14 July (the anniversary of Bastille Day) 1791, the Birmingham house of Joseph Priestley (1733-1804), the pioneer chemist, dissenter and defender of religious and civil liberty, was burnt to the ground in an outbreak of mob violence against 'Jacobinism'.[15] The mob duly made their way through the streets of Birmingham burning and pillaging, and then proceeded to Wolverhampton intending to burn down the old meeting house, or chapel, in John's Lane, believed to be a hotbed of Jacobin propaganda, of which Benjamin was the leading member, and then to burn down his house and property.

As the mob surged down John's Lane, the owner of the house next door to the chapel, a Dr Morrison, whose wife lay ill on the second floor, had the presence of mind to distract the mob's attention by coming to his front door and, taking off his hat and waving it, shouting at the top of his voice

Huzza my lads, Church and King forever!

This ruse saved the chapel from almost certain destruction and kept the invaders on the move. They rushed down the street to seek out the 'arch dissenter and embryo revolutionary', Benjamin Mander.

His grandson, Samuel Small Mander, wrote that Dr Morrison's shout gave a delay which

> had given my grandfather time to prepare for them and accordingly he posted himself at his front door with a drawn sword in his hand, and at the other entrance he placed one of his servants, a strong muscular man armed with a massive kitchen poker threatening to kill the man who should throw the first stone.

Benjamin lighted candles in the windows in order to identify his assailants which, together with 'the fierceness and courage he displayed', disconcerted the rioters. By his quick thinking he managed to hold back the rabble. The eight o'clock bell then rang as a curfew for the apprentices, so the crowd were compelled to disperse. They planned to meet the following day, when they expected to be reinforced by a large band of rioters from Birmingham. But by the next morning, troops of the cavalry militia had arrived preventing the crowd from reassembling, and the day was saved.

Bread and Circus: Benjamin Mander and the Union Mill, 1812

Benjamin Mander's interests were certainly diverse, perhaps too much so for his own profit as a businessman—and we shall see that he died leaving a meagre estate. His promotion in 1812 of the Wolverhampton Flour and Bread Company, which built and operated the Union Mill, together with the Union Poor House (a fine building to a radial plan which stood on the Cleveland Road) as a philanthropic adjunct, again led to notoriety.

The company was modelled on the more famous Birmingham Union Mill, largely as a charitable venture to provide cheap bread to the poor in the period of economic difficulty and social agitation which followed the Napoleonic wars.[16] In 1812 the labourers were suffering from a depression in agricultural prices and trade in a brutal climate of protection which favoured the landowners, and there was deep unrest, leading to rioting in the streets. Against a background of growing population and 35 years of war, piracy, and blockade, the price of bread had inexorably risen. There were years of dearth, as when in 1795 Pitt had taxed the use of flour in hair-powder, and then saw fit to forbid its use altogether. Since Benjamin had become a master baker, bread had gone from being the staple diet of the poor to being in some cases a luxury item. The Union Mill was founded on a sense of mission and high principle, intended to keep the price of good quality bread cheap.

The Union Mill project was launched when the promoters offered mass subscriptions to the public one market day in August 1812. The idea caught on immediately, and the public welcomed it by subscribing. Gerald Mander wrote:

> It came at a time too when steps were taken to enforce the Statute concerning the size and quality of bread in the county [which] perhaps reminded the authorities of their duties in this regard.
>
> It was perhaps fortunate that the baking of bread was such an everyday domestic affair, because the committee, strong in sentiment, was undoubtedly weak on the technical side. The notice:
>
> *WANTED, SEVERAL JOURNEYMEN BAKERS, who perfectly understand their Business*
>
> was not without meaning; for Benjamin Mander who, as managing-director, sought their services and was to study their characters for Integrity, Sobriety and Industry, was himself a japanner.

But the established millers and bakers were hostile to a scheme whose purpose, after all, was to undercut their prices, and wasted no time in retaliating. They brought a Bill of Indictment for conspiracy against

Benjamin and his committee of eight other promoters of the Mill at the Lent Assizes.

Benjamin and his committee were charged with illegal combination by the millers, stating they were annoyed by 'a scheme which was held out as a probable way to reduce the price of provisions, and be of great public benefit'. The case was brought to trial at Stafford in 1814 at the summer assizes before Sir Robert Dallas, and Benjamin, as chairman of the Mill, found himself as first defendant in 'The King *versus* B. Mander and eight others'. So he came to lead a celebrated trial on its behalf, the proceedings of which were published in full.[17]

The prosecution was founded on an Act passed in 1720 (6 Geo. I, c. 18, sec. 18, which the booksellers of the town and district were selling for 2*d.*) to prevent monopolistic trade combinations which were not in the public interest. The principle at issue was that enormous sums, here 15,000 shares of one pound each, could be held by as many subscribers, so that the Mill could sell its produce at a price scarcely exceeding that of the raw commodity. The legal question was whether the possible annihilation of the legitimate trade would be to the detriment of the public in general, or just one section of the public, i.e. the consumers.

In the proceedings, Benjamin, as principal manager of the Mill, is impugned as a japanner, ignorant of the trade of baker which he professed to carry on, 'an evil to a known and recognised trade', although on cross examination he pointed out he was, in fact, formerly a baker.

The evidence of the clerk to the Union, Abel Whitehouse, is of interest, giving insight into the general conditions of milling at the time. He stated that the Union Mill sold about 500 bushels of flour each week, three to four pair of stones being employed (four pair going and one pair dressing), and more flour was sold than bread. There were three ovens in general use, each of which would take about ten bushels per batch. The Union Mill was advantageous, he argued, to a town whose population had grown greatly in the last 15 years, with new coal and iron works, and an increase in buildings in the neighbourhood. There were excellent facilities to convey flour by water, and previously flour and corn had to be brought in from places as far apart as Liverpool and Worcestershire. There were few other mills of any size, just a few old mills on the streams about Wolverhampton, as the town lies high, so there had been a scarcity of bread.

For the Union it was argued that nine or ten thousand pounds had been spent on the mill, the greater part of which would have been lost if it were stopped. Great benefit had arisen from the preceding Union Mill in Birmingham. John Devey, a corn factor, stated that the idea was driven by the rise in the price of wheat: when the Mill started in August 1812, wheat was 23*s.* a bushel, but 'the people of Wolverhampton were much dissatisfied' when it rose to 26*s.*, and 'there was much murmuring', in consequence of which he supposed the Union Mill originated.

The bakers and millers made an impassioned case against the Union. One baker gave evidence—echoed by many others—to the effect that he was obliged to sell at reduced prices, or he could not sell at all. When the mill began, the profits were small, because flour was falling in price, yielding profits of 3*s.* 6*d.* a sack. In January 1814, the price of flour was 62*s.* 6*d.* Another baker, Thomas Wilkes, stated that whereas before the Union Mill he baked on average about nine sacks a week, now he only baked half that quantity, perhaps three of four sacks a week, losing his trade when the Union began to undersell.

When he complained to Mr Mander of his situation, and said what a sad thing it was to their trade, Mr Mander said he was sorry for it, but it could not be helped, and he advised him to give up baking. [Wilkes] asked him how he must live? and Mr Mander replied, 'Oh! go into the huckstering way, and sell flour for us'. 'Ah!' said Wilkes, 'but I know nothing of that, I was brought up a baker, and have been one almost all my life; besides my house is too large.' 'Why then,' said Mr Mander, 'you should take a smaller.'

Such arguments continued, and the trial lasted a full fourteen hours:

It proved a fiasco from the bakers' point of view, judge, jury and audience being for the defendants. It is possible that the prosecution was only half-hearted; counsel had only been briefed at the last moment, and vainly did his witnesses show that the Union Mill was 'unfair trading', 'a monopoly' and would drive the bakers to extinction.

The judge rather pertinently asked how the case differed from the decision given by Lord Ellenborough in 1811 in favour of the Birmingham Flour and Bread Company (The King *versus* Webb) and to that there was no answer.

The case was finally decided in favour of Benjamin Mander and the Mill, with shouts of 'Mander and the Union for ever!' He was pronounced the hero of a popular demonstration, which 'hailed him as the champion of justice and the poor'. Gerald Mander describes the upshot:[18]

The verdict of not guilty, that the company was not illegally associated, was a popular one; and though the news reached Wolverhampton at daybreak, the bells almost immediately commenced to ring and continued at intervals during the day.

The coach bringing the witnesses was met at Gosbrook and drawn through the town in triumph. The crowds assembled were immense, shouting 'Justice and Union for ever', 'The Big Loaf has won'. And yet the wildest rumours had been afloat; that B. Mander as ringleader was to be hanged and the rest transported for seven years; but 'it was a long and fair fought Battle and the Victory quite compleat! .... if we had not taken a single witness, we should have won.' (Family letter, 4 August, 1814).

There followed the inevitable 'dinner' at the Swan Hotel, with the usual long list of toasts, including on this occasion 'Sir John Chetwode and a Staffordshire jury', and 'The Union Mill, and may it always be found a public good'. It still grinds and a street has long borne its name.

The truth of Juvenal's dictum that the people never give concern for anything but '*panem et circenses*', bread and circuses, was shown in the sequel. Benjamin describes the effect of celebration in his workshop and in the town after the case was won in a letter to his son:

Now I must say the sooner you come home the better; our lads have got the Mill sickness and cannot work; in fact, there has been no work in town done this week.

But in the country at large it took a long time for the manufacturers to better the lot of the labourers, and bread riots and unrest persisted in the various towns and villages of early nineteenth-century England. The government's answer was harsh and blinkered, increasing the powers of the magistrates in a climate of widespread discontent which led up to the most unpopular of the Corn Laws imposed in the year of Waterloo (1815), fixing the price of home-grown wheat at 80*s*. a quarter and forbidding the import of foreign wheat until the home price reached that level. The effect was to keep the price of bread artificially high in the interests of the landowning classes, and it was of course to be a running sore for the government for the next generation or more.

The cause ran high in Wolverhampton. Richard Fryer, Radical, a local banker (and one of the first subscribers to the town Library with John and Benjamin) was also one of the first members to represent the borough in the Reform Parliament. He was the first to propose in the House of Commons the repeal of the Corn Laws. The House was lit with candles, and he smashed a pair of snuffers to pieces as he struck the table in a moment of heated debate, startling the members and forcing their attention. But the motion was defeated, and on the first opportunity he resigned his seat.

Benjamin Mander, swan flourish, 1792

Betsey Mander,
miniature by Mrs Morris, 1818

Benjamin married Elizabeth Hanbury Read of Kidderminster in 1776.[19] Known as 'Betsey' in the family, she was a skilled needlewoman: her childhood doll of about 1759, with the clothes made by her, and several examples of her needlework of expert quality, survive in the family.[20] Benjamin and Elizabeth had eleven children. Two sons, Charles, born in 1780, and Benjamin Parton, born in 1785, entered the business and became pillars of support to their father with the tinplating-japanning business and with the bakery. But both were to set out in different directions as industrialists.

Benjamin's letters are, after the fashion of the time, strained, misspelt and often barely legible, although written in a clearly artistic hand: Gerald describes it as 'pretty', 'an epithet one might hesitate to apply to the handwritings of some of his descendants'. He writes from London on 2 December 1809 to Betsey, while staying with his son-in-law, James Pearsall, a member of the London Common Council, and daughter, Rebecca, in Cheapside:

Betsey Mander's carved wooden doll, given to her by her uncle Dr Benjamin Hanbury c. 1759, with open robe, clothes and items made by her as a child.

Dear Betsey,
I am obliged to you for yours, I have said in Char[les's] that Rebi [Rebecca] is much better and James very well, you say how much you are pleasd that I have had some precious meals, it is a mercy & I desire to esteem it such to merit with some crumb, by the way, I wish the flavor did last longer, but so it is that our corrupt Meats & the various seens around us soon spoil our joys, steal our affection away from them that deserve our every thought and every love, but so it is & I fear will be in this wilderness state of life. Mr Scales does win upon ... you & many precious souls may he have much of the Lords presence and may the spirit seal this work to the souls of many and that a Cause that the Lord will plant & own may spring up in Wolverhampton, I have had some pleasant thoughts that I shall see Zion in prosperity & peace upon Israel if it is the Lord's will may I not be disappoint... you talk of dulness deadness & co. in spir... & affections, I find much of it, it is a mercy to be enabled to lament it may be drawn out to that precious fountain that can do all these things away, & supply all our needs may we look to him at all times, I intend if all is well to leave next week. Today I calld on Messrs N...h e & she send their respects if you sd be in Town will be glad to see you providence seems to appear for they must like you ... unless when I see you, the Lord does what he pleases with all his Creatures and all he does is well may we constantly view [h]is hand in all our concerns

Yours Aff^dy^ B. Mander

Another letter to his daughter, Sarah, describes the illuminations which followed the declaration of the Peace of Amiens, which was soon upset by the escape of Napoleon from Elba and renewed hostilities at Waterloo, in June 1815:

Wolverhampton, June 6th 1814.

Dear Sarah,
We have been expecting to hear from you some days—your Mother thinks you may find time. You have had the pleasure of having peace declared, suppose there is a deal of bustle, we have had nothing else since the news reached us, the people can't settle to work. Yesterday there was a grand illumination in Birmingham, and it is said there is to be another tonight, and one at Bilston. It is proposed to have ours on Friday week, and a general dinner for the poor and labouring people, men and women. A considerable subscription is on foot for the purpose. People in general want provisions lower—butchers' meat was never so dear, as at present, trade very indifferent, not near so good as it was twelve months ago. I hope the people will be enabled to see whence all mercies flow, and have hearts of gratitude given them, then we may expect showers of blessings.

How is the weather in London? It is very cold here—our fires are nearly as large as in Winter—I wonder anything grows—if the warm weather does not soon set in, the prospects will be awful. He that rules his own best and will do all things well through mercy.

Your dear Mother continues very comfortable, has been very bustling today and yesterday—it was our wash, some blame her but she is never so much in her element as when she is stirring about—may her useful life be long spared. I don't know her equal in most things—as a Mother, as a Wife, as a Neighbour. I would say to her daughters "go, and do thou likewise"—let us hear very soon from you—we long to hear of you all—give our love to your brother and Sister James and Ellen.

Your affectionate Father, Benj. Mander

Great preparation is making here for the illumination—it will be such an one as never was in Wolverhampton before.

Benjamin died in 1819 at the age of 67. In his life, according to his funeral panegyric, 'he courted not the smiles of the rich, nor did he regard their frowns; he watched to do good! To the poor and the distressed his ear was always open, and to his advice and even his purse (far beyond what prudence may have dictated) have they found relief.' His death was sudden:

He had long laboured under a complaint in his chest ... and had no doubt his dissolution would be sudden. On the day he departed he was in his usual spirits and made many calls, and although he felt more pain than common, he did not appear to apprehend the change, but in the midst of his usefulness was taken away without a sigh or a groan & sweetly fell asleep in Jesus and entered into the joy of his Lord.

Firescreen of the two spies returning from the land of Canaan, embroidered by Betsey Mander, c. 1775

Eighty years later Benjamin is described respectfully by Joseph Jones as 'a man of zeal and courage, ever ready to defend the weak against the strong, and stand up for right and liberty. At the same time, his kindness of heart was proverbial.'[21] He never made a will and his wife was given letters of administration. After a life of worthy industry, his estate was valued at just fifty pounds. The bakery died with him.[22]

John Mander, Chemist, 1773

John Mander (1754-1827) was the second (surviving) son of Thomas. (There was a third son, Thomas [1757-1813], who married Elizabeth, daughter of Edward Urwick of Felhampton Court, Wistanstow, Craven Arms, Shropshire, and settled in Birmingham.) He was born in John's Lane and almost certainly attended the Grammar School, with his brother Benjamin also, in the same street.[23]

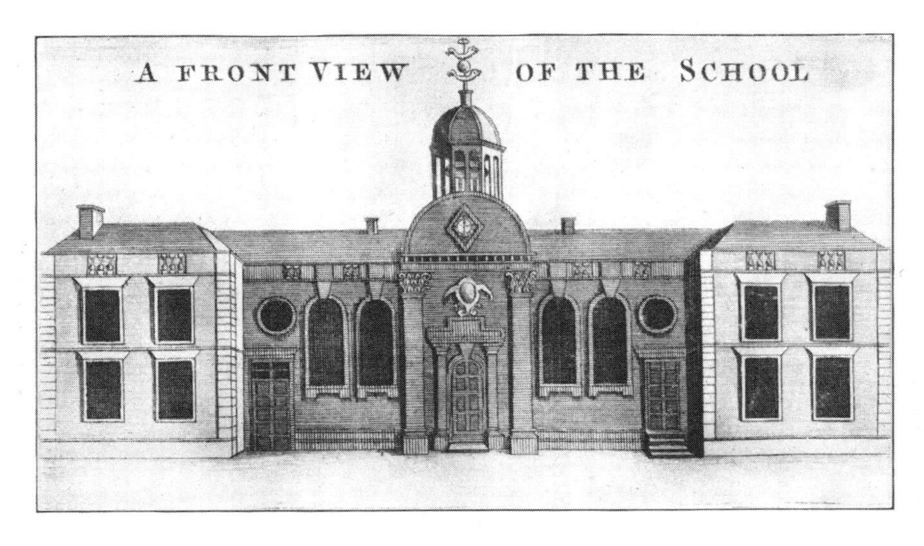

The Old Grammar School in John Street, 1750

John Mander, Benjamin's younger and, it has to be said, more commercially successful brother, was from the first apt and resourceful as a pioneer industrialist. John was apprenticed to the chemicals' trade. There is no record of the indenture (Barty-King suggests he may have served at the alkali works of William Small (1743-75), at Tipton). But he gained a sound knowledge of the new industrial chemistry of the post-Enlightenment, pioneered in the Midlands by men like John Roebuck (1718-94), Joseph Priestley and James Keir. He learnt his chemistry on the fringes of this enlightened circle, influential also on his political thought and religion.

They were all members of the great Lunar Society of Birmingham (*c.* 1766-1809), an informal group of fourteen men who formed a brilliant microcosm of a scattered community—'gigantic philosophers', empirical scientists, provincial manufacturers and professional men—who like him were typically religious dissenters and political radicals. They met in Birmingham on the Monday night nearest the full moon, when it was easier to travel, in order to discuss natural sciences and philosophy, and forge practical and commercial applications in manufacturing and industrial technology for the burgeoning innovations and discoveries of experimental science. They found England a rural society with an agrarian economy, and left it urban and industrial.[24]

We know that by 1773 (his twentieth year) John had finished his apprenticeship and accumulated enough capital to set up in business on his own as a manufacturing chemist and druggist in King Street. The chemicals works he founded was the first of its kind in Wolverhampton—it is still the only one in the *Directory* of 1781—and was effectively to prove the germ of a large and successful business.

According to family tradition, John, precocious in chemistry, had begun making chemical mixtures on a kitchen stove; he was soon exiled to the garden shed. Then, in 1778, the year he set up house as a married man, he bought property in Cock Street with Benjamin for £270 from one William Tomlinson. In about 1790, further expansion came when he took on the copyhold of new premises and moved his entire business to a site closer to Benjamin's activities, called (since at least 1675) The Brickhouse. He bought the four houses, two in Cock Street and two at the back adjoining 48 John's Lane, from one John Fowler for £600. On 11 May 1791, he announced that he was ready for business at the new factory: [25]

John Mander, Chemist and Druggist, respectfully informs his friends, the Faculty and Public at large, that he has moved his warehouse and Elaboratory from King Street into Cock Street, where he humbly solicits a continuance of their favours, both wholesale and retail.

It was a case of being in the right place at the right time, and business went well from the start. Over the coming years he gradually extended the site next to his brother Benjamin, until he occupied the land between Cock

Street and about a third of one side of John Street. He acquired further properties in 1800 (three dwelling houses which he converted into workshops) and 1803 (two or three cottages which he made into a drug mill and engine house, building a big chimney nearby). All this property was in due course, in the 1870s, acquired by Mander Brothers for their own expansion, to create a valuable town centre site.

Among his many ventures, John diversified into making varnish, japans and colours, supplying the japanning trade in general, and by 'horizontal integration', the japanning materials at cost to his brother's firm next door, Mander & Shepherd. The two brothers clearly worked closely together. An entry of 1794 shows: 'Sept. 19th Payd Mr Mander, of Wolverhampton, for Paint, Oil, Turpentine, etc., etc., £2 8*s.* 6*d.*'

The growing business led to the formation of a succession of partnerships. First, in 1790, he took into partnership William Bacon, 'a gentleman of fine business skills and considerable wealth'. Then John Weaver joined the firm in 1803. Weaver, who apparently came from Shropshire, 'was a man of great energy and application to business' and expanded the trade north into Lancashire and Yorkshire, and throughout the Midland counties. But he was a man of little sympathy:

> on one occasion it was reported to him that one of his employees had fallen down a hoist on the premises and been killed. He replied: 'Ah! in the midst of life we are in death; is the cart loaded for Birmingham?'

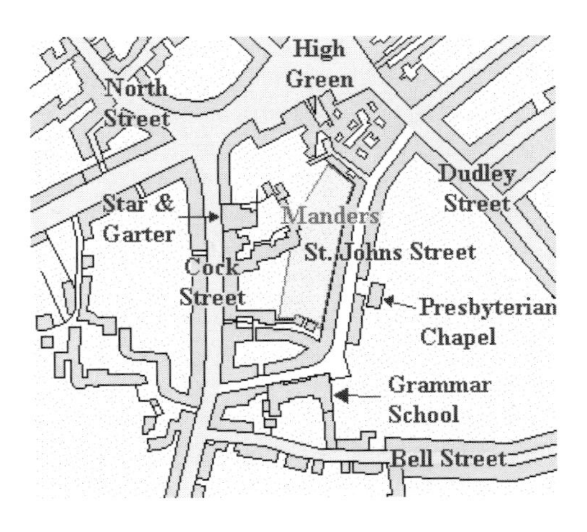

Map of the John Street area showing the Manders' works, drawn by Bev Parker

John's own son, also John, had no interest in the business, and joined the East India Company, where he was a lieutenant and adjutant in their Invalid Corps at the time of his early death in Bombay in 1821. So in 1818 his nephew, Benjamin Parton Mander, by then aged 33, was induced to quit working with his father, Benjamin, and brother, after 15 years, and to join his uncle's firm in Cock Street to secure the succession for the next generation. By that time, the capital in the firm of 'Mander, Weaver and Mander' amounted to £28,715. The Manders dropped out for good when Benjamin Parton died without heirs in 1835.

John was from the start a retail supplier. Traditionally, the tradesmen and artists had prepared their own pigments and paints, using chemicals, earths and vegetable dies as raw materials purchased from apothecary or herbalist shops. Recipes and mixing instructions were published in various handbooks, showing that making paints and pigment powders could be complex and tedious work. Then the 'colourmen' started in competition, recorded in London by the mid-eighteenth century supplying pigments for specialist trades, pre-made dried pigments in tied-off pouches of pigs' bladder 'about the bigness of walnuts', and hard, dried cakes of pre-mixed colour for artists and housepainters, stamped with the colourmen's names and wrapped in paper. These cakes were dissolved into paint by rubbing them in binders placed on special, china saucers or mussel shells. The cakes and saucers remained in use by many Victorian painters, for whom 'rubbing out one's colors' was a morning chore.

More importantly, John's main interest and success was as a manufacturing chemist. The work of the japanner and tinplate worker, exemplified by his brother, Benjamin, was confined to tinning the sheets of iron and soldering them together, and then coating and decorating the finished object. But he did not make the increasingly specialist materials which he applied, as a manufacturer of the coatings, gums and resins. There was a rapid growth of metallurgical industries with new technology, not just in tinplate working, but in all kinds of processes employed in the local trades such as children's tin toy making, enamelling,[26] iron braziers' trades, locks and safes.

The trades were often integrated, and John was well familiar with them. Both he and Benjamin senior knew at first hand the business of the tin-plate workers, who provided the containers, ovens and surfaces for the bakers like Benjamin, which had to be coated with tin to avoid being affected by salt and sugar, and who were important customers for the chemicals supplied by John.

John had identified a new market if he could successfully integrate the supply trades as well, both in Wolverhampton, and over the Black Country area from Bilston and Wednesbury to Birmingham. It was a niche opening which he had the capital, specialized chemical knowledge and, as it turned out, the entrepreneurial skill to exploit. *The Victoria County History* emphasizes: [27]

Ancillary to the japanning and enamel industries, there grew up in South Staffordshire a number of subsidiary trades producing colours, japans and varnishes. Of these the Wolverhampton firm of Mander Brothers was an outstanding representative.

His firm became one of the early Midland chemists who produced and supplied the growing array of specialist resins, rosins, copals, 'benjamins' (or 'benazoines'), tars, lacquers, spirits, turpentines, bronze powders and colour pigments, acids and grounds, from which every type of coating and stoving enamel could be prepared, and they became willy-nilly, without knowing it at the time, 'the founders of the modern coatings industry'.

Midland industry was sustained by this second, less visible layer of 'high-tech' activity in the firms that manufactured the chemicals used in the production of its famous wares, and which gave them the distinctive finishes which help to brand and market them. Plain japanning, giving the metal or papier mâché a single-colour shiny surface, was a simple matter. But with time designs became more elaborate, with painted decoration applied in burnished gold, pearl work, and 'crystallising' finishes to designs in the debased rococo of chinoiserie and tortoiseshell. Increasingly there were painted designs applied by trained artists. This demanded the use of an array of extravagant body colours, stains and mineral pigments. The 'chymists' were subsidiary trades to the japanning and enamel industries, supplying and manufacturing not just the varnishes and japans for the developing local japanned ware and allied trades, but also the colours, the specialized gums and drying oils, the solvents and thinners, the gum elemi, the cinnabar, verdigris and lake, used as colouring pigments by the artists.

John would have prepared the common chemical pigments for the local manufacturers, some requiring quite advanced chemical processes. They included muriatic acid, properly hydrochloric acid, a corrosive gaseous compound, very soluble in water; orpiment, an arsenic-sulphur combination (arsenic trisulphide) yielding a brilliant yellow known as 'king's yellow'; sal Ammoniac, a soluble ammonium chloride, white in colour, and vitreous; umber, a common natural pigment, hydrated ferric oxide, chestnut brown to liver brown in colour; litharge, the mineral form of lead monoxide, straw yellow (sometimes red) in colour, an additive used as a dryer in paint making; sulphate of lead, a mixture of lead carbonate and hydrated oxide; cinnabar (or vermilion), the bright red mineral form of mercuric sulphide, an ore of mercury found in crystals and powders; white and red lead; and many others still used by artists today.

High Green, showing 'big candlestick' gas column, looking southwest down Dudley Street, by Robert Noyes, c. 1835

John Mander's firm of 'wholesale chemists' prospered initially on the back of supplying the local trades. As it developed in complexity, size and product range, it extended to become most successful as a general manufacturing chemist, providing 'choice chemicals' for the London market; a term recalling that used in the company literature more recently, 'speciality coatings'. It was one of the first to make calomel and the various mercury compounds employed in medicine, the arts and the chemicals industry. The firm was also one of the first to trade in chemicals with the United States of America and, according to a contemporary newspaper account, 'had a large business with China and the East and West Indies, where their chemical preparations are held in high repute'. By 1851, its 'extensive chemical works' was best known for 'oil of vitriol, aquafortis, and a variety of preparations connected with medicine, manufactures, and the art of science'.[28]

John Mander's firm, trading as Mander, Weaver & Co., was also the first to manufacture gas in the town, to light their own factory and for chemical manufacturing processes requiring heat. In particular, the standard black pigment changed from lampblack to carbon black, prepared from gas. John's gas plant was still in use in the 1870s.[29] Having gained knowledge of the new technology at a time when city fathers were clubbing together to supply gas to the growing manufacturing towns created by the industrial revolution, Benjamin Parton Mander was one of two of the firm's partners listed among the 57 subscribers who formed 'The Wolverhampton Gas Light Company' by Act of Parliament on 22 June 1820, with a capital of £10,000 and the stated ambition of 'the better lighting of the Town'.[30]

The promoters pushed the enterprise actively through the summer and autumn of that year and, when two gasometers were ordered, the prospect of being able to offer gas in January 1821 'of the purest quality without smell or stain' was no small attraction.[31] A single giant iron column in fluted Doric, 40 feet high, known as the 'big candlestick', was erected in the middle of the main square at High Green, with a solitary light on top; 'like a carthorse holding up a butterfly', wrote a contemporary critic. But the conception was not an unqualified success, and it became 'a lounging-place for the most notoriously vicious and dissolute characters of both sexes'.

Regency soda jug by Mander, Weaver & Co., giving the date of foundation of the business as 1773

John became an entrepreneur of the early industrial revolution with a wide range of interests and investments. We see all the early Midland trades at this date—japanning, tin-plate working, chemical and varnish manufacture, even to a degree baking and malting—as organically interdependent, and the family emerging with involvement in a cluster of trades and ventures, maintaining the flexibility and the capital to move from one to the other. Among them, we find John Mander is recorded variously as a coal and ironmaster, apothecary, surgeon, druggist, a gas manufacturer, as well as being an investor in transport as a partner in the Wolverhampton Boat Co. in 1811. He was even making or commissioning 'Staffordshire' pottery at this time, which survives in the shape of a transfer ware soda jug with the 'Mander & Weaver of Wolverhampton' trade label, the first to give the foundation date of the business as 1773. This was to satisfy a European craze for soda and seltzer waters (as drunk by Byron, with hock) following Joseph Priestley's experiments in dissolving carbon dioxide under pressure in water. It is a craze which has never ceased.

John Mander married (firstly) Esther Lea of Kidderminster in 1778 and lived in an 'elegant villa' at The Elms, Penn Road, known familiarly as *Gallipot Hall*, 'an evident allusion to the trade carried on by its worthy owner'.[32] He also accumulated considerable property in and around the family holdings at John Street.

John's public career tracked that of his brother, Benjamin. Like him, he was a Town Commissioner, taking the chair thirteen times at the early meetings between 1805 and 1825. He was among those behind the foundation of the first 'Wolverhampton Library' towards the end of 1794, with Benjamin, and was elected to serve on the Committee. It was a subscription library, a project of self improvement rather than philanthropy 'for the mutual use and intellectual recreation of gentlemen', the subscription being a guinea a year. He acted as vice president in 1813, but appears never to have been president. In 1818, he was landlord of the property (in Princess Street) which the Library occupied.

Like his brother—and like many of Wolverhampton's rising business-men—he was a radical and liberal in politics. Characteristially, we find him campaigning against the slave trade. In 1814 he is among those who petitioned Parliament to protest against England allowing France to carry on the trade in slaves for five years or more. In January 1826 he calls and chairs a public meeting to support the government in the policy of the abolition of slavery in the colonies, 'particularly the British West Indies': 'we highly admire the Measures of His Majesty's Government for ameliorating the Condition of the Negroes, and eventually emancipating them; and equally reprobate the Manner in which these Measures have been met by the Colonists'.[33]

He was also a prominent local nonconformist, more fervent even than Benjamin. He helped to found the first Sunday School and various dissenting chapels in and around Wolverhampton. The Trinitarian congregation of the old meeting house in John's Lane was ejected by the minority of Unitarians in an unholy row in 1781. Part of the congregation moved to worship in a converted barn in Pountney's Fold (on the site of a sheep fold off Dudley Street), where they were served for the next sixteen years by students of the Countess of Huntingdon's Connexion. The Calvinist Charles Hunter with the Manders and their friends moved to worship in a little chapel in Grey Pea Walk (later Temple Street), where John and Benjamin both became deacons, and the births of Benjamin's children were registered in the late Georgian generation (1781-91).

Then in 1800 John bought a piece of land in Princess Street to build a bigger chapel. The Princess Street minute-book subsequently records: 'Mr and Mrs Benjamin Mander and Mr John Mander sit down with us as occasional members, considering themselves members of the church at [Grey Pea Walk]'. By 1819 they were admitted 'full and regular members' there. Perhaps they had tired of attending the services of the minister, John Godwin, a censorious man and very eccentric. It is said 'on good authority' that the sacrament was never administered during his 30 years ministry, as he did not consider his congregation to be Christians.[34] The Princess Street chapel had served its purpose well for twelve years when the premises were sold back to John for £400 to help finance a new Congregational chapel, while the old building became public offices where the town commissioners and the justices of the peace held their sessions.

The new chapel was built in Queen Street in 1812, again on land which John secured as 'a prominent and munificent supporter'.[35] He retained the vaults below, which were let 'to the scandal of the church' to a 'wine and brandy merchant'. One day some 'wag' posted the following verses on the cellar door:

There are spirits above and spirits below;
There are spirits of joy and spirits of woe.
The spirits above are the spirits divine;
The spirits below are the spirits of wine.

Gerald Mander commented that these[36]

ribald lines ... must have led to some head shakings in that strict and grave society. With what satisfaction must the Landlord, a regular attender in the chapel portion, have lent himself to his devotions secure in the knowledge that the basement was also paying its way!

In later life, John became a fashionable and benevolent figure about Regency Wolverhampton, involved in every aspect of its governance and especially in the proliferating nonconformist charities which became his métier. He was reputed to be the first to have a brougham carriage in Wolverhampton.[37] He died aged 73 in August 1827, marked by 'piety, virtue and intelligence'.[38] By then, the population of the town had grown to 23,000. He was a 'Georgian tycoon', writes Barty-King, who had established a durable mix of business, philanthropic and property interests, including 'one of the largest chemical elaboratories in the kingdom'.[39]

He died leaving the then considerable sum of £16,000.[40] He had drafted an eight-page will on 31 May 1827, leaving £2,000 to his second wife, Hannah (exclusive of the £1,000 left to her by her late husband), to be paid two years after his death. There was also an annuity. The £800 vested in trustees for his first wife, Esther, who had predeceased him, was transferred to his daughter, Amelia, who married a Chester wine merchant, John Williamson. He made detailed arrangements for the settling of his property all over Wolverhampton—in John Street, Queen Street, Princess Street and Can Lane. His obituary declared: [41]

He had been for about fifty years a prominent friend of religion and education, for which he was not only unsparingly munificent, but indefatigably active. Many a widow and her family have owed the comforts, and many young tradesmen their

successes, to his intelligence and generosity. The institutions which he founded will be his best monument, and the tale of the grateful his best panegyric.
His end was worthy of his life.

John was a capitalist entrepreneur first on the periphery of the great new scientific and politico-religious ideas fermenting in the West Midlands. His father, Thomas, had been born into a rural and agricultural society still recognisable as Shakespeare's Warwickshire. By the time of his death in 1827, John was contributing to an urban and industrial economy based on new applications for science in manufacturing technology and new structures of economic organisation which had caused a transformation in England and were fast converting her Midland towns into the premier workshop of the world.

Through the enterprise of brothers Benjamin and John, the Mander family was set up as a mercantile dynasty in Wolverhampton, whose fortunes were founded on the mix of businesses which continued to bear their name for over two centuries. The brothers had defined the family in the new, guiding political culture of Low Church, Calvinistic Protestantism which had triumphed in United States of America as well as England: commercially adept, militantly expansionist, firmly convinced that it represented a chosen people and a manifest destiny.[42]

[1] He is still listed as a 'baker, St John St' in the trade directories of 1781 and 1792.

[2] Venetian lacquer appeared just after the middle of the 17th century, the date attributed to one of the oldest Venetian pieces, a pair of *moretti* figures from Ham House, entered in an inventory of 1669. Filippo Bonani numbers ten different kinds of lacquer, used by the

English, French, Germans, Poles and Italians (*Tratatto sopra la vernice detta communete cinese,* 1720; Saul Levy, *Lacche Veneziane Settecentesche*).

[3] W.D. John and Anne Simcox, *Pontypool and Usk: Japanned Wares with the Early History of the Iron and Tinplate Industries at Pontypool,* Newport, 1966; Sir Richard Hanbury Tenison, *The Hanburys of Monmouthshire,* The National Library of Wales, 1995, pp. 48-9, 106.

[4] Dr Richard Pockocke, bishop of Meath and Ossory, writing in 1756, suggests the secret was learnt in Saxony (Hanbury Tenison, p. 106). W.H. Jones states tin plate was imported from there, Andrew Zarranton commencing production in the Forest of Dean about 1665.

[5] Charles Tomlinson, 'Illustrations of Trades', *The Tinman,* no. 22, 1860.

[6] W.E. Minchinton, *The British Tinplate Industry,* 1957, pp. 10-16.

[7] M.W. Thompson (ed.), *The Journeys of Sir Richard Colt Hoare through Wales and England 1793-1810,* Gloucester: Alan Sutton, 1983

[8] For an account of the local trade, see Yvonne Jones, *Georgian and Victorian Japanned Ware of the West Midlands, Catalogue of the permanent collection and a temporary exhibition,* Wolverhampton Art Gallery and Museums, 1982 [Mander Brothers, pp. 22-3].

[9] George Wallis, *Wolverhampton Chronicle,* 18 May 1860, reprinted for Charles Benjamin Mander as *Free Library and Practical School of Art.*

[10] The patent states that Clay had all rights to 'Making, in Paper, High Varnished Pannels or Roofs for Coaches, and all sorts of Wheel Carriages, and Sedan Chairs, Pannels for Rooms, Doors, and Cabbins of Ships, Cabinets, Bookcases, Screens, Chimney Pieces, Tables, Teatrays, and Waiters'.

[11] One son was Edwin (1833-93), tragedian and famous performer of Hamlet. The other, John Wilkes Booth, became outspoken in his advocacy of slavery and assassinated President Lincoln in a theatre box at the end of the Civil War, in April 1865, at the cue 'sockdolager' shouting, '*Sic semper tyrannis!* ['Thus with all tyrants', the state motto of Virginia] The South is avenged!'

[12] G.A. Godden, 'English Paper Trays, 1790-1815', *Connoisseur,* Aug. 1967, pp. 250-4, pl. 3.

[13] *Wolverhampton Chronicle,* 21 March 1793

[14] Marked 'Benjamin Mander & Son' and dating from *circa* 1792, it is illustrated in Geoffrey Godden, 'English Paper Trays', *The Connoisseur,* Aug., 1967, pp. 250-4, pl. 3. It is 30 x 22 inches. (Whereabouts unknown.)

[15] Other houses destroyed included Baskerville House, the Birmingham house in which John Baskerville had lived, which was set on fire and gutted on 15 July; the owner then was John Ryland. Baskerville was another dissenter and 'atheist'.

[16] Benjamin's daughter, Sarah Mander, still owned shares in the Birmingham Union Mill at her death in 1871.

[17] Benjamin Mander, *Wolverhampton Flour and Bread Co. Trial in 1814* , 1956

[18] *History of Wolverhampton,* p. 153.

[19] H. Barty-King suggests John Hanbury of Pontypool may well have been a forebear of Elizabeth, by which 'trade secrets' percolated to the Manders. But this seems unlikely, and the Bridgnorth/Kidderminster Hanburys were not closely connected (ex inf. Sir Richard Hanbury Tenison).

[20] The doll and the panel of 'The Two Spies returning from the Land of Canaan' are at Owlpen Manor.

[21] *Historical Sketch of the Art and Literary Institutions of Wolverhampton,* 1897, p. 6.

[22] The transcription of the grave markers in the family vault reads (transcribed 1935-6, in City archives, DX/186):

Thomas Mander the father of Benjamin, John and Thomas, died 1761, also Charles Hunter who married the widow of Thomas Mander, died 1788, also Joseph Mander son of John Mander 1800, also Esther Mander wife of John Mander died 1802, also Elizabeth mother of Benjamin, John and Thomas, died 1804. Also Benjamin Mander died 1819, also Elizabeth Hanbury Mander wife of Benjamin Mander died 1828.

Benjamin Parton Mander, aged 53, also Benjamin Mander younger son of Charles & Jemima Mander died 11th February 1842, aged 11, also Sophia Mander the wife of Charles Benjamin Mander, died 29th October 1869, aged 42, also Charles Benjamin Mander died August 1878, aged 59, also Jemima the wife of Charles Mander died 1st November 1834, aged 43, also Charles Mander 22nd December 1853, aged 73.

[23] The records for that time, with John's own papers, are lost, having gone to his own direct descendants.

[24] Roger E. Schofield, *The Lunar Society of Birmingham*, Oxford, 1963.

[25] *Wolverhampton Chronicle*

[26] Stephen Janssen opened the Battersea factory in 1753, bringing together the French designers and enamellers with the English transfer-printing process (probably invented by his manager, John Brooks). It closed after three years, when the focus of the trade moved to Bilston in the Midlands, where it had been established by 1749.

[27] *Victoria County History of Staffordshire.* An account of 'John Mander and Reade Brothers' was contributed by Thomas Reade to *The Wolverhampton Journal*, June 1907.

[28] William White, *History, Gazetteer and Directory of Staffordshire*, Sheffield, 1851

[29] George Lee, a Manchester cotton mill owner, was the first to order William Murdoch's industrial gas lighting for his factory in 1805.

[30] I Geo. IV, cap. viii.

[31] *Wolverhampton Chronicle,* 22 November 1820

[32] W. Pitt, 1817. A *gallipot* was an alembic, symbol of the apothecary and chemist (*OED.*). But *galipot* is also the residue from distilling Bordeaux turpentine.

[33] *The Wolverhampton Chronicle*, January 17 and 25 1826.

[34] GPM, *History of Wolverhampton*, p. 166: 'Note by SMM in their Church Book'.

[35] For the history of this church and its predecessor in Pountney's Fold, see Samuel Small Mander, 'Historical Sketch', *Queen Street Church Manual*, 1873; Henry Arthur May, *Queen St. Congregational Church, Wolverhampton: The Story of a Hundred Years, 1809-1909,* 1909; A.G. Matthews, *The Congregational Churches of Staffordshire*, 1924; and GPM, *History of Wolverhampton*, pp. 130-1.

[36] *History of Wolverhampton*, p. 149

[37] 'A closed four-wheel carriage drawn by one horse, very similar to the old growlers.' Although by some accounts the brougham, named after Lord Brougham (1778-1868), was not introduced until about 1838. (Joseph Aloysius Hansom [1803-82], the local architect, was inventor of the 'Hansom Patent Safety Cab' in 1834.)

[38] His memorial tablet has been moved from Queen Street Congregational Church to St Peter's Church (west end): 'THIS TABLET,| IN PERMANENT REMEMBRANCE OF | JOHN MANDER, GENT.| THE UNWEARIED AND MUNIFICENT FRIEND| OF RELIGION AND EDUCATION,| IS INSCRIBED| BY A GRATEFUL AND AFFECTIONATE CHURCH| AND CONGREGATION| AS A RECORD OF PIETY VIRTUE AND INTELLIGENCE.| HE DIED AUGUST XXII. MDCCCXXVII | AGED LXXIII.'

[39] John Smart, *Directory of Wolverhampton,* 1827

[40] Jane Austen writes in *Persuasion* that a gentleman must be worth at least £20,000.

[41] *The Wolverhampton Chronicle*, 29 August 1827

[42] Kevin Phillips, *The Cousins' Wars: Religion, Politics and the Triumph of Anglo-America*, 1998

CHARLES THE FIRST

3

CHARLES MANDER

1780-1853

Charles 'Primus' Mander was the first of (now) seven generations to bear the name Charles,[1] ever since used by the senior representative of the family. By early 1791 he was away at school, being educated with his aunts, the Miss Reads, who ran a dame school in Vicar Street, Kidderminster. Then he went to Mr Harrod's School at West Bromwich, 'where I was robbed of my precious time,' he wrote bitterly sixty years later, 'and have felt the loss of it all my life, to the present day ... in my 71st year.' As he left to boarding school, his mother, Betsey, offered him pious admonitions, typical of her letters written to him as a small boy, to 'behave well and remember that, be where you will, the greate God sees you and knows all your thoughts and actions. I beg you not to tell anything that is not true.'

Two Pence 1st Pair. G.R.

This Indenture Witnesseth That Charles Mander son of Benjamin Mander of Wolverhampton in the County of Stafford Baker, of his own freewill and accord doth put himself Apprentice to Benjamin Mander of Wolverhampton aforesaid Baker to learn his Art and with him (after the Manner of an Apprentice) to serve from the sixteenth Day of Febuary 1795 unto the full End and Term of seven Years, from thence next following, to be fully compleat and ended. DURING which Term, the said Apprentice his Master faithfully shall serve his secrets keep his lawful commands every where gladly do. he shall do no Damage to his said Master, nor see to be done of others; but to his Power, shall let, or forthwith give Warning to his said Master of the same. he shall not waste the Goods of his said Master nor lend them unlawfully to any. he shall not commit Fornication, nor contract Matrimony within the said Term. he shall not play at Cards, Dice, Tables or any other unlawful Games whereby his said Master may have any loss With his own Goods or others during the said Term without Licence of his said Master he shall neither buy nor sell. he shall not haunt Taverns or Play houses, nor absent himself from his said Master service Day or Night unlawfully. But in all things as a faithful Apprentice he shall behave himself towards his said Master and all his during the said Term. AND the said Benjamin Mander in consideration of the service aforesaid

his said Apprentice in the Art of Baker which he useth by the best Means that he can shall teach and instruct, or cause to be taught and instructed finding unto the said Apprentice sufficient Meat, Drink, Cloaths washing & Lodging and all other Necessaries during the said Term.

AND for the true Performances of all and every the said Covenants and Agreements either of the said Parties bindeth himself unto the other by these Presents In Witness whereof the Parties above named to these Indentures interchangeably have put their Hands and Seals the fifteenth Day of Febuary and in the Thirty fifth Year of the Reign of our Sovereign Lord George the Third by the Grace of God of Great Britain France and Ireland KING Defender of the Faith and in the Year of our LORD One Thousand Seven Hundred and ninety five

NB. The Indenture, Covenant, Article, or Contract, must bear date the day it is executed, & what Money or other thing is given or Contracted for with the Clerk or Apprentice, must be inserted in Words at Length; and the Duty paid to the Stamp Office, if in London, or within the Weekly Bills of Mortality; within one Month after the Execution, & if in the Country & out of the said Bills of Mortality within two Months, to a Distributor of the Stamps, or his Substitute otherwise the Indenture will be void, the Master or Mistress forfeit fifty Pounds, & another Penalty, & the Apprentice be disabled to follow h. Trade or be made free.

Signed Sealed and delivered being first duly stamped in the Presence of us · Samuel Bradley · Phebe Stones

Charles Mander

Benj. Mander

Indenture of apprenticeship of Charles to his father, Benjamin, Feb. 1795

He seems to have learned by these worthy precepts, as his conduct was grave and irreproachable to the end of his days. But his formal education was clearly brief. For, on 16 February 1795, aged fifteen, he was indentured for seven years as an apprentice baker, as trade practice required, to his father, Benjamin.[2] He then continued with his brother, Benjamin Parton Mander, for a while in business as a japanner and tin-plate worker. Thomas Shepherd was not proving great assistance, and left the partnership with Benjamin in 1799, creating an opening for the younger generation. From this time onwards, Charles (Primus) and Benjamin Parton (junior) became more closely involved in their father's japanning business, though it never really thrived.

He was known as 'Boots', 'on account of his boots'—at a time when such were an important article of dress. Charles, at a height of 5ft 6in (average for the time), according to his passport, with light brown hair, grey eyes, and wearing 'mixture', or tweed, was travelling to Ireland in April and again December 1800, at the time of the Rebellion. In 1808 he still describes himself as a 'japanner' first and foremost. But the two brothers gradually came to the conclusion that the future lay not in the restricted and traditional business of japanning alone, but in making japanning *materials*—in particular, varnish.

Varnish, 1803

Charles was already making varnish to supply the growing japanning business in the area by the age of 23, spurred on by his uncle John next door, who had been doing it for 30 years. It was the obvious 'high tech' development. The varnish book of the brothers has survived, with its first entry in Charles's hand bearing the date 1803:

Jan 13	Maddox	
	2 quarts fine Copal 32	16*s.*

In 1804, they were supplying O. & W. Rytons' japanning works, the most famous in the town, trading at the Old Hall:

2 gallons Var 32	£3 4*s.*
Can	2*s.* 4*d.*

It was the symbiosis of these two trades, japanned ware and then the varnish and chemicals to supply it, which led to the development of the Manders business.

Varnish making was a rising young industry, still developing under the experimental formulations and new processes of pioneers such as John and then Charles Mander. An impetus had been given by the publication in France of a book by Jean-Felix Watin called *L'Art du Peintre, Doreur et Vernisseur* of 1773. This inspired a host of experimenters in England, and several British patents were taken out. This was an arcanum where 'secret formulas' and techniques abounded, and elaborate precautions were taken to prevent their discovery. Because the Birmingham-Wolverhampton-Bilston area was the centre of the japanning, metalworking and tin-plate trades that used so much of it, it became also the centre of manufacture and innovation in the varnish industry, with the first varnish production organised on the factory system in Britain at this time. In France and Germany it came a generation later, in 1820-30.

The early days were not without difficulty, but Charles Mander was a man of scrupulous integrity in matters great and small. In the 1810 depression, trade was bad. 'In consequence', the record states, 'of acts not his own, he was found himself compelled to make a composition with his creditors', of thirteen shillings in the pound. Ten years afterwards, being in a position to do so, he honourably paid the remaining seven shillings, 'an example it would be well to find more frequently followed'.[3]

Business did prosper eventually though, and success was consolidated. The transparent varnish used by japanners was a gum copal varnish which contains less drying oil and more turpentine than ordinary painters' varnish. Charles's black 'japan' varnish was to become a phenomenally successful product in late Georgian and early Victorian England, cheap and strong and of good quality, used long after the decorated trays and furniture for which it was formulated had gone out of fashion.

Formula books survived into the 1970s of the firm's formulations of the 1830s, 'Varnish for Mander & Co.:[4]

best pale 4 lb Copal good 1/2 lb good Animi 2 1/2 lb of good thick green Oil with a little raw Oil in 2 oz sugar of Lead 4 Qu^{ts} turpentine sold at £9—0—0 pr Cw^{t}

There are formulas for 'Spirit Varnish', 'Lock Varnish', 'Pontepool Varnish' and 'Blk Japan for Mander'.

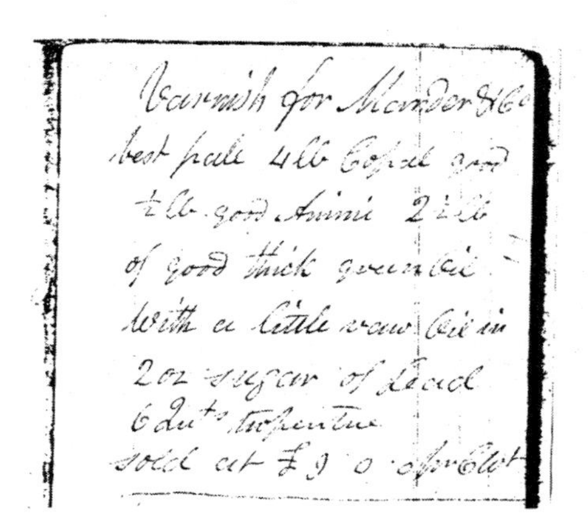
Varnish for Mander &Co
best pale 4 lb Copal good
½ lb good Animi 2½ lb
of good thick green Oil
with a little raw Oil in
2 oz sugar of Lead
6 Qu^{ts} turpentine
sold at £9 0 0 pr Cwt

By 1817 the twin varnish and japan works employed some 30 people. In 1818 Charles is still listed as a japanner, varnish maker and tin-plate worker. The works remained on a domestic scale, the manufactory arranged like 'the once beautiful back premises of a gentleman's house'. The works occupied the extensive spare land between Cock Street and Woolpack Alley (still existing up to the 1970s) which had been owned by John and Benjamin.

As well as organizing the works, Charles was travelling widely to sell and promote his varnish. Gerald Mander writes:

The death of Benjamin Mander in 1819 left his son to confront all the difficulties attached to a one-man show. It was not the easiest of things to keep up the manufacturing part and at the same time be away for days if not weeks at a time trying to sell varnish and establish a reputation for it. Foreign trade was at this time done through merchants; his own journeys did not take him further afield than Ireland.

Many of his letters travelling on business in the early years of the century survive and form an invaluable account of the life and high ideals of the early industrial families, operating among a network of nonconformist co-religionists throughout the Midland counties and the West. He is seen developing new markets, using varnishes for the decorated panels of coaches. We have a lively account of his efforts to sell carriage varnish in the West Country, dated 7 November 1817:

I wrote my beloved wife from Bristol on the 5th in which I informed her I purposed leaving there as yesterday morning. Agreeable thereto, I left at 6 o'clock, and arrived at Bridgwater soon after 12 o'clock, where the only coach-maker keeps an Inn, at which, of course, I dined.

Before dinner, I got an interview with the landlord (Mr. Sutton), with whom I had some difficulty to give my varnish a trial. He said he did all his business with Mr. Ives, and had done for more than 20 years, except when he had been persuaded to try some other, of which he had always repented. However, I must talk to his son, to whom he left the management of the business. I soon got the ear of the son, who took two quarts from me, and promised he would give it an immediate trial himself, and if he approved of it, the next time I came he would give me an order.

At two o'clock I left B-water for Taunton, where I arrived before four o'clock, in which place there are three coach-makers. With great difficulty I prevailed upon the principal to try the two quarts I had with me, and from each of the other two I got an order for one gallon of Body. At 7 o'clock I came on by the Mail Coach to this place [Exeter], where I arrived about 12 o'clock at night, rather tired I assure you.

This morning I sallied forth, and found there were six coach-makers, and having but two samples with me, I of course attacked the two best first. The first I called upon received me rather pleasantly, but said he could not try it without consulting his brother, who was out. I, however, talked to him till he said he had a body just ready for varnishing this morning, and if I would bring it him, he would have it immediately used, and if approved of would order when I came again.

From him I went to the next in point of consequence, and he positively told me he would have nothing to do with it; he bought all his varnish from one person, and would try none else, for he had been taken in too often. However, having a good brassy face, I was not to be put off with such trifles as those, and then I began to argue the point with him and to give him proof that I was no impostor, but understood what I was about. At last I succeeded so well with him that he, like the other, said he had a body just ready for varnishing, and if I would let him have it, he would give it the first coat this day. I found the third nearly as bad, but I talked the matter over with him, till he told me he would enquire from one of the others with whom he was intimate, and if he approved, perhaps he may write to me before I came again. From the two next I took an order for two gallons from each, and the last I did not press, as he appeared to be doing nothing, but left him my card.

Thus, my dear, I have given you an account of my two days' labour—but to whom must I attribute the success thereof? Not to myself I am sure, but to Him "who has the hearts of all men in His hands, and can turn them as rivers of water, which way so ever He pleases." I asked it at His hands, and blessed be His name, He has heard and answered my request! O! that I had a heart full of praise to His great name, who is the God of all my mercies.

I have taken an inside place (for it is very wet) to leave here at 8 o'clock tomorrow morning for Bath, where I hope to arrive about 9 o'clock and where I trust I shall find a letter from the Dear Partner of my life, and of all the comforts I can procure her, which I sincerely wish were more and better. Tomorrow I shall of course be journeying all the day.

O! that I may not only experience journeying mercies, which are indeed very great, but the presence of the Lord the Spirit communing with me by the way, till my heart shall burn within me! Then journeying mercies will be sweet indeed! I look forward with great desire to Sabbath Day. O that it may be a Sabbath indeed to my soul! May the presence of Jesus be felt by me, and by faith may I be enabled to call Him mine, then indeed will it be a Bethel to my soul never to be forgotten. A Sabbath began below, the blessed effect of which will never be lost through an eternity.

Blessed be His dear name, for the least desire I feel towards Him, I cannot procure this myself, but I want to feel more of it, to feel Him precious, and to know that He is my Lord and my God, to live wholly to His honour and His glory and to do more for His great name. 'Mine should the profit be, but His should be the praise.'

Wishing you every possible good, I must conclude with assuring you of my unceasing affection and believe me,

Your truly devoted husband,
Chas. Mander.

Please write me for Monday. Post to the Swan Inn, Bridge Street, Bristol, where I hope to be on Tuesday.

I have just heard since I wrote the above that the Princess Charlotte[5] is no more! Lord what is man? "At his best estate he is altogether vanity."

Charles Mander's trade letterhead

Charlotte Sophia (1744-1818), queen of George III, who died the following year, had been an early patron to Charles Mander. It was perhaps in fashionable Georgian Bath, a few years before, that he had clinched the sale of which he was most proud, when he managed to sell her a supply of varnish for her own carriages. From then on, throughout the nineteenth century, the firm's letterhead, indeed every communication from the firm, triumphantly bore her royal arms above the inscription *'Manufacturer to Her Majesty The Late Queen Charlotte'.*

The Royal Family are known to have patronised the Midland japanning industry. George III admired Henry Clay of Birmingham's techniques for lacquering on paper or slate (patented in 1778) to make buttons for himself, describing himself in the 1790s as 'George the button-maker'. Clay was also 'Japanner to the Queen', and in 1793, presented her with a sedan chair with papier mâché panels. The next royal warrant for Manders was awarded with greater formality by George V, nearly a century after the sale to Queen Charlotte.

The expansion of the business was not without its upsets. In the 1820s, the firm suffered a 'great fire' which nearly destroyed the whole of their property. Again Gerald Mander takes up the story:

> Strenuous as this was, there were also times of stress at home when he would work into the early morning at the office, 'his health better than usual' (1820). It was about the year 1824 (or perhaps later) when a great fire broke out in the works of Mander, Weaver and Mander, next door in John Street. The fire started in the morning and lasted the whole day; several lives were lost. The heat, an eye-witness says, was terrific, even the panes in the windows of the houses opposite were melted, machinery, iron, wooden floors and roofs were all destroyed; terror and confusion reigned throughout the whole town. Soldiers with fixed bayonets were placed at both ends of the street to keep the crowd back. Many ready helpers, men and women, carried water from the market place and other neighbouring pumps to pour on the ruins. Charles Mander's stock rooms adjoined the burning walls, but the only damage caused him was from the hasty removal of his goods. He was away at the time, and did not arrive back until all was in order again. The town pumps no doubt played their part. More interesting would be the parish beadle and the hand fire-engine solemnly squirting the blazing mass.

The varnish works had certainly been soundly established by 1831. One William Wiley had become in due course Charles's right-hand man as chief manager and invoicing clerk. Jemima died in November 1834 and, on January 17 of the following year, Charles Primus took Wiley into partnership, so that, with the accelerating 'whirl of business', he could concentrate on varnish making. It was to prove a disastrous mistake which was to unleash 'a lurking storm'. As senior partner, Charles Mander insisted that he should be free to 'barter with the paper tray makers and others varnish for paper trays and other things as he has heretofore been accustomed to do', and even stipulated that the new firm should buy all its paper trays from Mander at cash price.

Charles was clearly content to delegate the cares of the japanning side of the business. The partnership deed stipulated that Charles and his two sons would 'devote the whole of their time to the business of a Varnish Maker', while Wiley would handle the japanning business, which they foresaw would be abandoned when the 14 years' life of the partnership was up in 1849. The capital was fixed at £4,000, of which Charles had two thirds, probably indicating the rough weighting between the two trades.

An invoice of the following year (1835) describes Mander & Wiley on the letterhead as 'Japanners, Tin Plate Workers and Manufacturers of Fine Paper Goods, Fancy Pontypool Work & Co.' A Mander & Wiley invoice for Charles's 'varnish side', as it continued to be called well into the twentieth century, survives dated 4 February 1835:

6 gall	tar spirits
6 gall	turpentine
2 gall	gold size
1/2 pint	quick dry varnish

But the deed proved a most unworkable arrangement. Soon there arose a 'visible change' when, instead of 'harmony', 'there was opposition', and 'painful contentions', resulting in a disturbance in the workforce up to the point of 'a complete mutiny'. Wiley seems to have taken off for days at a stretch with what cash he could lay his hands on, and didn't live up to the 'trust and confidence' placed in him by the God-fearing and strict-living Charles. He was soon driving Charles to distraction. A note of his quoting the Second Book of Samuel appended to the family Bible (1730) reads:[6]

> This prayer suddenly darted into my mind as I was walking down John Street, Wolverhampton, at the time I was being so basely treated by Willm. Wiley. And I was immediately assured that I would be delivered out of His hand! And *it proved so. Blessed be the Lord!* He was never again permitted by me into the manufactory!

Sure enough, there was acrimony and, as Jemima Cox wrote, 'All disputes ended in dissolving the partnership'. When Benjamin Parton, Charles's brother, died aged 50 in 1835, he left his brother £3,000 'in consequence of the very distressing circumstances in which he has been placed by his late partnership with Mr Wiley'. The formal announcement of the dissolution after 18 months 'by mutual consent' was dated 10 June 1836.

Wiley set up on his own account, taking with him into partnership Charles Mander's chief ornamentor, Hancher, and other employees. The 1838 trade directory lists among 27 japanners active in the town: 'Wiley & Hancher, Japanners, Tin Plate Workers and Varnish Makers, Zoar Street, Wolverhampton'. We are told that they did not prosper, and in due course many of the employees they took with them wished to return.

Yet Charles Mander's japan ware trade plodded on successfully a little longer. At an exhibition of local manufactures held in Wolverhampton in 1839, a prize of one guinea was offered for 'the best piece of Japan Ware, the ornamental part being an original design'. Charles Mander entered two vases and shared second prize with another Wolverhampton firm, Edward Perry. The vases, one with a claret ground and the other with a green ground, were above two feet high and decorated by Mr Stockwin, one of Mander's artists. (First prize was won by the famous Old Hall works.)

But Charles was clearly losing interest, as the japanning and tin-plate businesses became decidedly secondary. It was varnish which evidently proved the more profitable business, and Charles, as he was reaching retirement, finally sold the japanning and tin-plate businesses altogether in order to concentrate on varnish making on 31 August 1840 to a Scotsman named William Shoolbred.

Shoolbred had learned the craft with the local japan master, Edward Perry. He continued in the business under various partnerships, notably with Henry Loveridge, to the 1870s. In 1848 they moved from John Street altogether on completion of the huge industrial buildings known as Merridale Works. There they installed the latest machinery and the firm in the third quarter of the nineteenth century became one of the biggest japanning firms in the country, trading as Henry Loveridge & Co.[7] It made both tin and paper wares but 'tended to concentrate on articles of utility rather than ornament', though it was well represented in the latter field by the artist Richard Stubbs. It finally closed in 1927.

The moment Charles chose to sell turned out to be well judged, as the Wolverhampton japanned ware trade never maintained its position and popularity. There was social unrest, with a tinplate worker's strike in 1850.[8] 'The tray branch of the trade does not stand as it did some 20 years ago, customs having changed, and fashions with them,' George Wallis was writing by 1860.

But the varnish trade continued to thrive. Charles was still on the road selling varnish for the firm in 1841, writing to his daughter, Elizabeth Smyth, apologising for tardy congratulations on the birth of her fifth child (she was only 26) on the grounds that he 'was fully engaged about the time looking after and obtaining the Names of respectable Persons with whom I may probably take some orders for Varnish':

> I opened 7 accounts for Varnish in Derby as I passed through it on my way home from Boston, and have already had another order from one of them to varnish a Church. I was in London nearly a month in September and took many orders, and have already had a much larger order from One Person there who exceedingly approves of it. I think it very probable that I shall, if spared, make a good trade of it, with much less anxiety than the Japan Trade.

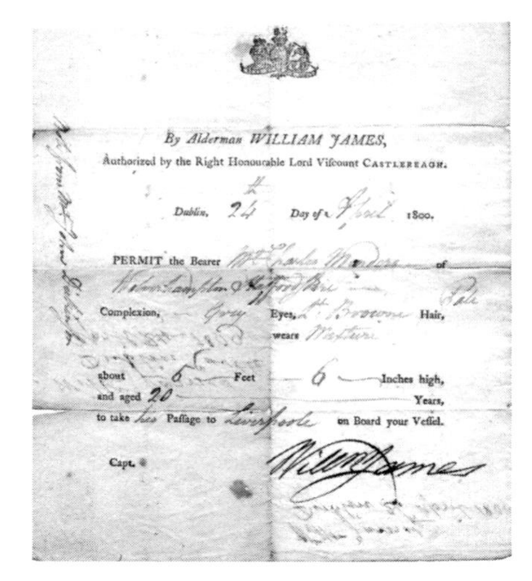

By Alderman WILLIAM JAMES,
Authorized by the Right Honourable Lord Viscount CASTLEREAGH.

Dublin, 24 Day of April 1800.

PERMIT the Bearer Mr Charles Mander of Wolverhampton Stafford Shire Pale Complexion, Grey Eyes, Lt Browne Hair, wears [illegible]

about 5 Feet 6 Inches high,
and aged 20 Years,
to take his Passage to Liverpoole on Board your Vessel.

Capt.

Willm James

Charles Mander, traveller—passport of 1800

Regulations for a Traveller, 1839

In the archives of Manders there survived until recently Charles Mander's *Regulations for a Traveller,* giving advice to a salesman representing the firm, dated about 1839. It is worth quoting at length for its earthy flavour of life and manners on the road in the days of the coaching inns, and the wise counsel of an experienced man of affairs freely given to a rising generation. Charles had travelled widely in Georgian England, sober in the days of wine dinners, when a bottle of port for each man after the midday meal was the norm, and dispensing hospitality to customers was part of the traveller's inducement. Alderman W.H. Jones, writing in 1900, recalls how the Wolverhampton japan masters would take their journeys only once a year, their samples packed in saddle bags slung across the backs of pack horses. When the master was about to depart on his annual journey, 'the work people used to crowd around, to give him a hearty send off, wishing him a successful journey, and a safe return home'.

The Paramount duties of a Traveller may be compressed in a narrow compass; the most essential in addition to his Assiduity, Temperance and an undeviating attention to the principles of Justice, between Employer and Representative, are:

Early Rising—which will be found conducive to the promotion of Health and Comfort and consequent longevity, together with the advantages of being prepared for actual business while others are wasting their time in slothful indolence, recovering in beds, the results of the previous night's intoxication or other bad practices—wasting the best part of the day in apathetic indifference, which ought to be usefully, rationally and industriously applied as a step to present happiness and the attainment of future comfort.

Sobriety—This does not require to be detailed upon, for if a young man is not governed by prudence appropriately of conduct, he is unfit for a Traveller—for it is an invariant axiom that the man who neglects his own duties and moral obligation is of too worthless a character to merit either esteem or confidence.

Punctuality—Is an indispensable requisite. For where there is not an universal attention to punctuality, there will be no respect paid to the individual, however talented he may be in every other respect; for confidence once lost, is rarely afterwards to be recovered or restored.

Honour—This admits of an extensive application: such as an undivided attachment to the interests of his Employer; the strictest care and integrity in the application of the property that may be placed in the possession of the Commercial Representative; obedience to all lawful commands; strict attention to all the relative duties.

If you travel in your own vehicle, start early to make a stage before breakfast and, if by coach and there is a choice, travel in those hours least suited for the transaction of business—carefully arranging to avoid the markets and if possible to arrive on the evening of it, or early the next morning—and be sure to *lose no time before* making your first call, as by so doing you will *save* much time, and frequently catch your customer before he leaves home—and if he has small journeys, may prevent wasting a day or perhaps losing time for the journey.

If you stop the night, see your room and have all you wish carried into it—as your packages are otherwise soon known by others and advertise your presence.

Avoid singing in a Commercial Room, for that will lead to your company to be courted not so much for your own personal gratification, but for the only pleasure of hearing your vocal powers, and that temporary pleasure, the indulgence of vain inclination which has led to the ruin of many who might otherwise have been the highest ornaments of commercial focus.

Avoid if possible to be the Chairman or Vice President of the dinner table, the ridiculous and absurd etiquette ruins health and is the destroyer of time, producing an empty purse and loss of reputation—nor sit more than 1 hr.—taking care to notice the wine, and call for the dinner bill before the full quantity is brought in... If there are more than [three] only, 1 bottle divided betwixt them, or glass of mixture each is usual.

Avoid political discussion and by all means religious controversy, for where you cannot convince it is useless to waste your time.

Firmness and integrity in principle and practise will be found the best shield for the protection of person and property. If you have any leisure time after the hours of business, exercise it usefully—and for the improvement of your mind by laying the foundation of future excellence by reading and reflection.

Dinner bills are often swelled by those who state good will to the house to be their motive—but it is nearly always the case, it is either a man *fond* of wine, or a *dealer* in it, or *spirits*—avoid them.

It will generally be that the servants or landlord notice those who carve economically and like them better than the dashing spenders—as *they* frequently destroy more than they use.

Suppers are unusual—a late tea with meat if you like it and a glass after is sufficient.

I usually found it necessary to use breakfast, to have it in good time—but if possible make engagements before breakfast and late in the day, so as to avoid the retail business hours as much as you can.

If you have a horse, take care to see he is attended to before you sit down to your meal—it saves time and keeps the ostler to his duty. *Always see it fed,* if you can, and bedded up in the evening; having a horse it is usual not to have any charge made for your own bed.

Servants are paid thus:
Ostler: horse only, 2d.; if a gig, 3d., and extras according to the trouble; 6d., oiling the wheels and washing the gig. Horse per day and night, 6d. Horse and Gig, 6d. *per meal;* 9d. per day and night.

Boots: 2d.; trouble, extra pay—for shoes *or* boots.

Chamber maid: 6d., if bed *is changed or not.* Extra trouble, extra pay, such as water for the feet, etc.

Waiter: 2d., or 6d. per day if only one meal; sometimes it's well to give 3d.

Coachman: 6d. per stage, or if you travel more than one change of horses, 6d. for about 20-30 miles. If 60-100, *guard:* much the same, but rather less, except if more than 40 or 60 of luggage, then payment accordingly, as it is under the guard's care.

If the coaches [leave] early or late or hours not convenient to customers, it saves much time. Be careful to learn from the coachman what coaches [leave] your next stage and use the limit as a reason to urge your friends quickly to transact your business.

If compliments are usual, keep up old customs, remembering if you [do so] it is [always] easy to retrace your steps.

In all cases treat servants with respect for their services—and carefully avoid familiarity with either male or female.

To spend the Sunday thus: Breakfast early if cold weather and the room is full; order a fire in your room (the usual charge: 1/-). I usually avoided the dinner table and took cold meat or chops or a steak about 1 o'clock. Tea about 5 o'clock; and a toast or jelly or something light or a small Welsh rarebit and a glass at night.

Carefully avoid walking the streets or leaving your inn after you have closed business for the day—take off your shoes and put on your slippers.

The Representative should be required to write home to his Employer at least twice every week, in addition to the orders required on the last day of the week, accompanying the Balance sheet statement of the current week. By this regulation, not less than three letters will be received weekly from the Representative, which must be a transcript of his order book and, on examination therewith at the close of the journey, be found strictly in accordance.

Should however any order be given to the Traveller of an extensive kind, or that require immediate attention ..., a letter should be sent home daily.

When you receive cash, let it be first entered into your order book before it is put into your purse, and invariably enter upon your tablet the cash you are going to pay before such payment is made.

Charles married Jemima Small (1791-1834), the daughter of a linen draper from Boston, Lincolnshire, who was orphaned before she was thirteen.[9] She matched him in piety and, Charles wrote proudly, she 'lived and died in the fear of the Lord'.

Gerald Mander relates the manner of their meeting in his *History*:

There was some romance in the meeting... He was travelling the eastern counties in [1808] and lost his way, which in the general absence of sign posts and A.A. men was confusing. The rider wisely left matters to his mount, and the old mare instinctively led him to Boston, where Mrs Charles Mander that was to be, dwelt, the eldest of a family of orphans, and aged [17]. But her uncle and guardian made her wait till 21.

Some of the early correspondence of their courtship is preserved, including the first letter the love-smitten Charles wrote to Jemima on 17 November 1808, when she was 17, letting rip a touchingly candid outburst of passion for one whose surviving letters, with much in the way of tedious prayers and preachings, usually show drear restraint:

Silhouette, family group, 1824
(attributed to Miss Clayton):
Benjamin Parton, Jemima, Betsey, Charles, sister

My dear, very dear Jemima!
It is now little more than a week since I left Boston in which sweet place I spent many happy hours; many more than I have since I left it. I am now more & more persuaded by experience that there is nothing like affection to bind one, either to a place or a People. It is an old observation & still remains a very true one, that 'where the treasure is, there will the heart be also' —indeed, I who have a heart so very hard, have found it so of late, if I never did before!

When, my dear, I reflect upon my first interview with you where and when I most instantly approved of you! upon my second in which I admired and esteemed you! and upon the third, in which I not only felt a love for you, and failed not to declare it, but for the first time ventured to kiss those sweet lips, from which afterwards I received so much pleasure; with the delightful seasons I afterwards experienced with you: I say when I reflect upon the train of events, connected with the very singular manner in which it pleased Providence to bring them about, I am really lost in astonishment!!

Being late before I left Boston, I only reached Bingham that evening, and that not till after it had been sometime dark. Upon my arrival there, to my great mortification it was their fair, and the house very full of company; so that, what with dancing and one strange noise and another, I was fearful I should spend a miserable evening, and have no time to myself for reflection; but all was much better than my fears, for the Old Lady very kindly put me into a room by myself, so that though I heard their clamour at a distance, I was not much annoyed by it.

And now my dear Girl! to convince you (that at a time I was thus surrounded with the vanity and bustle of the giddy multitude) I had not forgotten one so dear to me; I will give you, out of the abundance of my thoughts which that evening passed though my mind, a few... Can this be love? I must confess my dear Jemima I do really think it is! nay, if I am capable of judging from my own feelings, I am sure I love you! Well be it so, I must confess I feel very great pleasure in the reflection... May I not hope that some breach may be made in that strong citadel which you expressed yourself so capable, and determined of defending against all attacks of the enemy? May I not hope that I may yet find favour with the little sentinel! who keeps guard, and from him get possession of the keys, by which an easy access may be gained to ... the Castle?...

As I have formed so strong an attachment for you, that it is my wish to live and die with you, so it is also my most earnest desire, that we may live to him who is alone able to make us happy in life, in death, and to all eternity!

Charles also enclosed some powder for her friend, a Miss Hill, perhaps some new-manufactured cosmetic to conceal the ravages of the pox, which he was able to obtain in the Midlands:

I enclose the powder, and although it is very far from being a mill, to grind old women young; if properly applied, it may add to their beauty by taking away part of their deformity.

This arrived after ten days' journey, and Jemima acknowledges it curtly: 'We have ventured to inform Miss Hill of the Powder but have not yet dar'd to offer her any, tho we intend doing it under the excuse of accommodating her Friends'. He sent her copies of his favourite nonconformist tracts, *The Kingdom of Heaven Taken by Prayer*, and an autobiography by the eccentric divine, William Huntingdon (1745-1813).[10] These were clearly not her choices: 'there are Books I like much better', she half-heartedly replies.

Her reply is delayed, dated 3 December, a rebuff indicating that on the advice of her guardian, aunt and 'best friend', Mrs Lee, she should remain in her present situation, and wait four or five years, 'and indeed I'm firmly resolved not to engage with *any one* at present'.

You wish'd me to write an affectionate letter, that I cannot do, nor dare I even confess you sincere when I recollect what I said; but it will teach me for the future to be careful how I speak my mind before the Gentlemen.

Furthermore, she thinks that any liaison would be most unsuitable between her, as an Independent, and 'Mr Mander', a Calvinist, so that she professes herself 'unworthy your notice'.

Jemima Mander (1791-1834), 'with a bauble'

He continues to 'plague' her, as she complains, with long god-fearing letters, and sends her a pair of trays, doubtless Japan work of his own manufacture, as well as a cornelian clasp and brooch to wear on her gown, and a silver one for her pelisse:

Nothing I understand is more fashionable than the few trinkets herewith enclosed… the brooch for those sweet flowing ringlets must be placed where my little girl pleases.

Her portraits depict her as striking in a coy and severe Georgian manner; in one she is depicted 'with a bauble', perhaps the one given her by Charles. As Gerald Mander opines, any good looks which may survive in the family seem to have come from her. Charles, describing her upbringing in Boston, and her religious 'impressions', was obviously struck with her high moral and religious interests:

She was born in Boston in Lincolnshire, and from everything she could remember, and could learn about them, her parents, lived and died in the fear of the Lord, but both being removed by death, before she attained the age of 13 years, she was left in the hands of guardians.[11] Some years before this time, she had serious impressions, and would frequently leave her playfellows to listen to the conversation of those who were considered godly people, when she had an opportunity, and so much enjoyed those seasons that play was forgotten by her. She continued at times to have some concern about her immortal soul, and often feared the thoughts of dying. She was very moral in her outward conduct, and strictly careful always to tell the truth, and that even if she may suffer by so doing.

He was eleven years older, and lapses easily into a prissy, avuncular tone. He seems to have taken her on as a candidate to convert to his own doctrines as an earnest spiritual counsellor, with 'a zeal for the cause of God', and his conviction in a 'particular' providence, which was 'special', rather than a 'dangerous' free will:

But having embraced the dangerous doctrine of free will, she thought she could fall in with the offer of mercy and repent and believe when she pleased, and despised the free grace doctrines of the gospel.

In this state Mr Mander found her, when he was first brought to an acquaintance [with] her and for some time after he had formed an attachment to her, he thought he must have given her up on this account alone. But being persuaded that he was led by the special direction of providence to a knowledge of her and knowing that the Lord could if it pleased him, break down all prejudice against the truth, ?teach her, her utter helplessness, and ruin; and bring her to be willing to be saved in His own way. He frequently made her ease a matter of pray[er] and made the doctrines of free discriminating grace the principle topic of his letters, in reply to one of which she said, she was surprised he could say so much upon the inability of the creature. She could pray when she liked, repent when she liked, and believe when she liked. To this he replied, if you can, pray and repent, and believe when you like; you deserve to be damned if you don't. This coming from one who professed such great love to her, she thought very hard, but upon investigating the matter, she concluded he was right; for if she could, and would not, she certainly deserved to be lost. She therefore resolved on trying what she could do, and soon found to her great mortification she could do neither. All her boasting was put an end to, and soon began to be more and more out of love with herself.

Her uncle and guardian finally allowed Jemima to marry Charles at the church of St Botolph's, Boston, with its 'Stump' prominent over the flatlands, on 17 December 1812, aged 21 years and one month. Bills survive for the wedding cakes—'2 Plumb Cakes 20 1/4lbs @ 2/6 per lb', bought of M. Wilkes for £2 11*s.* 3*d.*—and then for their setting up house, including 'A Comp^{n} Set of Best Blue Painted Egyptian Landscape Containing 210 Pieces' bought of Mrs Rollason in Birmingham for £9 10*s.* 2*d.*

She was to die aged only 42, having had ten children, from typhus contracted while helping the poor in the Wolverhampton slums at Horseley Fields. An account of her death is preserved, from clinical detail to spiritual edification:

On Saturday 11 October 1834, she went down into the cellar and it is supposed took cold in consequence thereof. The next day, finding herself unwell, she only attended chapel twice, and Monday medical aid was called in, and Wednesday following, from the very painful state of her head, leeches were applied to her temples, by which the pain was removed, and she appeared so much better that her medical attendant said she may come downstairs on the following Sabbath. This proved to be more exercise and excitement than she could bear, and caused a relapse of her complaint.

She gradually became weaker until Friday evening October 31st ... after 8 o'clock, as her husband was sitting by her bedside, she ... said, "What a poor, vile, sinful wretch am I. Too bad to be spoken about." And a few minutes after she exclaimed, "Oh! How wonderful, that He who is the high and lofty one that inhabiteth eternity, whose name is holy, should condescend to take upon himself one creature to bleed and die for poor sinners, and for us!" turning, and looking with great expression at him as he sat by her.

About 10 o'clock she look[ed] at her husband with a sweet smile, and said, "All is well my Dear! All is well!" From which time she soon became insensible, fell into a sound sleep out of which she never awoke, or became conscious of anything; till she burst her prison with sweet surprise and awoke in Glory! about a quarter past nine o'clock on Saturday night November 1st.

Charles's loss was 'a heavy billow over his soul', according to Jemima Cox. But 'his sorrow was not as one without hope', because his deceased wife's younger sister, Elizabeth, came to assist in the household and 'was now a valuable help in his bereavement, taking all care off his hands'. She must have cared fondly, for he married her six years later, aged sixty, on 17 March 1840 at St Peter and Paul's Church, Aston, Warwickshire. Perhaps he was by then mellowing, in sympathy with the reviving Church of England. Elizabeth was 43 and, like Jemima, helped with the accounts and invoicing for the firm. She was described by Jemima Cox as 'a great economist [or housewife] and a real Christian'.

Ten years later, aged seventy, having set up his sons in partnership to follow him, Charles retired to the sea air of fashionable early Victorian Brighton.[12] He died suddenly of apoplexy in Croydon three years later, on 22 December 1853. His estate was valued at £16,154 12*s.* 3*d.*, including £4,000 in property and £3,750 in Mander Brothers. His obituary, no doubt guilty of fulsome hyperbole, declared that he was by then representative of 'the oldest family now in the Town'. In fact, there must have been many older; the family had been settled there little more than a century. The trade directories list him amongst the 'gentlemen'.

As member of the emerging merchant classes which were fast coming into political and economic prominence, Charles 'Boots' Mander had championed the philanthropic causes of the time as his conscience dictated for reform, but with his 'lovely countenance which beamed with kindness' captured in his portraits, he was by temperament quiescent, fastidious and benign, and never interested in the tiresome graft of official duties. His obituary notice in the *Wolverhampton Chronicle* remarked that he took little part in public affairs, as he was 'possessed of a Tyburn ticket'[13]—or mirror of one, feeling himself exempted from office by his early intervention to save the lives of the soldiers Hall and Morrison. He was a man of scrupulous integrity 'in the faithful discharge of whatever appeared to be his conscious duty'.[14] He was also an accomplished man of affairs, and his varnish business was to prosper and endure effectively to this day.

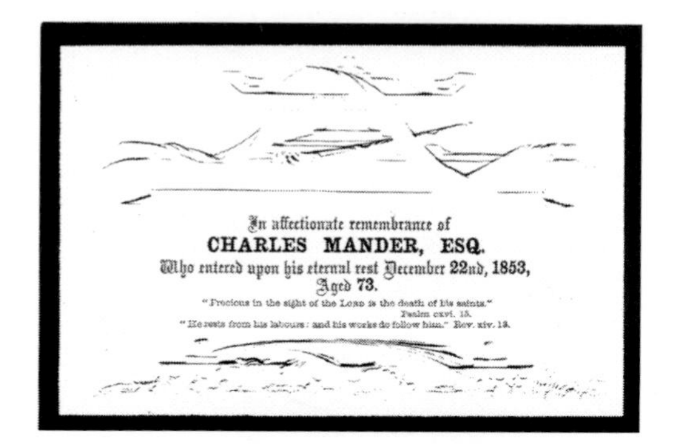

Charles Mander, funeral card of 1853

---

[1] Gerald Mander suggests he was named after the Scotsman, Charles Hunter, his step-grandfather (who had married Elizabeth [neé Clemson], widow of Thomas).

[2] The indenture of apprenticeship to his father and his passport survive in the Owlpen archives.

[3] *Wolverhampton Chronicle*, 28 December 1853

[4] The formula book of Mander, Weaver & Co. was inherited by Reade Brothers when they acquired the goodwill of the firm in 1873. 'It is likely that the first entries date from 20 years before 1853 and were made in the 1830s'. Mander & Co. would be Charles Mander's firm before it ceased japanning in 1840. (See H. Barty-King, 'Preliminary Survey for Mander Brothers of Wolverhampton to establish foundation as 1773', unpublished ms., 1971.)

[5] Princess Charlotte Augusta, daughter of the Prince Regent, was born in 1796 and died after giving birth to a stillborn son on 5 November 1817. The news caused an outburst of national grief which gave rise to the jingle: 'Never was sorrow more sincere| Than that which followed Charlotte's bier'.

[6] Chapter 15, verse 31: 'And one told David, saying, Ahithophel is among the conspirators with Absolom. And David said, O Lord, I pray thee, turn the counsel of Ahithophel into foolishness.'

[7] The Merridale Works was to have a new claim to fame when workshops there were taken by Sir Kenneth Corfield for the manufacture of photographic equipment. K.G. Corfield Ltd became the country's leading 35mm. camera manufacturer in the 1950s. The Works was demolished in 1973.

[8] It produced the ballad 'Song of a Strike', sung to the tune of 'King of Cannibal Island': 'There is a strike in Hampton town,| Caused by two men of great renown,| Who hope to do the tin-men down, |And so reduce their wages.'

[9] Dr William Small (1743-75) was a Scottish chemist and metallurgist, who succeeded John Roebuck (1718-94), the patron of James Watt and 'the father of Midlands chemistry'; Hugh Barty-King suggests he was related to Jemima.

[10] Huntington was a preacher who led an unconventional and scandalous life, styling himself a 'sinner saved'. He seduced a young woman, the daughter of a tailor at Frettenden, Kent, and decamped on the birth of their child to settle with a servant girl called Mary Short in Mortlake. He describes his experiences of a 'conversion', and later a vision of Christ, and became a Calvinistic Methodist, though his doctrine was flavoured with antinomianism, and claimed to be under the direct inspiration of God. After many reversals, he finally ran what he termed a 'Providence Chapel' in Gray's Inn in London. It seems that in early life Charles was prepared to be influenced by the fiery and unconventional nonconformist sects proliferating under the lethargy of the contemporary Church of England.

[11] Her father, Thomas Small (died 26 July 1803 'of an inflamation of the brain'), married at Raithby 1790 Elizabeth, née Harpham (born Low Taynton 16 July 1757—died 2 May 1803 'of a dropsy', aged 45). Her grandfather, Stephen Small, was accidentally drowned on 19 Jan 1806, aged 75.

[12] He conveyed the John Street property to his sons CBM and SSM 7 May 1846, and is described as 'now of Brighton, gent.' by 20 Aug. 1849 (Wolverhampton Archives, DSR/33/2).

[13] Granted to one who secured the conviction of a felon, so exempting him from all parochial duties *(OED.).*

[14] *The Wolverhampton Chronicle*, 28 December 1853

4

BLOOD MONEY

Two Soldiers Rescued from the Gallows, 1817

Charles Mander followed the emerging family tradition as a man of high public ideals and a zealous social reformer. Two cases were widely reported and caught the public imagination of contemporaries, one inspiring a minor novel and both leading directly or indirectly to Acts of Parliament.

The first concerns penal reform.[1] On 23 July 1817 two soldiers, John Hall and Patrick Morrison, billeted in the town on a detachment from the Ninety-Fifth Foot, were denounced by one George Roberts, the keeper of the House of Correction, or 'Whipping-House' as it was called, in Stafford Street. Their crime was to knock down John ('Jack') Read, a bricklayer's labourer, in a drunken brawl in St Peter's Old Church Yard and rob him of just 1*s.*1*d.*—a shilling coin and a bad penny. The incident seems venial, but this was then classed as highway robbery and so technically a capital offence. Following a lurid sequence of events, just six days later, on 29 July, they were condemned to death at Stafford Assizes.

The true story seems to be that Jack Read, an unemployed vagrant and 'blackguard' in his early fifties, had arrived in Wolverhampton on foot from Birmingham on Tuesday 22 July, looking for work. He spent the afternoon drinking in the Three Crowns in Dudley Street. After getting into a scrap, he went into another public house, drinking till nine, when, much the worse for wear, he was ejected by the publican after punching a soldier in the face; he staggered into the evening air, and lay down drunk in the main square. Short of money for a lodging, he eventually wandered into the churchyard sometime before midnight, where he went to sleep on one of the tombstones.

John Hall and Patrick Morrison were off duty, and spent the evening similarly drinking and smoking till nearly one o'clock in the morning, long after 'closing time' (at 11 p.m.), by which time they had been locked out of their lodgings at the Fox Inn. Perhaps the idea of spending the night in the churchyard occurred to them also. At all events, they wandered towards St Peter's, where they found Read in the churchyard, drunk and disorderly. They instantly recognised him as the drinking companion who had punched one of them earlier that evening.

Read, a bully who fancied his prowess as a wrestler, challenged them there and then to a fight. Hall, the younger, was game, and the two men grappled. In the second bout, Hall got the better of Read, who was thrown to the ground, inadvertently dropping two coins from his pocket as he fell. It was all the money Read had, and according to a witness, he tried to pick it up at once, but Patrick Morrison kicked his hand away and snatched both coins. Read demanded them back and, as the young soldiers absconded laughing, Morrison either flung them on the ground before him, or pretended to do so. Precisely which we shall never know. It remains one of the mysteries at the heart of this drama.[2]

Early the following morning, Read, with a 'dirty bloodstained face' after his 'bit of a skirmish' with the two soldiers, set off to look for one of the constables who were responsible for law and order in the town, muttering that 'two soldiers had been abusing him and had murdered him'. By half past eight, William Bell, a japanner passing by, had told George Roberts of the incident in the main square. Roberts showed 'considerable interest', saying 'It will be a good job for us'.

As the prison keeper, Roberts fancied he knew a little of the law, and seems immediately to have set about attempting to mould the events to fit the allegation, by making out that the incident had been in the eyes of the law a highway robbery—and a capital offence. By 'stage managing' a case, he hoped to secure the summary conviction of the soldiers as highwaymen. Then he and Read would be entitled to their fell reward as the price for bringing them to the gallows, sharing the 'blood money' between them.

Under the Parliamentary Rewards System, the so-called Blood Money Act (one of the statutes of 4th and 5th William and Mary, c. 8), anyone who succeeded in securing a conviction of another for felony such as duly led to their indictment and hanging was entitled to a reward as *blood money.* The rewards were intended to encourage private citizens to use the justice system in the fight against the epidemic of crime, but they became a temptation to frame the innocent and 'a fearful premium by which many judicial murders were committed ... and one of the worst Acts that had ever disgraced the Statute Book'.[3]

We know that as soon as Roberts heard of the incident, he seems to have sought out Read with desperation in order to concoct a plausible story and move false evidence against the soldiers. He went with Bell, Read and others to apprehend the men at the Fox Inn, handcuffing them and marching them away in their red coats as they were about to go on parade. The soldiers soon found themselves arraigned before a clerical magistrate, Mr Haden of Tettenhall. Read duly twisted his story, swearing blind that the soldiers had assaulted him and knocked him down unprovoked, robbing him of his money in the churchyard.

His perjury lead to its horrific upshot, with a rapid turn of events. The soldiers were immediately imprisoned in the miserable conditions of Roberts' 'Whipping House'. The magistrate duly committed them to be tried at the coming Assizes at Stafford and they were entered on the 'long and melancholy list' of those to stand trial before Sir William Garrow (1760-1840) on Saturday 26 July:

> John Hall, aged 22, and Patrick Morrison, aged 25,
> for assaulting J. Read in Wolverhampton.

Sir William was a hanging judge; one of the barons of the exchequer and sometime attorney general. Hall and Morrison were without witnesses and allowed no counsel to plead their case before him. Despite their previous good character and protestations of innocence, inevitably their case was poorly presented. They pleaded not guilty, foolishly attempting to perjure the court on the grounds of mistaken identity. The jurors found the accused guilty as charged:[4]

> The Jurors for our Lord the King upon their oath Present that John Hall and Patrick Morrison ... with force and arms in the King's highway there in and upon our John Read in the Peace of God and our said Lord the King then and there being feloniously did make an assault and the said John Read in corporal fear and danger of his life in the King's highway aforesaid then and there feloniously did put and one piece of silver Coin of the proper Coin of this realm called a shilling of the value of one shilling of the good chattels and monies of the said John Read... in the King's highway aforesaid then and there feloniously and violently did steal take and carry away against the Peace of our Lord the King his crown and dignity.

The Judge duly pronounced his sentence: 'For an highway robbery on John Read and violently taking from him a shilling his property. To be hanged.' The time and place set for execution was outside Stafford jail on the morning of Saturday 16 August.

The inhabitants of Wolverhampton soon heard news of the death sentence, writes Gerald Mander:

> Up to this point [they] had not been interested in the case. Soldiers were birds of passage at the best: if they chose to become gaol-birds it was their own affair. Disorderly conduct must be punished, property protected. Those who had considered the matter at all expected a conviction for common assault. But the disparity between the offence and the sentence came as a shock to sympathetic readers when they saw it much later (as the paper had to carry the news forward a week) in the Wednesday *Wolverhampton Chronicle* of August 6th 1817. Public opinion was stirred to protect the soldiers, and it was evident that speedy action also was needed if the death penalty was to be averted, for only nine days remained.

The news threw the town into a state of excitement. Peter Burke (1811-81) takes up the story in his detailed account of 1854:

> Their unjust condemnation became at once the loud subject of converse and comment in the Wolverhampton market-place. It chanced that an elderly gentle-

man, Mr Benjamin Mander, a highly respectable inhabitant of Wolverhampton, being then in the market, heard what was saying, and was struck with its momentous bearing. Returning home, he communicated the incident to his son, Mr Charles Mander, who became the instant champion of their cause. To the philanthropic zeal and activity of this Mr Charles Mander, the poor wretches owed, under God, the preservation of their lives. The country, too, was indebted to Mr Mander for relief from the dreadful calamity of putting the guiltless to death.

Charles's interest as a man of conscience was immediately aroused, and he decided to take up the cudgels on behalf of the soldiers. As Gerald Mander relates:

Charles Mander ... heard the news from his father, who had heard it in the market place, and knowing that legal process must be met in due form, they wisely sought legal advice, and in this case free advice, from their solicitor, Mr George Tompson. There must be a petition to the Prince Regent and a 'memorial' to the judge. Public support was forthcoming; people stirred their memories; additional affidavits were prepared.

There was no time to lose. Witnesses to an alibi were found and, in the course of the day, twenty people came forward to testify to their innocence.[5] Charles had their affidavits written and sworn before a magistrate by the Sunday. On Tuesday, at least eleven more persons gave evidence under oath and letters were dispatched to Whitehall. Charles straight away took the post the whole way to London, reaching London late that Tuesday night, 12 August. The following morning he went with his brother-in-law, James Pearsall, 'an eminent silk-mercer in Cheapside', to petition the Home Secretary, Henry Addington, Viscount Sidmouth, for a reprieve for the innocent men.

Sidmouth, accused by history as a man of mediocrity[6] and grave countenance, gave Charles Mander and James Pearsall instant admittance. A conference of some length ensued, Sidmouth paying every attention to what they had to say, and becoming deeply interested. So earnest were Charles Mander's pleas for the lives of the two condemned men that Sidmouth later declared that he had 'never in his life seen such an amount of interest exhibited in the fate of two men who were not related by domestic or other ties of affection to the individuals who were thus exerting themselves on their behalf'. At length, Sidmouth was persuaded to examine the affidavits.

When they returned that evening, Sidmouth told them he was impressed with their view of the case and that a respite had already been forwarded by special messenger to Stafford. Charles Mander insisted he should write out a copy lest the original should miscarry and, as his clerks had already gone home 'because of the lateness of the hour', this Lord Sidmouth did in his own hand:

Duplicate

Whitehall 13 August 1817

Sir

I am to signify to you His Highness the Prince Regent's Commands in the Name and on the Behalf of His Majesty, that the Execution of the Sentence of Death passed upon John Hall and Patrick Morrison, now in Gaol at Stafford, should be Respited until the further signification of His Royal Highness's Pleasure.

I am Sir

Your most obedient
humble Servant
Sidmouth

The High Sheriff of the
County of Stafford

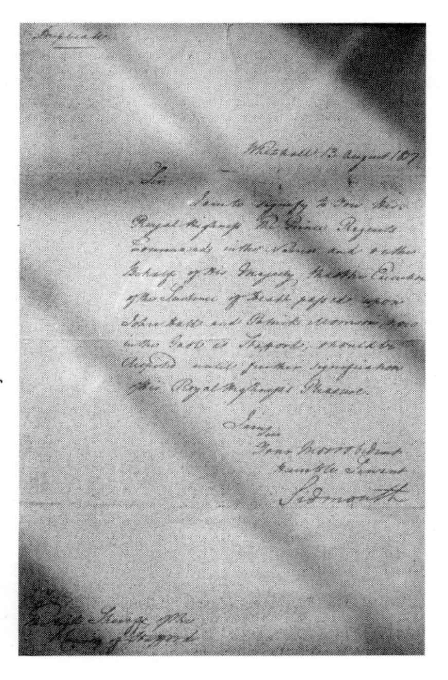

Meanwhile, John Guard, the Herefordshire vicar of Pembridge, the Hall family village, had done his own lobbying and also secured an introduction to Lord Sidmouth, from Lord Somers of Eastnor Castle.

The grim atrocity of the affair was becoming widely known in the Wolverhampton area, and causing a great deal of excitement. When Charles returned with a copy of the Reprieve for the High Sheriff of Staffordshire, there was a crowd of more than 2,000 people waiting in High Green, the main square of Wolverhampton, for the mail coach by which he was expected to arrive. He was able to read out Sidmouth's respite. It was greeted by tumultuous cheers and Charles became a hero overnight.

An abbreviated account abstracted from the contemporary sources is given by Gerald Mander:[7]

The people of Wolverhampton awaited the result expectantly and, the King's Messenger having passed through the town unnoticed (it is possible he went by the shorter, postal route), Charles Mander was the first to give tidings of his success to an eager throng. He was spared the melodramatic: a last minute reprieve from the scaffold, which retelling the story is apt to inspire, for the final spectacle was not staged, and his copy of the Reprieve was not used. It is preserved, with the affidavits and papers concerned, by his descendants.

The movement towards a free pardon was slower in taking shape, but it was signed a month later.

Indeed, a respite was a stay of execution, but not a pardon. There was no retrial. The judge, Sir William Garrow, read over the new evidence and advised the Prince Regent to issue a pardon on 31 August. But still the men were not released. The public became impatient. On 8 September a 'respectable requisition' calling for a public meeting was handed to the town constables signed by sixty citizens of the town—including of course Charles Mander. It was published in the *Chronicle* of 10 September and the meeting took place two days later. A unanimous resolution was passed, expressing surprise that Hall and Morrison were still in prison in spite of the considerable exertions which had been made to furnish Sir William with sworn statements they themselves had heard read. They asked the chairman, Francis Holyoake, to write to the Secretary of State soliciting a speedy determination to the case.

Whitehall wrote back to state that the pardon had already been forwarded to the High Sheriff. When the two men were finally freed from jail on 17 September, 'they came with their wives to Wolverhampton, and dined at Mr Mander's house. A large subscription was raised for them.'[8]

Holyoake had written to Sidmouth adding the opinion that 'the convicts if guilty cannot be pardoned at present without prejudice to the questions which have been raised against the character of Roberts'. An enquiry was held into the conduct of Roberts on 27 October, convened at the request of Lord Talbot, the Lord Lieutenant. Gerald Mander writes:

> The unexhausted part of public opinion turned its attention to an investigation into the conduct of George Roberts by the magistrates who appointed him. This caused some heated letter writing to the press. There was a die-hard reactionary, a point of view voiced by a long and violently worded letter by an eccentric lawyer who took on himself to cast doubt on the new affidavits and to point out that, had the victims only been sentenced to transportation, no one would have taken any notice.[9] How true!—but it was not the humane or considerate view. This was taken by the magistrates who 'resolved unanimously that it did not appear to them that Roberts was actuated by any corrupt or improper motives in the prosecution of Hall and Morrison and that in their opinion his character for humanity had not been in any way impeached.'
>
> And if they could not remove George Roberts, they could remove his post, for Nemesis overtook it. General William Dyott of Freeford, who in his retirement found interest in the question of prisons, when on his way to a visit at Wrottesley (15 March 1820) 'took Wolverhampton in my way, for the purpose of inspecting the house of Correction, which I found in a most filthy, dirty, shameful state' (*Diary*, i, 333). Later, at the Sessions, he writes 'I had a long debate after dinner to support my motion to discontinue the Wolverhampton House of Correction, but I carried my point without a division.' Later, the prison was advertised for sale.[10]

News of the case carried far and wide. Benjamin had been the first to encourage his son to intervene when he heard report of the impending execution in the market square. He was now rewarded publicly for his part in saving the men's lives. Son Charles and he were granted a number of Diplomas, including the Diploma of the London Vaccine Institution, founded under Sir James Shaw as Mayor of London in 1806, as a 'benefactor of humanity'. Hugh Beams writes presenting the Diploma on 10 November 1817:

Sir,

Under the consciousness of their Institution being a life preserving Establishment, the Managers have peculiar pleasure in seizing the occasions of marking their admiration of those Characters who distinguish themselves by their philanthropy in whatever Country.

The Diploma of their Metropolitan Establishment is therefore respectfully presented to you, Sir, as one of those gentlemen who by their happy exertions on a late occasion prevented atrocious homicide which the eye of office was found too dull to detect. Perhaps their families may hereafter consider this testimonial as a civic crown voted to their predecessors by a respectable Society.

I have the Honour to be, on behalf of the Managers,

Sir, Your mo ob humb servant

Hugh Beams. Secretary.

Charles wrote back to Mr Beams late, on 24 November, 'after an absence from home which had prevented him for expressing his warmest thanks', declaring he took great satisfaction, thankful that his efforts were crowned with success, although he 'only performed a duty I owed to them as my fellow creatures, in snatching them from an unmerited and ignominious death'.

The case won increasing notoriety, and the sense of outrage and public guilt remained. It was a time of much agitation for penal reform. Charles and his activists lobbied and manoeuvred behind the scenes. Scarcely a year later, in the next session of Parliament, his intervention led, with other similar cases that had preceded it, to the repeal of the iniquitous 'Blood Money Act' itself. First, the High Sheriff and the grand jurors of the county of Stafford presented a petition to Parliament imploring the House to do away with the evil of 'blood money' at the earliest opportunity.[11] Then the Conviction of Offenders Rewards Bill was introduced by Henry Grey Bennet, the radical Member for Shrewsbury in the next-door county. The Government was moved to act.

Sir Samuel Romilly (1757-1818), solicitor general (from 1806, in the administration of 'all talents'), was acquainted as Charles Mander's counsel in the John Street Chapel chancery case the year before. He now helped him to advance the cause in Parliament. He spoke to the bill on 4 May 1818, inveighing against the undoubted evils of the system of 'rewards':[12]

Rewards had the necessary effect of warping the evidence and of inducing informers to give a colour to their testimony, calculated to achieve their object in the conviction of a prisoner. The system, beside inducing persons to conspire against the lives of innocent individuals, created in witnesses an eagerness for the conviction of prisoners quite revolting...

It was one of Sir Samuel's last acts of philanthropy, as he died on 2 November in the same year when he slit his own throat with a razor 'in a fit of temporary derangement'—affecting Lord Eldon to tears.[13]

The repeal was passed on 13 June 1818 (58 Geo. III, cap. 70). Eventually, with the tide of reform in the country, the death penalty for many such petty offences was abolished. The case of 'the unmerited sufferings of two innocent men' was recounted long after. Most notably, it gave rise, writes Peter Burke, to the 'beautiful fiction' by the Methodist novelist, Samuel Warren (1807-77), *Now and Then*, published in 1847.[14] Henry Hylton is the chief character, the *honnête homme* and Charles Mander-figure, romanticized, elevated, and removed to a pastoral context: 'a man of good family; powerful industry; of accurate scholarship; deeply read in divinity; of great decision of character, and lofty independence of spirit; and fervent piety'. He is portrayed here as a worthy magistrate and clergyman, whose heroic intervention with the Secretary of State in London secures the respite at the eleventh hour of the goodly, innocent yeoman, Ayliffe, who had been condemned to hang for a midnight murder when circumstances pointed irrefragably to his guilt.

The real-life story formed a vivid drama with a happy outcome. Burke himself collected it among his compendium of the memorable and curious law cases of Georgian England.

---

[1] The case is recounted in Peter Burke, *The Romance of the Forum*, 1854, series 1, vol II, pp. 18 ff.; W.H. Jones, *History of the Congregational Churches of Wolverhampton*, 1894, pp. 43 ff.; G.P. Mander, *The History of Wolverhampton*, pp. 156-7; R. Swift, *Crime and Society in Wolverhampton, 1815-60*, Wolverhampton Public Libraries, 1987 (based on Ph.D. thesis, 'Crime, Law and Order in Two English Towns during the early nineteenth century: the experience of Wolverhampton and Exeter 1815-56', University of Birmingham, 1981); and John Ward, *Blood Money: an incident in Wolverhampton with national consequences*, Wolverhampton Public Libraries, 1988.

[2] Tompson's letter to the *Wolverhampton Chronicle*, 12 November 1817.

[3] *Wolverhampton Chronicle*, 28 December 1853.

[4] PRO: ASSI 5/137/17

[5] Twenty-seven affidavits (but not these ones) in the case have come to light in the PRO, rediscovered by Dr V.A.C. Gatrell, fellow of Gonville and Caius College, Cambridge. There is also further correspondence covering the case, giving a full background.

[6] Sidmouth, who had earlier (1804-11) replaced Pitt as prime minister, is now chiefly remembered to 'every schoolboy' for Canning's barbed quip: 'Pitt is to Addingtonl As London is to Paddington.'

[7] *History of Wolverhampton,* p.156. This series of affidavits is lost, but the Reprieve is preserved at Owlpen, together with the Diploma later awarded (see below).

[8] P. Burke, *Romance of the Forum*, p. 30. Hall was the only one married, to Jane, of Pembridge, Herefordshire. He had joined the army at the age of 15. Morrison was from county Mayo, Ireland. Both had already served in the West Indies.

[9] *Wolverhampton Chronicle*, 26 November 1817
[10] James Potter, a county surveyor, had made an inspector's report of its appalling conditions already in 1804, which survives (quoted at length in Ward, op. cit., p. 7).
[11] 10 April 1818. L. Radzinowicz, *A History of Criminal Law*, vol. 2, p. 75.
[12] *Parliamentary Debates*, Conviction of Offenders Rewards Bill, 4 May 1818, vol. 38, 1818, p. 503.
[13] Romilly was a penal reformer who took an active part in various philanthropic movements and who had pursued the cause of the amendment of the criminal law in his pamphlets and in Parliament. He had succeeded in abolishing the death penalty in cases of stealing from the person (1808), and in 1811 and the following years proposed several motions for the substitution of transportation for the death penalty for various offences. He was author of 'Observations on the Criminal Law of England, as it relates to Capital Punishment, and on the mode in which it is administered' (1810, 1811 and 1813).
[14] *Now and Then* opens as a social novel of criminality and the law, arguing the moral case for reform. Other practitioners in the genre were largely forgotten authors such as Pierce Egan, Ainsworth, Whitehead and Moncrieff. Warrren's narrative follows the Wolverhampton case in bare outline and occasionally in detail, but there is no mention of blood money as a motive.

The Methodist novel was arguing 'not from theories but from facts' and there is a strong undercurrent of realism. Lytton's character of Thornton in *Pelham* was drawn from life (from the actual murderer Thurtell). Warren was a practising barrister and jurist, editor of Blackstone's *Commentaries*. He demonstrates his sympathy for the criminal against a background of dire social conditions to preach his didactic purpose for the reform of the criminal code, inspired by men like the same Samuel Romilly. The fiction is interwoven with sentimental observations of scenes of rural distress and thin, pasteboard characterization, losing its way with *longeurs* in the second half of the novel.

The scene is set in the first chapters. The haughty nobleman 'of ancient lineage and vast possessions' in his castle; the 'reduced' yeoman, the fifth Adam Ayliffe, father to son, living in his neat freehold cottage at his gate; the cunning but callous steward who seeks to oust him of the poor remnant 'of his fathers' estate' which stands in the way of the earl's proposed improvements; the poverty and ever-present threat of the workhouse; the entrapment of the diligent but proud young Ayliffe by his acceptance of the gift of a hare at Christmas for his sick wife; his false accusation for poaching; the trial and consequent fine (paid by Mr Hylton); the sudden murder of the young heir to the earldom in the woods; Ayliffe's accusation and the blackness of the case; the melodramatic law court scene before the Lord Chief Justice himself; the guilty verdict and capital conviction; the establishment by Hylton of a motive for malice against the prisoner; his departure post haste at midnight for London; his visit to present new evidence to the Secretary of State; his 'noble and disinterested exertions' before the hesitating Lord Chief Justice; the respite issued in duplicate; his return awaited by an eager crowd. An awful murder mystery unfolds, worthy of Wilkie Collins (but more turgid) 'which baffled the impious daring of human conjecture, [but was] reconcilable with the ineffable wisdom and justice of the Almighty maker and governor of this world'...

5

THE GREAT FIGHT AT WOLVERHAMPTON

The John Street Chapel Case, 1816–39

The second Act of Parliament for which Charles Mander was at least in part responsible is where religious history again enters the story.[1] Like many early industrialists, Charles was a pious nonconformist whose business was run on paternalistic-religious lines, with prayers in the workshop to begin every day.

The flavour of life in his early factory is caught in the description by Jemima Cox, associated with the firm as a devoted and faithful servant for 54 years from September 1817. In 1871 she describes in her memoirs the fervour which governed all business dealings, and the pious regimen of the factory floor:

> My dear master had a zeal for the cause of God. A large parlour in front of his house had been used for Divine Service previous to the opening of the old Baptist Chapel. Many a happy hour have I had in that old Meeting House while listening to the truth. Mrs. Mander's sweet voice started the hymn tunes. I suppose my master's purse found a good share of the expenses of the supplies...
>
> After a portion of the Scripture read at breakfast time, prayers for blessings on the day followed, and for years a portion of the Scripture was read in every shop on the premises, in failure of which there was a fine to pay.

There were many groupings of dissenters following the Toleration Act of 1689, including Presbyterians, Baptists and Independents. Charles pondered long and hard over his successive allegiances, changing denomination from Unitarian to Trinitarian, until in later life he became a Baptist, and finally a 'Particular' Baptist.[2] He was throughout a courageous defender of religious freedoms. His tendencies hardened over time solidly against the emerging 'new' Unitarianism,[3] espoused by many similar trading families of the rising urban middle classes. He found comfort in the more Calvinist and traditionalist Trinitarian doctrines, which became aligned more closely with the evangelical revival in late Hanoverian Anglicanism, as expressed for example in the Clapham sect.

The background is complex. The Toleration Act had formalized the acceptance of Dissent, but it became narrower and less structured in polity. Increasingly it focused on the self-governing meeting house and congregation rather than a national church as the unit of association, with ministers as the head of a congregation of believers, and financial control in the hands of lay trustees. The result was that the deacons and richer members of the congregation often dictated to the minister himself, and the trustees who controlled the endowments became an unaccountable, self-perpetuating oligarchy.[4]

In doctrine, Dissent had shifted from the enthusiasm of the mid-seventeenth century, to the rationalism, materialism and latitudinarianism of the early eighteenth, and in the process often leaned dangerously towards heresy. Already by the mid-seventeenth century, Unitarianism in particular was becoming dangerously anti-trinitarian. Unitarians, 'denying the doctrine of the blessed Trinity', were excluded from the benefits of the Toleration Act. Under the Blasphemy Act of 1698, they were liable for three years' imprisonment for propagating such doctrines. A schism started to widen between the Trinitarians and the Unitarians, with their emphasis on intellectual 'necessitarianism' and polemic for rational Christianity, as well as political reform. Unitarianism became associated in its extreme form with a schematic framework of the denial of the divinity of Christ, departing from the primitive 'Socinian' tradition, which had been textual: Bible-centred and exegetical.[5]

The Midlands, with its burgeoning middle class wealth and the education that went with it, was a focus of Unitarian activity.[6] Its doctrines were developed and debated there by members of the intelligensia. Coleridge observed that Joseph Priestley, with his avowal of Socinian Christianity and his indefatigable proselytising at this time in Birmingham, 'must be considered the author of modern Unitarianism'.[7] Perhaps John Mander, sharing a broad professional interest also in the new experimental chemistry, attended the meetings of Priestley and his circle. The father of William Hazlitt, the essayist, was Unitarian minister at Wem, in Shropshire. He was visited by Coleridge, who was planning in 1798 to replace Mr Rowe as full-time Unitarian minister at Shrewsbury nearby.

The origins of Unitarianism in Wolverhampton go back further, to the ejection of the minister, John Reynolds, from his living at the main Collegiate Church in 1662. The local history of Dissent had focussed on the John Street chapel, built in 1701 as a Presbyterian 'meeting house', when his followers congregated under the care of John Stubbs.

Gerald Mander takes up the story from the arrival of John Cole as 'settled' minister in Wolverhampton in 1759:

It was during the ministry of Rev. John Cole that further trouble arose to agitate this small religious body, but this time trouble came from within and not without. It was also at this time that the Mander family, whose property lay near the

Meeting House, became interested in the movement and in August 1772 the name of Benjamin Mander, together with that of Peter Pearson, was added to list of trustees. The friction which agitated and divided the small congregation of the Meeting House in John Street arose from questions of doctrine. Unitarianism was becoming popular (although in fact it was still proscribed) and Mr. Cole leaned towards this new line of thought.

Matters came to a head in September 1780 when the Calvinist section under John Mander (the brother of Benjamin), his cousin John Hanbury and one Joseph Linney sent an ultimatum to Mr. Cole demanding his resignation. But Mr. Cole was a man of peace and decided to go rather than fight the issue. On his suggestion, Mr. William Jameson, who had preached eight probationary sermons, was appointed and, on 24th April 1781, he arrived with his family and all his worldly possessions to take up his appointment.

The situation was not working out as the Calvinist Trinitarians under the Manders and their friends wished, but the Unitarians under Joseph Pearson[8] and his son Peter seemed to be in complete possession. Charles Hunter, stepfather of Benjamin and John Mander, and a Scottish Presbyterian by upbringing and training, sought to take possession of the chapel, but found the Unitarians under Pearson entrenched, and had to retire, leaving them masters of the situation. A new chapel was started in Grey Pea Walk (now Temple Street) and to that place Charles Hunter, his friend and fellow-countryman John Smith 'late of Creigmuie, Linen Merchant' and the Manders transferred their support.

In due course, at the John Street chapel itself, violent scenes took place during which it was successively occupied and reoccupied by the warring parties under respectively the Manders and the Pearsons. The Rev. William Jameson found the doors locked against him on 24 April 1781; the rioters assembled in the chapel in 1791, and hooted; and then the Socinian Unitarians shouted abuse on Sunday 6 October 1816, and followed their precedent of barring out the minister on the 19 October, when the Trinitarian Calvinists forced an entry the next day, and tumult reigned.

These events had important consequences for the history of Dissent when the Mander faction in the meeting house began proceedings which soon threatened the Unitarian movement at its heart, just when it was gathering strength and respectability in Parliament, local government, the professions, and in the movement for social reform. The Mander law suit became unwittingly a national cause: 'The Great Fight at Wolverhampton'.[9] It was one of the most widely reported of several cases at the time which came to challenge in the courts the tenure of all nonconformist chapels and endowments.

The strength of Charles's convictions was never in doubt. He claimed to act out of 'enlightened and cordial attachment to the great principles of religious liberty', founded on the rights of conscience and the word of God. On these principles, he pursued, financed personally, and finally won (as something of a pyrrhic victory) a chancery suit for recovery of funds belonging to the chapel which lasted intermittently for 23 years, from 1816 to 1839. With appeals and awards, the litigation lasted decades longer.

Gerald Mander writes, 'Around this building the consuming heats of the Court of Chancery smouldered from 1816 until they finally burnt themselves out in 1863'.

The Manders fought their corner hard, seeking the best legal counsel from the start. Benjamin as paterfamilias early sought a conference with John Wilks (c. 1765-1854),[10] august secretary of The Protestant Society for the Protection of Religious Freedom, who was later member of Parliament for Boston, home town of Jemima Mander. His first opinion written to Benjamin Mander is dated 14 November 1816:

> Your estimable son-in-law [Mr Pearsall] ... brought me the papers relating to the disputes as to the Meeting House—has intimated your determination to assert your rights as a Trustee ... especially for the protection of the Revd Mr Steward... I cannot but feel personally interested in your case. The conduct of your opponents manifests a persecuting and intolerant spirit which I must disapprove and your opposition therefore acquires an importance which produces a peculiar solicitude for your success... To be firm but cautious—To be decided but reserved—To evince the most determinate resolution with Christian gentleness is the conduct which I respectfully advise and which I am persuaded you will display.

From this point the most eminent lawyers in the land were involved in the case. Sir Samuel Romilly, himself a reformer, was duly instructed as counsel for the Mander faction and fought the case with the obdurate determination advised by Wilks. Romilly argued that Unitarian-ism was illegal at common law, and so no endowments made for its support could be lawful. The Unitarians, too, saw it as a crusade for religious liberty in the age of reform. Counsel for the Pearson faction was also an eminent lawyer, if not a great speaker, Sir Robert Gifford (1779-1826).[11]

The case at Chancery was finally heard before the Lord Chancellor, Lord Eldon, himself. It came to trial on 14 July 1817, and took four days. Eldon was conscientious, but indecisive in court; proverbially known as 'Old Bags' from his habit of carrying home in different bags the cases still pending his judgment. This case was no exception, and he reserved judgement. He eventually found (at great length) that the law was strictly on Charles Mander's side and ordered the Unitarians to vacate the chapel until the further order of the court.

The progress of litigation surrounding the 'Great Fight' was widely reported and excited long-standing national interest in a wealth of records. Among nonconformists, the case rapidly became something of a cause célèbre, filling many columns of turgid print in the nonconformist-liberal magazines of the day, namely the *Congregational* and *Evangelical Magazines* and the (Unitarian) *Monthly Repository*.[12] The furious pamphlet war which paralleled the case in the tracts and journals, and the privately-sponsored publications of Dissent was prolific, and often irreligiously vitriolic. It gives a valuable insight into the depth of feelings inspired by a religious controversy rooted in socio-economic change—and possibly arrièrespensées to do with the personal rivalries, prestige and property of the litigants themselves.

An array of publications found their way into print. Charles Mander the feuilletonist launched into his polemic with *An Appeal to the Public* in 1818, swiftly followed by *An Appendix to an Appeal to the Public.* These exacted an anonymous reply from Joseph Pearson, his Unitarian adversary; *Remarks on an Appendix to an Appeal,* in 1819, and finally his *Addenda* to the remarks on the appendix to the appeal to the public. Charles Mander rejoined with his fullest diatribe yet, an enlarged edition titled *A Minute Detail of Circumstances relative to the Old Meeting House in John Street, Wolverhampton* in March 1819. The inevitable retort was *An Answer to the Calumnies contained in Mr C. Mander's Minute Detail,* and a pamphlet by one mysterious 'Verax' entitled *Facts connected with the Case of the Old Meeting House in Wolverhampton in reply to a statement which appeared in Monthly Repository for March 1818.* The Rev. J. Robertson then published *Religious Liberty applied to the case of the Old Meeting House, Wolverhampton* and *Infringement of Religious Liberty exposed in the case of the Meeting House, John Street, Wolverhampton.*

In addition to the pamphlets, topical in heated debate, numerous pages of law reports followed the case. Accounts of the proceedings of the protracted litigation—which outlived all the parties originally involved —continued to be rehearsed ad nauseam throughout the century, in such books as T.S. James, *Presbyterian Chapels and Charities* (1867), the germ which grew into his compendious tome, *The History of Legislation on Presbyterian Chapels* (1869).

In due course, judgment went in favour of Charles Mander, when in February 1835 the Vice-Chancellor Shadwell dismissed the appeals of the Unitarians. They promptly appealed again to the Lord Chancellor, Lord Cottenham, who heard the case in January 1836. He reserved judgment pending the pronouncement of the House of Lords on the Dame Sarah Hewley's Charity Trust case, a test case on the whole question of the rights of Unitarians to the old meeting houses and their endowments. The two cases threatened to create a precedent in charity law which would seriously affect nearly all Unitarian chapels in the country—all but twenty or thirty. When the Lords decided against the Unitarians in 1842, the Lord Chancellor dismissed the appeals one more time in favour of Mander. But it presented an alarming decision for the Unitarians, when they recognised that 200-300 similar cases could immediately come before the courts if Parliament failed to intervene with statutory measures.

As the century progressed, the Unitarians were becoming less radical, and more liberal and middle of the road, after 1832 with increasing political representation. Opinion in high places, including that of the prime minister, Robert Peel, also by now of a manufacturing background (in his case, Manchester cotton, and estated in Staffordshire), and the Lord Chancellor Eldon, shifted to their side. The affair culminated in the Tory government introducing the Dissenters' Chapels Act of 1844 which limited the rights of Trinitarians in chapels occupied by Unitarians, securing chapels to the congregations who had worshipped in them for the previous 25 years. It roused support in many quarters, and Lord John Russell, Peel and Gladstone all spoke to the bill when it was raised in Parliament. Despite many petitions from the orthodox, it passed both Houses with large majorities.

The Act had no retrospective effect, of course, and did not reverse the decision in the Wolverhampton case; there the former Unitarian congregation lost both their endowments and the chapel. Charles Mander had repaired the chapel building in 1828, probably when he became a Baptist. Eventually the chapel had to be sold to pay the costs of the action, at £773 to Mander. In 1871 it became a chapel-of-ease (by purchase) known as St Michael and All Angels to St Peter's church. Its final fate was to be absorbed into the Manders' paint and varnish works in 1890, as their premises continued to ramify down John Street. The shell of its four walls remained, and there was a yard to mark the spot in my childhood. Today its site is buried somewhere under the Mander Shopping Centre.

The Old John Street Chapel

[1] I am indebted to Stella M. Blazier, author of 'The Wolverhampton Chapel Case', unpublished M.A. thesis, Polytechnic of Wolverhampton, 1985, for assistance and for supplying copies of numerous contemporary pamphlets covering this case.
[2] The General Baptists were Arminians, believing in the doctrine of general atonement, that Christ's death was for all men, and not only for the elect, i.e. those predestined to be saved. The Particular Baptists originated in non-Separatist independency and believed that only believers (not infants) should be baptised. In theology they were strict Calvinists, who held to the doctrine of *particular* atonement; that Christ only died for, and salvation was only available to, the Elect.
[3] The term 'Unitarian' had been in use on the Continent of Europe since 1600, appearing in England in Henry Hedworth's writings in 1673. Hedworth writes that Unitarians are so called because they 'own but one Person, and one substance or Essence of the most High and Independent God and to distinguish them from other Christians, that hold three Persons and one Essence of God, and are therefore denominated Trinitarians.' (Quoted in H.J. McLachlan, *Socianianism in Seventeenth-Century England* [1952], p. 312.)
[4] R.E. Richey, 'The Effect of Toleration on Eighteenth-Century Dissent', *Journal of Religious History*, 1975, vol. 8 (Dec.), p. 350.
[5] Faustus Socinius (1539-1604) was the author of *De Christo servatore,* where he denies the doctrine of atonement, that Christ appeased God's wrath by suffering the penalty that was the just due of man.
[6] For Birmingham Unitarianism, see E. Bushrod, *The History of Unitarianism in Birmingham from the Middle of the Eighteenth Century to 1893*, 1954. Coleridge later rejected Unitarianism altogether, which, 'in its immediate intelligential ... consequences, is Atheism or Spinosism' (*Table Talk*, 23 June 1834).
[7] Letter to Clarkson, 13 Oct. 1806; *Collected Letters*, ed. E.L. Griggs, Oxford, 1956, ii, p. 1166; T. McFarland, *Coleridge and the Pantheist Tradition*, Oxford, 1969, p. 182.
[8] Pearson was another eminent and worthy citizen, a brassfounder in Snow Hill of 'enlightened views', responsible for founding the Mechanics' Institute. His eldest daughter married Sir Rowland Hill, who instituted the penny postage. When he died in 1742, John Weaver proposed to place a bust by Chantrey in the Library as a memorial.
[9] A.G. Matthews, *The Congregationalist Churches of Staffordshire*, 1924, p. 9.
[10] His son, also John Wilks and an M.P., known as 'Bubble' Wilks, was a notorious swindler who floated a number of joint stock companies, all of which failed.
[11] Later first baron Gifford, he was solicitor general in May 1817, attorney general in 1819 and lord chief justice of the common pleas in 1824, and sat as a deputy to Eldon, whom he was groomed to succeed, as lord chancellor in the Lords. He prosecuted the Cato Street conspirators in April 1820.
[12] Francis E. Minelca, *The Dissidence of Dissent: The Monthly Repository 1806-39 under the editorship of Robert Apsland, W.J. Fox, R.H. Home and Leigh Hunt*, Octagon, 1972.

6

THE NARRATIVE OF JEMIMA COX, 1871

Gerald Mander unearthed and edited a first-hand account of Charles Mander's early nineteenth-century business and its ways. He writes:

In the year 1871, the life of a devout and faithful servant of the firm was fast approaching its allotted span, and Jemima Cox [born in 1805], as she was named, set out to write a narrative of her fifty-four years' association with it. Written in the plain, homely language of the times, it affords a privileged insight into the character of the pioneers of the business.

The original manuscript, from which this is taken is '*Dedicated to C.B. Mander, Esq., also S.S. Mander, Esq. Narrative of Events connected with their late beloved Father, C. Mander, Esq.*', to quote from its title page.

In the year of our Lord 1817, one bright September noon I found myself in the presence of the late Charles Mander [1780-1853], who was asking many questions, and testing my abilities in reading and writing. I felt rather timid in answering, being in the twelfth year of my age. He had on a blue suit, and brown paper cap. This was his varnish-making dress (leaving the varnish a few minutes to see me). A more smiling countenance I thought I never saw—which gave me great encouragement in my answers, especially those of a religious character. He wrote the word "*understanding*," and desired me to copy it, which I did quickly, to his great satisfaction.

Addressing the person who was to be my instructor: 'Mary, I believe this child will be a blessing to us. This situation may be for your lifetime, but be sure to be ever truthful. When you are in fault, or forget some of your little duties, speak out and confess them, then they are done with, but a lie brings a curse and leads into much trouble and sin.'

Here I would remark this counsel sunk very deep in my heart and saved me many a sorrow which a lie would have caused me, and by the blessing of God, up to this day, have experienced the happy result of telling the truth and fearing a lie more than a fault.

The warehouse was very beautiful in my sight, three windows filled with beautiful geraniums in full bloom, and flowers. No walls or order compartments to be seen, all was draped over with green baize, and the floor clean enough to count the grain in the boards. I thought, oh! how nice, I shall be very happy here, I'm sure I shall, and above all go to Chapel every Sabbath Day.

Next morning I went to work at 7 o'clock. Alas! for anticipated pleasure in my new situation. My first duty was to assist in cleaning five lamps, and trimming them ready for lighting and hanging in their appointed places at night. No gas in Wolverhampton at that time, nor for many years after. How disappointed I felt; the lamp oil made me sick: what a contrast to going to school in a little pink lilac frock and apron, to the gingham apron I was obliged to don! The next thing was to descend into the fire-hole with a long-handled shovel, and carry fire up two and sometimes three pair steps, not only choking me, but smoking my face and hair, besides nearly blinding me, as I was very small in stature. Sweeping and dusting came next, not so disagreeable as the fire and lamp exercise. By 9 o'clock the Counting House, Warehouse and passages were in order, as I found them the day before.

Thus my first quarter of the day was accomplished. I was not happy and while at breakfast felt sick at the thought of lamp oil odour. Mother, observing my sorrowful countenance, asked me if I thought I should like my place.

'No, mother, no, I cannot and will not trim lamps,' was my answer. 'Making fires is bad enough, but the lamps. . .'; and I gave vent to a shower of tears.

I then felt lighter hearted, and after a good wash, dressed in my school garments and resumed my second quarter of the day. I was again delighted with the appearance of the warehouse, and assisted in putting candlesticks into white paper, which I thought very pleasant. I found also my instructress a very good, cheerful young woman. I was taught by my mother that religion was a path of peace. I felt very happy till the thought of the first quarter duties rose in my mind. What rebellion there is even in the heart of a child, not then knowing it was my Heavenly Father's will, it was the way He would have me walk in.

The rest of the day passed very pleasant in the changes of duties. At night Mr. Mander asked me how I liked my place, remembering his admonition about the truth, I at once told him. 'Very well, except the lamps and fire business'. He smiled and said, 'You will not think so much about it when you forget you were a little Miss'; and helping mother to support me, he bid us goodnight. His residence then was Chapel Ash. Mary, that was my teacher's name, asked me if I could sing, so after a few verses of the evening hymn, first and second treble, we parted very much pleased with each other.

Each day brought a new variety of work, all of which I did cheerfully. At last, Saturday, no mention of wages had been made and I often wondered how much I should have. At 6 o'clock I called the people to settle, no bell was needful, a trip up the three or four *flights* of steps with the word 'settle' was quite sufficient. The long wished-for moment came, I was called to receive my first week's wages; with beating heart I stood before my master and teacher. 'What are we to give the little girl, Mary? Do you think she will suit you?' asked Mr. Mander. 'Yes, sir, I do, besides she writes so well, indeed near as good as my own. Give her 3s. because she is a scholar.' Half crazy with joy, I carried the thirty-six old copper pennies, ornamented with fish scales, as the change was had from Bosworth's, Dudley Street, and casting the money on mother's ironing table at which she stood, I exclaimed, 'All this and my Sunday, too, all my own, my Sunday, my Sunday.'

Dear reader, the Sabbath seemed to me more valuable than the money, the love of that Sabbath caused me to go through six days' toil and lamp-trimming with ease. That Holy returning Sabbath has been my pole star, and has borne me through fifty-four years' heart service of one situation, and fifty years in His sanctuary in sacred melody. Give God the praise, God is a God of providence as well as a God of grace.

Through many dangers, toils and snares
I have already come;
'Twas He that led me safe thus far,
And Grace will lead me home.

Mr. Mander's counsel and Mary's consistent works had great influence over me, so that I did not care for the companionship of the girls in the establishment. Though prudent everyone in their several stations, they lived the Sabbath different to mine, opening it in their own pursuits.

It is time for me to give a slight sketch of the St. John Street manufactory. The dwelling of Mr. Mander was in Front Street once, and was now occupied by C. Thorpe and family, the Black Varnish Maker. A range of stoves, quite new, covered with cherry trees on the right hand of a large square yard—the left hand upper and lower stoves in operation—two oil varnishers, one woman, two girls lower stoves, a colour grinder who filled up her time in picking gum, the gum-room being under the old counting-house. One long shop containing four or five men and several apprentices completed that department. A room under Japan Shop to keep iron blanks and retail varnishes.

A long row of shopping at the top of the yard finished the square. A man, his wife, and several children, with two apprentices were the only operatives. The Varnish House filled a corner joining the new stoves; forgot to say several Varnish Stock Rooms were under the upper tin shops. The whole of ground floor of yard was laid with large white flags now covered over in many places with green moss. Two oval flower beds were in the centre, out of which several tall poplars reared their spiral branches toward the skies, nodding in windy weather in very many fantastic shapes, and many a time I have watched them. I forgot to say there were four black polishers, and a woman to polish bottle stands and round waiters and a lathe—three or four finish polishers I believe were the only operatives.

A year or two passed away and the lovely yard still bore the appearance of the once beautiful back premises of a gentleman's house. At that time I spent many pleasant seasons at Mr. Mander's house with his dear children [four sons and three daughters survived infancy] whom I dearly loved, and romped about the hayfields with great delight teaching and singing to them verses of Watts' hymns. How sweet is the memory of those days even now, how delightful it will be to see again in Glory the lovely countenance of dear Mr. Mander! I have gazed upon it while he has given me good advice, which beamed with kindness and ennobled by grace in the heart.

Mr. Mander was now more frequent in the Varnish House and Mrs. [Jemima] Mander was obliged to be amongst us often as the invoicing clerk. Dear, kind lady, I think I see her on a winter night with her muff on her arm waiting for master to go home with her, cheerful and uncomplaining.

My dear master had a zeal for the cause of God. A large parlour in front of his house had been used for Divine Service previous to the opening of the old Baptist Chapel. Many a happy hour I have had in that old Meeting House while listening to the truth. Mrs. Mander's sweet voice started the hymn tunes. I suppose my master's purse found a good share of the expenses for supplies; there was no regular minister at that time. Happy period of my life, the like I shall not see again.

Two sons and two daughters were then my master's family. Mr. Mander found it needful to leave his nice country house for a residence in Queen Street in consequence of the long walks in the dark after business hours. Early closing at that time was out of the question, and there were no rail roads. I have known waggoners wait until ten at night to get off goods by what was called springtime.

I well remember master's first journey on voyage by steamship to Dublin. On his return he said, 'Surely the world is turned upside down, the vessel was like a Leviathan, waited neither for wind nor tide, but went on ploughing, nothing obstructing.'

Soon after this my instructress married Mr. Wiley, one of the japanners, and was engaged as a foreman. It was impossible to do without her as the business increased so much. This alteration entirely freed Mrs. Mander from business. Another daughter was added to the family circle, so we seldom saw Mrs. Mander, except on Wednesday evenings when she called to invite us to chapel. Bright examples of genuine Christianity were Mr. and Mrs. Mander carrying out their profession in all their walk and ways, hearts and hands to sympathise and help in time of need to the utmost of their power, truly serving the living faithful God of Israel. Their characters and conduct shone bright in deed and truth in those dark days of erroneous teaching. They are now reaping their reward through the merits of Jesus.

I know by dear master's earnest prayers he had great difficulties to cope with, for after a portion of Scripture read at breakfast time, prayers for blessings on the day followed, and for years a portion of Scripture was read in every shop on the premises, in failure of which there was a fine to pay. The whirl of business soon swept away this duty, but these rules and practices left a good impression on many.

New shops soon filled up our once pleasant yard. 'Bricks and mortar again' soon became a proverb, leaving only room enough for a barrow to pass.

A dreadful fire broke out on the works of Mander, Weaver and Co., and several lives were lost. Great danger was apprehended from the heat—the houses opposite had some of their panes melted—to our stock rooms joining the burning walls which were left bare. Machinery, iron, wood floors and roofs were destroyed. Great terror and confusion in the whole town; soldiers were placed top and bottom of the street to prevent intruders. With great difficulty I got permission to pass through the ranks, and one of the soldiers threatened me with a bayonet if I persisted. I told him I belonged to the place and wanted to assist. I found our people all in haste moving books to a place of safety.

A wonderful scene presented itself in the street, houses and chimneys and all the pavements covered with red, black, blue, white, green, while many other coloured minerals were scattered about by the wind. The poor people could not keep the diversified colour out of their dwellings with all their efforts. Here was a remarkable instance of God's great protection, nothing belonging to Mr. Mander was injured except in the hurry of removing goods, which was trifling. We were very thankful our dear master was spared all anguish of witnessing such a scene of danger and confusion, being absent till we were in order again.

Mr. Wilks' men, Warners' shopmen, with many others on the Market Place, assisted lustily in carrying water from the surrounding pumps. The street was crowded with spectators of ruins; a solemn sight to see two dead men extricated at four in the noon from the burning rubbish.

With heavy but thankful hearts Mr. Wiley and family, with assistants, sat down to tea at five in the evening, the first refreshment tasted that day. The first rest we had from four in the morning, we could not help smiling at each other's appearance, like a meeting of Oddfellows; one had a patch of blue, another black, some all colours. We were too tired to pay any attention to a tea-party dress. Mr. Wiley returned thanks to God for His special care and mercy towards us.

From this time increasing duties were laid upon me, as the health of Mrs. Wiley began to decline, owing to the untimely birth of her first born caused by fright she received at the fire. In her absence I had to give out materials for tin men and japanners, look after polishers and very often had to pay the people. I think I have had a little of everything to do, except polish and sand stones. Many a time I have sat entering orders opposite my master, and trembling lest I should make an error; in short, the entire management of the warehouse was on my hands at the age of seventeen. At this period I had to encounter many trials, the polishers especially did not like a 'young thin' like me to find fault, threats and enticements to pass bad work. I stood like a flint to see my master done right by, so deeply sunk in my heart was the first counsel of my master—'Be truthful, and you will have nothing to fear.' A tender conscience was the blessed result. I have shed many tears and had many restless nights through their want of principle, yet, thank God, a clear conscience bore me up, and no weapon formed against me ever prospered.

Business increased so much that we were obliged to give up going to chapel week nights, but my Sabbath made amends for the six days' toil and anxiety, sweeping away all care. We seldom saw any of the master's family; the sons were at school. If I remember right Miss Small [Elizabeth Small, b. 1797], Mrs. Mander's sister, taught the young ladies. A very excellent lady, but very strict in all her ways, yet kind hearted and a very great help to Mrs. Mander in domestic affairs.

A year or two quickly passed, bringing more business. Mr. Wiley became chief manager and invoicing clerk, his poor wife, my teacher, got weaker, and after giving birth to a second son she was very little in the warehouse with me now. I was much grieved about her, feeling sure that I should miss her valuable society. When I was very young, I often thought her rebukes rather severe, but proved all was for my good.

An assistant was found me, a very disagreeable one too, unwilling to learn and subtle as Satan, one of those eye-service men-pleasers. This caused me new trouble; so artful was she, everything appeared to be right when all was wrong.

My dear master, hearing a man paying addresses to me, was not very well pleased, and I frequently smarted under his somewhat hasty reproofs. My unprincipled rival still grew in favour by her duplicity. I felt Mr. Mander would find her out I ere long. I could not convince him of her deceit and hypocrisy. Thus grieved at my dear master's seeming carelessness, whether I stayed or left, I was the more easily persuaded to marry. When my dear instructress lay on her death bed, she sent for me and wished me to postpone my marriage, and stay where I was till she was out of the way. I would willingly have done so for it was a great grief to me to see her almost last wish unfulfilled. Mr. Mander also wished me to stay, but my arrangements were made, and I could not break my promise.

Dear Mrs. Wiley died a Saint indeed in July, and the September following I married, and after an absence of two years, at the earnest wish of Mr. Mander, I accepted again my former post and position.

My malicious rival was found to be worse than I represented, and was sent off the premises at a moment's notice, Mr. Mander having found her and her mother house rent free.

Very often the innocent suffer for the guilty, but God is His own interpreter, and He will make it plain.

Our Blessed Redeemer suffered for doing good, let us be content to follow in His Steps. Soon after my return the premises were enlarged and a poor man was engaged to look after the Black Department. Mr. Wiley kindly taught him to write sufficient to keep a stock book. My time was taken up in collecting packages and looking after the finishers' work and books. Mr. Mander was now entirely occupied in varnish making and journeys. The young gents returned from school. Master C.B. [Charles Benjamin Mander] soon set to work and became a first-rate artist. Master S.S. [Samuel Small Mander] could not endure his department, looking over polished black work. I have seen him writhing under the task, so disagreeable it was to him, and many times helped him out of difficulties, very much regretting his superior genius ought to be better employed. Soon after he was wanted in the counting house entirely, and gave up to a young woman who understood the business well—Sarah Minett.

Mr. Mander now thought proper to take Mr. Wiley into partnership, and for a time all went on well. Tranquillity in this world—how short. Frequently when we think our best concerted plans are going on prosperously, there is a lurking storm beneath the surface of smooth waters.

The disciples of Jesus passed a happy day with their beloved Master; at night the winds and waves threatened their destruction, but Jesus appeared for them and there was a great calm.

I must pass over many painful incidents and relate how Jesus was with our beloved master in two heavy trials which closely followed each other. The first was the loss of his beloved wife [Jemima Mander] in the year 1834. This was a heavy billow over his soul. A very short illness took away the desire of his eyes and treasure of his heart. His sorrow was not as one without hope. She was a bright testimony of the power of the gospel and love of God the Father in Jesus.

Miss Small [i.e., Jemima's younger sister, Elizabeth] was now a valuable help in his bereavement, taking all care off his hands in domestic affairs. So the Lord is with them that put their trust in Him. Miss Small was a great economist and a real Christian, and ultimately became the second wife of Mr. M.

The young gents [Charles Benjamin, Samuel Small, Joseph and Benjamin] increased in stature, knowledge and perseverance. Another clerk was added to assist, and the whole manufactory lighted with gas. This was a great pleasure to me after so many years endurance of smoke and lamp oil. I shouted for joy in the presence of my master, who laughed heartily at my exultation. The first evening the works looked cheerful in the silvery light. What a variety of changes in business, how uncertain of success, anxieties, disappointments, perplexities; all attend even the man who would gain the world though he lost his soul.

Although my master committed all his ways to the great Disposer of Events, and taught his children to walk in the right way, yet he had great trials, I am sorry to say. The most grateful person ought to have been his partner who turned (may I use the term) ungrateful and covetous.

I cannot proceed with my narrative without very briefly entering into some of the circumstances for the good of both parties. Mr. Mander consented to take Wiley partner; for a time all went well. I never enquired what was the cause of a visible change between the two masters. There were rumours of dissatisfaction, then there appeared a complete mutiny among the people, and it was difficult to get work done as it ought to be. Oh! the weary days and wakeful nights I spent; instead of harmony all was opposition. Covetousness and avarice caused all the mischief which followed the steps of the double-minded. Cole, the stove manager, took part with everyone who behaved wrongfully against my dear, kind-hearted master, whom I felt convinced was quite right.

Dear reader, judge what I had to pass through, from a child I looked up to Mr. Wiley as an elder brother, receiving many good admonitions and spent many happy hours in his family circle—I had all this to read from heart, I found many a pang in so doing—I was able to stand firm to what I was sure was the right cause. Prayers, tears, yea, even fasting became familiar to me. I well remember one night crossing the old churchyard (then open to west), the evening star was sparkling and brilliant in the sky; oh how heartily I prayed and wrestled like Jacob of old that the Creator of the Universe would restore peace. Many months passed ere there was any peace. During those months painful contentions and explanations, worst of all, partners in trade and brethren in the Church. Meetings and discussions as to which was right and which was wrong; happily for me I was quite ignorant of the first cause of the unhappy convulsion, therefore could stand, though with heavy heart, with clean bands touching the miserable treachery which surrounded us.

I must now introduce the name of one not before mentioned, the good brother of my master, Mr. Benjamin [Parton] Mander [1785-1835], who often comforted me with scripture quotations. 'Stand fast in that which is right', he would say; again, 'Who shall harm you if ye be followers of that which is good'. 'Fear not man whose breath is in his nostrils, the fear of man bringeth a snare, but who so putteth his trust in the Lord shall be safe'. These and many others were the exhortations of the only spiritual friend I had to console me. Cole and his accomplices did all they could to annoy me—texts of scripture sent in secret judging me as a man pleaser with all sorts of accusations I was entirely ignorant of. All this brought me nearer a throne of grace and have good reasons to thank God for guiding me with His counsel.

All disputes ended in dissolving partnership. Wiley set up for himself and as many of the people who chose joined him. Hanshen, chief ornamentor, also left and became his partner. After all this there was little peace. Cole wanted to join Wiley, but Mr. Mander was determined he would serve his time (being hired). I was much surprised one day when my mother questioned me about my discourteous behaviour to Cole, who threw down his cap and declared he would not transact business with such a woman. He would rather serve in prison; but the Lord was on my side giving me utterance of speech and proving by facts that Cole was working against the interests of my master's business to get his dismissal and join Wiley. Soon after this another clerk was engaged, Mr. Parkes, though unacquainted with our work knew quite well how business ought to be conducted. Cole still persevered in his frustrations, causing delays and countermands. It soon became evident to the newcomer all was not right, as the people under Cole's management worked or played, just as it pleased, without any rebuke. 'The wicked fall into the pit they had dug for others' was soon manifest in the case of this man. Being left to the depravity of his own heart he never could invent a slander so black against a person so chaste in all his ways and conversation as Mr. Mander. Everyone was disgusted at the report, even his own accomplices trembled at the thought of being brought before him.

Did my dear master faint under this addition of the craft and subtlety of the devil and man, which seemed to work against him? No, in the presence of proper witnesses the cowardly inventor confessed he had not the slightest reason for impeaching the character of so just a man, Judas like, and asked for forgiveness, signed a paper as to the intent of his conduct, saying it was only a joke. Had it not been for the sake of his wife and family he would have found it cost him more than all the jokes of his lifetime.

Cole had to leave, no good seemed to be in him, hindrances were more frequent, and at last he became obnoxious to all and left to join the firm of Wiley and Hanshen. What he was to their firm I never knew. It was reported the co-workers were going to ruin the old John Street factory.

The Lord in His Word declares 'All false ways I utterly abhor'—the way of the wicked He turneth upside down—so it was with them; their counsel like David's enemies was turned into foolishness, they prospered not. Many of their followers wanted to come back, their firm broke up and they wanted bread. To this day I believe Cole to be at the foundation of all the mischief. I believe Wiley truly repented in his heart toward God, and became a Minister of the Gospel. As for the rest they tried hard to return. How they could turn against so kind a master I know not; an open hand, a sympathising heart, and he never turned a deaf ear to the wants of his people. I have known him lend money to shoe the people's families, and also to relieve them in every case of distress with kind admonition, and we can truly say of him as it was of job: 'When the car hears him then it blessed him, He delivered the poor that cried and him that had none to help him'.

New stamps and workers were engaged, the young gents were now in the varnish department. All the old hands did their best to cope with the influx of trade. Messrs. Parkes and Evans, tin foremen, did their best and held a strong rein. The management, our beloved master, worked very hard all my time. Quick in execution, persevering I should think from a youth.

What was to be done today was not put off till tomorrow. This example of his has been beneficial to me. Avoiding procrastination, remorse, etc., presents many difficulties. Faithfully blessed in his life the three-fold golden girdle set forth by St. Paul: 'Diligent in business, fervent in spirit, serving the Lord'. He never on any account neglected the service of God, public or private. Surely while we remain in the valley of tears he is now enjoying the sweet rest which remains for the people of God.

To my great sorrow one day I was told the business had passed into other hands. [The japanning business was sold in 1840.] My master told me I need not fear, God would be with me. He has. Tin and Japan trade turned over to Shoolbred and Son. 'My days are closing,' my dear master said, 'and I shall do well to set my "House in order".' Rapid changes took place, all prospered well under new hands— outsiders were engaged, a new partner, Mr. H. Loveridge, added to the firm. It now became my chief business to attend to patterns. The manufactory became too straight for both parties, and the foundation stone was laid for Merridale Works entered upon in 1848 with all the busy bees of St. John Street.

What manifold changes in life. Merridale Works prospered. How St. John Street prospered you well know. A great pleasure to an old servant to be able to say goodness and mercies have followed them all their days, and I am sure I may say with truth the Scripture has been fulfilled in your case—'The generation of the faithful shall be blessed'. Upwards of thirty years my life was spent in your service and always in your family, you will not then be offended at the liberty I have taken in giving a retrospect. My days are fast closing, a service of fifty-four years altogether in John Street and the Merridale Works.

May you, dear gentlemen, and your families live long in a crooked and perverse generation as lights, and when called to your Great Account hear the words of our Blessed Redeemer: 'Come ye blessed of my Father inherit the Kingdom prepared for you from the foundation of the world'. Matthew XXV., 24th verse.

Yours faithfully in Jesus,
JEMIMA COX,

December, 1871.

CHARLES THE SECOND

7

CHARLES BENJAMIN

1819-1878

Charles ['Secundus'] Benjamin Mander was born at the family's 'fine country house' in Chapel Ash in 1819. When he was nine, in 1828, his mother, Jemima, was writing to his elder sister, Elizabeth, then a child of 13 away at school in Aberystwyth, doubting that her sons Charles and Samuel were good pupils. 'They are quite well', she said,

> though I do not expect they are making much progress in their studies—at least, I fear my dear Charles is not, as I know he has not much application.

Elizabeth (1815-65) married John Field Smyth in 1835; he came from her mother's town of Boston, Lincolnshire, and their descendants worked in the firm, although it was no sinecure for poor relations. Charles was artistic rather than academic. Years later (in 1863) when he had his own children, his wife Sophia wrote to their son, Charles Tertius, with tender admonitions to work hard, noting that 'your Papa, when a boy, was not made to work by his master, and now he is a man he is very sorry for it'.

Mander Brothers, 1845

But Jemima need not have been concerned. When he was 21 in 1840, he joined his father, Charles Primus, as a partner in the varnish business, while his younger brother, Samuel Small, was apprenticed for the second time to John Morton, 'a factor in all its branches', for three years, after which he too joined the partnership with the two Charleses, senior and junior.[1] Jemima Cox wrote of these years:

> Master S.S. could not endure his department, looking over polished black work. I have seen him writhing under the task, so disagreeable was it to him, and many times have helped him out of difficulties very much regretting his superior genius ought to be better employed.

Whatever his application as a young scholar, as a businessman Charles Benjamin proved meticulous, entrepreneurial and efficient. In the first five years working with his father and brother (1840 to 1845), he kept an order book showing the high standards he sought in products and services. An extract from 1843 had Samuel's comments entered (here in italics):

July 1st—If more ordered must consult father before sent.
Augt 7th—If this is not excellent, will be returned.
Augt 9th—If not excellent, shall lose them.
Augt 11th—Soon and excellent. *Never sent, this was an unaccountable mistake. SSM.*
Sept. 20th—This 6 Galls must be sent & *not charged* as the last would not dry under 4 or 5 days & will be returned. *One of the first Houses in Manchester.*
Novr. 23rd—The quickest & best you have, will do if dries *hard* in 6 or 8 hours. *Consult Father on his return. SSM.*

By 1845, Charles senior was 65 and trusted that the business was now established on a sound enough footing to enable him to retire to the sidelines and leave matters to his sons, Charles Benjamin and Samuel, aged 25 and 23 respectively. The two brothers made local history when they 'entered' on business as a formal partnership called Mander Brothers on 1 February 1845. On that day, they posted printed letters to their clients, including one to Robert Pegg, colour maker of Derby:

Sir,
Upon entering into the business so long carried out by our much beloved Father, we beg to say that no exertions on our part shall be wanting to maintain that high character as Manufacturers of Varnishes which has ever distinguished him; and to render ourselves worthy of that confidence and support which we now earnestly and respectfully solicit. Our practical knowledge of the business is very considerable, it having been under our almost entire management for several years, and we can assure you that it shall ever be our aim to merit your approval by care and promptitude in the execution of orders. The business will in future be carried on under the firm of 'Mander Brothers' to and by whom all accounts must be paid.

We are, sir, your obedient servants,
Charles B. Mander Samuel S. Mander

The firm was well established, and by 1861 already described as 'the oldest now engaged in the trade which has been carried on here upon the same premises since 1803'. Under the new partnership the business of the Mander Brothers' firm developed along with the rapid industrial expansion of Victorian Britain in the two decades following the Great Exhibition in 1851. Wolverhampton was itself emerging as a major manufacturing town, well placed in the centre of England to supply the Midlands metal industries, not only the japanning and tin plate industries, but the growing panoply of engineering works and factories.

Varnish was becoming a key product here, with a myriad of new industrial applications supplanting its traditional domestic ones. Its uses for house painting, furnishings and decoration, its local uses in the japanning, enamelling and metal trades, its age-old use to give lustre and protection to precious items from oil paintings to violins, paled into insignificance as new varnishes were being augmented with applications in virtually every new product and invention of the industrial revolution, and on a far larger scale than ever before. A vast range of new manufactured goods required finishing, often by being coated in specific formulations of varnishes, typically the best black 'japan', giving a surface which shone 'with the lustre of glass': stoves and kitchen ranges, fenders and grates, advertising signs and tablets, Wolverhampton locks and safes, deed and cash boxes and uniform trunks, biscuit tins (with gold stoving varnish), Birmingham tools and toys, umbrella furniture, agricultural implements, buckles and boot eyelets, stationery and paperclips, even matchboxes: 'iron bedsteads, brass foundery, bird cages and general wire work, etc.'[2] Significantly for the long term, higher-technology coatings began to be used in machinery, from the nuts and bolts that held them together to the furnaces and boilers that forged the steel, and in a host of industrial processes, from treating leather, oil cloth and linoleum to, for example, the colour printing of fabrics, where the healds in cotton weaving were varnished. We learn that it is used upon 'the new American leather cloth which has been brought into such general use for covering chairs &c. as a substitute for leather'. The gloss of varnish was undoubtedly fashionable and versatile, whether on the pitch pine pews of the new Commissioners' churches or the decking, marine instruments and dials of the merchant ships of the Empire.

Most importantly in this mid-century era, the coach-makers who had been early customers of Charles Mander's varnish for their panels and 'bodies' were rapidly superseded on an unprecedented scale with the development of one of the century's most successful industries, the railways, as a decisive fillip. Contemporaries recognised this: 'The universal adoption of the system of railway travelling has given a considerable impetus to the trade', wrote the local *Official Advertiser* in 1861, adding that 'in consequence to the demand from railway companies for their carriages, upon which varnish is necessarily much used'.

Manders always had a firm base in the Midlands. But markets were becoming national and international, and Mander Brothers intended to remain at the forefront, already laying down with good timing the basis of an extensive overseas trade in the 'sixties. The *Great Western Railway Guide* was writing of Mander Brothers in 1860:

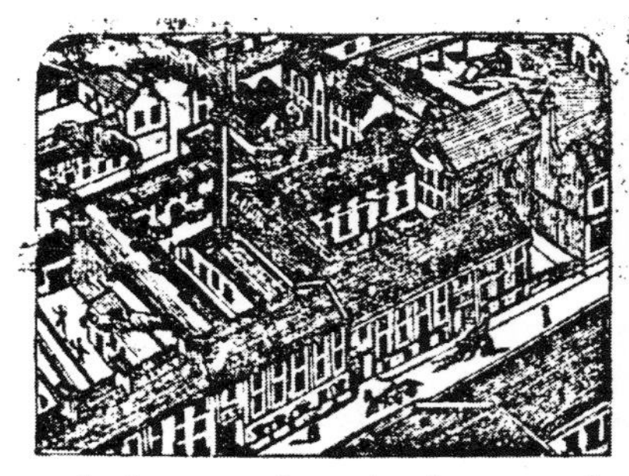

Black varnish and colour works

Copal varnish works

The reputation of English varnish is very high on the Continent, and generally throughout our colonies; little, indeed, being used upon carriages, or the higher class of work of any kind, but what is imported from this country: this doubtless results from the greater care which has been bestowed upon its manufacture here, and the judicious selection of the gums and other material used therein.

First a London depot was opened on 25 March 1861 at 363 Oxford Street, 'opposite the Princess's Theatre', where it took in the first year £628 on account and £170 in cash. A clerk from John Street was in attendance, named A.W. Pounce. The traveller was George Ring, 'a hard working, plodding traveller with good address and very regular business habits'. By 1861 Mander Brothers 'varnish and japan manufacturers' had depots also in Dublin (Sackville Place) and Paris (16 cour des Petites Écuries).

Throughout the decade trade with the Continent of Europe and the United States was steadfastly developed, giving the partners for the first time opportunities for regular foreign travel. The minute books record in January 1864 Charles Benjamin's travels in Italy, where he would have indulged his passion for art, and the appointment of increasing numbers of agents all over the world. By 1865 the two brothers as partners were discussing with Henry Clarke, their manager, the setting up of new overseas agencies in Hamburg, Dublin, Odessa, St Petersburg, Bombay, Spain and Australia. The foreign business was foremost in the partners' minds in a minute of the partners' meeting of 20 August 1866, which ran:

The Prussian War being over and it appearing that we had probably reached the limit of the rapid development of the Home Trade and the quick returns with the Foreign Trade presenting a great advantage, it was definitely decided that no further time should be lost in extending our business on the Continent, and in the United States... That Mr Charles should give the Spring to the United States and that Spain and Portugal should be visited afterwards.

By the spring of 1867, true to this decision, Charles Benjamin was visiting the United States 'in the face of the falling off of business', to be ready for trade when the country returned to normal after the Civil War.

In the space of a few months he visited New York to appoint American agents, and Paris to arrange displays for The Paris Exhibition—the effort was rewarded, as Mander Brothers won another *medaille d' honneur*—while Samuel Small went to Hamburg, Berlin (as well as Paris). They wanted agents in all the big cities of every country in the world, not just a representative in each capital.

A proper London office, in addition to the depot established seven years previously, was opened in 1868 in the heart of the City at 17 Gracechurch Street (after bombing in the Blitz, it became the head offices of Barclays Bank). Henry Clarke was put in charge, and from here he conducted the London and increasingly the international, or 'foreign', business until 1901 with a high degree of autonomy, 'fostered by the repeated visits abroad of the partners, and not least, of Mr Henry Clarke'. There were 34 overseas agents when Clarke took over and he immediately decided to appoint 33 more. In his first year of trading (1868/9), the London office had a turnover of £30,466—£12,772 home and £17,684 foreign. He dispatched 5,600 letters—hand written, of course. He travelled 13,000 miles, visiting nine cities in Italy, Palermo in Sicily, Alexandria, Cairo, Beirut, Smyrna, Constantinople, Athens, Stockholm, Helsingfors, St Petersburg, Moscow, Warsaw, Brussels, Paris... He targeted particularly the railway companies, now extending operations all over the Continent. He reported

The competition increases every year and has a natural tendency to reduce prices. Our policy is to maintain them as firmly as possible short of losing accounts. Our great strength must be in our quality; with superiority we can preserve present quotations, with bad varnish we should be powerless to stem the current low prices.

By 1869, Henry George Harper of Ludlow, brother-in-law of Charles Benjamin and Samuel Small, joined Clarke in London, where the office was conducted as 'Harper & Clarke'. Harper had married Janetta (she had a bad stammer as a child), the younger sister of the two partners, in 1844 and first set up in business as a wine merchant in Chester.[3] By 1855 he had 'tired of tempting persons to drink', and was no doubt induced, writes Gerald Mander, to join the firm by Samuel Mander, 'a supporter of temperance of the driest kind'. Harper had a long and serious illness in 1872 and so the brothers decided to recall him to Wolverhampton to help them to manage the firm. Charles and Samuel made him a salaried partner and drew up an arrangement dated 31 December 1873 by which he was to receive a salary of £1,023 plus five per cent of the profits. He complained that it was not enough, at £700 less than he was already earning as a partner with Harper & Clarke, so by another indenture of the following year, they upped his share to 10% of the profits, and guaranteed to keep his salary always £200 above Clarke's.

In 1871 there was war on the Continent again, and Clarke reports to the partners in Wolverhampton of the events in France in 1871:

The commencement of this year found Paris invaded by the Prussian Army and, although peace was effected with the Foreign Invader, yet owing to the far more calamitous [sic] insurrection of the Communists, Paris was again in a state of siege, and all commerce was interrupted until May this year when Messrs Lévy & Finger's [the Paris agents] operations were again resumed to a trifling extent... Thus owing to this disastrous war the trade was robbed of some eight or nine months' business.

Not content to sit in London and write reports, he went to Paris at once and had 'long discussions fraught with difficulties and requiring most careful handling' with customs officials over import duties. Messrs. Lévy and Finger had deposited their wives and families in England and, as soon as the blockade was over, they came and collected them. Clarke resumes:

It is impossible to conjecture how long France will remain in such a state of quietude, as alone admits of mercantile prosperity and progress, but after the bloody events of the past eighteen months, and drawing conclusions from parallel events in the previous history of that Country, it may fairly be presumed that should another change of Government take place, which is most likely, that the transition will be rapid, prompt and, after what has occurred, possibly bloodless.

The wars, political realignments, unifications and annexations of the nineteenth century are evident in the developing pattern of the firm's trade. 'The Italian Business' was established in Florence in 1862:

What was in 1864 called Tuscany became later our 'Florence' depot (later Milan), now understood as 'Italy'. Austria was a fairly large customer until the Prussian war of 1864 fixed attention to Berlin. The American market was watched with anxiety so soon as its civil war allowed its country to settle down. But it was not until the Franco-Prussian conflict in 1870 cut off our principal agency that the 'opening of a really extensive trade [in the U.S.A.] became the event of the year,' as Mr Felkin records.

During the communistic struggle in Paris in 1871 our stock 'had a simply miraculous escape, having been discovered by the leaders of the commune only a few hours before the final events of the blood strife'.[4]

Back in Wolverhampton, the John Street works was developing. Much of the works was devoted to the secret weighing and mixing of chemicals, of natural gums and resins with exotic proprietary names, like *Seed Lac, Animi, Elemi, Dragon's Blood, Gamboge, Kauri* and *Isinglass,* with linseed, poppy seed and other vegetable oils for drying, and solvents and thinners of alcohol, turpentine and even lavender oil. The processes were still more like brewing or wine-making than modern industrial chemistry, involving letting the mixtures stand in huge vats, like solera sherries, sometimes for years, to mature and settle from impurities. This took up a great deal of room, and beneath John Street a labyrinth of cellars and tunnels extended where vats of amber and black varnishes, enamels, glazes and lacquers were securely serried. These products were given quaint descriptive names and dates (seemingly indicating the year of their formulation) like *Box Bottom 1799, Sacking Black 1856, Hook and Eye for Iron 1801. Dead Black 1773* seems to refer to an original receipt of John Mander and is described in a notebook labelled *Sundry Black Varnishes* as 'Air drying in 1 hour—quite dear. Used for stoves etc.'

Raw materials, gums and resins often formed as natural secretions from insects or exudates of exotic trees—lacs, ambers, balsams, rosins—were delivered in increasing quantities on barges along the canals, and after 1851 by the London and North Western Railway, into John Street from all over the Empire (and elsewhere), and the manufactured varnish exported back in tins and barrels to developed markets.[5] In the early days, varnish was delivered in copper vessels, which were returned to John Street.

The best asphalts for japan varnish, like bituminous pitch, came from Trinidad. Early varnishes used amber, the fossil gum from Samland in the Baltic; cast up by the sea, collected at ebb tide with nets, or brought up by divers and dredging. The copals, lustrous in spangly shades of yellow and brown, were the oldest substitute for amber; sub-fossil or semi-fossil gums exuded by trees, 'chiefly of the torrid zone', which shed them as 'tears'.

Charles Benjamin and Samuel used principally the hard West African copals, from Sierra Leone; also Cameroon, Angola and Accra. At one time, in 1873, Charles Benjamin found the 'natural curiosity' of a live insect preserved in a nodule in a solid piece of Sierra Leone copal, and contacted the British Museum. Their Richard Owen wrote back in August:

The occurrence of a living insect in a solid piece of copal would need more evidence to make it rank as a 'scientific fact'. The presence of dead insects in both recent and fossil (amber) gum-resins is usually ascribed to their sticking to the recent exudation and so becoming enveloped in succeeding out-flows. I do not know any instance of the egg-laying and breeding of an insect in a lump of copal...

Copal from New Zealand became increasingly popular, prized out laboriously from bogs of kauri pine, *Agathis australis.* A classic account of the kauri gum-digging industry, the gumdiggers probing the ground with gum spears, then digging it up with spades, as the surface pieces were used up, is given in Jane Mander's (1877-1949) novel, *Allen Adair* (1925), set in the Kaipara harbour, where her father, Frank, took his family to mill the kauri in the 1890s. She describes these giant timber trees of New Zealand towering arrogantly above all else, like the colossal pillars of the ancient halls of Karnak, seemingly as eternal as the hills, losing themselves without a knot or branch in a roof of impenetrable green. Jane, now considered one of New Zealand's foremost women novelists, was only distantly related.[6]

Later, in the early twentieth century, African copals came in from the Belgian Congo (Zaire) in the vast hinterlands of West Africa, or Zanzibar, in the east. Congo copal would be picked by natives from the swamps, whole families of gum pickers working together wading waist deep, and sometimes up to the neck, in the pestilential swamps, probing about the floor with a spear, or ducking down into the water to gather it in baskets on their backs at the rate of 60 to 80 pounds a week for a man working with his wife and children. By the 1920s, the Congo had become by far the largest producer in the world. Zanzibar copal came in fossil form, mined a few feet down from the earth. Soft copals came from 'the Manillas' and Dammar in south Asia, too; and some of the best came from Mexico, Colombia and Brazil. 'They range in value from one shilling to four shillings per pound'. A rare form of copalite or 'Highgate' copal was found in the London clays at Richmond and Highgate.

Shellac was another gum, brought from Burma, and derived from the secretions of a lac insect, like an English greenfly; they were scraped from the twigs of trees into a cauldron and boiled up in a mixture to be poured out onto cold metal plates. There the sticky mass would condense to form amber flakes, ready to be loaded for Wolverhampton where its elasticity was exploited as a soft natural thermoplastic agent which flowed under pressure, useful before the synthetic vinyls were developed in the 1930s. Then there were the rarer gums, the milky resins from the Japanese varnish tree, *Rhus vernicifera,* from which lacquer is obtained, the wood-oil tree, and many others—traded from as far away as eastern Tibet.

Turpentine is a natural 'oleoresin', gathered typically from pine trees. The essential oil thickens and solidifies in air, commercially separated by distillation to form a solid resin—rosin or colophony—giving off also the volatile 'spirits of turpentine', the solvent thinner used for paint and varnish. In classical times the best was produced from the terebinth of Chios, which gave it its name. According to Theophrastus, 'it sets firm, is the most fragrant, and has a delicate smell'.[7] Early turpentines were traded from Virginia and the loblolly tree of the Carolinas, the price fluctuating with the harvest of the yellowish, viscous exudate tapped each fall. During the American War of Independence, varnish manufacturers had to resort to smuggling to keep up their supplies, paying off profiteering sea captains. Norway was an obvious source mentioned in the Manders' company literature of the mid-century. 'Venice' turpentine became one of the most esteemed, in fact from the Tyrol; producing a pale green, sticky fluid collected from the European larch, *Larix decidua*, or *europaea*. Bordeaux turpentine was gathered from the *Pinus pinaster*, the cluster pine of the vast forests of Les Landes. Many conifers yield prized qualities of turpentines, from Strasbourg to Corsica and Cyprus, and even into Central Asia.

The most important source of vegetable 'drying oil' was linseed, the variety of flax cultivated for the yield of its oil. Manders used chiefly the finest quality linseed oil crushed from flax grown on the shores of the Baltic provinces of Russia, but sources of supply proliferated through the nineteenth century: the East Indies, the Argentine, 'the countries bordering upon the Black Sea', Canada. Then there were always small quantities of exotic gums to be bought and traded: the balsams and benzoins of Siam and Java, gamboges, sandarac, copaiba from the West Indies and the Amazon, anim, gum tragacanth...

As the technology of varnish making underwent dramatic changes by the mid-nineteenth century, so Manders had to become more industrial, necessitating an ever larger scale of operations. The alcohol-based spirit varnishes, where the 'soft' resin is dissolved in spirits of wine, began to be augmented or replaced by 'fixed' or 'cooked oil' varnishes, where the resin is melted in a hot oil, frequently with a metallic drier. These were easier to use and far more durable, promoting the widespread use of high quality coatings on a host of new industrial products, no longer just the specialised output of the Midland trades.

But the chemical processes of treating the natural gums like the copals to make them soluble and then heating them with the linseed or other semi-drying vegetable oils, often employing highly volatile solvents, to controlled and stable temperatures, and making accurate additions, dispersions and mixtures on a large scale, always avoiding the attendant fire hazards, required investment in new buildings, plant and expertise. The basic process of varnish manufacture involved washing and partly bleaching the gums, and then fusing them into a molten mass. When perfectly liquid, the linseed oil is added together (according to the firm's contemporary account) with 'certain oxides of lead, as red lead and litharge, to impart a drying quality. The whole is boiled together in a suitable vessel'.

THE WORKS OF MESSRS. MANDER BROTHERS, WOLVERHAMPTON.

Mander Brothers' John Street factory, with projected 'Guelph' chimney tower, from George Measom's Railway Guide, *1860*

After cooling, the turpentine is added in proportion, according to the formulation. 'After the varnish is made, great age is required for fining down the more expensive kinds, which are stored in large vats or cisterns for periods of six months to two years'. Also, all the ingredients and chemical compounds have to be carefully selected, measured and stored.

The Brothers drew up ambitious plans to extend and modernise the varnish factory. The volume of trade was increasing and space was needed for all the kettles and storage vats. Edward Banks was the architect who in Wolverhampton had designed the School for Practical Art opened in 1853 with which Charles Benjamin Mander was so closely involved, as well as the administration building for the London and North Western Railway in 1851. The Mander partners engaged him as architect to produce a new factory, an overblown fantasy in Lombard-Italianate gothic, a moral statement of adornment and clean renewal, and fitting as a flagship for a major manufacturing house, with a giant chimney proposed as a prominent landmark rising like a Guelph tower over the sprawling town.

John Street in the Sixties had a number of pubs and no drains, and Gerald Mander points out, 'to build such edifices among such surroundings of drear decay and dirt must needs have helped to the moral brightening of the whole street'. The open ditch sewers were improved with a deep drainage system which, 'after much misgiving, was passed and carried through' by Charles Benjamin's borough council in 1868.

The mid-nineteenth-century works as reordered by Banks was engraved for George Measom's *Great Western Railway Guide* in 1860, as if it were one of the sights of the manufacturing town. It is described as[8]

> a bird's-eye view ... which exhibits the whole of their present works, with the new frontage which is now in the progress of erection, together with the tower which is intended to carry off the whole of the smoke and gaseous vapours emitted in the process of manufacture... An ordinary chimney shaft, 120 feet high, would be very objectionable from its unsightly character... With a public spirit, therefore, which is deserving of the highest praise, Messrs. Mander Brothers have determined to erect a tower which shall subserve all the purposes of trade, and which, from its great altitude and situated upon the summit of the hill upon which the town stands, will be at the same time a great ornament to the town and a conspicuous object for miles around it.

Banks' plans—notably the chimney tower—were (according to Gerald Mander) never completed. One block stood 'heavy, imposing, a massive fraud, as sample of what might have been (had not gracious providence forbade) which has never ceased to be a marvel to all subsequent architects and builders, both clerical and lay'. The conglomeration of ramshackle offices and sheds which had grown up on the west side of John Street in the course of 70 years of continuous expansion and adaptation was transformed. Existing buildings were refaced, straightened out, embellished and enlarged. In 1862 property was acquired on the opposite (east) side of

the street as the Mander Brothers site extended relentlessly to form an island site in the middle of the town.

Mander Brothers' next opportunity to acquire property was not till 1873, when John Mander's original chemicals' works was sold. This was now an extensive site with buildings and outbuildings, still including the original old gas works which had supplied the gas lighting and power to the Georgian factory. John Weaver, who had become a partner in 1803 with William Bacon and Benjamin Parton Mander, had died in 1849, and his place had been taken by his son, Frederick Weaver. In 1873 Frederick sold the firm to Thomas Reade and his brother, who promptly removed the works from the site it had occupied for 82 years to new premises. These were in Cock Street—a name apparently offensive to nineteenth-century propriety, renamed 'Victoria Street' to commemorate the impromptu visit of the Queen to Wolverhampton in 1866. Here they continued to trade under the name of Reade Brothers into the late twentieth century.

The varnish product range was experimentally perfected and improved, new lines constantly devised, and complaints had always to be met. In 1861, Mr Schmid, the varnish works' manager, introduced two successful new products. The white 'Coburg' varnish was 'for white and delicate decorations ... far superior to anything yet produced'. 'Warranted Varnish for Seats of Churches &c.' was 'a brilliant and durable, hard-drying, and tackless varnish for painted and stained work'. There were spirited discussions on the best formulations of black varnish for hairpins and horse vans, and a cheaper version for gas meters. Blooming was a recurring problem. Their Brussels agents complained in 1862 that their japan was '*trop mince, et coulé*'. It was not as black as Harland's, but flowed better. There was a loss of lustre and it seemed to be drying too quickly, and cracking. A note in the *Memorandum Book* of 1864 stated that, as regards blooming which affects [most] of our varnishes, we are inclined to think that the cause may arise from our practice of chicking with fine oil. We have decided therefore to test this theory by omitting any chicking oil.

The confidence of customers had always to be nurtured. Manders offered a written warranty that their varnishes possessed every good quality attributed to them, 'a security never yet attempted to be given by any other House, in view of the great annoyance which has so frequently occasioned by the failure of Varnish upon the seats of Public Edifices from its not hardening'. The *Official Advertiser* of 1861 picked up this point:

There is great competition in this trade, but as the quality of the article can only be ascertained by a practical trial, the trade must remain one of confidence; the feeling between the buyer and the manufacturer being akin to that between patient and physician.

Mander, Weaver & Co., works in 1858

Paint, 1864

The big new development of the mid-nineteenth century was the diversification into the so-called 'colour' trade, which was to become so crucial to the mix of operations. Colour pigments had been manufactured by John Mander, of course, as soon as he established his chemicals works in John Street in 1791. Now the partners met on midsummer day 1864 with Henry Clarke to discuss formally a natural extension of the operations:

24 June 1864. *Colour Trade.*—Resolved that this matter may be made a valuable adjunct to the Varnish business, and that steps should be taken, immediately, for discovering the best makers of each colour, as at first it would be better not to make it ourselves.

Henry Clarke opined that colours would materially assist the sale of varnish among shippers, and Samuel Mander proposed to confine the sale of colour to them alone. They sought the advice, among others, of T.H. Suffield of the Birmingham Colour Company, one of the firm's varnish customers. Lewis Berger & Co. were another manufacturer suggested as a possible supplier, and Charles Benjamin visited them both, finding the Birmingham Colour Company prices were cheaper. The minutes of the partners' meeting of 30 August record 'it was finally determined to go into the colour trade... Mr Mander stated that the question of capital need not enter into the consideration as he could get plenty'.

The Mander Brothers' product described as *colour* was distinguished from paint. In the trade the word 'colour' indicated both *colours* and *dry colours*. *Colours* were the stiff pastes consisting of pigments ground in linseed oil or turpentine spirit to which the decorator would add oil to give gloss or spirits of turpentine to thin, blending it with other colours, the resultant mixture being 'paint'. *Dry colours* were the colour pigments themselves, which gave their hue to paint, inks and stain. The next stage was for the progressive varnish manufacturers to begin for the first time to mix the two ingredients of paint, the pigment or colour and the vehicle or binder, typically linseed oil, and market them as one product in a tin. Manders developed distinctive packaging, their famous 'green can' bashed out in the Works, with its conical top, which became a hallmark of their paint brand. Manders now had the premises, technology and know-how to enter the modern paint industry.

The firm was already beginning its practice of taking care of more distant relations. Robert Felkin was appointed the commercial manager. Charles Benjamin wished to appoint Mander John Smyth, son of his sister Elizabeth, in charge of the colour project as a separate department. But he did not get his way, as Henry Clarke complained that the 24-year-old was too young. But Smyth assumed another vital post to the firm when he became chief chemist, a position he held successfully for many years.

He kept a little note book of 'Varnish Trials, Experiments, Recipes, etc.' in which he recorded such observations as the darkening effect of tin cans on spirit varnishes; a method of making glass-coloured transparent show plates; and a way of making a varnish for preserving stone and bricks: 8 pints of raw linseed oil and one pint of sulphur heated to 278 degrees Fahrenheit. He recorded the effects of spattering varnish with mud from John Street one day. He noted: 'Sandersons inform us that the best Body Varnish they know is composed of 2 pts W.H. & Co. and 1 pt. Th. B's. The mixture is better than either of the constituents. It stands wonderfully well.' Another observation concerns the use in the North of half and half Japan and [Best Black] for Pin Varnish; and Birmingham umbrella furniture makers used Dipping, and thinned it.

Family Group circa *1856*

Seated left to right: Dr John Weaver (of Chester); Amy Mander (his granddaughter, born 1851); Sophia Mander (wife of CBM)
wet collodion (glass negative) process introduced in 1851, requiring about 10 seconds exposure

In public life, Charles Benjamin was a magistrate and a town commissioner of Wolverhampton, then a councillor when a Charter granted borough status for the first time in March 1848—'although he passed the chair', wrote his son later. He took a close interest in a number of high-minded philanthropic and educational initiatives. In one week, for example, in February 1859, we find him engaged in the administration of the poor laws, speaking for the formation of a 'workhouse visiting society' of ladies to assist the overworked chaplain, Mr Hastie, to provide 'not only for the material, but also the moral and spiritual welfare of inmates of workhouses', and also moving 'That the drinking water fountain erected in the High Green at the expense of Mr. Councillor Mander be henceforth the property of, and be supplied with water by, the Corporation'.

This refers to an earlier scheme when he provided for a drinking fountain to be erected in the market place—reinstated after demolitions of 1961 in the gable end of the stables at Wightwick. Such schemes expressed a typically Victorian movement for greater standards of temperance and hygiene in the crowded cities created by the industrial revolution, where in Wolverhampton the cholera epidemic of 1848 had shocked locals when it resulted in 500 deaths. He may have been inspired by other philanthropists like Mr Merry of Liverpool, who had provided a whole system of 42 drinking fountains there at his own cost.

A new waterworks system had been installed in Wolverhampton in 1858, resulting in expensive litigation between the town Corporation and the private waterworks company which bankrupted the Council, the bailiffs taking possession of the Town Hall in scenes of high drama. On this occasion, speaking for his motion, Charles Benjamin stated he was 'ashamed of the depraved condition of his native town'. He had made investigations, accumulating an impressive number of statistics showing that there were at that time 211 public houses and gin shops and 225 beerhouses in a town of 60,000 people, equivalent to one public house for every 142 men, women and children. An immense amount of money was being wasted 'when the small wages men earned must to a great extent be spent in public houses and gin shops'. This was leading to degrading poverty which would be relieved only if the borough were to provide free drinking water where 'labouring men could obtain a plentiful supply of water free of cost... If drinking water fountains were placed at the corners of our streets, working men would prefer to slake their thirst at them instead of visiting public houses', he added, somewhat optimistically.

Henry Fowler, another high-minded progressive, supporting him, pointed out that the corporation did little for the working people of the town, which was almost alone in its absence of free institutions, 'such as baths and wash houses, free libraries, and public parks'. Free water would remove them from 'a great degradation, from that which was their curse, and the curse of the district'. Surprisingly in retrospect, after heated debate, the motion was only carried by a majority of three: 14 to 11.

Mander Brothers of the mid-nineteenth century reflected the enlightened concerns of its partners, following these humanitarian developments. There was a 'Workpeople's Library', with a bookplate later (in 1896) designed by the pre-Raphaelite artist, Robert Anning Bell (1863-1933), which states the terms:

The workpeople employed in our various factories are at liberty to take out books, only one book can be withdrawn at once and may be kept a reasonable time, but must be returned, in any case immediately on request of the Librarian.

There was also the provision of free medical help for employees. The Minute Book shows that at a partnership meeting with Henry Clark on 27 November 1865:

H.C. proposed that it might be advisable to pay a Medical man a fixed stipend to furnish attendance and medicine to all the workpeople and that his certificate should be required when anyone may be absent through ill health.

This was confirmed early the following year (22 January 1866):

It was agreed that all persons on the works should be provided with Medical attendance gratis.

The Wolverhampton Schools of Art, 1852-71

A man of artistic temperament and tastes, CBM's major public work in Wolverhampton was involved with the establishment of the local Schools of Art in the 1850s. The educational debate into which he entered was dominant in Victorian middle England. Education was seen as the best means of improving the moral character and conduct of citizens, both of students and the wider community. Art education for craftsmen in particular was advocated as a necessity to improve the design of manufactured products in a climate of increasing competition.

CBM was secretary of the first Wolverhampton School of Art, the Government School of Design, founded in Castle Street in 1852, and then became secretary, treasurer and prime mover of its successor, the new School of Practical Art in Darlington Street, which followed in 1854. This was to be the first purpose-built institution for art education in Britain, and became a vital and controversial issue in the Wolverhampton of the 1850s and '60s.[9] Wolverhampton already had a Tradesmen's and Mechanics' Institute founded in 1827, based on one founded in Glasgow four years earlier, set up by local nonconformists, 'thorough-going' liberals and businessmen —the Manders prominent among them.[10] By the mid-century it was already inadequate. In 1851, the Great Exhibition came as a 'revelation' and produced a 'profound sensation in Wolverhampton', writes Alderman Jones. Again, some of the leading public figures were inspired to set up the first Government School of Design in Castle Street.

This School of Design was still a small affair, and lasted as first conceived only a matter of years. CBM was the founding secretary, whose lot was to draw up a prospectus towards the end of 1851, setting out the aims, a model of worthy philanthropy in art education:[11]

The primary object is to furnish the means whereby our artisans can acquire, at a small individual expense, a knowledge of ornamental art, and have the advantage of a complete and systematic course of education in relation to every kind of decorative work ... the characteristic aim of the School being to fit the students to apply the information thus acquired, to the various branches of manufacture in which they may be engaged.

The School will be supported by subscriptions and donations, and by fees... The government will make an annual grant equal in value to the amount of subscriptions...

[It] will be the advent of a new era in the history of the artisans of this neighbourhood, when, through its agency they will have, not only the skill to execute, but the talent to invent, and when they and their employers will no longer occupy their present humiliating position as buyers and copyists of the works and designs of others, because unable to originate for themselves...

Independently, a School of Design will be particularly valuable to the manufacturer, the merchant, and the ironmaster, and beneficial to the interests of all... The moral influence ... has been found to be great ... enlarging the minds of the pupils, and drawing them off from the debasing and injurious influences which might otherwise contaminate them.

A full-time art master named Thomas Chittenden was appointed by the end of 1851. But the School needed a to be housed fittingly. As treasurer, CBM soon set to work on raising funds to complete the Greek revival building designed by his friend Edward Banks, the same local architect who designed the high-blown extensions to the Mander Brothers' factory. He wasted no time, and the foundation stone was laid in a grand ceremony on a rainy day in June 1853. Charles Benjamin and the other worthies, including Sir Robert Peel (son of the prime minister, who had a Staffordshire estate), were standing on a specially-erected platform to superintend the laying on of mortar with trowel. But the occasion turned into a fiasco when the platform and everybody on it collapsed in the glare of publicity.[12]

CBM organised a less eventful follow-up ceremony just over a year later for the official opening on 1 August 1854 by Lord Granville in the presence of county figures, MPs, and the leading national personalities in public art education in his day. They included Henry Cole, secretary to the Department of Art and Science, and George Wallis (1811-91),[13] a Wulfrunian who had been Deputy Commissioner of the Great Exhibition and later became Keeper of the South Kensington Museum (now the 'V&A'), an institution which exemplified his interest in art education as applied to design for art manufacture and decoration.

CBM's publicity broadsheet for the opening describes the School officially as 'the first erected in England devoted to the cause of Education in Art and Science ... destined to confer solid and lasting benefit on this town and neighbourhood'. It was intended to be a model for the nation.

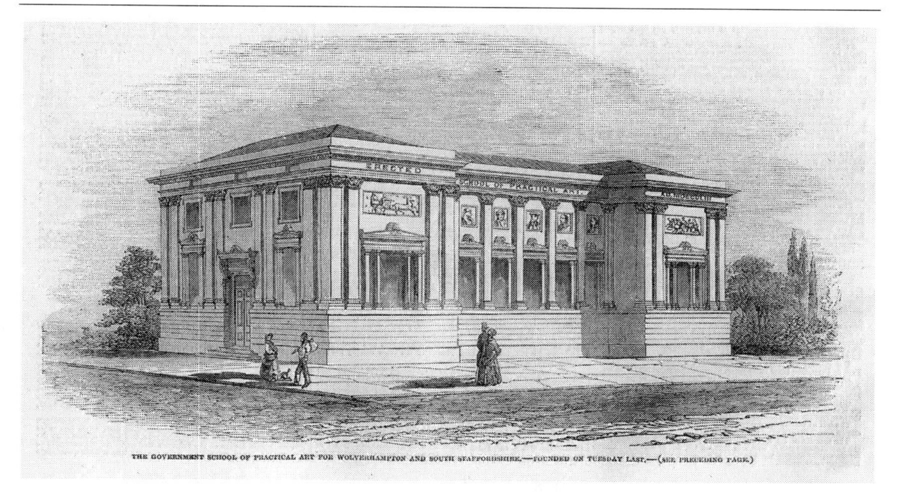

The Wolverhampton School of Art, 1854

The School was a success in its objects 'in spreading a taste of art, and in developing the artistic abilities of the young people of the town'. But it came to depend on CBM's financial initiatives, patronage and energy, from which in old age he found it ever more difficult to extricate himself. The building was partly financed by public subscription, but some £1,600 of the total cost of £4,000 had to be raised through mortgage. Despite all the initial enthusiasm, the trustees found themselves over committed, and already by May 1855 the Art School was in financial difficulty due to mortgage repayments and Chittenden's wages.[14] The latter at £200 per annum were high, and by far the biggest item of expenditure.[15]

Part of the premises was leased to the Methodists for use as a meeting room, and the school yard was sub-let to a builder. CBM increasingly involved members of the county gentry in the School, in the hope of attracting more donations and patronage. He again succeeded, and by 1858 the list of 'Honorary Governors' of the (renamed) School of Practical Art included two Dukes, one Earl, two Lords, as well as Sir Robert Peel.[16] But all this failed to bring in the funds required and had the effect of increasing the alienation between the august managing body and the ordinary people of Wolverhampton, who played no part whatsoever in the organisation and administration of the School.

CBM, always one of the principle benefactors behind the School, sought to establish it securely for the long term by placing it under the funding of what proved a reluctant and suspicious borough. This had become technically possible under The Public Libraries Act of 1855, itself an amendment of the Museums Act of 1845, which would allow its future running costs to be thrown upon the rates. It provided a tidy and timely solution, for under its provisions, if only the borough could be persuaded to adopt it, the Council was empowered to use the penny rate to purchase the Art School, which would then house a Public Library as well.

Acting in his capacity as a Town Councillor, the Tory CBM called upon the Mayor to convene a meeting of ratepayers with a view to adopting the Public Libraries Act in Wolverhampton. At the Meeting of the Town Council in May 1860, he moved a resolution to the effect that

The Mayor (B. Hicklin, Esq.) be respectfully requested to convene a public meeting of the burgesses of the borough in order to ascertain whether, in the opinion of such burgesses, the Public Libraries Act (1855) shall be adopted for the Wolverhampton Borough.

In the Council Chamber CBM made little secret of the fact that he saw the adoption of the Act as a means of saving his cherished Art School. The matter had to be decided by the burgesses, who were empowered to vote a rate of a penny in the pound for the purpose of maintaining a Free Library, Museum and School of Art, which he calculated would bring in a revenue of £500. This he worked out was plenty to support both the School of Art, which cost about £120 a year, and a Free Library at £220 a year, the balance of £160 being used to pay off the mortgage on the building of the Art School on favourable terms. He was willing to sell the School to the Council for use as a Public Library for £2,500, which was the amount of money then owed by the School to its creditors.[17]

But two thirds of the burgesses had to vote in favour before the proposal could be adopted. Charles Benjamin set to work galvanizing support. His publicity campaign was typically thorough. He promptly had various posters and bills prepared and distributed around the borough, 'as an old inhabitant, having an interest in my native town'. His publicity urged 'every intelligent artisan' to support the imposition of a rate, following the success of the scheme in neighbouring towns like Birmingham, Lichfield and Walsall, 'to escape the blighting influences of drink and ignorance, which have so long demoralised our working population'.[18] He wrote laboured dialogues between local working men promulgating the sound economic merits of enlightened Ruskinian public art education:[19]

George.—Schools of Art are very useful in manufacturing places ... in the japan trade artists are constantly employed to make designs for trays and other things... Everyone now looks out for the pretty and useful; ugly things have gone out of fashion... There are many of our designs which ought to benefit by the teaching of the School of Art, and new designs for locks, bolts, hinges, &c. that combine the beautiful with the useful would be sure to sell best...

The Free Library went in tandem:

It will be a good thing for a working man, after a day's work to look into the Library, which will be made very comfortable, and sit and read an hour or so, and then take a book home to read to his wife and children.

At first, public books, such as a collection of patents given by the Commissioners of Patents from 1855, had been stored in a room in the School of Art. The only public libraries at the time were the subscription libraries for the 'educated classes' in Waterloo Road, and that of the old Mechanics' Institution, which cost more than most working men could afford to pay. Charles Benjamin became the first to propose practical measures for the provision of a library in the town, although his chief concern was to rescue the School of Art from its accumulated debts, so that the Free Library would become 'a supporting adjunct to the School of Art'.

Charles Benjamin's posters also emphasise the 'vagrancy consequent on lack of education':

The great proportion of criminals who now fill our jails can neither read nor write. Our Workhouses are filled with the thoughtless and improvident of our population, who have descended ... from ignorance and intemperance until ... they become a permanent burden upon the public purse.

He harnessed the campaigning skills of George Wallis, who entered the press campaign on his behalf. Wallis pointed out in the *Wolverhampton Chronicle* of 18 May 1860 that 'there were sound practical reasons to support art education for working men in Wolverhampton', arguing passionately his conviction that 'the prosperity of the town would depend on its trade, and so developing the skills of its artisans'. This was particularly important in an industrial town like Wolverhampton, he states, which was involved in 'a number of industries like japanning, iron and brass casting, lock manufacture, and furnishing—all of which depended on skills in design and ornament to keep abreast of growing competition'. The traditional local japanning trade based on trays was falling back, so that new articles 'which ingenious men might construct of paper' were needed.

A lengthy correspondence followed, pro and con, in the coming weeks. In the event, the public meeting convened by the Mayor for the 26 June at St George's Hall was described as being 'one of the most boisterous held in Wolverhampton for several years'. Despite CBM's careful marshalling of support, a large proportion of the audience had evidently come 'with the determination not to listen to any argument to be brought before them, but to vote against it with as little discussion as possible'. There was 'a perfect torrent of groans and ironical cheering', and the greatest disorder prevailed.

When the Mayor was at last able to propose that 'a Free Library in connection with the School of Art would add greatly to the commercial prosperity of the town', he was greeted by 'a loud and almost unanimous shout from all parts of the room of "We don't want it, and we won't have it." ' A more direct proposal: 'Would they have a Free Library or would they not?' was answered with shouts of 'No! No!'.[20]

The chief opposition to the scheme came from James Walker, the future first Chairman of the Free Library, and of the local Liberal Party. Walker objected to what he saw as a misuse of the spirit of the Library Act in the purchase and maintenance of an Art School. The Liberals won the day. The first attempt at having Ewart's Acts adopted in Wolverhampton ended in rumbustious acrimony and stalemate. It has been argued that there was a genuine fear of the financial burden of the penny rate and this was the main reason for opposition to CBM's proposal.[21]

Charles Benjamin's manoeuvres in 1860 were of limited success in the short term, and had met only with apathy from the local manufacturers. He kept the School going, as he felt he should, but the times were against him and he resigned as secretary and treasurer of the Wolverhampton School of Practical Art in 1863, 'having stood by it for ten years through good and evil report with a large sacrifice of time and not a little of money'. If he had kept it afloat hand to mouth by his private benefactions and enthusiasm, he had failed to secure its long-term future with public funding after him. The School was to have 'an unvarying run of ill fortune', he wrote with evident dismay. Henry Cole was invited to open a trade exhibition, promising a large grant from the Department of Art and Science to pay off the accumulated debts.

On February 1871, Charles Benjamin, still much involved, wrote to the Department in London:

> When I ceased to act as Secretary on Lady Day, 1863, there was a balance of £630. due to the Bank, for which the Trustees were liable: they took legal powers to obtain possession of the Property, but the times appeared unpropitious for a Sale, and they were so reluctant to harm the School, which Mr Loveridge was endeavouring to maintain, although at great personal sacrifice, that they abstained from action…
>
> A meeting of the Trustees of the School has been held to consult on the question; but although two or three might have been willing to pay their quota of the liability, two of them determinably refused, unless the whole School property was offered by Auction, when they would pay their proportions, more or less.
>
> The effect of this extreme but justifiable course would certainly be to close the School which would be a grievous result after so many years of labour and cost. But what can be done as the Trustees are definitely resolved to make a firm stand at once?…

Our only hope is in some action of the Department, for unquestionably the School was built under the old system of annual grants, and we had every reason to rely upon provisional assistance, without which the Effort to establish the School would not have been made, and it was at the opening of the School by Mr. Cole that the altered plans of the Department were announced, which under the circumstances in which we were placed, with a considerable debt, have caused all our difficulty.

The School nearly closed in these conditions of crisis, debt, change of Government policy and ill fortune, exacerbated by his early death in 1879. Soon after, the Wolverhampton Corporation Act at last allowed it to be taken over by the borough in terms such as he had envisaged, and a new school was eventually built to replace it.

Like the local public libraries, the art schools were something of a Mander project. One of the leading lights who saw through the new art school on this occasion was Theodore Mander, builder of Wightwick and chairman of the Art Committee (1885-1900) of the Borough Council. He made a speech at the ceremony to open the new School of Art buildings in St. Peter's Close on 21 July 1885. A.J. Mundella, the member of Parliament, performed the official opening, with the promise of a grant of £1,000 from the Education Department of central government towards the cost of £5,570. Joseph Jones 'paid high tribute to the energy and devotion to the new school, of Mr Mander. He was worthy of all honour—(applause)—for without his efforts the new school would never have been built. (Applause.)'[22]

The Mount, August 1883, watercolour by Jack Mander, aged 14

Charles Benjamin, April 1872

In looks Charles Benjamin was High Victorian, bearded, bewhiskered, majestic as an Old Testament prophet, with a high brow dented with care; stern perhaps, but with a genial twinkle in his eyes. His features are captured tellingly in a portrait by the pioneer Swedish photographer, Oscar Rejlander.[23] He married Sophia, daughter of Dr John Weaver[24] of Chester, in Chester Cathedral in April 1850.

He was 'a first-rate artist', with an informed interest in the arts. Several of his pencil sketches, drawn to a professional standard with a fine line, often with a moralizing narrative, hang at Owlpen. He travelled widely in the cities of Italy, where his visits to agents could be extended to family holidays in Florence and Rome. Apart from his pioneering interest in local art education, he had a hobby of *improving* the Old Master paintings in his collection 'to their great gain'. He was proud of a picture of a French priest bought in France, attributed to Greuze.

Pencil sketch by CBM

Few of his letters to his children survive, but his first to Charles Tertius, addressed from Kingstown, Ireland, on 3 April 1858, when CTM was not yet six years old, is typical of his kindly, fatherly good humour:

My dear Charlie boy,
This is the very first letter that I have written to my little boy, and that is not because I do not love you very dearly, only because you have not been able to read my letters; and even now I am afraid you will not be able to read a single word. If you would wish to hear from Papa when he goes from home, you must learn very fast to read both books and letters, because I dare not write any secrets while nurse has to read them to you.

You are now growing a big boy, and will soon have to wear a coat and trousers like mine, and big boys, when they become men, look silly if they have not become wise, and learned a very great many things from books which have been written and printed for them to read.

Now many little boys have no one to teach them and they grow up ignorant and often very wicked men, and we ought to be sorry for them, because they are often taught to do wrong by people who do not care for them. You have many kind friends and teachers who will always help you to do right; and when you become a man, you too may have a little boy, and perhaps if I live long enough I shall see you writing *him* a letter as I am writing you and telling him to love his books more than play or he will never be a great and good man.

I wish you were with Mamma and me, for where we are, we can see a great many ships, one a very large one which belongs to the Queen and that has *sixty* big canons for shooting her enemies with when she goes to war.

Ask Miss Walters to show you upon the map what part of Ireland we are in. You will see that we are upon an island which Amy can tell you is land surrounded by water; from Dublin, which is the chief town in Ireland, we go to Belfast to see your aunt Mrs Shaw, (who is your Mama's sister) and from that place we shall have to go in a steam packet over the water again to Liverpool before we can get home.

Now there is one little secret I will tell you, which you can get Miss Walters or nurse to whisper in your ear, and what do you think it is?—Why, it is this,—that I have not seen a little boy anywhere since I left home, that I love half or a quarter as much as I do my dear little Charlie, nor any little girls like Amy, Jenny, Sophie or baby [Julie], there now, what do you think of that? Don't tell anyone, and in my next letter I will tell you another secret.

I hope when we arrive at home that we shall hear what a good boy you have been, and that you have left off crying when a fly looks at you, or some other equally silly thing, for little *men* never cry and you will never be a man until you can bear pain or being teased without acting like a baby.

I could write you a much longer letter, but I dare say you will like me to write best when you can read it yourself and so I wait a little until then.

Mamma joins me in love to yourself, all your sisters and Miss Walters—and may God bless you my dear little boy, make you happy on earth and eternally happy in Heaven. Oh! that will be joyful!

Your very loving Papa, Chas. B. Mander

Charles Benjamin and Sophia were the first members of the family to move out of the centre of Wolverhampton with their growing family, purchasing The Mount in 1862. The site commands the highest point (at 560 feet) of Tettenhall Wood, and the views remain spectacular. In turn, the deodars he planted are giants prominent for miles around. The ridge to the west of the growing town (the population was now over 60,000) was to become the favoured resort of the leading Wolverhampton families. They included manufacturers enriched by the industrial revolution, like the Thorneycrofts, the Hickmans, the Fowlers, the Felkins, later the Marstons (of Sunbeam motors)—many of them connected by marriage with the Manders over the years. The distant views look utterly rural in the family watercolours of the Victorian period. They rebuilt the old Regency villa and extended it during the ensuing years to form a large and comfortable mid-century house. The Mount remained the principal family house for ninety years. In 1992, a blue plaque to commemorate CBM's life was placed on the porch by the Wolverhampton Civic Society.

Having had a large Victorian family—of three sons and five daughters—Sophia died in 1869, aged just 42, two months after Jack's birth. After a proper interval, five years later, Charles Benjamin married his children's governess, Harriet Spooner, known to them as 'the Mater'. But he was already worn out and frail.

He retired from the partnership aged 57 in 1876 on the grounds of ill health, which had been 'without hope of cure' for a year or more. But he had 'made his pile', as CTM was to put it. By June of that year he had some £55,278 capital in the firm, bearing interest at 5%, as well as his share of the partnership.[25] Neither he nor his brother, Samuel, lived to be sixty.

Sophia Mander (1827-1869): attributed to pioneer photographer Oscar Rejlander

Family group at The Mount, late 1880s
Standing: ?Neville, Amy, Sophie. Seated (right): Harriet, Edward Weaver

Mander Brothers, the firm of which they were founding partners, was overseen by their brother-in-law, Henry Harper, during the interregnum from 1873 until the younger generation of cousins, the brothers' eldest sons, Charles Tertius and Samuel Theodore, should attain the age and business maturity to take control. By January 1875 the partners were making an agreement to take on Charles Tertius and Theodore at a salary of £1,875, and the two cousins began to acquaint themselves with every aspect of the business.

'Uncle Harper' lived at Wightwick House, next door to Wightwick Manor. Gerald writes:

How little there is to tell about him! Once however when travelling into Italy before the railways (and that came late in Italy) the coach was set upon by the usual bandits, to the dismay of some R.C. priests who were bringing some gold for the Pope. Mr Harper was equal to the occasion and stuffed his boots with the gold, and adopted a demeanour which put the bandits to flight. I suppose he took his boots off, as the priests expressed their great satisfaction at the turn of events. This period was the acme of the Englishman abroad.

Family records suggest the priests were Irish, the amount was £60, the year was 1856, and Harper was shot within an inch of his nose. He had an audience of the Pope, *Pio Nono,* to convey his personal thanks.

By 1891, the tables were turned and his nephew, Charles Tertius was already in charge. He wrote to old Uncle Harper cheekily on 14 January of that year, seemingly enclosing a final distribution from a family trust:

> I enclose a small windfall in the shape of a cheque… It appears you were not as careful a trustee as you should have been… Be very careful how you invest it. Avoid Argentines.

Uncle Harper

[1] Samuel Small's indenture of apprenticeship to his father dated 3 September 1834, when he was 12, is in the William Salt Library, Stafford.
[2] Richard Timmins, *Birmingham and the Midland Hardware District*, 1866
[3] Her aunt, Amelia, had married another Chester wine merchant, John Williamson (it may have been the same firm).
[4] *The History of Mander Brothers*, p. 17
[5] The first railway station was opened at Wednesfield Heath in 1837, one and a half miles outside the town. But canal navigations were advanced, and Smart's 1827 *Directory* reports that the canals linked Wolverhampton with 73 major towns of Britain.
[6] Jane (1878-1945) was dau. of Francis Mander, MP for Marsden, N.Z., son of John Jordan Mander of Worcester, who descended from Henry and Anne of Aston Cantlow.
[7] *Enquiry into Plants*, trans. Sir A. Hort, IX. ii. 2, Loeb C.L., vol. II, 1916, p. 223
[8] George Measom, *The Official Illustrated Guide to the Great Western Railway*, London: Richard Griffin, n.d. [1860]; 2nd ed., Griffin Bohn & Co., n.d. [1861], pp. 450-4; *The Official Advertiser*, p. 80.
[9] Joseph Jones, *The Historical Sketch of the Art and Literary Institutions of Wolverhampton: from the year 1794 to 1897* (unpublished, Wolverhampton Library archive section); research of Jane Cooksey of the University of Wolverhampton.
[10] N. Fogerty, 'An Analysis of the Reasons behind the Decline and Ultimate Collapse of the Wolverhampton Athenaeum and Mechanics' Library', *West Midland Studies*, IV, 1979, 35
[11] 25 November 1851
[12] *Illustrated London News*, 25 June 1853, vol. xxii, no. 629, p. 515
[13] Wallis lectured on the principles of decorative art and organized the first exhibition of art manufactures in Manchester in 1845. He published *Schools of Art, their Constitution and Management*, 1857.
[14] Minutes of the School of Art, 22 May 1855.
[15] Letter from CBM to W.J. Hinkley, 24 May 1855.
[16] Report of the School of Practical Art, 1858.
[17] J. Jones, op. cit., p. 80
[18] Poster entitled 'Free Library and School of Art to the Burgesses of Wolverhampton', 9 June 1860
[19] *A Dialogue between Thos Giles and Geo. Tomkins about The Free Library and School of Art.*
[20] J. Jones, op. cit., p. 82
[21] A.J.Rowberry, *A History of the Wolverhampton Public Library 1868-1900*, 1967, p. 3.
[22] *Birmingham Daily Post*, 21 July 1885.
[23] Oscar Gustav Rejlander (1817-1875), after studying art in Italy, settled in Wolverhampton, with a studio at 42 Darlington St. in the 1840s. One of several to be claimed as 'the father of photography', he was patronized by Prince Albert and Charles Darwin. He is said to have judged his exposures, sometimes of over two hours, by observing the degree of dilation of the pupils on the eyes of his cat. Sophia Mander was also photographed by him.
[24] The Weaver family were settled in the Wever valley, Cheshire, by the late C13. One line has been traced to Cunedda the Great, a Roman officer, by birth half Welsh, who became King of the Welsh about AD 400. The genealogy was researched by H. Baillie Weaver, a barrister, c. 1900. (See: Lucius E. Weaver, *History and Genealogy of a Branch of the Weaver Family*, Rochester, New York: Du Bois Press, 1928.)

Hugh Barty-King suggests these 'Cheshire' Weavers were connected to the Weavers who were business partners of John Mander in the early 19th century; but there is no evidence for this. There is a lengthy account of the wedding in a letter published in the *History of Mander Brothers.* The portrait of Sophia's uncle, Lt William Weaver (1795-1857), is at Owlpen.
[25] Multiply by a factor of 35 to reach 1990 prices.

CHARLES TERTIUS

8

CHARLES TERTIUS

1852-1929

Charles Tertius ('the Third') Mander was the Edwardian patriarch, dignified, even military, in bearing, with curly moustaches and a monocle. He was successful both in public life and as an industrialist; efficient and thorough in detail, confident, and pleased with himself in ebullient charm. He consolidated Mander Brothers as its first chairman and the rank of the family as gentlemen—leisured, estated, beneficent, keeping a respectable distance from their origins smeared in trade and toil.[1]

'Charlie' Mander was the eldest of three sons of Charles Benjamin and Sophia, born on 16 July 1852. His first letter with its litany of eager questions, 'written without assistance' when he was scarcely six, is dated 25 November 1858:

My dear Papa
Are your little children better? Have you a nice garden? Have you pretty flowers? Do they smell sweet? Are your children good? Have you horses and a field? Is the gun ready to be seen? Are you sorry Bruce is lost? When shall I go to Chester? I hope I shall be a good boy. Give my love to Mama.
I remain dear Papa your affec^{ate} son CT Mander

'CTM', as the family called him, was educated at private schools: Miss Reach's dame school—where his cousin Theodore followed him—and then Miss Hill's in Duoro Villas, Cheltenham. He then went to Rugby which, after Arnold's reforms, was perhaps the premier public school in the country for the sons of gentlemen and the fathers of gentlemen, liberal and Anglican, and with a place for the sciences in the curriculum. Dr Frederick Temple, its great headmaster at the time (1857-69), was famously described as 'a beast, but a just beast'.[2]

A letter written from Rugby on 30 June 1867, a month after his entry aged nearly 15, to his governess, Harriet Spooner, brings to life the excitement of a junior boy at the time of the Tercentenary celebrations:[3]

We had an awful' cute stodge on Thursday night. Only the worst of it was that I had to sit on a very swell position amongst the swells... All the fellows squashed into the common seats and left no room for us so after standing up for about 5 minutes we had to go to another table a smaller one where the fellows in the 11 and the 22 sat, and fellows who had their caps. And I had to sit in chair at the end of the table and had to carve some lamb. I had to carve it like mutton instead of lengthways, because I had not a proper knife and fork and because there were such a lot of things on the table that I was afraid of knocking over the knife very blunt. Well after cutting the lamb I had to cut a tipsy cake and jellies and help strawberries and cherries etc etc. We had awful good grub ices and iced puddings of all sorts. Blamanges, jellies, tarts, creams, and that sort of bubbly stuf quite white I don't know what you call it.

I should like to go to Germany very much indeed.

I am 31st this week, that is 3 places higher than last. I might have been higher only we have not had regular work it being the tercentenary week and the old Rugby match and one thing and another having interfered with the work of the School. Mind you remember to give Neville an half holliday because of the tercentenary and also to teach him to say *Tum Tum Little Tum Tummy.*

He won prizes at Rugby for vaulting, an early enthusiasm on which he had prepared his own illustrated manual, *Gymnastic Positions executed by Master Charles Mander,* aged eight, ending with the admonition: 'Never attempt any difficult feats without Papa's assistance. Never play during the exercises as Gymnastics require attention and a firm Resolution'.

He went up to Corpus Christi, Cambridge's smallest college, in 1872.[4] He has left no record of his academic attainments—except his annotated copies of Cicero. When he was distributing prizes at a school later in life, he referred to his degree of Master of Arts, 'but with cheerful candour he admitted that he did not quite know how he had obtained it'. But he joined the Military Volunteers and he certainly distinguished himself as a sportsman. He was one of the first team to play rugby football at Cambridge; he also represented his college at cricket, rowing and athletics. In the 1870s, he also played full-back for the Wolverhampton Rugby Football Club, of which he later became President.

After Cambridge, in training for his entry into the family firm, he spent a year attached to the office of the firm's accountant in Birmingham, Mr Bayfield. His father promised him a hunter if he succeeded in catching the train from Wolverhampton to Birmingham every day at the right time without fail. It worked. He got the train, and the hunter—or watch? In 1873, when he was twenty-one, he entered Mander Brothers to begin a lifetime's work at John Street.

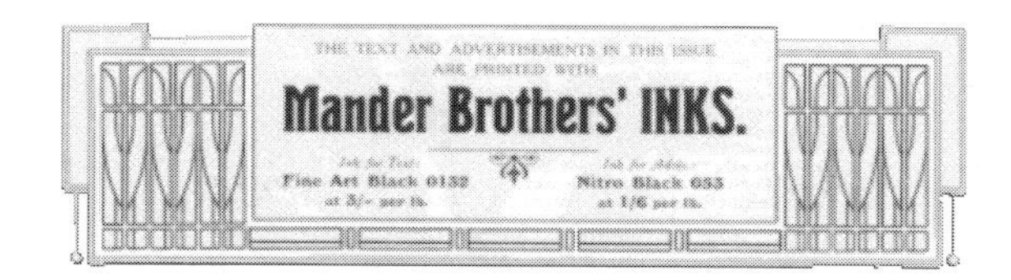

THE TEXT AND ADVERTISEMENTS IN THIS ISSUE
ARE PRINTED WITH
Mander Brothers' INKS.

Ink, 1880

In the event his father died young, only five years later, aged 59, in August 1878. Samuel Small, also in bad health, retired soon after, and a new partnership deed was drawn up dated May 1879 between the young first cousins of the next generation; Charles Tertius and Samuel Theodore, and their uncle by marriage, Henry Harper. As was the custom of the day, the cousins gave a grand dinner at The Exchange, Wolverhampton, 'In Celebration of Their Entrance into the Firm of Mander Brothers', shortly before Christmas of that year.

By the time of Charles Tertius's entry into the firm, the House of Mander was established as manufacturers of varnish and colours of repute. The third diversification of the product range came naturally in about 1880 with the advent of printing inks. Varnish was the common constituent. It had been made in the first instance to supply the firm's japanning trade and for selling to other more or less local japanners; then for selling to carriage and coach builders nationwide; finally to railways internationally; then there was the trade supplying paint manufacturers and house decorators; latterly there was the trade of making their own paints from the colour pigments also manufactured by the firm, or supplied to the makers of artists' colours. As the trade grew, more speciality varnishes were being made for industrial processes, foremost among them those to supply the profitable printing ink trade. The market in Victorian newspapers and illustrated magazines, not to mention printed books, was burgeoning, particularly with the advent of the offset lithography process. The logical development was for the firm to launch its own range of printing inks: letterpress and litho inks, photogravure, tint and gloss inks, ink dryers, embossing and relief-stamping colours, and printing lacquers (for tin).

A printing ink department was certainly in existence by 1882. There is a photograph of its full complement—a staff of manager, two girls and six men—taken in the yard of John Street in that year. A first mention of printing ink appears in Henry Clarke's annual report from the London office for the year 1883. He states the sum of £134 as the ink turnover, out of a gross turnover for his office of £72,270.

Printing ink is not fluid, as the familiar liquids for use with pen and brush. It is a glutinous, adhesive mass, suitable to transfer from types, engraved plates of copper and steel, blocks of stone or boxwood, and similar surfaces. Its ingredients are not the tannin-yielding nutgalls, the iron salts and gums, of common writing ink, nor the carbon soots and lampblacks ground with the gelatins and glues of the more primitive Indian inks. Printing inks, since the moveable type experiments of Johannes Gutenburg in the 1440s, had been essentially mixtures of varnish as the vehicle, with some pigment dispersed, the whole ground to an impalpable fineness. The early printing inks were made of boiled linseed oil, as old as possible, with tung, perilla or walnut drying oils which were given body by heating. Organic resins were added, such as a black or amber rosin or dammar, and soapy coal tar solvents; finally, colour pigments, such as indigo or Prussian blue (for blue and black inks), carmine or cochineal (for red), lead chromate (for yellow); synthetic dies had come in the 1860s.

At the time Manders entered the market, chemical drying agents were being developed, making possible the use of a wider variety of pigments for coloured inks. Castor oil and fish oil were tried out, blown with air, cracked with heat, experimentally reacted with natural resins and glycerine. Varnishes of varying degrees of stiffness were developed to make inks adapted for different surfaces and presses. The technology developed by varying the composition, viscosity, density, volatility and diffusion to adapt to the specialized printing presses involved, their speed and the material printed upon. It was becoming a high technology chemical-industrial process for which Manders had the resources of capital and expertise to exploit.[5]

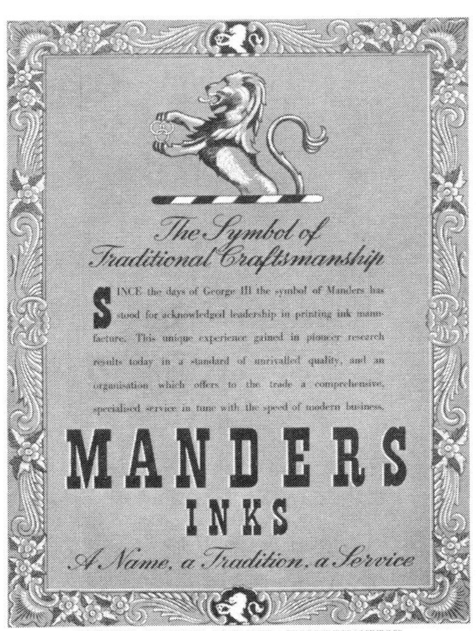

The Symbol of
Traditional Craftsmanship
SINCE the days of George III the symbol of Manders has stood for acknowledged leadership in printing ink manufacture. This unique experience gained in pioneer research results today in a standard of unrivalled quality, and an organisation which offers to the trade a comprehensive, specialised service in tune with the speed of modern business.
MANDERS
INKS
A Name, a Tradition, a Service
MANDERS PRINTING INKS LTD., WOLVERHAMPTON.

The first Mander inks were launched underwritten by the cachet of the brand name of 'Manders Varnishes' and met all the requirements of the comparatively low-speed printing machinery, letterpress and lithographic, of the day. But ink making was rapidly changing from a craft undertaking where raw materials were mixed by the printer himself, to a complicated chemical-industrial process. Here Manders immediately established a reputation for high quality. Manders Inks was to prove the most durable of their divisions, dominating the industry in Britain and outlasting the sale of the decorative paints division in the late twentieth century.

Works, 1908

In December 1892, as Charles Tertius, aged 40, took up office as Mayor of Wolverhampton, it was the turn of Neville and Howard Mander, the younger brothers of the senior partners (himself and Samuel Theodore respectively), to hold their bumper dinner at the Exchange to celebrate their entrance into the partnership—and their marriages. Uncle Harper, who had presided over the transition, died in retirement in Bournemouth in August 1894, leaving the new generation in command. The four partners made an indenture of co-partnership with Henry Clarke, establishing London offices as 'varnish, colour and printing ink merchants' at 17 Gracechurch Street. In Wolverhampton, the fourth generation had set up their positions they were to occupy for the next 30 years—the last all-Mander partnership.

In fact, Howard was by this time owner (as mortgagee) of the Exchange where such grand gatherings were held.[6] And, though nominally a partner of Mander Brothers, he spent his youth with a series of jobs in America, including helping to lay the Denver to Maine railroad. Neville took his turn as best he could. But he had delicate health and an impediment in his speech, and contributed little. His share was bought out by his elder brother CTM, 'for a lunch'. He went on to build his own Arts and Crafts house at The Woodlands, Penn (now a nursing home), and spent his time indulging his loves of shooting, and collecting Georgian furniture.

In 1894, Mander Brothers acquired new premises off Well Lane, Wednesfield, on the outskirts to the north west of Wolverhampton, where they set up a factory for the manufacture of the new products: printing inks and litho varnishes. These 'new auxiliary works' are described in full in *The British Printer* (December 1908):

Manders' New Auxiliary Works.
As further testifying to the remarkably strong position attained by the house of Mander—not merely in respect to varnishes, colours and paints, in all of which directions its output is of huge proportions, but more particularly in the printing ink section and its essentials in respect to colour, varnish and so on—have we pleasure in placing on record some impressions of the establishment gleaned during a visit early in November last.

The headquarters and chief works are situated round and about St. John's Street, but out at Wednesfield, some two or three miles away, is situated a further large establishment, in itself much larger than most factories associated with the allied industries. [Here] a seven-acre piece of land, bordered by a canal on one side and railway on the other, easily reached also by the electrical tramway, is the property of Messrs. Mander Bros., and a very considerable area of ground is covered by various specially-erected buildings.

We find that since our visit of some years ago the buildings have been entirely re-modelled and large new departments added. The firm is in the enviable position of possessing ample accommodation to carry out its own ideas in respect to the most desirable arrangement of works, and we are to find that the aims and ideas of experts have been actually carried out here. The premises are regarded as the ideal of their class.

The main buildings run along the water-side, with others at right angles. The first are devoted to colour mixing and to ink making, in fact, forming an ink making plant complete; the other series of buildings nearer the railway is allotted to varnish manufacture, also complete. These works are, we understand, chiefly used for supplying the materials made up at the Wolverhampton departments.

A tree-bordered main road sweeps round two sides of the works area, and affords access for vans to all parts. Each of the buildings is allowed ample space round about, and the structures, more particularly the new ink works, are most substantially built, with stone staircases, concrete floors, and fireproof generally.

The electric light is used throughout, and, as at the Wolverhampton works, a marvellous degree of cleanliness and tidiness prevails, for although all departments are evidently very busy, untidiness is never apparent, and many a printing office with far less excuse for the appearance of its rooms might take a lesson from the ink maker. The general scheme with regard to these works seems to be the elimination of dry colour from the grinding rooms, realizing that dust floating in the air and being deposited on grinding rollers may seriously neutralize the efforts to provide thoroughly pure and finely-ground colour. Thus a long room is devoted entirely to ink grinding, a heavy door shutting off the ink-mixing department with its closed-up machinery. Printers will appreciate this point. A low screen across the centre with the driving motors to left and right divides the floor area. Around and against the walls, with ample space about, is arranged a continuous series of large three-cylindered ink-grinding machines, a battery of some five-and-twenty of large size being already in full operation.

It is interesting to go from machine to machine and to note well-known colours in soft, oily curves rolling away from the pressure of the cylinders, the white coated operators, each with his magic broad-bladed knife charming or threatening his machine into uniform pressure and even flow. Well-known blacks, blues, and greens in one section are shown as on regular order for well-known magazines, whilst other colours are equally popular for illustrated work. The facility for handling cans, for frequent tests and arrangement generally, speak of an ideal system. Driving is obtained by short belts driven from overhead shaft on either side of the room, power being supplied by a couple of 50h.p. motors.

Contrasted with the roar and roll of so many grinding machines, the mixing department alongside is positively restful. Judging by the piping which comes from the ceiling, the tall mixing machines are fed from above, and we find this to be the case, varnish and dry colours being fed through their respective channels. This further explains the entire absence of dust, that is dry colour, in the air. The mixers are mechanically operated, the cleverly arranged blades of the paddle mixers making short work of the compounds of oil and colour. Besides the series of large sizes there are smaller cylindrical mixers, and we note particularly the curious looking litho blacks in their steam-heated pans. This department is devoted to blacks.

Colours In the next building across the yard is a department much more pictorial in effect. Again carrying out the idea of freedom from dry colour or dust, this room is fitted down one side and the centre with a series of bins with closely fitting lids. In these bins dry colours are stored, and the effect is to keep one colour to itself when the supply is being drawn upon, for, of course, neighbouring stocks would not be opened at one and the same time. Along the further side of the wall is a series of mixers, and we find these to embody some very ingenious ideas in apparatus for mixing. There are small-sized circular mixers ready to tackle small quantities of special colour fitted with scientifically arranged knives which scrape the sides, vessel and knives being revolved separately. To complete this as a mixing department, on a third side is a row of varnish tanks holding the pale, transparent varnish used for mixing colour. This department, as with the others, is self-contained, and possesses its own motor for driving purposes.

Stores Stepping now into a large roomy building, shelved from floor to ceiling along the walls, and with tables and benches, we find a can and drum store. The familiar tins in a variety of sizes are arranged in their respective sections, and all readily accessible. This is not a tin store, but an ink warehouse, and in spite of the chief chemist's confidence as to the absolute uniformity of new inks and those made for some time, it is quite clear that he makes no mistake as to keeping up substantial stocks of all colours. This we are glad to see, for we know only too well how commercial conditions so frequently require the printer to order inks for immediate use. Here once again we have the assurance that the laboratory maintains rigid fulfilment to standards, so that absolute reliance may be placed on receiving the same colour at any time of ordering.

The floor above is used as a storeroom for important sundries such as pomade and ink-easers. A steam-heated pan for solidifying oil is also noticed, the odour of the place being rather pleasant than otherwise. On looking out from the crane platform at the far end a fine view of hedge-bordered fields is obtained, for we are really on the fringe of the country here, with all the real country advantages of fresh air and spaciousness generally. An adjacent room, the dry black room, is situated directly over the black mixers, to which earlier reference is made. The whitewashed walls are rapidly assuming the artistic mottled effect of a busy chimneysweep's countenance through contact with the piled-up sacks of carbon blacks lodged here. The receptacles over the mixing cylinders are filled from here, and again there is every facility for minimizing any waste and preventing dust and trouble resulting there from.

The isolation of blocks of buildings is carried out with a thoroughness which must be the envy of those confined within small and often cramped areas. To reach the place of storage where the casks of colour, tins, and supplies of this character are safely put out of the way, and yet easy of access, we cross the yard again and enter a long single story building filled with casks and crates, tins and drums.

The Varnish Side In totally distinct buildings, separated by considerable yard space, is carried on the operations concerned with varnish making. First to the actual cooking... The varnish-boiling works show a long row of pans set in brick with closed fires. A large cowl or hood is fitted to each to carry off fumes, and conspicuously placed thermometers record temperatures. Conscientiously climbing the steps to sniff at the odours each successive one surely more pungent than its predecessor we are able to note the great heat used, and to observe the working generally, returning with an enhanced impression of the infinite care taken to prepare varnish.

At the rear of this building is one of similar size, the tubing whence escapes the fumes from the pans being here in evidence, and we are shown a clever device automatically coming into operation at each pan in case of fire from any individual boiler. Following the varnish as it runs off in pipes across the yard to the oil stores, we find on the second floor of a substantial building several dozen thousand gallon tanks, each equipped with gauge for showing depth of varnish contained in the tall cylinders, and with pump for filling or removal of the contents. Large as would appear to be this stock, as we are aware from visits to varnish stores, this represents but a fraction of the tremendous amount of oil always maturing in the firm's stores.

Fire Fighting The various buildings are disconnected, partly for convenience for manufacturing purposes and largely to minimise the risk of and the scope of damage by fire. Expecting to find full provision made to meet emergencies, for the fire fiend is ever a possible foe where oils are being treated, we found that every possible safeguard was adopted and each section provided with appliances for fighting that which is a good servant but a bad master. The works also possess their own fire brigade-already tried once on their own area and again at a neighbouring concern. Whilst we were present an alarm was raised and instantly men swarmed out of the buildings, each to his allotted task seizing section after section of hose pipe, bucket, or 'stood by' hydrants exactly where duty required, and all with a celerity which it would be difficult to surpass.

Black ink mixing

The District Would appear decidedly popular with the workpeople, and so healthy as to form quite a sanatorium for those employed at headquarters. Leaving the works we are struck by the appearance of a fine new building, an attractively built school in style, with a handsome villa attached. Inquiry as to this led to the production of keys, the opening of doors, and we found the building to be a mess-room for the workpeople. The floor is coated with a special linoleum-like terracotta coloured concrete, warm and clean in appearance. The tables and seats are painted a pleasant green and with the large cloakroom and lavatory make up an eminently neat and attractive picture.

To Sum Up We come away with the impression that 'this is surely Mander-like'—well thought out, well carried out, sound in conception, finished in every detail. No wonder the house maintains its place in the confidence of friends and customers.

In 1898, Manders again sought premises for the other successful new product of the time: colour. They were found within sight of John Street at Townwell Fold, where the 'Townwell Works' were set up. Chrome pigments were manufactured in the northern section, linked to the southern section by a tunnel, where dark pigments were made in 'The Blue Plant'. There were stables from which a horse and dray delivered their products every day to Birmingham. Noah Butler was manager, and under him the colour works prospered to become a major part of the business. Again the works are described in *The British Printer:*

To refresh our memories in respect to colour, we look in at the Town Well and School Street Works paying special attention to the department devoted to colour making. These show open, single-story rooms with gallery, enormous vats at one end, and a long row of huge tanks of colourful length of the floor.

After filtering, tramlines bear the trucks carrying the colour into steam-heated or vacuum chambers. The lighter colours, the deeper lakes, and the darker shades are confined to their respective departments, and it is very interesting to note how, after mixing, the development of colours is succeeded by unnumbered washings of pure water, whilst from beginning to end is felt the control exercised by the laboratory.

The chemists' department seems to us to be one of the most striking features of these works. It controls test by test, all supplies of goods coming into the works, all results obtained at the various stages of manufacture, warrants the sale of the finished article, whilst, above and beyond this, it is constantly at work on new colours, colour combinations, new methods of treating colours and oils, of suiting inks to papers. The permanency of colour seems to be an ever present aim, and, walking out on to the flat roof facing the laboratory windows, we notice many slips of paper attached to the windows, all bearing colours under test in some degree for permanence in connection with atmospheric effects. Some of the slips are dated nine and twelve months ago.

Cousin Mander John Smyth was the chief chemist here, the formidable technician behind the formulation of Manders' colours and varnishes. In 1898, he provided each traveller with a little manual with information on *The Four Trades*—varnishes, colours, paints and japans. The difference between oil and spirit varnish is defined, with ready answers to complaints about the processes of sleepiness, pinholing, shrivelling and cissing in varnish. Under the heading 'colours' he gives advice on dry colours, paints, pulp or water colours, and spirit or turpentine colours.

Manders Brothers' published trade catalogues, specimen books and booklets of the late nineteenth and early twentieth centuries are period pieces, and continued, with Gerald Mander's good taste as a bibliophile, between the wars.[7] For customers, Robert Gregory, commercial manager, produced a series of finely-produced catalogues demonstrating each type of application. The innovative lake-making plant is described, showing how advanced Manders were in the manufacture of madders, cochineal lakes, reds (including their famous 'carminette'), and the colours employed by the coach painter. Manders' dry colours were sold in powder, lump or 'drop' versions, and were distributed in a fine impalpable state which would require little grinding.

The packaging endorsed the quality, with Manders' patent screw tins, moulded glass bottles, and the famous green cans which were bashed out noisily in the firms' own tin works until after the second world war. These had a conical funnel top closed by a blue and silver capsule bearing a debased version of the Mander crest which is used (straining against heraldic propriety) as a logo to this day. In due course, the distinctive 'green can' by which the firm's products were recognised all over the world became the obvious name and symbol for the firm's house magazine.[8]

Manders began to market their 'ready-mix' paints in the 1890s; convenient, easy to use, sold in retail quantities and well-designed packaging. The catalogue for 'pound colours' demonstrates that these were produced from pigments in Manders' own factories in Wolverhampton and prepared in appropriate media which made them quick drying and flat on the surface. The colours were

> mixed for use with readiness and certainty and without disagreement with themselves and the thinners which often occurs with ordinary Colours and the Binders used in the old-fashioned way.

Prices ranged from carmine lake at 24*s.* a pound to Brunswick green at 1*s.*3*d.* Customers were reminded of the medals and awards which Manders' paints and varnishes had won at the international exhibitions, as if they were buying bottles of fine cognac: London 1862, Paris 1867, Naples 1871, Lyons 1872, Vienna 1873, Paris 1878, Brussels 1897...

The Green Can
THE HOUSE JOURNAL
OF
MANDER BROTHERS, LTD.,
WOLVERHAMPTON.
VOLUME IX.
MAY, 1929.
No. 5.

Varnish King

CTM's position as senior partner was dominant and unchallenged. He was described by contemporaries as one of the 'merchant princes of Wolverhampton, [whose] interests were bound up with the interests of the town'.[9] Considered a good businessman, the record does not indicate that he was heavily committed to the day-to-day management of affairs, for the Manders' company was run effectively by its various heads of department. Sir Alfred Hickman referred to his 'leisure', even by the lackadaisical standards of the times. The secure management seems to have relaxed into a climate of prosperity and ease, with a regime of long holidays and travels by the partners, constant hunting and shooting—or botonizing in the case of Theodore—and a complete dedication to time-consuming public affairs.

But under his watchful and animating direction, Mander Brothers became a leading company, exporting its products throughout the Empire and Europe. It maintained its own branches in London, Berlin (29 Kurstrasse), Vienna (111 Ungarstrasse), Paris (6 rue de l'Entrepôt), Florence (11 Piazza S.M. Novella), then after 1910 Milan, and by 1904 Montreal (218 St Paul Street), besides agencies in 'the enlightened countries of the world'. The firm and implicitly the family were of course 'stakeholders' in the local economy, as one of the largest employers and rate-payers in the borough, and CTM personally had a finger in many pies. Even the smell of varnish compounds dominated the air of the town as travellers arrived at one of the two rival railway stations: the London & North Western 'High Level' (1852) and the Great Western 'Low Level' (1854). It was said that locals could tell which way the wind was blowing by sniffing the distinct varnish aromas which wafted in the town air.

The firm was progressive, and had been early to internationalise its markets. Manders varnishes were now employed in car bodies, typewriters, optical instruments, bicycles, and machine tools in rapidly industrializing new cities from Stuttgart to Detroit. The markets for many kinds of varnish and protective coatings continued to expand into higher technology areas, with nearly 200 industrial processes in which varnishes were used: for example, as an insulating coating on copper electrical conductors in dynamos and in armature winding.

The late Victorian and Edwardian years when Charles Tertius presided were the heyday of the firm and family, and the town of Wolverhampton, and the Empire—where the Manders' brand reigned indomitable as a household world, the subject of *Punch* cartoons. In addition to the warrant of Queen Charlotte, still proudly displayed, in 1910 Manders were appointed 'Manufacturers of Varnishes and Colours' by Royal Warrant to King George V. Buckingham Palace was painted in their products. Downing Street was another regular customer, and the famous front door

with fanlight of Number Ten was always painted in Manders paint. The firm sponsored Captain Scott's expedition to the South Pole, and Scott came to dine at Wightwick. For in the years up to 1917 Manders Paint and Varnishes were the prestige brand, Number One in Britain—and therefore the world.

But there were already threats to Manders' supremacy. Early to internationalise, the first world war dislocated its markets decisively, and reduced the size and scope of the firm's operations so drastically that it never again assumed the stature of the pre-war Mander Brothers. During the war the place of the 'foreign', mainly European, trade was taken by orders from the Government for coatings for shells and munitions—where varnish coatings were required in huge quantities to prevent chemical action between the explosive mixture and the metal of the shell—fuses, grenades, bombs, propellers, vehicles, munition huts, hospitals. But Daisy observes in 1917: 'Mander Bros have had £51,000 less foreign trade this year. Mr King distracted, but not allowed to send abroad even where we could.' Orders for the war effort were small compensation for all Manders lost by the Great War overseas.

Already by the turn of the century it was becoming clear that the firm needed a new and up-to-date corporate structure. The delicate management arrangements were defined in partnership deeds in 1882, 1892 and 1896. But the untimely death of Samuel Theodore in 1900 led to complications which long outlived him, as under the partnership deed of 1896 a deceased partner's capital had to remain locked in the firm, where it always earned 5% interest *before* any profits were declared. The provisions of Theodore's will were even more complicated, under which the rights of his sons to become partners were scrupulously upheld by zealous trustees. The will could only be set aside by court order, in order to allow for the trustees to accept preference shares in the proposed company in lieu of the guaranteed interest payments due to them as partners. The firm had been run as a patriarchal family estate, which it was the intention of the deed and the will to perpetuate.

The partnership minutes have a japing undergraduate ring, with the air of the debating society or junior common room (possibly imparted by Gerald):

March 12, 1924—It was pointed out to the chairman that the arrival of A seemed to have dislocated D who was now floating between wind and water. It was admitted that at present an Ararat had not been found.

A draft memorandum and articles of association were drawn up in 1907 for a company to be called 'Mander Brothers Limited'. The idea of a company structure had been mooted even earlier, after CTM's hunting accident in 1904, but it took 20 years, virtually till the next generation in 1924, for all the obstacles—legal, financial and personal—to be cleared in order to dissolve the old partnership structure and set up a private limited company instead. Of course, all the shares in the new company were held by members of the Mander family, and of course CTM became the first chairman and 'governing director'.

---

[1] For instance, before the baronetcy, the family is one of the only Wolverhampton dynasties, with the Hickmans, to receive an entry in such standard directories as *Walford's County Families of the United Kingdom or Royal Manual of the Titled and Untitled Aristocracy*, 1904. The editor writes: 'in countries like our own [...] mainly owing to the influence of trade and commerce, individuals and families are constantly crossing and re-crossing the narrow line which severs the aristocracy from the commonalty'.

[2] P. Hinchliff, *Frederick Temple, Archbishop of Canterbury: A life*, Oxford, 1998

[3] Rugby was founded and endowed in 1567 under the will of Laurence Sheriff. The game of rugby was first played there in 1823. Thomas Arnold was the headmaster 1828-42 who raised it to the rank of a great public school. For the tercentenary, subscriptions were raised for a number of building projects and scholarships. His brother, Jack, followed him to Rugby. CTM entered on 27 May, and left in 1868 (*Rugby School Register*, vol. 2, Aug 1842-Jan 1874, revised and annotated A.T. Mitchell, Rugby, 1902).

[4] He was a contemporary of Sir Horace Edmund Avory (1851-1935), captain of boats, a criminal lawyer and senior judge of the King's bench division. He figured in many sensational trials and became a household word as the most dreaded 'hanging judge' of his age: 'thin lipped, cold, utterly unemotional, silent, and humorless, and relentless towards lying witnesses and brutal criminals'. The family saw a human face. He was a lifelong friend and visitor at The Mount, and godfather of Charles Arthur Mander. (See Gordon Lang, *Mr Justice Avory*, 1935 and B. O'Donnell, *The Trials of Mr Justice Avory*, 1935. He writes to Daisy shortly before his death, enclosing a copy of the latter (28 March 1935): 'It was written and published without my permission or communication with me.')

[5] The first specialized accounts of the industry appear at this time, notably William Savage, *Printing Ink, Both Black and Coloured*, 1882.

[6] The Exchange was built in 1850-1, when the prospectus set out the advantages of such a building to agriculturists and corn merchants: 'the approaching railways to the counties of Worcester, Hereford, and Salop will complete a chain of circumstances that will shortly render the market of Wolverhampton second to none in the Empire.' In the event, the venture lost money. Howard found himself representing the mortgagee when it failed to sell at auction in 1888. He carried on the Exchange until 1898, when he sold it to the Wolverhampton Corporation for £2,500, on condition that the building should be demolished within six months, and the land levelled, railed off, and paved.

[7] *Price List and Printing Inks, & c. manufactured by Mander Brothers, Wolverhampton, England*, 1891, is the earliest Mander Brothers' specimen book listed in St Bride's Institute catalogue. Supplements to *The British Printer: A collection of ornamental supplements and advertisement plates*, London, 1893-94, include specimens in different Mander Brothers colour printing inks.

[8] There are collections of the firm's late Victorian and Edwardian packaging in the Bantock Museum, and on display at Wightwick Manor.

[9] At the presentation dinner held in his honour on being granted the baronetcy.

Alderman Charles Tertius Mander, D.L., J.P., *1897*

portrait by the Hon. John Collier,
'presented by his fellow Townsmen and other friends',
aged 44, after serving uniquely four times as Mayor of Wolverhampton.
He wears Levée Order in Hussar style, with frogged cord loops across the front,
newly introduced busby, and sabretache

9

BART

Mayor and Alderman, 1892-6

CTM was an astute, no-nonsense, businessman, controlling diverse commercial interests as an industrialist, a Galsworthian 'Bart' and man of property. But from the first he was active in public life, in local, municipal and charitable affairs. He entered Wolverhampton Council as a Conservative representing St Peter's ward. He served uniquely four times in succession as Mayor of Wolverhampton (1892-6), 'a record number of years of office for any mayor of the town'.[1]

It was an age when the mayor was a prominent social figure, with the means and standing to maintain the dignity of his office, expected to pay for his own civic entertaining at receptions, balls and feasts, to make numerous speeches and presentations, and to take the initiative in public appeals, contributing if necessary to the poor and unemployed out of his own pocket. Councillors required 'character, ability, wealth and a well-known name which entitled them to respect'.[2] He threw a dinner for one thousand people at the Agricultural Hall, mainly for destitute children and the poor, and entertained the merchant classes royally in the drill hall. A concern was the appalling winter of 1893, which was 'disastrous' for the less fortunate among Wolverhampton's inhabitants: 'It drew forth his sympathy for the poor. By his exertions the clothing of destitute children was organised into a society, and the good work was carried on for six years. Mr Mander liberally subscribed to it... By this means 2,408 poor children were clothed during the cold winter months.'

In 1888 Wolverhampton was established as one of the original county boroughs. It was fast becoming one of the richest and most populous of them in the country (82,662 in 1891). As mayor he was determined it should stay that way, and that he would take it into the twentieth century.

CTM was chairman of the Council's Lighting Committee (1893-1902), instrumental in promoting the first municipal electricity supply against an unconvinced opposition. As an unabashed pioneer, who had already installed electricity in his house and works, he 'was one of the earliest and most active advocates of the electric lighting of the borough'.[3] 'His first plunge into matters electrical' had been to present the town with an electric 'time ball' in 1887, sited on the tallest building in the main square, activated when the Post Office supplied electric current from Greenwich at 10 a.m. every day so that the townsmen should know the correct time. Then, as mayor, in 1895 he persuaded Lord Kelvin,[4] President of the Royal Society and, among many things, inventor of the absolute temperature scale cited in degrees Kelvin, to come and open the Corporation electricity works in Commercial Road. On 30 January he set up a stage-managed display when 1,000 electric lights blazed as they were turned on in unprecedented synchrony in Queen's Square and the surrounding streets. All the while there was a group of vociferous cynics who confidently predicted that such gimmickry would be a failure.

According to his daughter, Daisy, he 'started' the Wolverhampton Wanderers 'Wolves' Football Club. The claim may be a slight exaggeration, but we know he was Vice-President. (He was also President of the Wolverhampton Rugby Football Club and Vice-President of the Wolverhampton and District Football League.) During his first year of office as mayor, Wolves won the English Cup for the first time, shortly after adopting their distinctive gold-and-black stripes. It set the tone of a term of office which was regarded as 'a gratifying success' and for a career in public service which was 'meteoric':[5]

> Elected four years in succession as Mayor of the borough, he fulfilled the duties of that office in a manner which—both in regard to the tact he displayed on several occasions in presiding over the debates in the Council Chamber; his initiation of important undertakings for the improvement of the town, notably the introduction of the electric lighting system, which he so skilfully piloted to success; and last, but not least, his geniality and general hospitality during the long period of his Mayoralty—earned for him the respect and esteem of the inhabitants generally...

By 1896 he was said to have 'surpassed all other Mayors'. On his retirement in 1897, he was made an honorary Freeman of the borough 'in recognition of the eminent services rendered by you during the four years of your Mayoralty'. His lady mayoress was presented by the ladies of Wolverhampton with a diamond tiara. To commemorate the occasion, CTM for his part presented the Wolverhampton Corporation with a rosewater dish,[6] and his Cambridge College with a set of candlesticks.[7] He showed he could still master the epigraphic style instilled by a classical education when he had them both inscribed in Latin.

As Mayor and alderman of the expanding borough, CTM was the efficient force behind the local tramway services, which became a contentious matter in Edwardian Wolverhampton. With a Cambridge education and evident interests in practical science and gadgetry, he was said to have 'tramways on his brain'. He was chairman of the Transport Committee, and elected first chairman of the Tramways' Committee of the Council when it was set up in October 1896. He remained so for a quarter century (till 1920), taking an interest in every detail of operations—even donating seasonal presents to the staff, such as warm underwear for cabmen, tram conductors and drivers.

The Corporation took over the existing tramways in the borough with the compulsory purchase of the Wolverhampton Horse Tramways Company under its own bill, the Wolverhampton Corporation Act of 1899. They proposed to reconstruct the entire system, extending the routes within and beyond the borough boundaries, converting to a narrower gauge and electrifying the tramways. The Wolverhampton Corporation Tramways Department officially began operating on 1 May 1900, now revitalised in smart military order under the watchful eye of CTM:[8]

> There was in some senses nothing short of a transformation. The passengers found on mounting the car that the driver and conductor were literally metamorphosed. They wore for the first time a uniform of blue serge, with orange braid, from head to foot they were smartness personified. Inspectors wore a suit similarly cut, with gold trimmings.
>
> All the day the cars have been profusely decorated and have attracted considerable attention along the different routes. The horses were gaily decked in ribbons, and on one of the cars were the words "Success to the Wolverhampton Corporation Tramways", in which every Wulfrunian will heartily join.

The system of traction led to heated controversy, with various rivals on the market between which CTM had to adjudicate with characteristic thoroughness. The Committee assessed the respective merits of the overhead, conduit and accumulator systems, finally recommending the overhead system, used by the tramways of the surrounding areas, in its report back to the Council in July 1898. Various experimental lengths of track were installed and tried out. The Electric Street Car Syndicate Ltd. constructed a surface contact system of its own invention, but in October 1900 the Committee was still recommending the overhead system.

CTM was not convinced, and became a partisan opponent. In March 1901, he reported that as a traveller his attention had been drawn to the Dolter 'surface contact' system, which had been experimentally installed in Paris the year before, in May 1900. In due course the Committee visited Paris in his train and inspected the system in operation. They examined tenders in March 1901 for the original overhead system and another submitted by the Dolter Company for their rival surface contact system.

But the Committee were even more confused, and deferred accepting any of them. In April, at a special meeting, he explained the working of the Brown, or 'Lorain', surface contact system of 'direct-contact traction', manufactured by the Lorain Steel Co. of Ohio, USA, to the Committee. The various manufacturers were given an opportunity to demonstrate and explain the merits of all their competing systems.

CTM was by now championing the superiority of the virtually untried Lorain system. This propelled the trams by means of electrical impulses picked up by the tram through an arm fixed underneath it, which came into contact with plates set in the middle of the tracks. It was still a pioneering technology, used on just one section of the Washington, DC, tramway system in 1898. Even there it was only used for a short period, before it was taken over by another company using a conduit system. On the one hand, the Lorain system was expensive and involved potentially dangerous live contact boxes set between the tramlines in the streets; in its favour, supporters pointed out that it avoided unsightly overhead wires and traction poles. As CTM remarked, 'I have no wish for the centre of our town to resemble a bird cage'.

Ever practical, in the face of entrenched opposition, he prepared a working model to demonstrate the 'Lorain' system in public. He was a forceful advocate, and took the Committee with him until the Committee finally recommended it to the Council. The Council resolved to accept a trial, contracting to equip some eleven miles of track; although in the first place a length of less than a mile was to be set up for an experimental period of 30 days. If it fulfilled certain stipulations, the Council bound itself to adopt it.

He broke the first ground of the new Wolverhampton tramways on 20 May 1901 with a silver-plated pick, and the first mile of experimental Lorain fitted track was completed on 13 January 1902. The opening ceremony for Wolverhampton's first electric trams was fixed for 6 February that year when, just before 12.30 p.m. a conductor boarded a double-decker car calling, 'all the way for a penny'.

CTM proclaimed the success of the experiment, although not all the conditions had been precisely fulfilled. There were threats of litigation by the Lorain Company if the Council refused to adopt the system. The Council felt CTM had bounced them into a decision, and the Lorain question 'keenly divided the Council and the Town'. One councillor said: 'I never remember being present at a meeting of the Council at which I have heard language so strong'.[9] But CTM had his way. The Committee agreed that the contract for the first eleven miles or so of Lorain track should be completed. A few other tramway authorities did use surface contact systems which lasted some years, but Wolverhampton became the only city to use this system for any period of time; at least 20 years.

High Sheriff, 1903

CTM was 'pricked' as High Sheriff of Staffordshire, the first Mander and one of the first Wulfrunians and manufacturers to so serve, in 1903-4. Correspondence with other county figures is revealing of the punctilious etiquette of provision of state coaches for the assizes, with their coats of arms in heraldic blazons on the door panels, the second carriage for the judges, 'barouche or Victoria generally', the liveries for coachman, two footmen and trumpeter with his banner.[10] Ridges & Sons of Wolverhampton gave estimates for his shrievalty equipage in December 1901:

To provide Elliptic spring coach as State Carriage, for the Judge's use for Year of Office, with Full Dress, Hammercloth, Hind Standards, and with Heraldry, properly emblazoned on panels, £37 6*s*.
To provide a full body, Cee spring State Coach to match your own colours, with Sheriff's Hammercloth, Hind Standards. And with Heraldry emblazoned on panels, for your year of Office. £57 10*s*.

When his equipage appeared in all its splendour at the Opening of the Summer Assizes on 30 July 1903, the locals were impressed by the way he performed his duties 'in style', already the incarnation of a bygone age:

The High Sheriff's equipage was a very smart turn-out, and drawn by a handsome team of four light bays from his own stable. The body of the carriage was enamelled blue, with light yellow wheels, these being the High Sheriff's colours, and his coat-of-arms was also emblazoned on the sides of the carriage. The livery of the coachmen and footmen was in the same colours. The former wore a powdered wig, three-cornered hat with the cockade at the side, blue coat with yellow facings and gold buttons, yellow plush breeches, and white silk stockings and black shoes with silver buckles; the footmen being similarly attired with the exception of the hats, which were of the Court variety with the cockade in the front. The High Sheriff wore the uniform of a Major in the Staffordshire Imperial Yeomanry. Mr Justice Bruce was driven to the Judges' House, and later in the evening was joined by Mr Justice Ridley,[11] who arrived privately from London.

The judicial procession from shire town to shire town was an awesome pageant, when the judge's party was met on horseback at the city limits by the sheriff and his footmen, with their cocked hats braided in silver, one with a silver-topped mace in his hand; then escorted with hangman, chaplain and entourage into the town centre, to be heralded by a flourish of trumpets. The Red Judges in surviving photographs look severe and altogether ancient in their full-bottomed wigs, raised in Regency England. At the next Assize, the press wrote: 'His horses and carriage are one of the sights of the county town when the Assizes are held, for the horses are really four splendid animals. The Sheriff's coachman looks a picture... He differs from the famous Lord Mayor of London's coachman inasmuch as he is not stout, but a slim and sharp-faced man'.

The press remarked that as 'Lord High Executioner', CTM was liable to be called on to supervise executions: but 'to the unfortunate criminal on whom it may be his duty to see the last dread sentence of the law carried out, the genial presence of Alderman Mander cannot but prove a cheering support on "the way to dusty death".' This duty he had to discharge when the death sentence was duly pronounced at the Winter 1904 Assizes, when the Jury returned a verdict of 'Guilty' on Henry Jones (50), a collier who had wilfully taken the life of his mistress, Mary Gilbert, of Hanley. Mr Justice Kennedy

> appeared to be much distressed, as his clerk put on the black cap, whilst Prebendary Penny stood up.[12] The Judge said that the prisoner, animated by jealousy, had taken the life of the woman whilst she lay sleeping. He did not desire to do anything, but make as short as possible the prisoner's suspense. He then passed sentence of death, and Prebendary Penny added, 'Amen'. The prisoner, who uttered not a word, turned round quietly, and walked down the steps of the dock.

Mary, his wife, attended the Quarter Sessions one morning with the daughter of the Recorder of Wolverhampton, Abel Ram. He writes to Daisy: 'She is a very nice girl, about 21, but she looks more. Your mother and she went into Court but it was very prosy and I don't think that they got much out of it. Charlie Bailey's burglar got three years and had to finish another sentence, so he had about four years in all. Charlie Bailey got 7*s.* 6*d.* for attending two days, which he gave to the policeman.'

The Assizes were graver occasions, when the High Sheriff had to provide ringers, curate, clerk and choir at St Mary's, hall keeper, wine for the judges' associate in the summer assizes, chaplain's court robes, and to provide luncheon for juries (thirty shillings a day, when ordered by the Court), unless they were locked up, in which case it was paid for by the Treasury. He also paid for the bailiff's attendance on the jury. But the county paid for the police, the Treasury repaying the county.

Despite the pomp and circumstance of such ceremonials, 'Charlie' Mander was always approachable to ordinary people. A reporter describes his appearance at the Assizes:

> I was at Stafford recently while the Assizes were in full swing, and the High Sheriff, who had just 'partaken of luncheon', was returning to the vitiated atmosphere of Court where Mr Justice Kennedy was presiding. The figure under the nodding plumes, despite the cigarette stuck jauntily between the lips, was traversing the ground with a martial stride—there was however no trace of affectation in the gait—that was in exquisite harmony with the resplendent uniform, which cost something like a hundred guineas.

There gazed after this gorgeous apparition, which was fading in the distance, a gentleman whose expression appeared to be vacant. How sometimes we are deceived by appearances, to be sure! With lips framed to impart information, as I imagined, this gentleman turned to me. In a flash I conjectured the fellow was going to say, 'There goes the High Sheriff.' He merely remarked without the slightest hesitation, 'Did you notice Charlie Mander?'

How pregnant with suggestion was that single query! The full force of the comment would not have been felt had the High Sheriff been clad in the sober garb of everyday life... Had Alderman Mander been born the Mikado of Japan—which Heaven forfend with one of his might—he would be known by the Japanese equivalent of 'Charlie.' And the trappings of the sacred ruler of the Japs are no whit behind those of a High Sheriff in their gorgeous conglomeration of all colours, primary or otherwise. The fact may be adduced, that a man who is thus known as 'Charlie' may have many opponents, but you cannot find that he has a real enemy... I know not the man who is such a striking monument to the futility of human applause and human decoration...this personality which can rise superior to all the absurd accoutrements of state.

He liked to order matters correctly, and insisted on revising his armorials for emblazoning his state carriage with the correct differences, as the arms the family was using hitherto clearly had a slightly bogus hint of parvenu impropriety. The heraldic revisions had to be established with due sanction of the College of Arms. On 10 February 1903, he wrote to C.H. Athill, Richmond Herald:

Dear Sir,
Referring to your letter of 17 [June] 1901, I duly received patent for Armorial Bearings.[13] I know the College of Arms would not grant me the use of the crest I had worn for so many years & my father & grandfather before me (a demi lion couped holding 3 annulets interlaced) as that was already held by another family of Mander to whom you could not trace any direct descent, but at any rate I thought you made a distinct difference by *adding* 2 buffalo horns; you also allowed the 3 rings on the coat of arms, with a difference on the ground.

My reason for re-opening the question is that I shall most probably be pricked for High Sheriff of the County next month & shall have my coat of arms painted on the coach. That is not a matter of much moment, but if the crest on the Coat of Arms has only 2 rings on the coach, I shall have to alter the crest on my harness & livery buttons to match.

What I again ask is, cannot the crest be altered to 3 rings, same as on the coat of arms of course with the difference of the buffalo horns added so that I may not have to make so radical a change as deleting one ring? The buffalo horns can more easily be cut on my signet ring, etc.

I can send up the Patent for alteration any time you could make out a new one.

Please reply at your earliest convenience, as there is no time to waste.

Yours faithfully, C.T.M.

On 29 March he is following up, already preparing a pedigree:

I have sorted out from my neighbour (son of my late Cousin Theodore Mander of Wightwick) a Family Bible, belonging to *Mr. Mander his book 1742* (Benjamin Mander?)

Also a packet of documents which my cousin unearthed at Aston Cantlow in 1874, a packet of Birth & Baptisms same date & a Roll of Pedigrees compiled, same date or earlier.

My neighbour will send these documents to you tomorrow.

I am off to Biarritz on Thursday till end of April. If you want to write me after Thursday my address will be: Grand Hotel, Biarritz.[14]

The College of Arms was clearly a dilatory organization that tried his patience sorely. He writes reprovingly on 3 January 1904:

It is now 3 years since you granted me a new coat of arms, & as far as I remember a year since I gave you a cheque to pay for getting out a genealogy, & nothing has been done. I told you at the time that you would have to find out particulars of dates of births & marriages from the parsons & referred you to the Rector of St Peter's Wolverhampton for some of the later ones. A long time ago you sent me down a list of riddles & I asked for a copy as I had sent it on to one of my sisters & it has been mislaid.

However you did *not* send me a copy, but I fail to see what my sister's cousins & aunts have to do with my genealogy.

You really must buck up & do something for the money I gave you.

With the compliments of the season, believe me

Yours ever truly, C.T.M.

Finally, Athill's family tree, still the starting point for family genealogy, finely engrossed with armorials in its official red Morocco dispatch box with cypher, arrived later that year. Gerald Mander was establishing himself as an antiquarian, and spent many years compiling genealogies of collateral and antecedent families, poring over parish records and (upside down) over recumbent tombstones, and publishing some of the results of his researches in antiquarian journals.

Victorian etiquette had to be observed punctiliously, but its niceties were clearly mystifying even to those heavily involved in public life. He wrote to 'The Right Hon^{ourable} The Lord Chamberlain' on 12 February 1904:

My Lord,

I have the honour to request that I may be allowed to pay my respects to His Majesty at an early date, before the termination of my Shrievalty.

May I at the same time have the privilege of presenting my chaplain, The Rev Alfred Penny, Rural Dean & Prebendary of Lichfield Cathedral?

Since I last attended a Levée His Majesty has honoured me by making me a Deputy Lieutenant. May I enquire if it be necessary for me to be re-presented? If so, by whom?

State coach at Stafford Assizes, 1903

Coronation Honours, 1911

He had already written to Mr Alderman Bantock on 30 October 1892, with information for the book he was editing of the county families of Staffordshire, giving a succinct account of himself and the family:

Dear Mr Bantock
Agreeably with my promise I beg to hand you the following note about myself and family which you may make what use of you please on the 9th prox.

I am one of the fifth generation of Mander's of this town, my great great grandfather having settled in about 1750. He married a Miss Clemson of Bridgnorth, through whom some of the property in John's Lane (now belonging to my firm) came into the family. His son Benjamin was a Town Commissioner in the reign of George III about 1777 and both he and his brother John, together with my grandfather Charles & my great uncle Benjamin Parton, were Commissioners in 1814 (i.e. four).

I am the head of the firm of Mander Brothers "Varnish and Colour Manufacturers" of this town. We have a house in London, Berlin and Florence besides agencies in Paris, Melbourne & in fact most of the countries of the world.

The business was founded at the end of the last century or early this by Benjamin Mander my great grandfather.

My grandfather was also a japanner but many years ago retired from that business which was sold to Mr Shoolbred and eventually passed on to the late Henry Loveridge.

Mander Brothers are nearly if not quite the largest private rate-payers in the borough and employ a considerable number of hands.

Passing to the next generation, my father Charles Benjamin Mander was a J.P. and a member of the Council, but never passed the chair; he was much interested in art & had a great deal to do with the establishment of the old School of Art in 185[2] of which he was Treasurer for many years.

To revert to my humble self, I was born in Wolverhampton & was duly taught by Miss Reach. I eventually went to Rugby and afterwards to Cambridge where I took my degree ... in 1875. I subsequently took my M.A. in 1879.

I am a Lieutenant in the Q.O.R.R. (i.e. the Staffordshire Yeomanry) & am attached to the Himley Troop, than which there is no smarter in the service.

I am V.P. of the Chamber of Commerce, Treasurer of the Blue Coat School, on the Board of the Hospital and also of the Orphanage, was one of the lay secretaries of the church congress in 1887. I am as you know a churchman and a staunch Conservative.

I married in 1882 the daughter of Henry Paint of Halifax, Nova Scotia, an M.P. of the Canadian Dominion Parliament & a member of an old Guernsey family.

I was elected to the Council in 1886 (August) & have twice been re-elected unopposed. I serve on several Committees as you know with but indifferent success.

Referring again to my grandfather, I have in my possession a duplicate of a Reprieve (he was instrumental getting in 1817) for 2 men who were about to be hanged for stealing 1/6. On the back is a cutting from the W'hampton Chronicle of 1853 in which is stated that my grandfather was a representative of the "oldest family now in the Town", so I suppose I am equally, only more so. Should you wish to see it, it is very much at your service.

I hope you will forgive this long and somewhat egotistical letter.

I forgot to say that my father married in 1850 a daughter of Dr Weaver of Chester, an old Cheshire family.

The letter was written when he was forty. In the end he was senior Alderman who served on the Town Council for 41 years without a break, was a magistrate for the borough and county, was involved, as he states, with innumerable local charities, and was a Deputy Lieutenant for the county. He was a formidable and energetic figure, 'genial, frank and hearty',[15] prominent in the public life of the Midlands and the wider business world of late Victorian/Edwardian times. He was made a baronet for his public services, and implicitly those of the family over the generations, in George V's Coronation honours of 1911.

He professed to be a 'churchman', his side of the family for some time reunited to the established Church of England. He doesn't seem to have been as diligent a sabbatarian as his forefathers, writing (December 1904):

I went to church today for a change and saw the new curate, who is a fairly old man with a big moustache and beard (say 32). He preached and gave us a sermon of 17 minutes 12 seconds, which is at least five minutes more than he should have given. There were mighty few people in church.

He was 'the leading Conservative of the town'. He described his politics with a typically vital oxymoron as those of 'a staunch Conservative who held strong political views in a mild way'. He believed there were only two kinds of politics—Conservatism, and 'the other sort'. But he often said he hated politics; he was unideological and pragmatic, not partisan, especially in municipal matters. Soon after he had finished his distinguished term as mayor, there were murmurings in the neighbourhood that he should stand for Parliament to succeed Sir Alfred Hickman. Hickman[16] wrote on 12 October 1893 asking him to represent Wolverhampton West:

I look to you with confidence as my successor in the representation of Wolverhampton. You have leisure, abundance of means, and the great success which has attended your Municipal career will certainly lead you to look to the larger Parliament...

The question arose again when he was asked to stand in 1899-1900. He wrote to Colonel Tom Thorneycroft[17] on 10 September 1900:

My dear Colonel,
... I should consider it a very great honour to represent the division of the County in Parliament & if it is the wish of the heads of the Party here that I should stand for the Constituency I shall be very pleased to do so. I was however under the impression that Colonel Webb had consented to stand. He would romp in. If he stands I shall gladly give him every assistance in my power as I know he would on the other hand give me. I don't think your Committee would be likely to ask me any questions which you could not readily answer on my behalf. Election expenses are a detail about which there need be no question.

In the event, Hickman soldiered on until defeated by a trade unionist in 1906, and CTM never stood.[18] Perhaps he felt he was 'above politics', or lacked the temperament to perform as a democratic politician. The family were politically viable in the Midlands. Theodore Mander was asked to stand for Mid-Worcester, in his case in the Liberal interest, about the same time (June 1895). William Woodings of The Midland Liberal Federation wrote to him:

Your name would be well known and you have almost a local connection... The constituency is Liberal in tendency and is not difficult to work.

In the desperate period after the first war he seems to have shifted to the Right. As a manufacturer CTM was a natural imperialist. By the 1918 election he was listed as one of a number of prominent figures who supported the controversial National Party formed by Sir Henry Page Croft, the first baron Croft (1881-1947), as a new and radical right-wing party which advocated a limited role of the state in society and the economy, the stabilisation of Europe as a British market, the strengthening of imperial ties, and keeping a safe distance from the Russian bear.

Riding out from The Mount stables: Daisy, Gerald, Mary, CTM, Arthur, groom and guest

[1] A standard account of his mayoralty is given in William H. Jones, *Story of the Municipal Life of Wolverhampton*, 1903, chaps. 20-1.

[2] Quoted in G.W. Jones, *Borough Politics*, 1969, p. 151
[3] *The Midland Evening News*, 20 June 1911
[4] William Thomson, first baron Kelvin of Largs (1824-1907). He was also involved in the laying of the first Atlantic cable and invented a receiver for the submarine telegraph. The first electric street lighting in Britain was at Holborn Viaduct in 1878.
[5] *Express and Star*, 13 November 1902
[6] The inscription (original in Latin) reads: 'C.T. Mander presented this rosewater dish to his fellow-citizens, in pleasant and grateful remembrance of being elected by their grace and suffrages to fulfil the high office of mayor for four successive years, 1896.' (See W.H. Jones, 243.)
[7] CAROLUS TERTIUS MANDER AM, HUJIUS COLEGII OLIM ALUMNUS, SUMMO WULFRUNIENSIUM MAGISTRATE QUATUOR JAM FUNCTUS, VASA IGNIFERA IN CONCLAVIS HUJIUS USUM AMICITIAE MONUMENTUM DD MENSI DECEMBRI MDCCCXCVIII. His own translation reads: 'CTM, once a student of this college, who has borne, now four times the highest official dignity of the town of Wolverhampton, presents these fire-bearing vessels for the use of this chamber as a memorial of friendship'.
[8] *Express and Star,* quoted in S. Webb and P. Addenbrooke, *A History of Wolverhampton Transport*, vol. 1, 1833-1930, Birmingham, n.d., p. 23; J.S. Webb, *Tramways of the Black Country,* Bloxwich, 1954.
[9] *Wolverhampton Chronicle*, 14 October 1903 and 15 May 1903
[10] Letter from R. Copeland, potter, of Kiblestone Hall, Stone, dated 11 August 1902.
[11] Sir Edward Ridley (1843-1928), PC, MP, married a local, Alice Bromley-Davenport.
[12] Alfred Penny (b. 1845), author of *Ten Years in Melanesia*, was rector of St Peter's, Wolverhampton, 1895-1919, and canon residentiary of Lichfield Cathedral, 1919. He m. 2nd 1895 the dau. of the Rev. Ralph Bourne Baker, of Hasfield Ct, Glos.
[13] The revised armorial bearings, 'legally established and recorded', were granted and assigned to descendants of Charles Benjamin and Samuel Small by Sir Arthur William Woods, Garter, and George Edward Cockayne, Clarenceux (see Appendix III). The new buffalo horns may be a canting reference to the Turkish for 'buffalo': *manda.*
[14] Theodore's correspondence of 1874 is quoted in *A Private Heritage.* The Family Bible, probably of Thomas Mander, is one of the oldest Mander books to survive after the loss of the 'Read' bible.
[15] *The County of Stafford and Many of its Family Records*, Exeter, 1897
[16] Hickman (b. Tipton 1830) was known as the 'iron king'. The Hickmans were another patrician Wolverhampton family about whom there was some family doggerel: *Who appears grander,/ Hickman or Mander?* The Manders later married into the Hickmans, when Brenda, daughter of Howard Mander of Trysull Manor, married Alfred Edward Hickman, the second baronet, in 1919. (The third baronet, Howard Hickman, married Beryl, former wife of Sir Dennis Thatcher (subsequently baronet) in 1940.)
[17] Thorneycroft (1822-1902), of Tettenhall Towers, poet, inventor, eccentric, industrialist, veteran of Spion Kop. His brother, J.B. Thorneycroft, invented the 'Thorneycroft' short rifle. Their father, George Benjamin (1791-1851) was first mayor of Wolverhampton (1848). The family were connected by marriage when Philippa, daughter of Philip Mander, married John Thorneycroft in 1965.
[18] Wolverhampton West was represented (1910-22) by Alfred Bird, a Birmingham custard manufacturer, whose son, Sir Robert (b. 1876), 2nd Bt., held it after him until 1945. Through Charles Arthur Mander's good offices as local party President, his son-in-law, Patrick Stirling, was selected prospective Conservative candidate for the 1950 election. But with boundary changes, Enoch Powell was to represent the new South-West Division continuously to 1974. Stirling subsequently sat on the Westminster City Council, and was twice mayor of Westminster. His reception for the Queen with Churchill at the Royal Academy in 1953 was one of her first official engagements in London after the Coronation.

10

THE MOUNT

1891 and 1908

CTM made a family arrangement to acquire The Mount for just £5,000 from the ever-cautious trustees of his father, Charles Benjamin, in 1890. The family obviously thought the price for a large house, even then, derisory, and he was nearly 'choked off trading' after haggling with the trustees. He wrote in his bumptious manner on 6 January 1890, trying to play down its attractions, to his younger sister Julia's husband, Robert Turnbull.[1] He was the property man of the family as head agent for Lord Carlisle to the Naworth Castle, Morpeth and Castle Howard estates, a huge tract of land across the north of England. He lived at Four Gables, Brampton, in Cumberland, a model house of the Arts and Crafts movement (dated 1876-8), designed by William Morris architect friend, Philip Webb. It was through such channels that the Manders developed an informed interest in the new 'artistic' style (as Daisy calls it). Robert Turnbull remonstrated over the price, saying that £7,000 was the lowest price that would be acceptable to his wife. CTM took issue:

> As regards the price of the Mount, I am not satisfied with it myself and consider its value is under rather than over £5,000. I should like to know how you can value 5 acres of land and a poor house at more. (The two paddocks of back land are not worth consideration, say £150 an acre, i.e. £300 in all.)
>
> I tell you candidly that if I had been offered the Mount for £5,000 a few months ago, I should have refused the offer, as I was then thinking of going elsewhere...[2]

In the end, he managed to buy the house on favourable terms and feverishly set about altering and extending it, renting Tettenhall Manor meanwhile to supervise his building works. His cousin Theodore was building Wightwick at the same time, and they complement one another. Wightwick is set by the old canal, and The Mount is well sited on the top of the sandstone ridge. From the early pictures, it is not clear what he did to the house, an unremarkable Regency villa which had been extended by his father in the 1860s. It was transformed to give a strongly Gothic Revival, fairy-tale impression, 'to [his] own ideas',[3] he said, in 1891. The style was Norman Shaw, with an impressive two-story hall, staircase wing, stained glass, rich plasterwork and lofty ceilings, turrets and a Tower with his astronomical observatory. As at Wightwick, from the start there was an electric plant, a prototype for the municipal works he had encouraged.

He often dealt with many of the tradesmen himself, and found it difficult to brook their minor inefficiencies, writing to B. Verity & Sons, of London, for example, on 14 July 1891:

I never had the misfortune of doing business with such disappointing people as you are. You seem incapable of executing an order as given.

The copper tulips to hand today are *exactly* like the brass ones in shape, whereas I distinctly ordered them to be much shorter & your clerk made a sketch in his order book of what I wanted. The whole house is being delayed in finishing because you will not execute your orders properly. It is most annoying. Kindly ... put in hand a sample copper tulip for fear you get it wrong again.

He writes to B. Burnet & Co. in London for fittings on 7 June:

I accept your contract for the fittings, which please order at once, also all the curtains, with the exception of the Hall, corridors & stairs & the small bay in the drawing room.

He buys a grate from Bennett Brothers in Liverpool, enclosing one of his own sketches, with which so many of his letters are admirably illustrated:

July 7 [18]91

You may put the grate in hand at once as per sketch enclosed @ £27.10.0 on condition that you take the grate made by Warings into stock at cost price (should they refuse to take it back) as agreed with Mr Ould last week.

The Mount, after the alterations of 1891

The family cousinage worked closely together, sitting in the partnership room, deliberating on many of the same committees, donating to the same causes, shooting and hunting together, often attending the same schools and Cambridge colleges, and were involved together in their many charities, and house building and gardening projects. CTM is found supervising work on the Wightwick estate for his cousin, Theodore. He wrote to the Liverpool architect, Edward Ould, on 3 April 1891:

I have seen Bishop [head gardener at Wightwick] this morning & he is much pleased with the plans of cottage... His only comments were that he thought the rooms should not be less than 8 feet high & that the living room (on the east side) was possibly larger than necessary.

On 17 April he is writing to Henry Willcock, the builder, to accept his price:

I beg to accept your tender to build a cottage at Wightwick manor for £468 & shall be glad if you will at once order the bricks.

When the works to The Mount were nearing completion in October 1891, he must have thought his improvements were reflected by an increase in value, and he arranged insurance of the buildings with the Atlas Fire Co. for £10,000 and the contents for £4,000 through F.W. Smyth :

I am not at all satisfied with the Policy of the Atlas Fire Co.

...There is some error in the contents of stables. I keep no Harriers. The last sum is ridiculous... The value of the whole electric plant is at least £1,000, & the bulk of the wires, electroliers, fittings etc. are situate in the house & of necessity a part of the buildings included in the £10,000 on the House. Your Company seem to ignore the fact that there is less risk on a house lighted by electricity & should consequently be done at a cheaper rate.

I may mention that you say the house is heated by hot water apparatus. It would be well to consider that there are ordinary coal fires in all the rooms with the exception of 5 or 6 which have gas fires.

I herewith return the Policy for correction & reduction of Premium. In case your company cannot see their way to make a substantial reduction I must look elsewhere.

Later in the year he is evidently furnishing the enlarged house, writing to a Miss C. Cromonchin in London on 25 November:

Referring to our conversation about the real old Chippendale wardrobe which I told you I thought was oak but you said was mahogany. I have carefully examined it again & find it is made of walnut; well, I don't like walnut & in fact shall have no room to put it in.

Under the circumstances, I must ask you to take it back again, especially as I bought it from your description & sketch only. It is undoubtedly a very fine piece of furniture, but made of the wrong wood to suit me... I am really sorry to have to give you so much trouble.

The finished house was illustrated with engravings of its towering halls and languid bystanders in the architectural journals of the day, as a fashionable example of the high Victorian country house. His licence of 1893 shows that by then he had an establishment with eight male servants, five carriages and six dogs; the females did not need a licence. By 1899, his daughter records: 'We have about ten dogs, one cat and fourteen horses.' Pictures included a developing collection of old masters, like *St Sebastian* attributed dubiously to van Dyke and an *Old Man with a tambourine* to Gerard van Honthorst, which had no doubt been the victims of confident if unscholarly 'improvements' by his father, and an early Renaissance Florentine 'portrait of a lady' which Mary Mander bought later in Messina.

He was restless and far from satisfied, and altered The Mount again, much more radically, in 1908; again under the supervision of Ould, who had by then worked so successfully for his cousin Theodore at Wightwick. Ould seems to have become something of a family friend, his spidery signature occurring in the autograph book. But he was obviously not given a free hand when he superintended the 1891 works, as CTM had his own strong opinions on matters architectural. We know Ould wrote complaining when the new additions and alterations were proposed in 1908:

I hope you are going to let me have a chance this time of doing some thing that I need not apologise for, and if you will only leave it to Mrs Mander ... & me, I will promise that you shall have something that you will be proud of, & your son after you.

The main work was the addition of a 55-foot 'Jacobethan' library; in fact a two-story Edwardian living hall with a sprung floor for ballroom dancing, a cabin and music gallery, a secret staircase 'carried up in the fireplace recess', with ceilings again by Leonard Shuffrey, all pendant bosses and armatures on wood bracketing, armorial carvings by Edward Griffiths of Chester (who carved the drawing room chimney panelling at Wightwick), Jacobean-style panelling with pillars and balusters (proposed) in walnut by the Liverpool artist James Parkinson, and heraldic glass from the Stourbridge firm Bryans & Webb. The new room and improvements were completed at a cost of £6,251. This compared to the cost of Wightwick of £8,630 for the first phase of 1887, including renovating the Old Manor and outbuildings—always built out of income, of course.

Details of fenestration were modelled on Kirby Hall, Northamptonshire, where, Ould wrote, you will see 'all my windows and other absurdities in an old semi-ruinous building'. This had been a key building in the English Renaissance from Sir Thomas Graham 'Anglo' Jackson's use of a Jacobean hybrid of Gothic style and classical orders in the Oxford

Examination Schools (1876-82), another well-lit building. In the search for national prototypes, rooted in English domestic architecture, the Jacobean was becoming a standard solution, marking a different eclecticism in the transition from Old English to Edwardian baroque, with its imperial styles and neo-classical monumentality.

Ould refronted the garden side of the house with the hard Ruarbon brick he had used at Wightwick, altering the dormers to shallow-pitched Jacobean gables and inserting more 'correct' mullion windows and leaded lights, with string courses, coats of arms and CTM's omnipresent monogram, stone dressings and pattern-work banding. The result was to integrate the whole untidy facade, setting off the more-glass-than-wall library and transforming the effective statement of the house from Gothic Revival to a quieter, more dignified English Renaissance. When shown the plans, CTM was obviously complaining that the proposals were still too much in the neo-Tudor style of his father's time. Ould wrote back on 3 December 1907:

> There is no Tudor or Plantagenet architecture about our design. It is not Early Victorian but it is the same as your Dining Room, Porch, Staircase and Tower. I prefer that it should match these rather than the sad display of architectural fireworks on the West Front.

The library was an impressive room, like one of Ould's Cambridge college halls,[4] with its storied oriel bay and heraldry stained in glass and carved in wood, and 41 pairs of curtains. Its very name suggests the centrality of bookish self-improvement—though the bookcases were concealed behind panelling. It was admired by contemporaries. This time it was illustrated in *The Studio*, the Bible of the Arts and Crafts architect-designers, praising Ould's work for 'the refinement and distinction reminiscent of the stately halls of Tudor times, characteristic of this and similar interiors designed by Mr Ould'.[5] But for the rest it is clear that Ould was not as assured or energetic as he was in his crafted half-timber mode, and it tends to the later classical swagger of the Lutyens of Empire. It was his last work, and Ould, a frequent guest by this time at the house, died the following year, in 1909.

The Mount from the Mawson terraces, after the alterations by Edward Ould of 1908, including the addition of the Library (left)

There is evidence that Thomas H. Mawson[6] advised on works to the gardens, designing arched shelters and terraces with sandstone balustrades; steps led down to a pond with an island at the bottom of the hill, where skating was a popular pastime in the winter. A coracle and Canadian canoe were kept. A favourite ploy of his meaner grandchildren later was to row unsuspecting guests out to the island, and leave them stranded.

The Mount when completed is remembered as light, lavish and convenient, the interiors furnished and decorated in the 'Old English' revival style—like Wightwick. The two houses used the same architect and builders,[7] and many of the same craftsmen, and both had the Mawson terraces. But there are striking contrasts between Wightwick's best room, the Great Parlour of 1893 in eclectic Cheshire vernacular, with its timbering, colour highlights and Kempe frieze to Ovidian themes, and The Mount's Library of 1908 in purer English Renaissance, more restrained, with baroque Mannerist conflations.

The Mount was a grander house of a bluffer, military, hunting Tory, a clubbable patriarch and paterfamilias, extrovert, stylish and competent, where Wightwick, was Whig-Liberal, brooding, refined, intellectual, more intricately wrought and ultimately astringent.[8] The Mount was High Anglican, establishment, where Wightwick was nonconformist; The Mount was built for comfort and entertaining on the grand scale, reputed for its French food and wine, where Wightwick was austere and all but teetotal—The Mount had a tradition of 'punishing the port', where at

Wightwick Rosalie Mander would dispense Cornish mead, or Sunday morning sherry in jars saved from potted shrimps, as Ricketts himself might have done.

At Owlpen, the heights of seventeenth-century children are inscribed in graffiti on door jambs and fireplaces. An Edwardian tradition at The Mount was for the gentlemen to record the variations in their weights as meticulously as their billiards' scores, on the cloakroom Avery scales. Before and after dinner or before and after a 'Friday to Monday' house party, they noted the percentage of total weight gained, sometimes with curious results. Arthur notes that he put on more than average (at 2.87 lbs. per day) one Sunday in 1907: 'On Sunday, eat invariably less, so must have drunk more!' The cloakroom had patent 'voider' basins, without plugholes, which pivoted on gimbals to spill the dirty water down the drains.

The Mount library is often described as one of the finest Edwardian rooms in the Midlands. With its sprung floor in Canadian maple, it was a magnificent setting for hunt balls, fancy dress balls, *bals poudrés,* still (just) remembered between the wars.

On 19 September 1909, there was an altercation when Mr Lockley intruded, a trespasser who came with his family to spy on the proceedings of a society ball. Charles Tertius wrote him a stern letter. We hear the uncompromising voice of an Edwardian patriarch, not to be trifled with:

> I understand you & your children, together with Mrs King, were trespassing in my garden on the night of the 10th instant, when I had a Ball at my house, & in spite of being ordered off by my coachman, continued to try & look in through the windows of my Library, moving some vases to stand on in order to do so.
>
> One of the vases was broken, & unless you do not pay, say, £2, in compensation of the value, I will summon the lot of you for trespass.

He follows it up on 20th September:

> You admit your gross piece of impudence & you can arrange with "some more people" to compensate me for the damage done, otherwise you can "face it out" in the Police Court.

In CTM's case, there are records of his being prosecuted as a magistrate for allowing two of his dogs to contravene a muzzling order. The case provoked a letter to the newspaper from a Fred Nutt of Heath Town:[9]

> I noticed that a Mr C.T. Mander of Tettenhall Wood was fined the ridiculous sum of 1s. and costs for allowing two dogs to go about without a muzzle. This is in the face of so many cases where a fine of 5s. had been imposed for allowing only one dog to go loose.
>
> Personally I am very much against the muzzling order. So long as it is in force, however, it should press as hard on the rich as on the poor.

Visit of Duke and Duchess of York, c. 1906

Of the ten dogs Daisy records at The Mount in 1893, a number would have been foxhound puppies. In April 1903, CTM won the three first prizes for puppy walkers in the dog, bitch and couple classes with a dog called Gulliver, and a bitch, Guilty. Thanking for the prize for his hat trick, the papers reported:

> remembered that he once walked a puppy named Cardinal in the time of the muzzling order, and the puppy went about with a muzzle on. One day Mr Kettle obliged him by riding one of his horses, and the puppy followed Mr Kettle to the meet. The puppy joined the hounds with a muzzle on—[laughter]—and was the third to come out of one of Lord Dartmouth's coverts in a run the hounds had, but when the puppy was caught, he became violently sick.

Houses like The Mount had public functions, and CTM entertained lavishly in the area, officially as well as privately. His *Times* obituary records: 'It often fell to him to entertain political speakers at his residence'. Many national figures visited. Lloyd George was his guest as prime minister within a fortnight of the Armistice, when he announced the 'coupon election' campaign on 24 November 1918.

Now honours 'rained gold boxes' on Lloyd George—as they had on Pitt—and he was in Wolverhampton ostensibly to receive the Freedom of the borough. He seized the occasion to throw down the gauntlet with his postwar manifesto, seeking a mandate to negotiate the Peace and for a programme of reconstruction—although his demagogic conduct of the election campaign did his reputation permanent harm. The Wolverhampton speech of that day turned out to be the most quoted of his career: 'What is our task? To make Britain a fit country for heroes to live in!'

Daisy, the daughter of the house, catches the spirit of the occasion in a letter to her brother, Charles Arthur, who was still on service with the Yeomanry in Palestine, waiting for a boat back from Haifa:

Dearest A.,
Meant to write you from London, but hadn't time. We—Madré, Louise [Hellier[10]] and I—went up to London by the one o'clock train on the Wednesday Nov: 20th and from Oxford on it was most fearfully foggy, and by the time we did get to London, an old fashioned fog was on, yellow, but not quite so bad as when you got home two years ago. L. had never seen a yellow one before, and thought it a novel experience. Worst of it was taxis vanished, and we actually had to take bus, so the time lost was appalling. Mollie Hay née Lysaght lunched with us and her vivacious daughter about 18?—such a nice girl full of life and great chatterbox.[11] She is very keen on Art and wants to have a studio at Chelsea, but her mother says she must first have a season in India, where she hasn't been since she was a little girl.

Then C.T.M. got word the Prime Minister, Mrs Lloyd George, Captain Guest,[12] Coalition Whip, two secretaries, valet, two detectives, were turning up on the Friday, so L. of course decided to stay over the week-end.

We took first train Friday a.m. and arrived about two hours or so before they all did, so had time to do flowers, change books in their rooms and rush around! M. was quite excited; she said it really was rather thrilling to hear the crowd cheering outside before he arrived at the door. C.T.M. came up with them, secretaries followed, all having been met at the station by the Mayor and Town Clerk, etc. Mr Bantock lent us his closed car, had three Sunbeam men working on it for him, rather disappointing for Storrar [the chauffeur], but everyone got tipped £1, Mrs Allum included, so that the P.M. must be popular when he stays about. But the secretary dished it out.

We hadn't time to get anybody extra in for dinner, so L. sat on his other side, a thing she could never have done in London had she dined out to meet him at any time. She was afraid Lady Dartmouth might have come! However I had him next day at breakfast, which fewer still can say they have done! And he took quantities of sugar in his coffee, and had 1a cups!

Louise made a great hit with him and he asked her questions nearly all evening. He is really awfully nice to meet, one quite forgot he was P.M., he had such a sense of humour and was so jolly and amusing.

Capt. Guest seemed *very* preoccupied and self important, but I suppose his job is wearing, as he must know everything that the P.M. may wish to find out about. Louise was awfully sick at Capt. G.'s democratic views, such rot a man *talking* so big with a millionaire for a father-in-law, a house in Park Lane, etc.[13] We both felt rather antagonistic to him, although he really made himself very pleasant.

It really was too amusing to think of such a party in this house [which was of course Conservative], and the P.M. thoroughly appreciated the fact and rotted C.T.M., and they got on awfully well together!! C.T.M. simply *would* say his say and the P.M. always listened to him and told others to, in fact we had a very jolly evening all snugly by the Library fire, as we had it specially heated for him, and it really seemed quite pre-war. The dinner too was perfect: so hot, thick soup, fried sole, turkey, cream mould (you know the kind of thing) and excellent bonnes bouches of cheese. But what the P.M. really enjoyed were muscats.

He signed three books for me, and wrote his signature for Mrs E.B.'s autograph collection. There were 25 at lunch next day at the Town Hall, L. and I being there, but Miss Bird pushed in *uninvited*, and Sir Horatio[14] refused to squeeze himself in, although we begged him to—far too old fashioned and polite to do such a thing, we were annoyed. I was *not* thrilled by the great speech at the [Grand Theatre], though expected to be. General Hickman[15] got the applause with his Alien policy, a dash of clapping, and he spoke very well and to the point, and his voice sounded delightful, place jammed with people. L. and I sat a little to the left, front row, so saw everyone perfectly far better that having a back seat on the platform. G.P.M. hadn't a ticket, so got in with Mr Davies, the secretary, as of course he had to be there, and sat just behind P.M., as so did the valet!!

Then after lunch the Freedom was given and I never heard a more appalling voice than the poor Mayor had, it simply could *not* have been worse, and he looked such a squirt too, poor man, almost his first appearance and such a big occasion for him, it was hard lines. The P.M. spoke quite differently from the morning and I am sure people enjoyed it.

Then we all went off to tea in the Mayor's parlour whilst the P.M. rested (incidentally, had a sketch made by Phoenix) and we messed about till five, and then accompanied them off to Lower Level for 5.22 back to town (though personally I think they would have stayed the two nights had C.T.M. not pointed out Sunday trains were not so good as the others, stupid of him). Such a lovely saloon, a drawing room in pale grey, detective's room, kitchen and dining room, just the five of them.

Left to Right: Margaret and David Lloyd George, CTM, Mary Mander at The Mount on the occasion of calling the 'coupon' election, 1918

The group taken by Bennett Clark is excellent—even Gerald came over for it with his kids. It is so nice of M[adre]. I am having her head taken out and enlarged and, of course, heaps of copies will be ordered. In fact, the whole visit was a great success.

I shall be glad when Christmas is over. I seem to have such a lot to do, have hardly *read* a thing, and feel I would do anything to be abroad somewhere and *laze*.

The sequel at The Mount, too, was happier. Theodore and Flora of Wightwick both died aged 47, and the house was shuttered and for long periods little used, or loved. It was advertised for sale in 1920 as a genuine old Tudor house, with no takers. Eventually, Geoffrey Mander set up house, as a political fortress, or a retreat for weekends away from his London parliamentary interests, although he was chairman of the family business for 33 years.

At The Mount CTM was always a county or Midlands figure, popular, hale and active, who lived on to 1929. Then his widow, Mary, presided with a retinue of footmen in slowly-fading Victorian splendour, reduced in the lean war years to a cockney cook and butler, a chauffeur, and daily help. 'Rochester used to drive very badly in a temper, if he had been done out of a cooked lunch and only had a sandwich... But at the end he and his wife were the last people to stay and look after my grandmother. No domestic chore was too belittling for them', recalls Gerald's daughter, Hilary. Mary survived into her dotage, dying aged 92 in 1951, having outlived her sister, Flora, of Wightwick by nearly half a century.

There were 24 comfortable bedrooms for the Friday-to-Monday house parties of the fin-de-siècle era, which have made it adapt well as a hotel. William Peveril Turnbull, Julia Mander's brother-in-law and a fellow of Trinity, Cambridge, seems to have stayed at The Mount on several occasions, before it was extended, in the 1880s. He records in November 1881: 'I was at the Mount lately. Never was such a house for rotation of bedrooms; I daresay I have had nine.'

Mary Mander was described by Edward Ould, a little obsequiously perhaps, as having 'more taste than any *lady* I have met'. Her collections were voraciously catholic, if indiscriminate. The 'Old English' aestheticism of the 'nineties fell victim to successive reorderings, and it became increasingly over furnished. The rooms were more cluttered and fussy than Wightwick—at least the Wightwick of today, which has been simplified since Victorian times along the lines of a purer Morris-inspired medievalism. Collections consisting of innumerable *objets*—Chinese and Delft blue-and-white porcelain, maiolica and faience, textiles, fans and dolls, snuff and tobacco boxes and curios—covered every surface, to be carefully dusted by a retinue of parlour maids. There was a special emphasis on objects of Midland manufacture: enamels from Battersea and Bilston, Staffordshire china ornaments, the polished steel jewellery, misers' purses and 'toys' of Wolverhampton, japanned ware made by the old family firm, a Stuart horn book found 'tucked away in the wall of an old house in John Street which was being pulled down' in 1862—all lent about periodically to exhibitions.[16]

Drawers were stuffed till they were wedged tight shut with stuff; textiles, examples of needlework, lace, beadwork, tatting. Chairs were upholstered and tapestries worked at leisure by the hands of Mary and Daisy Mander. The Library windows had antique Indian cretonne curtains, but there was a good deal of carpets and curtains supplied by William Morris & Co., mainly in less grand upstairs bedrooms, as well as Morris furniture and upholstered chairs, mixed with the antique furniture and rugs. As at Wightwick, there was early Continental furniture and more exotic acquisitions: Mary Mander's annotated inventories list the prices paid to dealers for seemingly untransportable items culled on travels energetically pursued in Taormina, Granada, Russia, Cairo, Tunis, Khartoum, Fez, Cuba and Brazil, many long before the first world war.

Both Wightwick and The Mount were technically advanced and comfortable by the standards of the day, with central heating, electric light, above all ingenious planning; the admirable domesticity of the Arts and Crafts style is often emphasised. The Victorian dream-houses—even Wightwick—with their picturesque revival of details and precious, self-conscious historicism, tend towards a ponderous churchy gloom, even if such was 'not sadness', but what Morris called (writing of Kelmscott) a 'melancholy born of beauty'.

Mary Mander, collector, in the Library of The Mount, c. 1935

The next generation were less positive. Monica Mander always hated The Mount, making it a condition of her marriage to its heir that she would never have to live there. Rosalie Mander admitted she never liked Wightwick, either. She later described how, finding Wightwick 'a monument to Victorian standards of practical inconvenience', they looked for a smaller house in the countryside.

Mount house party, 1908

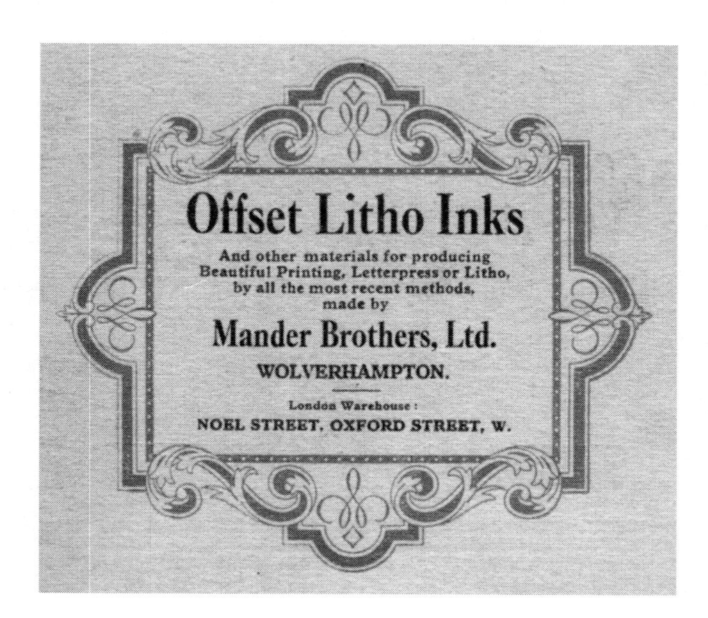

[1] Robert Edward Turnbull married Annie Julia in 1879, when he took his first farm at East Park, Burton Constable; in 1892 he became a partner in the firm of Alfred Mansell & Co., in Shrewsbury. His father, also Robert (1812-91), of Low Hall, Hackness, was agent for nearly 57 years to Harcourt, first lord Derwent, for the Hackness estate; he was author of an *Index of British Plants.*
[2] According to Daisy Mander and then Amy Stokes, he was treating to buy the Rudge estate near Pattingham, where he took the shooting for many years from the Wight-Boycotts.
[3] Much information is derived from CTM's letter books in the Owlpen archives.
[4] Ould worked at Selwyn (1908) and Trinity Hall, Cambridge (Gothic roof to 'restored' and extended Hall, master's lodge with simple Jacobean facades). George Haswell Grayson (b. 1871—d. 1951), like the Manders, was Cambridge educated, and joined the partnership in 1896, completing the Thornton Building at Trinity Hall after Ould's death. (See C. Crawley and G. Storey, *Trinity Hall*, Cambridge, 1992, pp. 240-1.) Ould's other work on this scale was for James Darcy Lever at Thornton House (1895).
[5] *The Studio,* 1909, vol. 2, 140.
[6] Thomas Mawson, garden designer and architect of London and Lancaster, worked in Wolverhampton, and also with Ould for Lord Leverhulme and at Wightwick Manor for the Mander family (see below); author of *The Art and Craft of Garden Making.*
[7] Henry Willcock & Co. of Wolverhampton. But Lovatt is mentioned as the contractor of Wightwick in *The Builder* account, 24 May 1889, p. 720. It mentions an old farmhouse on the estate being restored for a gardener's house, which provided 'richly-moulded and carved oak framing ... refixed in the hall and boudoir'.
[8] Ex inf. Peter Nevile (b. 1912), grandchild of Theodore Mander and one of the last to remember both as functioning houses in the aftermath of the first world war.
[9] *Express & Star,* January 1899; reprinted 8 January 1999, 'Write back in time'.
[10] A life-long American friend of Daisy's. Count Serra told CTM in 1917 that Louise's father had made £62,000 a year from his Kentucky coal mine.
[11] Mary Louisa, dau. of William Lysaght of Beechmount, co. Cork, m. 1909 Lt-Col. Arthur Sydney Hay, DSO (b. Dharwar, India, 1879); Indian Army. She d. 1925.
[12] Frederick ('Freddie') Guest (b. 1875—d. 1937), third son of the first baron Wimborne, was MP for East Dorset (and later for Stroud, Glos), chief whip of the Liberal members of the coalition government and sometime Secretary of State for Air and patronage secretary. He was private secretary to (and a cousin of) Churchill. The Guests, originally ironmasters from Shropshire, by this time had their main business in Glamorgan.
[13] He m. 1905, Amy, dau. of Henry Phipps, of 5th Avenue; Philadelphia iron and steel manufacturer associated with the Carnegies, who was a dir. of Mellon National Bank and founder of the Phipps Institute at the University of Pennsylvania.
[14] Sir Horatio Brevitt (b. 1847), was solicitor, Town Clerk and Clerk of the Peace for the borough of Wolverhampton, 1882-1919, and a JP 1919. He resided at The Leasowes, Tettenhall, and was an expert on heraldry.
[15] Brig-Gen. Thomas Edgcumbe Hickman, CB, DSO, DL (b. 1859—d. 1930), 2nd son of Sir Alfred Hickman, was MP for Wolverhampton South and for Bilston (1918-22), and a veteran of the Egyptian and Sudanese campaigns, the Boer War and World War I.
[16] Much of this remains at Owlpen, or local museums. The horn book is illustrated in Gerald Mander, *History of Wolverhampton School,* f.p. 264.

11

SQUIRE AND COLONEL

CTM was a confident industrialist dedicated to every aspect of municipal life, without aspirations as a serious rural landowner. In a time of declining agricultural rents, his capital was always better employed in his business. But his interests, demeanour and manner of living were those of a country squire, knowledgeable and enthusiastic about country affairs and field sports, the yeomanry, the Bench, dogs and horses.

He still owned, malgré lui, some 25 houses and cottages, and farm land totalling at this time 'about 500 acres', including the Dippons and Red House farms, adjoining The Mount.[1] He also owned investment property in Canada, in British Columbia (640 acres at Yale[2]) and in Nova Scotia, including gypsum and plaster of Paris properties at Brierley Brook in Antigonish and building land in Halifax. Then there was property (for the firm's depot) at Neal Street in London and shops at Queen's Arcade in Wolverhampton. A charitable venture was the purchase in 1918 of the timbered fifteenth-century Guild House at Aston Cantlow, Warwickshire, the village where the family had lived in the seventeenth century, which he put it into repair for the use of the village.[3]

Letters to tenants and land agents show his close interest in the detail of affairs. He writes to Robert Arthur at the Theatre Royal in October 1891:

I was looking over Mount Cottage this afternoon & found a considerable amount of dilapidation even since you ceased to live there.

If no fires are kept in the house the coming winter, you will soon run up a bill for repairs. I have no wish to be too exacting, but I must insist on you acting up to the spirit of your lease... I give you fair warning that I shall charge you with whatever expense I may be put to.

He was a military man. While at Cambridge he had served in the Military Volunteers. He joined 'D' Squadron of the Himley Troop of the Staffordshire Yeomanry—'than which', he would proudly declare, 'there is no smarter in the service'—and in due course became Colonel of the Regiment. He was interested in rifle shooting, winning the regimental cup. Letters reveal him continuing to take a keen interest in the Yeomanry shooting team, including technical matters of marksmanship, sighting the rifles and competition rules. He arranged the subalterns' escorts for royal visits, like that of Princess Louise to the Dartmouths at Patsull in October 1891, and for the Duke and Duchess of York during Theodore's mayoralty in 1900. He loved his visits to Yeomanry camps, parading his motor cars, saying that 'many of the happiest weeks of my life have been spent in camp'. The poetaster 'Pen' records in 'Our Gallant Yeomen' the impression of his troop setting off to Camp from the Victoria Hotel in May 1905:

And no mistake they looked a smart and dapper little crew,
Major Mander and his troopers, and his Sergeant-Major too,
The Major looked as if he'd do whatever man would dare,
And his Sergeant-Major on his own would charge a blooming square.

Colonel Mander: CTM wears the officers' pattern khaki serge frock, with a khaki cover to the top of his blue and scarlet 'dress' forage cap

Boer War

He was very proud to belong to the Queen's Own Royal Yeomanry, 'as it was the only one in the world'. His swagger portraits by John Collier show him in his hussar's dolman, with sabretache and clutching his busby. In 1899 he wrote to Colonel Lord Chesham to present the regiment with Maxim guns for use in the Boer War, explaining that he was unable to serve because of his public duties.

> I have the honour to inform you that, as I am not volunteering to serve with your force at the moment, I am prepared to present to The Imperial Yeomanry a fully equipped Maxim gun.
>
> I understand that a galloping Maxim is not considered suitable to the country and that guns carried on mule back are now recommended.
>
> I have only one request to make, if I may be allowed to do so; that, if at the end of the Campaign you bring the gun home again, you may be pleased to recommend to the authorities to hand it to my Regiment as an interesting momento of the active service of some of its members.

He was so overjoyed at hearing the news of the Relief of Mafeking that he gave sovereigns to those who brought it him. The family did have connections with South Africa and its bitter imperial conflict. Charles Tertius's sister, Janetta, was a professional artist in oils and watercolours, several of whose landscapes are in public collections in South Africa. She married Henry Sparke Stabb, who died suddenly during the Zulu wars at Pietermaritzburg, Natal. At the time of his death on 22 October 1888, he was Brigadier-General commanding H.M. Troops in Natal and Zululand, Deputy Governor of Natal and Commissioner of Justice for Zululand.[4] His death, according to Miss Colenso,[5] 'was a great misfortune to that country and the British Empire'.

Charles Tertius's youngest brother, Jack,[6] was a young captain in the Boer War, gazetted like his brother-in-law in the Duke of Cornwall's Light Infantry. Later he became Chief Constable of Cambridgeshire and the Isle of Ely, and finally (1915) of Norfolk. He married Elinor Lloyd Philipps of Dale Castle, Pembrokeshire (and Mabys, Cardigan). Their elder daughter, Cecily, was to marry in turn Francis Phillips (different spelling), the younger son of the 'Randlord', Sir Lionel Phillips,[7] the partner of Cecil Rhodes, and his wife Florence. Cecily Phillips was known in the family for her pearls rather than her diamonds. Members of the family recollect being introduced to her two eligible, blushing daughters in London in the Thirties, with a hint of match making.

Jack Mander (1869-1927), Chief Constable of Norfolk

'Captain' Jack was mentioned in dispatches in the Boer War. A letter from hospital dated 1 March 1900 gives his stirring account of difficulties in the field in the period of British reversals after Spion Kop, just as the fortunes of war were about to turn with the arrival of reinforcements:

No. 1 Hospital
Wynberg [near Cape Town]

My dear Charlie,
Very many thanks for your nice long letter which I have just this morning received. As you have seen in the papers ere now, I got punctured at Paardesburg and ought to have been killed, but thank God I was not. Our Colonel got the order to turn them out of the river bed with the bayonet, which meant charging over 600 yards of absolutely flat open ground against any number (up to

thousands) of the enemy behind bushes on the river bank. It was absolutely insane and I objected as much as I could to the C.O., as I said it was impossible to get there in one rush, the men could not last so far. But the C.O. would not have it. We were formed up, my company in front, and Grants Rhodes and Harvey's behind with 100 yards interval, and three paces between men.

When we got up to the firing line of Canadians, etc., we told them our orders, we all fixed bayonets, the Col. gave the order, and off we started, cheering. We had not gone 50 yards when the air turned blue with bullets, but luckily very high. I got one through my helmet just grazing my head. After we had got about 400 yards, there were very few of us left. Finally, when about 120 yards from the bushes, I suddenly saw the C.O. drop and about ten men round me all at once, and found no one else coming, so threw myself down, luckily in a slight hollow. I at once unfixed bayonets and set to work, lying perfectly still and flat, to scrape up earth in front of my head. In five minutes I had about ten inches of cover and a small hole in which I buried my head and lay still and prayed. There I lay for an hour, then I got an awful blow on the shoulder and back, but managed not to move, so I think they thought I was dead. Bullets flew all round, hitting the ground almost touching me, but no more hit me and finally in two more hours dark came, when I crawled back on my stomach 200 yards and then on my knees and finally got out to the firing line.

The bullet went through the back of my shoulder and came out by my waist without doing much harm, thank goodness, but I lost a lot of blood. It was a horrible experience for one's first show. About 20 men lay round me at first, most of them writhing with pain, but the Boers went on firing at them till they killed them all off round me. The C.O. was killed about ten yards ahead of me. Thank goodness most of my company were in a small hollow which saved them, but one section of 25 men who started had nine killed and ten wounded. Altogether my company lost about twelve killed and twenty wounded out of 100 who went in. Poor Wardlaw who married Miss Seckham and Newbury, a captain, were also killed in other parts of the fight.

My poor servant, Viney, a most excellent fellow, was killed. I ordered him not to come, but to have some food for us when we got back, as he was my company mess cook. But he begged to be allowed to go in to this our first fight. He was shot in three places and was not brought in till the next day, when he died of exhaustion and shock. Fife, my sub, was also wounded. You might show this account to Neville, as it will interest him. To get back to Hospital I had to wade a rapid river up to my waist in the pitch dark, but I got two men in my regiment to help me. That's what made it impossible to get the wounded in unless they could walk till next day. The result of the chill of the river was to bring on dysentery again, but I think I have thrown that off now. We had to travel about 45 miles in ox carts with no springs which took three whole nights of awful jolting to get to the Modder river where we joined the ambulance train and got into comfort. It was very annoying to see the others eating good food and having a good drink and I was still at milk only.

I was very interested in your yeomanry work. I have argued for two years now that our sights wanted altering, as I always had to allow as you say from two to three feet at 500 yards and about six inches at 200 yards, also the sighting is always undersighted. In my company I always started by telling the men this and allowing for it. Now a fuss has been made about it the government have had to do something.

From what I can hear, those Colt guns are excellent and I hope yours will be a success. We want mounted men out there, the more the better. The distances are too great for us poor feet fellows. We fairly did leg it. I did the following marches and you must understand that ten miles on the veldt equals at least fifteen at home, and if by day, more: We first did 16 to concentrate from Wittefonts to Mapleleaf camp. Then only four to Graaspan. Then the whole Ninth Division started. We did 11 or 12 to Ram dam starting at 4 a.m. arriving at one o'clock in sweltering heat. Started 5 a.m. twelve miles to Vaterfall drift twelve miles around 12.30, myself, rest of battalion at 2 o'clock. Next day only eight and half miles to Wegdiai drift where we watched the others div shelling Jacobsdal. Next day started under arms 3.30… Left Saturday night 4.30 and we just cooking breakfasts when battle started, so had to pack up and men got nothing and battle went on all day. So we were fairly pushed. Especially as the men lay all night just 500 yards form the enemy and got nothing to eat till next day 48 hours without food. The food was with the transport but it was impossible to get it out to the regiment, which was split up all over the place. Little do the volunteers know what they are volunteering for. It is no Omdurman medals this time.

It is very good you sending me that serge coat … as of course the drill gets so cold when wet at night.

Bertie Hawker I just hear wrote to mother to ask if I would like a horse because if so he would send me a good charger from Australia. Mother wrote to say she did not know but thought a horse would be useful. So he has wired for one to be sent me. It is awfully good of him, but I don't know how I am to get it up to the front… Then when there it is most difficult to feed them in some places. On Pilcher's column I rode a pony for some time. I really don't know what to do about the horse unless I lend it to Rhodie, who by the way I hear has been recommended for the V.C. by his Colonel for rescuing two men at Rensturg…

There is an officer in the Welch in my ward who had a bullet through his left temple, behind the eye and out through the lobe of his right ear. He was only hit the same time as me and beyond not being able to open his mouth to eat he is quite well. He went off into Cape Town yesterday without leave to do some shopping. Sir W. McCormac and a lot of 'bugs' came to examine him as a curio and he could not be found.

I hope now we have got old Croje and his 4,000 and quite another 2,000 of them killed, we will begin to break up the Free State, and after that the bully Boers. But they may settle to fight a guerrilla warfare in which case it may still last months. I do hope we won't be left as part of the army of occupation…

I never got a shot at a Boer the other day. If I had moved to shoot, I should have had 100 rifles at me at once, so I lay doggo, though I saw one Boer in a trip which was a temptation when I first lay down. I dug a shelter instead. If I had fired, I should not have been here.

News has just come here that Buller has got into Ladysmith which I hope is true. I hope the government won't let these Exeter Hull people press for easy terms. People don't realize in England what a deep plot has been going on between Reitz, Steyn, Kruger, Molteno, Hotmeyer, Sauer & co. The ordinary Boer thinks he is fighting for independence, but the schemers have been driving for 15 years at having a S.A. Republic with the Dutch at the top and no English rule at all, and what is more, if the war had not come for a year or two, they would have either done it, or else we would have begun our fighting at Cape Town and Port Elizabeth and Durban. In fact this time if they had not tried to capture Rhodes in Kimberley but had marched down on Orange River and De Aar, they could have easily captured all our stores at De Aar, and we should have had a fight in the Karroo mountains, which would have been most difficult, in fact like relieving Ladysmith. The whole of that Hollander, Poond, crew would have been plotting for the overthrow of English rule and they devilish nearly succeeded.

I had a long talk in Cape Town with 'Baby' Moltero, a noted rebel. I did not know till after who he was, but we found we had been at Cambridge together, so palled up. But I became appalled at his rebellious views and finally angry, so left him lest I should be rude. I afterwards heard what he was. If I had known before I would have told him a thing or two...

Yours ever, Jack

CTM, as a man of his class and age, in some matters is revealed less than perspicacious. As the first world war broke out, in August 1914, he wrote to his younger brother, Neville:

This war is a terrible matter, but it is a fight to a finish & the German Empire must be destroyed. There will be an awful loss of life on both sides, but it cannot last more than a month or two. Russia ought to be in Berlin in less than that, & there should be a revolution in Germany for lack of food which the Government cannot get or pay gold for even if it did get in.

He spent the war going back and forth to London to advise the Government on munitions. Perhaps there was trade for Mander Brothers in this, but they were short handed when 100 men had been called up by early 1915. There was hope that Mander Smyth could work between military duties, while he was adjutant in Wolverhampton.

The war caused domestic difficulties, too, as it raged far beyond his forecast. Apart from the usual servant problems, his eldest son Arthur had enlisted, and was on active service in Egypt and Palestine for years at a stretch, causing his mother worry at home: 'It is only a matter of time before he gets hit'. He left behind his young wife, Monica ('Barbadoo' in the family), and their daughter, Marietta. Their first house at Kingslow was in due course closed up, and he writes to his daughter-in-law on 19 January 1916:

My dear Barbadoo,
Referring to your letter to your Aunt Charlie & Daisy & my letter to Marietta, I am certain that your intention to take. Lodgings for her in London is most unwise.

I naturally take no exception to both of you staying as long as you like at Stake Farm [her family home at Godden Green, Kent], neither would Arthur, although I promised him before he went abroad that I would make a Home for you both at

The Mount, & take the greatest care of you until the end of the War, ie until he returned from active service & reopened Kingslow. Neither could he or I object Marietta living at Egerton Terrace, if Mrs Neame [mother to Monica Mander] put some rooms there at your entire disposal, but the very idea of your putting Marietta in lodgings near Egerton Terrace, however good, (& it is a question whether you could get any good enough) is utterly unthinkable both to your Aunt Charlie & myself, & I am sure it would cause much distress & worry to Arthur, in spite of any letters he may write you, putting a brave face on it. In May or June it might be an entirely different matter.

You are causing your Aunt Charlie great distress, & she worries about Marietta all day long & often falls into tears, both day & night, which worries me very much. I beg of you to again think this matter over & not run counter to Arthur's expressed wishes to me.

Your ever loving "Uncle Charlie"

Give Marietta a kiss from me.

In the event, she and Marietta never returned to Kingslow, but went up to stay at Neasham, near Darlington, with her sister Gwen Wrightson—who also had a little boy, John—or with the Neames at Stake Farm.

CTM was 'an outdoors' man', a dedicated field sportsman, 'both an excellent rider to hounds and a fine shot'. He got 'decidedly bored in London', Daisy felt. A contemporary biographer states his version of muscular Christianity:

He considers that were it not for the sports of the field, effeminacy and deterioration would ensue, and earnestly hopes that the day may be distant when no longer 'the horn of the hunter is heard on the hill'... for it will mean that sloth has taken the place of energy.

He maintained his shoots at The Mount and Rudge in Staffordshire and Shropshire, and at Tyndwfr, near Llangollen in mid Wales, with characteristic efficiency revealed in his letters to gamekeepers, tenants and landowners. His gamebooks show him shooting three or four times a week in the season, making one wonder how he ever did any 'work', with hunting as well; observing in detail the placing of guns, planting of cover, new techniques of 'cross driving' his moors and rearing 'Hungarians', and the presentation of game to the guns. He was not interested in the massive bags slaughtered by the Edwardian big shots. Often he shoots a half day, or with just four guns, all members of the family, getting a mixed bag of partridge and pheasant, rabbits, hares, woodcock and various. Partridge were plentiful. In September 1911 he writes:

I went out shooting with Neville at Gatacre yesterday and what do you think we got driving seven guns? We got 112½ brace of Partridges and he got 91 brace on another beat on Wednesday, a long way a record for Gatacre. Two or three of the guns said they had never had such a day before, no more had I at Partridge.

He always enjoys his shoot at Llangollen, writing in October 1904:

We had a ripping time at Tyndwfr last week ... lovely Indian summer weather. But I found all the soldier men equally chuckleheaded and in spite of having taken the trouble to have a map for each gun, they were generally in their wrong places. It was early days for pheasant shooting as the leaves were still on the trees and the fern was high, so that the pheasants did not show as well as I expected. However we got 148 one day and 149 the next, i.e. about 300 in the two days, but at least 1500 cartridges were fired off and everybody enjoyed themselves muchly. Arthur shot 83 cartridges and killed 39 pheasants, which was much above the average.

There was no Lodge, and the domestic arrangements were not ideal:

We went down to Llangollen to shoot and had a very cheery party at the Royal Hotel, where they did us very well indeed. It was mighty cold there however. There was a good fire in it when we went to bed, but in the morning you could see your breath and you may be sure I did not stay messing about in my tub long. Sam Loveridge was to have come but at the last moment ran in, and stayed at Davies Court as old Mrs Loveridge was dying any moment; she was unconscious for 2 or 3 weeks and had lived on nothing but morphia.

CTM, an informal portrait, relaxing on the shooting field

On 27 August 1900, his cousin Theodore was taken ill while fishing, after a day's grouse shooting with him at Llangollen, an illness from which 'he never rallied'. Short term, this seems to have disturbed CTM's shooting arrangements, for he notes on 29 August: 'not enough guns, birds went over empty butts'.

In October 1904, Daisy remarks: 'Fancy Uncle Neville peppering three people. I wonder what CTM's remarks were?' A year later, a gamebook note (10 November 1905) tersely records an accident which understandably shocked the family: 'Grainger [a head keeper] shot his left foot off a week ago and died in Hospital yesterday.' Arthur writes from Cambridge: 'It is indeed a judgment on his getting drunk, poor man; I can't imagine how it happened unless he was half tight at the time'. On 12 December he still wants to know more:

You never told me how Grainger shot his foot off. It's like Mac's story of the American on board ship who was dying to know why the man's arm was gone, and was told, on condition that he ask no more leading questions, that it was 'bit off'. Well, all I know is that Grainger's foot was shot off!

CTM writes disapprovingly to a land agent through whom he rented some adjoining coverts on 27 January 1908:

I went through "Calf Heath" yesterday to shoot cocks, but it was an absolute farce, it would not hold pheasants at all, as there was no undergrowth anywhere.

The least thing you can do is to plant suitable undergrowth *at once* for some distance at the end of each beat ... otherwise it is only fair to make a substantial reduction in the rent.

I am putting down 1,000 brace of Hungarians this winter & going to buy 1,000 pheasant eggs, but it is ridiculous to rear a lot of pheasants if you cannot turn any down in Calf Heath.

As ever, the sports of hunting and shooting could cause conflict, and on the same day he writes to his friend, Colonel Goulburn, D.S.O., of Somerford Hall,[8] after hounds had ruined one of his best drives:

I did not care to say anything when you came through Somerford Big Wood, as I was shooting yesterday; but it was most annoying to my guests, one of whom, Major Milbourne, came down specially from Aldershot.

It is rather absurd to think, that it was only the 3rd time I have shot the Big Wood this season & you have, say, 120 days to choose from, & that hounds should run through at the same time my beaters were beating the coverts.

The usual thing would have been to whip off hounds.

It was rather rough too on Morrison, who naturally wishes to show birds, that the best beat in the coverts should have been spoilt the first time (when you were there) by 3 or 4 foxes, & that the same beat should be absolutely ruined the third time by hounds running through & driving all the birds out, & not only so, but

they ran through the other beats which we were going to shoot subsequently, some of which we abandoned altogether.
Two stray hounds were left behind hunting in the coverts all afternoon.

Colonel Goulburn wrote back by return

I regret extremely that the hounds ran into Somerford on Saturday. Had *anyone* taken the trouble to let me know you were shooting I should of course have given orders to stop hounds. Morrison was told (I understand) to stop Calf Heath as the original intention was to go to Hilton and back on Calf Heath, so he has no excuse for not sending me word that you were shooting.
I got a wire on Friday evening from Mr Verum to say he would not be back from Bournemouth so we had to alter the draw to Chillington way. If Morrison had standing orders to always send word up here when you are shooting humanly speaking this would never occur but you know as well as I do that sometimes hounds get away and can not be stopped but on a bad scenting day like last Saturday it would have been easy.

The shooting went on regularly through the first world war, sometimes to the consternation of his family. Daisy complains of it in 1917: 'CTM is keeping Wrottesley on again. Feel so mad about it, with no one to ask to shoot anyway; throwing away of £1,500. He might have put it into War Loan, or bought bandage materials. Too sickening.' But one day in October that year he and Sir Horace Avory shot and walked near Trescott all day, but actually only got one pheasant: a record! Another day was more satisfactory, when he shot 25 rooks.

He wrote on 17 October 1890 to the Wolverhampton station master for the London and Western Railway Co., after a horse had been injured in August while in the care of the company:

The horse in question has repeatedly travelled by rail & has always been easy to manage. I consider that there was great negligence on your part, in keeping the box at Stafford for so long a time & shunting it so many times... I imagine it was during such shunting that the horse slipped up & got cut, probably through some defect in the flooring boards. Anyway it was quite evident to me that the horse cut his hind fetlocks with the heels of his fore shoes while he was under your care, & that the damage was not caused by the sports at Atherstone.
I may say that the horse in question was a valuable hunter, for which I gave £250, & which had been having regular exercise at the time of the accident.

He follows it up on 25 November with a letter to G.P Neale, as director of the company in London:

Herewith please find written statements from Sgt-Major Aston & Corpl Lane giving their version of what occurred on Aug 4th when my horse was injured while under the care of your company... I may say that the horse is quite fit now, & the hair on his hip has grown to the same colour as formerly so that there is no blemish. I beg to leave the matter now in your hands.

Knowledgeable as a Cavalry officer in matters concerning horses, he enjoyed 'messing the gees' himself: 'I have just come in from sugaring the nags and did not know t'other from which. One at the far end nearly had my finger off, he snapped at the sugar so.' He hunted with the Albrighton pack. The local papers record each meet, invariably commending his exceptionally smart mounts: on 23 February 1903 'prominent members of the hunt included ... Mr C.T. Mander and party in a well-appointed equipage'. On 24 February, CTM was present 'in a splendid turnout'...

His courage was put to the test when 'he met with a very serious accident whilst riding to hounds' in March 1904. He had just gone through a wicket gate when his horse seems to have stumbled over some wire. He was catapulted head first onto the ground, losing consciousness for several days in a condition reported in the press to be 'extremely critical': 'Alderman Mander ... is an accomplished horse-man and few are more devoted to the delights of the chase than he'. *The Field* reported:

> The horse recovered itself and got away, and the groom immediately went to his master's assistance, at the same time doing all he could to attract additional help. He unbuttoned Mr Mander's waistbelt, collar, and shirt, but he showed no signs of consciousness, and some ten minutes elapsed before anyone arrived on the scene. Ultimately three medical gentlemen who were out with the hounds rendered all the help they could, and then they sent the injured gentleman home.
>
> Dr Deasnsley was immediately called in, and he afterwards secured the attendance of Dr Victor Horsley, [of Cavendish Square, London, W., the author of 'Brain Surgery']. During the past week the injured gentleman partially recovered consciousness and the symptoms are favourable of his gradual recovery. A large number of sympathetic messages have been received, and numerous ladies and gentlemen have called at The Mount to make kindly enquiries. Throughout the town the utmost sympathy has been expressed for Mr Mander and his family.

Bulletins continued to appear in the local and national papers until his condition stabilized: 'Mr Mander continues to make satisfactory progress, and no unfavourable symptoms have appeared'. But the accident seems to have left him short tempered for the rest of his life.

CTM was a keen traveller, of the first generation for whom foreign travel, languages, cosmopolitan society and culture, art and collecting, could be indulged as a way of life for the growing numbers of the leisured and affluent middle classes. He crossed the Atlantic frequently in the great age of ocean liners. The first time recorded was for his marriage and honeymoon in 1882, when the young couple traversed the American continent. They visited the Niagara Falls in June, staying four nights at the Clifton House Hotel, and then, after crossing the Rockies, took four days in a coach and four to make the journey from San Francisco to Yosemite. He was cosmopolitan in his outlook and interests, patronizing the great

Edwardian city hotels in Nice, Paris, Biarritz (in the Edwardian period he would stay for weeks on end at the Grand Hotel, playing golf, hunting and making motoring excursions into Spain), Berlin, New York, Palm Beach, and the cruise liners to North Africa and South America.

Egypt was remarkably accessible by sea from Nice. A letter in the neat writing of the illiterate and grovelling style from his dragoman there is dated 1 March 1913, before travel was curtailed by the war:

to his Lordship Sir Charles Mander
Excuse me Sir for taking the liberty to write these few lines, hopping that you are all injoining the best health. and arrived safly back to Assouan... I shall be very happy to meet you all again and explains you about Isis. Osiris and the other great God Horus... I beg you kindly Lordship that I have allready spocken to you that I wish to be under your service in Cairo, to show you sight seens ect...and I pray the great Lord of heavens so keeps you all in long life and return again and again on the classic Nil and may your virgins to the world will wider then ever. Sacred eye of Horus protect you all from evil eye, with thousand 1000 salams,

I remain your obb. Servant
Mohamed Abudi Dragoman (Luxor)

Typical of his generation, he was an assiduous correspondent. Just three of his bound letter books survive, a small proportion of the total; they contain damp-press duplicates of some 1,000 letters on fine and brittle paper, revealing him as a practical man of affairs, capable, assertive and outspoken.

[1] He paid £12,500 for 235 acres, including the Red House and The Dippons Farms, in 1895.
[2] G.E. Bryden of Norristown, Pennsylvania, writes in 1900 about the gold mines in British Columbia, 'the richest group of which he states have been named after Theodore, you [?Flora], Geoffrey and Lionel'.
[3] *VCH Warwicks*, 1945, vol. 3, p 37. His trustees continued as lords of the manor after him. A guild was in existence temp. Henry VI. As late as 1770 the upper room was reserved for manorial courts.
[4] According to Amy Mander's memoir (Feb. 1917), his rank was Hon. Colonel, acting Brigadier-General and first on the official list to be General; 'he was to have received a KCB' (as Sir Arthur Havelock, Governor of Natal, with whom he served as lieutenant in the Relief of Lucknow, told her at The Mount). Janetta therefore received a Brigadier-General's pension and was offered apartments at Hampton Court. At the time of their marriage, he was colonel commanding the Duke of Cornwall's Light Infantry. He had an immense knowledge of the various South African tribes who held him in high affection, and was one of the first big game hunters in South Africa.

Henry was the son of NicholasSparke Stabb (1835-1900) of St John's, Newfoundland. His brother, Sir Newton John Stabb, KB, OBE (1868-1931) of Furnham Hall, Saxmundam, was one of the founders and chief manager of the Hong Kong and Shanghai Banking Corporation. (Ex inf. the late Peter Mander Mills of Highfields, Liphook.)
[5] She was the daughter of John William Colenso (1814-1883), the first bishop of Natal, who famously first questioned the literalism of the Bible on behalf of the 'intelligent Zulu', was 'father of the Zulu people', and author of a Zulu grammar, etc.
[6] John ('Jack') Howard Mander, OBE (1869-1927), of Thorpe St Andrew, Norwich, was educated at Rugby and Trinity Hall, Cambridge. He first joined the North Staffordshire Regiment, and ended up as Brigade-Major in the Durham Light Infantry.
[7] Born in 1855, Lionel Phillips had had the good fortune to be taken up as a penniless young diamond prospector on the banks of the Orange River by Alfred Beit, one of the founders with Cecil Rhodes of De Beers Consolidated Mines. In due course he made his fortune with his brilliant grasp of mining engineering, becoming a partner with Cecil Rhodes in Wernher Beit & Co. He was exiled to England in 1896 for his complicity in the Jameson Raid, the abortive attempt by Rhodes to annex the Transvaal by force. He then acquired Tylney Hall in Hampshire, which he rebuilt and furnished in the grand Rothschild manner, now appropriate, like The Mount, in its adaptation as a hotel. Florence established a reputation as one of the great hostesses of the age, and in the years after 1917 they rebuilt Vergelegen on the Western Cape. (M. Hall, 'Vergelegen', *Country Life*, vol. cxcii, no. 47, 19 November 1998, 66-71.)
[8] Col. (later Brig.-Gen.) Cuthbert Edward Goulburn, RA, DSO, born 1860 (son of Col. Edward Goulburn of Betchworth House, Surrey, Grenadier Guards, who d. 1887). He m. Grace, dau. of W.H. Foster of Apley Park, Bridgnorth, and was MFH of the Albrighton Hounds 1905-10.

12

PATERFAMILIAS

CTM was an astute and competent manager, running the firm, the community, the town, the regiment, his household and his family with imperious authority. He would help out his relations where he could. He writes to an (unspecified) aunt:

July 28 1889

My dear Aunt,
... I have much pleasure in handing you cheque for Herbert value £100 to be repaid at his convenience and in the meantime bear interest at 6%.

There is no need for me to refer ... for a character, as Herbert comes from an honest stock and I can therefore trust him. I am glad as far as possible to be of assistance to my poorer relations and hope that with this small start Herbert will soon make his pile.

I saw uncle William [?Weaver] the other day; he has gone very grey but otherwise looks as sound as ever.

I was very nearly coming out to Canada 2 or 3 years ago, in fact took my ticket, but had to give it up.

Mary joins me in much love to you and yours.

I am your affect[e] nephew, C.T.M.

But as he got older and richer, he seems to have been less liberal with indigent and pestering relations, with all manner of hollow-sounding prevarication.

He writes on 25 November 1902:

Dear Willie,
I am really very sorry for you & it is most distasteful to me to refuse you, but you entirely misunderstand my position. We are not making half the profits in our business as formerly. Most materials have increased in price very much & we cannot sell at increased prices so that although our returns keep up our expenses are greater. Your last loan I had to borrow from my bank & I still owe them for it. This cannot go on indefinitely. The education of my children is a great expense too, besides my cousin Theodore having died, we have to pay out large sums to his Trustees, so that I am not justified in advancing money now, however good the security.

I shall have many calls on me next year too, when I shall be high Sheriff, so that however much I may wish to help my relations, my wife & children have first call.

Your affectate Cousin, Charles T. Mander

He bought a house in Hereford in 1905 for his sister Louise, whose husband, Dr George Leeper of Dublin, had died aged about 45 leaving her with four children. Her son, Dermot, was sent off to America as a young man with her introduction to Alexander Graham Bell (in Nova Scotia). CTM writes of him disapprovingly in a rage in December 1908:

My dear Louie,
I am very annoyed to think that you have sent Dermot £40. He has done nothing but deceive you & me ever since he went out [to the U.S.A.].

He wrote me a most pitiful yarn last week about being liable to be put in prison for cashing another man's cheque, which was a false one. That was much too thin, & he must consider me an idiot to believe such a yarn. In the same letter he referred to his girl & said she is a darling, forgetting that he cabled me some weeks ago for money to bury his baby. The fact is he tells so many lies he gets mixed.

I wrote him a long letter yesterday to the effect that I have no more faith in him & shall not send him another cent, & that he ought to be thoroughly ashamed of himself, bleeding you for money, when he ought to be sending you money to educate his sisters & paying you back the money which he has had from you on specious promises, not to mention what he owes me and Neville.

As for your rent, that is a detail. I cannot expect to get my rent if you are fool enough to squander it on Dermot.

I hope that Nora will soon be all right & sound directly, as well as Mervyn.

His immediate family were also soundly dealt with. Geoffrey was a constant source of irritation and trouble as a youth, apparently 'a champion slacker', with a needling manner. CTM was probably suspicious of his 'Rad' politics, and he aroused his anger by his bad time keeping. He wrote to Geoffrey's guardian, Aldwin Soames (a cousin by marriage) on 11 November 1906, 'very indignant about his conduct':

My dear Aldwin,
I have told you repeatedly what an impossible young cub Geoffrey is, & has been ever since his father & mother died.

I have had little or nothing to do with him at the Works, as I don't believe in too many Partners interfering. He has been entirely under the supervision of his uncle Howard, & in Howard's absence Neville has undertaken him.

A month or so before he sailed for Canada we carpeted him in my office & had a very bad quarter of an hour. He had never mentioned to any of us how long he wished to have for his honeymoon. Neville & Howard both told him that they had a month only, & that they were both Partners at the time they were married. Anyway we would stretch a point & give him 6 weeks. That meant that he would have to be back at the Works on November 2.

He made no comment at the time nor has he written a word to any of us since, but has absolutely ignored our wishes. It was only from my son that I casually heard that he was sailing from New York on Nov. 6, ie that he has calmly taken a week or two longer than we gave him leave for.

This is absolutely absurd & we cannot allow a mere clerk or employee (for that is what he is now, whatever he may be later on) to ride roughshod over us, it is time we brought him up with a round turn.

The result of his ignoring our wishes is that the Firm wrote him a letter, to await his arrival, that we should not require his services until Jan 1st.

What he will do remains to be seen & probably he may write to you as his guardian, & as such I think you should know the facts of the case at first hand.

Howard and Neville have remonstrated with him dozens of times, but it has had no result & I am looking forward to a great deal of trouble with him in 3 months' time when he becomes a Partner.

I am very sorry for him; he is very self opinionated, has no judgement or tact & is much too big for his boots & has been ever since his father died.

Yours very truly,
Charles T. Mander

A few days earlier, he had been complaining about him to his daughter, Daisy, still in America:

Geoffrey is a hopeless chap and how he will get on later remains to be seen. He has made no arrangement about putting up his bride when she comes home, not even the room they will have, I believe. He might have arranged for the Dining Room ceiling to be whitewashed and also the back stair Comfit repaired too, etc. Where he got the money to buy a diamond necklace and earrings, goodness knows. He ought to live very quietly for some years anyway...

He is terribly slack about his own house. Miss Smith showed Mary a letter from Florence, saying that they wished to occupy Flora's room, and that they wished the old double bed to be put back there again. The bed was sold years ago. She said that they were sailing on November 6th, but by what line or boat goodness only knows, or when they will arrive.

Clearly Gerald, his younger son born in 1886, who suffered from persistent ill health, was another who was not spared his temper:

Feb 1 1909

I am sorry that I lost my temper tonight, but your behaviour for months past, off & on, has been enough to make a saint swear.

I am writing this carefully, so that you may calmly think over your position without interruption.

It is a pity I did not pull you up with a round turn years ago, but I always thought your three cornered temper was the result of ill health, & let matters slide.

At times your temper was angelic, but many times of late you have been so surly and infernally rude to your mother & sister that I have been surprised that I have stood it. We have all given way to you in every way for years owing to your ill health.

Personally I have spared no expense on your education & have done my best to bring you up as an English Gentleman.

I have given you the choice of any profession you liked, but you elected to go into my Works, & as head of the Firm I expect you to behave as a gentleman, & act up to & be proud of the name you bear.

I have no wish to rub it in further & consider that you are smart enough to read between the lines. By nature I never bear ill will, & if you express your regret, will let bygones be bygones & never refer to the matter again.

Your loving father
Charles T. Mander

The reply from Gerald is in this case preserved:

2 February 1909

My dear father,

Yours to hand. I am sorry for the incident.

It appears I suffer from suppressed gout in the head, which is not always apparent but shows itself frequently enough however and I don't see how to avoid it very well.

Of course, you have always been very good to me and I am afraid that I very often return this with ill will, tho' (as in your case) there is no malice afore- or after-thought.

For all this trouble I sincerely apologize. In the future I must try and leave all arguing with you alone, as it is pretty evident that we rarely agree; and confine myself to the Biblical "nay nay or yea yea".

And I think should I live up to this resolution it might work well enough.

Yours ever,
Gerald

Again he confided in Daisy in April 1911: 'Wonders will never cease, Gerald last night actually *apologised* to me after dinner for having rounded on me and been rude to me at dinner. Of course I was very pleased and shall tell Arthur to tell him so and point a moral.' On another occasion he describes to Daisy his mother's concern (October 1906): 'Your mother is in a great stew about Gerald. He has been out in the rain for an hour or more, messing with drains. She is lying in wait for him like a spider, to bundle him into a hot bath; whether he will have one or not, depends.'

As an industrialist, CTM was an enthusiastic amateur of technology, with an interest in all the new-fangled machines and gadgets of his time. He was an early advocate of electricity. The Manders had been among the promoters of the first gas works in Wolverhampton in 1820, but sixty years later gas was being replaced by electricity, domestically. Cragside (National Trust) of 1880 is often cited as one of the first examples of a house to be lit by electricity. Certainly by the mid-1890s gas was becoming antiquated in fashionable houses—although suppliers of country house gas works were still advertising in 1911.[1] In December 1890 CTM was complaining about the gas supply, clearly not a man to be meddled with, and he wrote to the manager of the Wolverhampton Gas Company:

I have again to complain of the gas, and give you notice that from this day I refuse to pay for any gas which may pass through my meter until you provide me with a proper pressure and candle power, as at present it is not worth having.

Perhaps it was an excuse, as he was wanting a new local company, the Electric Construction Corporation, to install an electric system. Wasting no time, the same month he was writing to their London office to contract for a 'complete installation for lighting'. He was obviously convinced by the technology himself, and bought shares in the company, sharply proposing to offset the dividend against the cost of works in a letter to their chief accountant:

Nov 16 1890

Your company has contracted to supply me with a complete installation for electric lighting at The Mount and have only within the last four days commenced the work. When you have completed the contract to my satisfaction, I shall have pleasure in sending you a cheque. Meanwhile the dividend, which I presume your company propose to pay soon, should more than balance any contra a/c you many have against me.

He had soon installed the gleaming electrical plant, batteries and dynamos, employing an engineer to maintain them, a marvel he could show his dinner guests after the port, and using his influence to promote the technology in the borough. He upgraded the system in 1895/6, when the steam-driven generator was supplying 100 volts DC for the lighting. By 1904, he could dispense with the engineer as he connected up to the mains, writing to Daisy in December in Berlin:

We have had our house fixed up with the 'Ocker Hill' electric light, same as Wightwick and Sir Alfred [Hickman] have, and for that matter same as Uncle Neville... The engine broke down the other day again, and so I would not be bothered with it and arranged to take the other on. It gives a capital light and won't cost more than making it myself, but I shall have to find a job for Poyner, otherwise he will have to walk about all day with his hand at the salute. I might send him to act as courier for you. You know he has travelled some.

'Honest' Tom Parker was the developer of the first rechargeable battery and one of the first to build large dynamos and put them to practical use. He was the inventive genius behind the Electrical Construction Company, one of the largest manufacturers of generators and electrical plant, who exported all over the Empire, producing the first electric sparking plug and an electric car with hydraulic brakes and four-wheel steering. Charles Tertius helped him set up his own company, Thomas Parker Limited, in 1894, with new works in Wednesfield Road, becoming its first chairman. The company developed centrifugal turbine pumps.

He was also a pioneer motorist. In the early motoring days there were rival technologies. At the turn of the century, he was convinced by the superiority of steam, which accounted for some 40% of vehicles at the time, being praised for their speed, smoothness of operation and hill-climbing ability. The White Sewing Machine Company of Cleveland, Ohio, introduced their first steam car in 1901. He tried out and ordered his first White 'steamer', a 10-HP limousine, on 30 January 1904. He writes with his deposit:

Limousine seems to be more particular about cash with order than Tonneau. Anyhow, I have pleasure in enclosing a cheque for £200, which is more than a third...

You said you would not object to my firm's materials. As I am a varnish and colour manufacturer, I certainly desire that my own materials should be used on my own car. It would be a totally different matter if I bought a ready made car at the Crystal Palace Show or direct from your House in America.

I am recommended to have Michelin hollow tyres in front and solid (Artillery) tyres with soft rubber centres on the hind wheels. What is your opinion about this?

You seem to be mighty particular about my signing an order, but you are not so particular about what you put in the order.

By 18 March the car had arrived, registration number E200, and he was already a keen motorist, entering into copious correspondence with Whites:

My wife & I both like the car immensely. As I told you before, I had a drive the other day, but got very mixed up in the steering. I had another go today and got on better.

I find that people take no notice of the gong & have bought a hooter @ 12/- but it is left-handed & will not fit on the steering rod.

On 3 April he writes to Mr Edwards, the coach-builder in Ashford:

I heard from the White Steam Car people that you would require my car back again for a fortnight to build the Limousine top on it. I want it back again complete by the end of 1st week in May ... as I am going to Camp for the yeomanry training ... & even if I don't want to use it, my wife would want to run over to camp from time to time.

By the way, the door bends at the top. This you will no doubt look to.

By October, he had trained the head groom, Storrar, to 'exchange the reins for the wheel' and there are reports in the papers that the car caught fire. He writes to Daisy: 'My own motor car is in dock, being painted up after the fire Storrar had with it lately. You heard of Captain Cousins tumbling out of it and leaving his lunch and flask behind. The car skidded and one of the wheels was buckled, so that will have to be put right while it is in dock.' Later in the month, he reports: 'The motor car has come back entirely done up and I hear is going ripping.'

By November, he is sold on the motoring experience, and all set on upgrading to their latest 15-HP model. He writes Daisy with evident excitement on 25 November:

When in London I went to the White steam car place and Arthur met me there. We had a very good run on their new 15 H.P. car, which has many improvements on the 10 H.P. car I have now, besides having more room in the tonneau. It is 6 or 8 inches wider and 14 or 15 inches deeper, i.e. in front of your knees.

We were very pleased with it indeed. It went up a hill, steeper then the Compton Holloway, very well, but Mr Coleman (the manager) who drove us was not satisfied with its show and took us round a long way and eventually came to the same hill again; it went up it like smoke, quite 10 or 12 miles an hour!

I have ordered a new 15 H.P. car which may arrive in Jan or Feb. I shall have it made with new dodges of sorts and expect you will be delighted with it.

This time it was to be painted like his carriages in the family livery:

I think we shall decide to have our new steam car painted white instead of grey, probably with blue and yellow lines on it, as in the other one. I shall not have a limousine top on (i.e., a Brougham), but a cover to put on with curtains all round.

By September the following year, he decides to train up another of his men as a mechanic and chauffeur:

We have thought of a new scheme, i.e. to send Charles up to London for a month or so to learn the guts of the Cars and then to become Head Shuvver. He seems very tickled at the idea and if they agree Charles will go up on Tuesday.

Chauffeur Charles with White 'steamer' at The Mount, 1904

A month later, he writes: 'Charles drove the blue motor back from London on Thursday. It is going A1 and I shall send it into Clarks tomorrow to have it properly fixed up by the time you are back.' By 1907, he had again traded up, with two steamers, a 15-HP model and an 18-HP 3/4 limousine, for which Clark & Son of Chapel Ash made bodies for £60. Horns were a new idea which he was soon to take up, writing to the Motor Supply Co. in London on 25 July 1909:

I duly received the loud horn but ... I find it most awkward to fit on my cars, as it is in the way of the Lamps or the Bonnet.
 Are they not made or can you not have one made with the horn straight instead of at right angles so that it can lie along the chassis at the side of the bonnet?

By January 1908, the steamers were proving unreliable and he was writing to Mr Coleman at White's:

What a farce it is! King has been here 5 or 6 weeks putting my 2 cars right, a week or so after they were left in perfect order by your previous fitter.
 Your steam cars are a perfect worry to me & I am beginning to hate the sight of them or talking about them.

Petrol cars were beginning to get the upper hand by now, and he seems to have realized pretty quickly that he was backing a loser. Whites stopped making their steamers in 1910. He had decisively abandoned his steamers for more trusty technology, ordering in 1908 one of the first petrol Rolls Royces when the Silver Ghost was launched. Charles Rolls, one of the founders, had been at Trinity just before Charles Arthur, hanging up in his rooms the famous summons he had been served with for failing to have a man with a red flag walking in front of his car, as the law then required.

Early in the war the chauffeur Storrar was threatening to enlist as a motor driver. In 1916, CTM was writing patriotically to Colonel Holden at the War Office to offer his 40/5 Silver Ghost, for which he had paid 'over £1,000' in 1911, 'as a staff car for conveying generals at the Front'. Rolls Royce, always sticklers for quality, used Manders paints on their motor cars, long after sought out by enthusiasts to repaint their vintage models.

In the early days of motoring CTM was a supporter of driving on the left in the Wolverhampton area, where there was no standard convention, and some advocated driving along the middle of the road: 'In the olden days, men used to meet to the left at tournaments, and cavalry men always meet sword arm to sword arm'. He suggested pedestrians, too, should keep to the left: 'If you stick to the left you are sure to be right, and if you keep to the right you are sure to be wrong.' Long after the age of the motor, he continued to enjoy driving four-in-hand with his carriages and to take a pony and trap into Wolverhampton, a hazard to pedestrians as he drove hell-for-leather to his Works or the station.

His scientific enthusiasms were diverse. He had an astronomical observatory at the top of his house, set on an eminence from which he could survey the stars by night and a panorama of seven counties by day, as far as the Malverns and the Clee and Clent hills. He would point out Habberley Hill, Kinver Edge, Barr Beacon, the Wrekin, the Welsh hills by Welshpool, Cannock Chase, Stafford Castle. He practised photography early, had his own well-equipped darkroom and, putting his money where his mouth was, was one of the first subscribers to stock in Eastman Kodak. He plagued his family with his magic lantern slides. Daisy records in 1915: 'CTM tried to work the magic lantern, but electricity is worse than the last machine affair, so we saw little'.

His obituaries state that he was a keen horticulturist, 'having taken prizes in competition with some of the best horticulturists in the country'. Daisy accuses him of having an obsession for weeding: 'most extraordinary man!' More typically, The Mount garden contained a collection of erratic sandstone boulders moved to the neighbourhood in the ice ages, subsequently set up with their origins identified at Wightwick Manor, where they remain today.[2]

As a personality CTM is remembered in later life as a stern, direct and rather frightening Victorian paterfamilias, even by the standards of his contemporaries. His granddaughter, Jill Wallis, writes:

> Grandpa was rosy-faced with merry blue eyes, and could be abrupt (but not to us children). He had a large gold pocket watch on a chain on his waistcoat, which always intrigued me.He would suddenly pull it out, flip open the lid and ask me to tell the time. If the nursery governess politely intervened and gave the answer, he was furious and told her to be quiet. 'That's enough, Charlie', Dandan would say firmly.

His *Times* obituary said of him:

> He was fearless and absolutely straightforward in his doings, without tact and finesse. When he gave offence, as he often did, it was without intention, as it was usually by him unperceived. Many of his public statements, as he was a bold and unskilled speaker, were toned down by a merciful Press.[3]

One incident of the sort of brush with the press suggested here occurred when he was first elected mayor in December 1892. He soon found himself in confrontation with them when a group of reporters united against him for treating them in 'an ungentlemanly manner' by holding them up to ridicule at public gatherings. He craved their indulgence, hoping they would 'deal lightly with my inexperience as a public speaker'. But they only made a vote of censure:

That we as members of the Institute of Journalists, incorporated by Royal Charter, beg respectfully to protest against the continued observations of His Worship the Mayor of Wolverhampton (Charles T. Mander, Esq.) in his frequent designations at public gatherings of the members of our honourable profession as "wretched reporters," "scribblers," and "inaccurate reporters hanging around," to the discrediting of the representatives of the Press of London, the provinces generally, and Wolverhampton in particular... We are quite ready to believe that his Worship may mean nothing by his jocular observations ... but we cannot suffer ourselves to be continually held up to ridicule by the chief citizen of this borough in public assemblies to which we are invited.

CTM back-pedalled rather feebly, claiming that he used the term 'wretched reporters ... more as a term of endearment than anything else', and chaffed with his usual facetiousness at an unofficial interview that he had used the term 'immaculate reporters' (not 'inaccurate reporters'). But the reporters were not to be hoodwinked and still took exception, formally asking that he unreservedly withdraw his offensive language 'in as public a manner as he had uttered it'.

A contemporary reporter who clearly bore him some affection describes his public speaking:[4]

Charley Mander is not a good speaker. I once heard him say publicly, with an abandon which did not trouble to correct itself, that a certain firm's goods had a world-wide reputation throughout the length and breadth of England.

But this very implication of ineptitude constitutes his charm as a public speaker. I don't care who is in the room, on the platform or in the audience, but as soon as Charley Mander rises to his feet his hearers settle down with that peculiar rustle which denotes anticipation of something enjoyable, to hear what he has to say—or rather to listen to what he does not say.

As a speaker he is never disappointing. Were he fluent he would spoil everything. His disclaimers—and he always has something to disclaim—are delicious, his capacity for saying the wrong thing at the right moment is exquisite, his arguments are astounding... Perhaps Alderman Mander is seen and heard at his best when conjouring with figures, not employed as arguments, but by way of illustration. As he backs his fancy with variegated sporting terms, and makes the digits dance before one's dazzled eyes, who can doubt the cogency of his reasoning? The speaker knows what he has been talking about evidently, the arguments of those who would confound him have spoken through their hats, and so—well, there you are!

He had a direct, straight from the shoulder, turn of phrase, never mincing words or mealy mouthed with 'anaemic language', as his son Arthur put it. 'It's all tommy rot', he would say in the Council chamber, with a sportsman's terse phrase, and sit down. He was remembered for his 'bluff downrightness': 'Sir Charles, in appearance distinguished and dignified, possessed mannerisms and methods of expression which, at times, surprised, and even alarmed those who met him for the first time as a stranger… Fond of a joke, and racy in conversation, it might be worth while to make a collection of the many unusual expressions of his vocabulary or, at any rate, such as are printable.'

Charles Arthur did jot down a list of family expressions—not all CTM's—current at the turn of the century, 'compiled for visitors to The Mount'. Many have achieved recognition, or appear innocuous enough today:

Bobble—to move slowly. Boost—to assist with force, generally from behind.
A smell—a short distance, generally less than six inches.
A bit "niffy" (billiards)—rather "smelly", cf. above i.e., "a close shave".
Ach!—exclamation of contempt or displeasure.
Ink—a species of drink circulated after dinner.
Get—derived from go, went, gone. *Imperat.*
Desolute—vacant, uninhabited (of island).
Raise Cain to—dispassionately inquire into a subject, generally with regard to causes of contretemps.
Raise *absolute* Cain to—if you hear this, "look out" first, and then see above.
Poyner—black sheep, or scapegoat, generally found near dog kennel.
Smell your hat—to latecomers at meals, is equivalent to, "Grace has already been said; you must make your own benediction".
Sweat blood—try one's hardest.
Gooseberry bush—any arboreal growth.
Mutty—sand for tee at golf.
Kivver to kivver—cover to cover.
To coffee house—chatter.
"The fine-olly was that, etc."—the result.
Débris—applied to murderer under death sentence: *"Holloa, Sheriff, have you got rid of your débris yet?"*
Squirt (generally in conjunction with "bit of a"); *"He's a bit of a squirt"*—"He's a second-rate person".
"Give him the run of his teeth."
"Tell another while your mouth's wet."
I'm going "to lie down a bit"—to bed.
Myther (v.a.)—to be long winded about, without reaching the point in a speech or story, to be verbose.
Skew-whiff—lopsided, out of alignment.
Duds—clothing, male or female.
Dig out—investigate.
It went into the pocket "like shit off a shovel".
Gizzard—internal organs, or health generally: *"How's your gizzard?"*

CTM died on 8 April 1929, aged 76, bequeathing one year's wages, reported *The Times*, to each of his servants at The Mount who had been in his employ for more than a year.[5] He had a civic funeral at St Peter's Collegiate Church, Wolverhampton, the Union Jack serving as his pall.

Today his life is commemorated among other Mander memorials there[6] by a fine storied internal porch, a striking Comperesque perpendicular design by the Birmingham architect, James A. Swann, a good friend of Gerald's.

With crocketed gables in limed oak which has mellowed to blend with the stone, it was made by Panchieri & Hack of Bromsgrove, and was dedicated in March 1932. It bears the arms of Mander, Paint and the Corporation of Wolverhampton, with inscriptions either side from the *Sanctus* prayer which introduces the Canon, apposite in commemoration of a genial patriarch: *gratia cum omnibus*, and *sursum corda*: 'let us lift up our hearts'.

The Mander Porch, CTM Memorial at St Peter's Collegiate Church

CTM's funeral

[1] M. Humphrys, *Construction and Management of Small Gasworks*, 1911.
[2] Kelly's *Directory of Staffordshire*, 1924 states: 'Many years ago, Mr Mander (father of Mr C.T. Mander of Tettenhall, Wolverhampton) collected examples of the finer erratic blocks at Tettenhall where (by kind permission of his son) they were visited by and gave much pleasure to the members of the Geologists' Association in 1898.'
[3] *The Times*, 10 April 1929. Other biographies include: *Express & Star*, 21 June 1911 (baronetcy); *Express & Star*, 20 Sept. 1935; *Wolverhampton Chronicle*, 10 April 1929 (obit.); *Wolverhampton Chronicle*, 17 Apr 1929 (funeral); *Express & Star*, 20 Sept. 1935 (biography)
[4] *Impressions of an Alderman*, 1904
[5] *The Times*, 15 July 1929, reported he left estate of the value of £258,160, with net personalty £157,612.
[6] The Shell Guide to *Staffordshire* (1978) comments: 'of special interest are [the memorials] to the Mander family' (p. 186). The family vault is in the curtailed churchyard outside, fenced in to the north. Benjamin, Charles Benjamin and Charles Arthur are commemorated in Wolverhampton by blue and white plaques by Rudi Herbert installed under the aegis of the Wolverhampton Civic Society.

Mary in her library in old age

13

PAINT OF NOVA SCOTIA, 1817

CTM married a Canadian, Mary Le Mesurier Paint (1859-1951). In 1920, her father Henry Nicholas Paint (1830-1921)[1] recalled the day 'I put you on the train for Rimouski to embark on the Allen steamer for Liverpool in 1881'. The wedding was a year later, in her home town of Halifax, Nova Scotia. It was an age of transatlantic marriages —including many rather grand ones. Her elder sister, Flora, had been sent to Europe to attend a finishing school with Theodore Mander's sisters in Clapham, south London, in 1873. She ended up marrying Theodore, builder of Wightwick Manor, in May 1879.

Guernseymen had been trading in the Cape Breton area of Nova Scotia since the seventeenth century.[2] Settlement began in earnest when it was cleared of its French Acadian population after the Seven Years' War (1763), which left it an unpopulated waste land. The tragic diaspora of 'peasants of Normandy' to Louisiana and the tiny offshore islands was immortalized in Henry Wadsworth Longfellow's narrative lament, *Evangeline* (1847):

> *Scattered like dust and the leaves, when the mighty blasts of October*
> *Seize them, and whirl them aloft, and sprinkle them far o'er the ocean.*

An idyll in jingling hexameters of the American landscape—goodly acres and forests primeval of murmuring pines and hemlocks bearded with moss —emerges as a solemn threnody of lovers reunited in death.

Guernsey fish merchants soon established seasonal settlements, trading cod with the remaining Acadians and returning each fall with their cargoes via a triangular trade with the Basque country of northern Spain.[3] A Guernsey firm had set up a fishery business at Arichat in Cape Breton by 1764, where it prospered until the American Revolution. Gradually, the settlements evolved into permanent villages. From the mid-eighteenth century, as more complex trading patterns developed and the British began to root out the historic smuggling and entrepôt privileges of St Peter Port, the Guernsey capital, we find the names of Channel Island families seeking a new life in Nova Scotia, and around the Gaspé Peninsula of Québec.

Some of these families were connected to the Paints. The Le Mesuriers,[4] with whom they had intermarried several times over the generations, were settled in Gaspé by 1789, at the time of the visit of Bishop Charles Inglis. He recorded several brothers Le Mesurier; 'natives of Guernsey. They generally catch from 10,000 to 12,000 quintals of fish every year and sometimes bring over 100 fishermen from Guernsey for the season'. (A quintal is about 112 lbs.)

On 15 May 1806 another group from St Peter Port reached Charlottetown, the chief settlement carved out of the primeval forests of Prince Edward Island in the Gulf of St Lawrence. They were mainly Methodists, inspired by the excitement of John Wesley's visit to Guernsey in 1787. One of their leaders, settling at the place which became known as Guernsey Cove, was Henry Bréhaut, of another island family close to the Paints. Henry Paint writes:

My mother's name was Mary Le Messurier [1786-1864]. My father's mother was Rachel Bréhaut. Three of the Bréhauts during two centuries at intervals were Bailiffs or Governors of Guernsey, likewise several Le Messuriers...

In Guernsey there were three judges of that name; Peter 1598, John Bréhaut 1637 and John Bréhaut 1661... I got this from Berry's *History of Guernsey* [1815] presented by F.B. Tupper to my father at Arichat in 1820. There are some Bréhauts at Murray Harbour, Prince Edward Island—rich farmer, I have been told.

Henry Paint married a Scot, Christiana St Clair McVean (1824-91). He writes of Christiana's parentage to his daughter Mary in July 1918:

...The name/surname of your Scotch grandmother was Ann D[o]ckendorf [of] Colonsay, Argyllshire, who died in 1850, on her tomb stone in Camp Hill Cemetery, Halifax. Her husband Donald McVean was a merchant of Glasgow [who] emigrated to Georgetown, Prince Edward Island, in 1815 and died at Halifax in 1840; tombstone in the old Cemetery Halifax. The ship landed the family at Sydney, Cape Breton, where they resided until they moved to P.E. Island.

About 1850, I met some old gentlemen from Sydney who told me Flora McVean (your mother's sister) was the best-looking young woman they had ever seen. She died in 1852—as indicated on the marble that marks her grave in Camp Hill Cemetery. Good and true devout Christian girl!

Members of the clan McVean were already established in Prince Edward Island by the end of the eighteenth century,[5] at the same time as the Dockendorff name occurs there. We know one at least married an emigrant from the island of Colonsay, off the coast of Argyll, which remains one of the most remote communities in the British Isles. Almost a quarter of the population (150 people) was forced out in September 1791, at the time of the infamous Clearances. The Colonsay emigrants settled in Pictou county Nova Scotia and across the Straits in Prince Edward Island.[6]

Jacob Dockendorff[7] came from Bad Kreuznach in the Rhineland in 1753 and secured land near Lincoln, Maine, whence two of his children migrated to Prince Edward Island about 1790. According to family tradition, they were attracted there because two of their uncles had over-wintered at Port La Joi (the original French settlement dating to 1720, by entrance to the harbour of Charlottetown), before they were killed in the capture of Québec in 1759. There was much intercourse between Argyll and Nova Scotia, and one of their descendants in the next generation must have moved back to Colonsay to breed.

The Paints were an old family of Guernsey seafarers. They would have set out on the westing keel-paths with the April winds, fishing for the rich harvest of cod off the Grand Banks and the shores of Cape Breton; trading, smuggling, privateering and exploring the indented coasts of Nova Scotia. A 'Paint Island' is already recorded at Cape Porcupine off the Straits of Canso by 1750.[8] In the nineteenth century, we are told, they became 'one of the principle families associated with the early development and commercial life of Port Hawkesbury'.

Port Hawkesbury, a sheltered inlet known as 'Ship Habour' before 1860, commands the straits dividing Cape Breton Island from the mainland of Nova Scotia, at the 'gut' of Canceau, or Canso. It is a mountainous, pristine and rocky country, carved by glaciers, covered with fir trees, a landscape familiar to the predominantly Highland settlers, who long remained Gaelic speaking in country districts. Almost all the houses are white, with rugged thatch to withstand the harsh winters. Near the southern end of the Strait of Canso, lies Janvrin Island and the much larger Isle Madame, with its small township of Arichat.

By 1815, Henry's father, Nicholas Paint (1790-1832),[9] was acting as agent for the Arichat and Gaspé Society, an association of merchants managed (and largely owned) by the Janvrin family of Jersey. He returned to Guernsey in January 1817, obviously intent on making moves to quit and set up on his own, on condition his father would advance him the money. The following month the Janvrins got wind of Nicholas's plans and wrote to their Guernsey partners, Cartaret Priaulx & Co., asking them to sound out Nicholas Paint and try to secure him to continue as agent, 'as we are more or less at his mercy'; they felt that they must plead with Nicholas to remain at Arichat for at least five more years.[10]

But while working for the Arichat and Gaspé Society, Nicholas Paint had clearly spent the time paving the way for his own future success. By 5 February 1817, he had fallen out with the Janvrins, who were writing bitterly: 'we have had a visit from Mr Paint, to whom we gave the reception he deserves and would not pay him a farthing's salary before we were compelled to it by law.'

Nicholas was evidently already beginning to work in direct competition with the Janvrins. By mid-February 1817, Janvrins were writing that

Nicholas had engaged some captains as well as men, and was reported to be establishing at Canso, or perhaps Gaspé; in addition he had purchased the brig *Charles of Guernsey*, at 182 tons, as well as a vessel expected from Gibraltar with a cargo of salt.

Meanwhile, Nicholas had successfully petitioned for two town lots in 1816 to settle permanently as a merchant in the shipping trade. He set up in trade partly on his own account and also in partnership with the Guernsey firm of Thoume, Moullin & Co., on whose behalf he acquired a further nine lots on the waterfront, including two water lots, in 1817. In 1818 he started building his house. By 1820 he was an established resident of the growing community and was appointed justice of the peace for Cape Breton by Sir James Kempt. He was soon building and commissioning a number of vessels: first the brig *Unity* of 131 tons; in 1831 the brig *Rewano* of 121 tons launched by T. Embrée; then the brig *Lord Saumarez* of 154 tons built by G. Billows the following year.

Henry wrote several surviving letters to his grandchildren on the theme of his father's exploits, sometimes differing from what we know from other sources.[11] One dated 3 April 1914, written to his granddaughter Daisy in a shaky and spidery hand when he was 84, is typically informative:

Belle Vue, Staits of Canso, 1818, silkwork picture by Daisy Mander, 1927
The flanking pentices are a typical Guernsey feature.

Halifax, N.S.,

On the 12th March 1859 when your mother arrived at midnight, one of the greatest blizzards was raging outside. I had rented the four acres House—two storeys, nine rooms, stable, wharves and warehouses—and remained there until I moved to Halifax.

In 1817 my father [Nicholas Paint] arrived at Hawkesbury from Guernsey in the full-rigged ship *Charles of Guernsey* with his staff, and remained manager and Agent of the new Company for ten years. My father married in 1814 in Guernsey. On his return from fighting in Buenos Ayres, when England was trying to detach that Colony from Spain, as France and Spain were under Napoleon aiming to sink England; but Canning's scheme of sending emissaries to stir up the Spaniards in Spain followed by money & Wellington helped to put Napoleon in Elba. As soon as we agreed to aid Spain, we could not in conscience try to capture one of her colonies, so about 1810 or 1811 my father paid £90 for his passage to England and offered his services to Wellington. As he was well versed in Spanish, French and English, he was put in the secret service to travel in the French towns and transmit information to Wellington via England, or direct. This he did for 3 years and escaped being shot.

My father was educated in England, in London [at Miss Legais' school]. In 1815 he engaged with Janvrin de Lisle & Janvrin of London and Jersey to go to Arichat, Richmond County, as High Agent—that is Agent over their other Agents—in different localities in the Gulf of St Lawrence; and about 1817 Ferdinand Brock Tupper, the father of the Miss Tuppers in Guernsey, succeeded him. My father built and managed a number of ships trading to the Brazils, British Guyana, West Indies, Spain, Italy, Portugal &c.

Now a little more family history. My father in 1818 began to build a stone house four great chimneys a double roof brick and some of the stone imported from England in his ships. He went home every autumn to see his family and returned every spring, finally the residence being completed on 130 acres of land on the beautiful shores of the strait of Canso called 'Belle Vue'. In March 1823, my father, mother, two sons, two daughters, and a Governess embarked on board the good ship *Mayflower Capt David.* They touched at Azores and saw the boiling fountains.

My father was a strong powerful man highly tempered, challenged on different occasions to fight duels, but always refused; being a famous boxer was always on the ground with the weapons nature had given him. I have been told that my mother could lead him as gently as a child, but nobody else until the storm was over.

You will say, well Grand Pa has spun a long yarn but poorly twisted...

After Nicholas's decease, a cousin, Peter Paint Senior, who had come out from Guernsey in 1822, looked after the estate for his widow till 1855, when his son, Peter Junior (later the first mayor of Port Hawkesbury) took over in partnership with Henry Nicholas. Henry later moved to Halifax and set up in the firm of Fraser, Paint & Co. A post-war letter to Mary is preserved, going over similar ground:

Cape Breton Island, Point Tupper
23 August 1919

My dear daughter,
Your long and interesting letter was most gratifying, coming from my beloved daughter Mary, reviving as it does an old life...

This very morning my eyes rest on the spot where my father built six ships from 1817 to about 1832, when at Philadelphia the cholera cut him off with my brother John, aged ten. The first of these ships were named the *Rachel and Mary* after your two aunts, and all traded to Rio, Bahia, Santos, Spain, Portugal, Naples and Buenos Ayres.

My grandfather Nicholas Paint was registered a shipowner in Guernsey in 1835 of a fine new full-rigged brig named *Lord Saumarez*, 151 tons.[12] This vessel's keel was laid when my father died and my mother completed the ship and [December 1832] sent the vessel to Guernsey consigned to my grandfather with Rachel and Eliza to school; Rachel three years and Eliza six. Miss Martin, their governess, had Rachel for six years before this.

The Paints are described as 'men of push and substance' in their philanthropic contribution to charities, education and religion in the Port Hawkesbury region—like the Manders in the Midlands. Henry writes to Mary after the First World War, in November 1919: 'The Manders ... according to what Theodore was in the habit of telling me, relied upon what the Bible taught, and so did the Paints. Let us pursue the same journey still. The results of the War should confirm us absolutely in this course. You remember I never made any undue fuss as regards religion in our family except to pay every regard to the teachings of the Bible.' The family had moved from Anglicanism to practice as Baptists, as there was no Anglican Church at the Straits. Peter Paint Senior provided a new school house in 1867; his wife the site for a temperance hall in 1898. Marie, Nicholas Paint's widow, gave land for the Baptist Church at Belle Vue, and left funds for its completion after she died.

After schooling in Guernsey and then at the Wolfville Academy, Henry was commissioned as a lieutenant-captain in the Canadian militia (1853-69) and fought in the Fenian raids in the 1860s, when nationalists tried to hold Canada to ransom in exchange for a free Ireland. He was awarded his gallantry medal by Sir Frederick Williams, 'the Hero of Kars'. In his fifties, he became a member of the Dominion Parliament of Canada for Richmond county (1882-91) in Cape Breton Island, giving steady support to Sir John Macdonald, the first prime minister of Canada. He built up the industry of Port Hawkesbury, writing boastfully of the projects there due to his efforts: the Dominion Warehouse and Wharf, the Strait of Canso Marine Railway, also the first crossing of the mails at Port Hawkesbury, the first steam ferry across the Strait, the line of steamers from Boston, 'also other public works in different parts of Cape Breton'.

Aged ninety, old Henry set out his political reminiscences in a letter headed 'Facts for the Public' written from 3 Artillery Place, Halifax (1920):

How Sir John Thompson became Premier of Canada: communicated by H.N. Paint

Paint began his canvas by sending four Roman Catholic boys to Horton Academy. The majority of the population of Richmond were Catholics, and this created some astonishment. The religious part of the population were anxious about the salvation of the boys at a Baptist school, and in course of time the Roman Catholic Bishop, sided by an Irish Priest, called me to account and wanted me to remove the boys. I answered, 'The tares and the wheat grow together until harvest'. He urged their removal, and I answered, 'I will try to gratify you'.

I then went to Horton, saw the boys, and explained the purport of my mission. They refused to leave. I then asked them, 'Are you Roman Catholic boys?' They answered, 'Yes'. 'Then', I said, 'pay respect to your Bishop. Here is the money. Go to Antigonish and see the Bishop and say to him the last thing Mr Paint said to us was: "Plead with the Bishop to be sent back."' There are about twelve or more Protestant boys at St Francis Xavier and we must have reciprocity, so he sent them back.

To my surprise, Sir Hibbert Tupper [member of Parliament and Solicitor General in 1896, during the premiership of his father, Sir John Tupper, 1821-1915] landed in the County. I saluted him, and inquired what brought him. He replied, 'I have come here to regulate the politics of this County'. I replied, 'The steamer that has just landed you will leave in about five minutes. Get on board and leave. I have charge of this County, and you have no crew to put me out'. He left.

Next day, Sir John Thompson arrived. I showed him my nomination. He read the names and assured me he had not come to interfere with my nomination in any shape whatever. We dined together at the Finlay Hotel, Arichat. He left the table before I did, made a polite bow, and attended a private meeting against me.

Next morning, a large delegation went to Descouse, where a large gathering took place, and he and his friends filled the Assembly Room—a strong opposition to me—with a number of friends from Sydney to lend him assistance in favour of Mr William R. Cutler, solicitor. They were all assembled when I came into the meeting, and I inquired of the Chairman if I could say half a dozen words. He said, 'Yes'. I inquired of the Chairman if I could rely on his signature and that of his four sons to my nomination, and he replied, 'You may, Sir'. I then turned round and addressed my opponent: 'That is my answer, you contemptible lot!'

I left, and went into an adjoining field. Thompson then came out to meet me, and said, 'How much money will induce you to retire?' I replied, 'I am not for sale'.

Thompson and his party then took the ferry to St Peter's—thirteen miles. I drove around in my carriage to St Peter's—28 miles—and arrived there at eight o'clock, when a meeting was in progress.

Thompson was speaking. He then said, 'Mr Chairman, I perceive the Candidate has come in, and I have this to say; that there will be no business done while he is present, and if he does not retire, we will find a way to make him'.

The hall was crowded, and I retorted, 'Gentlemen, if you are my friends, give an expression of it'. And the audience shouted, 'Paint or none'. I then said, 'Is it a man who never paid a cent of taxes in your County or owned a foot of land, that has the cheek to tell you who you are to vote for? I will tell you what to do with this meeting. Be guided by me: blow out the lights and smash up this meeting'. And the audience walked out.

I then met Sir John McDonald [1815-1891, first prime minister of Canada, who created the Liberal-Conservative Party], and I said to him, 'Let us strengthen our party'. 'How do you propose to do it?' he said. I replied, 'Get Angus McIsaac to retire in Antigonish, and run Thompson'. Sir John answered, 'Can that be done?' 'I think it can'. 'Who do you propose to do it?'

In a few minutes I answered. Sir John said, 'A most dangerous proceeding. Mr Isaac will rise in the House and endeavour to make a smart man of himself by saying, "Mr Speaker, I am offered a bribe". And both your names will be in every newspaper tomorrow morning'.

McIsaac asked if that was an official offer. I answered, 'You have five minutes to decide. Goodbye'. And I retired to the Conservative side of the House, as I had been sitting behind Laurier and Blake among the Liberals.

The next intelligence was a tirade from Cartwright, who attacked the Conservatives for having purchased McIsaac. But Antigonish was open, and Thompson ran, and became Premier of the Dominion.

He also lists his own achievements as a politician, 'the enterprises that I initiated in 1883, when a member of the Dominion Parliament':

I carried a committee on Inter-Provincial trade in opposition to Edward Blake and his party, aided by John A. McDonald and the Conservative members. The committee consisted of eleven members, four of whom were Cabinet Ministers, and they appointed me chairman. I advocated a bridge from Lennox Passage to Arichat, and a railroad to Arichat. The bridge has been completed by Premier Murray, and is now in operation at a cost of $100,000. The question of building a railway to Arichat harbor, I advocated and had a perfect survey made. I secured the purchase of water lots and a site for the Richmond County Public Building and Wharf at Arichat harbor.

Long before I was a member, I took three of the Cabinet Ministers and three of their young friends in my small steamer through St Peter's Canal—at that time 16 feet wide; now 46 feet wide and 18 feet on the sill, thanks to Mr Finn, MP, and Premier McKenzie—and we got them to agree to support a vote of $100,000 for the widening of the canal, and to erect the important lighthouses at Cape St George, Grand Narrows and Boularderie Island, and one on the South Bar, Sydney Harbor. I got them conveyed to Ingonish harbor, Victoria County, and at their request sounded the waters of that harbor and found 14 fathoms. Only narrow boats could go in at that time; now sailing vessels can use it freely. I gave my support for $100,000 to open up the channel, and now it is a success.

I then advocated strenuously the cultivation of the West India trade with the Dominion, and obtained the support of seventy members of the House of Commons, who signed a memorial which I presented to the Under Secretary of State, Mr Powell, and with that support the Cabinet provided a guarantee of a liberal subsidy, which enabled Messrs Pickford & Black to put on the Norwegian steamers as freight carriers; and since then the business has so increased that we have four British steamers laden, from the Dominion and back, with passengers and freight, touching at all the islands and making St John and Halifax their headquarters, with increasing trade.

I also established in Richmond County, while I was a member, twenty post offices, and fourteen lighthouses; was a member of the Hudson Bay Railway committee and inquiry into the feasibility of its navigation, with the result that 150 miles more would take it to Port Nelson, Hudson Bay. It is then hoped that we shall get a share of the Western grain and freight trade to Liverpool, and the whale oil and fur trade to the United States.

With all this guarantee of my usefulness, they turned me out, and I ran for election since and they rejected me on four occasions. But Premier Murray gave them this bridge last year. Now I am too aged to contest the County, but I shall, if Providence permits, advise my son to take my place, as he is back from the war and is preparing himself for public life...

Henry lost money in his political career following his election failure in 1891, and became poor in his old age, trying to subsist on $300 a year. From that point on, he kept writing shameless begging letters to his more prosperous Mander sons-in-law, CTM and Theodore, asking them for help in his political career—CTM paid him £50 towards his election expenses in 1899. He sought backing for his speculative schemes, vainly assuring them they would turn to account for his great-grandchildren, at least: notably leases on coal mines (the 'Paint seam' was near the bituminous Victoria mine) and gypsum properties at Brierley Brook, in Antigonish county.

He soldiered on in politics, writing as he returned from the capital in August 1904, 'The electors are coming to my support en masse, and no moonshine... No blandishment will turn my head. By going to Ottawa I renewed dozens of acquaintances among the best people, and all servants, messengers and officials hoped to see me back an M.P... Now to successfully defend the water grants and win the election I require £100.'

But he lost both the election and the water grants for his land at Point Tupper guaranteed by the Government, worth some $25,000; even though 'the Premier of Nova Scotia, the Hon[ble] Geo. H. Murray, stated to me in private, "It is the King, we dare not" [and] the Attorney General said to me, "The King will not break his seal."' He was left all but bankrupt. He writes to Flora at Wightwick on 28 January 1905, to say that he has just lost the election, and that now he has no income, no position in politics, and no property.

His grandson Arthur writes that he 'was countycourted by creditors to the tune of $21,000':

> properties were sold, the deeds of which were still in his name. However, he came to an agreement with the trustees of the creditors—the Deaf and Dumb Institute (who were creditors themselves)—not to sell any more land ... and he proposed to pay 35 cents in the dollar on the total liabilities.

CTM was bounced into investing unwisely in various hare-brained property speculations devised by Henry. One was a grandiose new residential development 'exceedingly well situated for trade', involving the laying out of a new township to be called 'Guernsey' at Point Tupper in 'romantic scenery' at the entrance to the Straits of Canso. Here Henry had bought 45 acres of land in 1863 a few miles outside Port Hawkesbury, on a site named by Sir James Kempt after Ferdinand Brock Tupper, the Guernsey historian. The land was surveyed and soon subdivided into 236 lots along a grid of streets; Mander Street, Paint Street and a string of others named after connected families, mainly in Guernsey. The investment must have been pretty substantial:[13]

> The situation of the town is described as one of great natural beauty, and it is also very healthy. Railway wharves are being opened up, extensive coal wharves are in preparation, and every care is being taken to secure for the place a prosperous and successful commercial future.

The lots seem to have sold slowly in the following 50 years. He sold one parcel to Emelia Tupper and another to Henrietta Tupper in 1874, 'on condition that no spirituous or intoxicating liquors should at any time be sold or kept for sale on the premises'. 'I am here at Point Tupper selling lots when I can at a profit', he is still writing in 1918.

The local heritage association museum is today housed in an old Methodist church in Henry Paint Street at Point Tupper, 'once a vibrant community and the main entry point between mainland Nova Scotia and Cape Breton Island'. Henry was ahead of his time, and the area did not see the booming development he had envisioned until the 1960s, too late to save him. Then there appeared in swift succession a pulp-and-paper mill, a deep water port with a gypsum shipping terminal, a new ferry crossing, a heavy water (deuterium) plant run by English Electric, a thermal generating plant and an oil refinery. The gently-rolling, forested landscape which had so attracted Henry Paint, dotted with babbling brooks and pristine springs, is no more, and the community is reduced to eight families, where a wallboard plant completed in 1990 occupies the jutting headland.

In spite or because of his yarns, his bruised optimism and begging, the family were patronizing, and clearly regarded Henry as a bore. His grandson Charles Arthur describes meeting old Henry in Canada when he was attending Geoffrey's wedding in October 1906:

> After breakfast, had a long talk with Grandpa P., or rather he did the talking, and I listened. He gave several extracts from speeches he and others had made on different famous occasions, thumping his palm with much effect, and causing considerable surprise to the people sitting around...
>
> Mrs P. is very common, like a cook... Geoff says he won't have her at the wedding... Mother and aunty Flora have never really forgiven him for marrying her... [She] seems to manage Mr P. very well, who has much collapsed and looks 90—very wrinkled.

Geoffrey had clearly offended the old Paints on that occasion. Daisy wrote, 'Marjorie [Geoffrey's sister] took Mander a silver watch, and we had *such* an interview, which ended all right after a very unpleasant conversation, and I hope Geoffrey will feel small about it'. CTM replied later in the month: 'What an ass Geoff made of himself with Pa and his wife! He has no tact whatever, and apparently let Arthur into the trouble too, not to mention you and Marjorie. The watch was a great scheme on your part and I hope it calmed your step-G. and that she thinks better of you both anyway.' Henry's own memories of the occasion were warmer, as he writes at the time to his emollient granddaughters, Daisy and Marjorie:

> My deep regret is that we scarcely had a quiet chat, every minute appeared to overlap the next one, a restless tide carried us along, and now we are separated for ever, possibly. The gratifying part is that I met and had a few words of conversation with five grandchildren in America assembled to witness an important function, the marriage of the eldest son of one family [Geoffrey Mander] to a Canadian girl [Flora Caverhill]. What the future has in store for each one of us is uncertain, unless we accept God's promises as written in his Holy Bible with faith and prayer. This I have striven to do, at times with failure, I admit. It was this carried our forefathers through—can be traced for seven centuries, but without a break for six, as your brother Gerald has proven. Let us follow with confident step!

Although his son by his second marriage to Ella Cowdray of New York, proudly named Mander Paint, seems never to have lived up to his father's promise in Dominion politics, Henry and his wife enjoyed respect in their old age in Halifax. When women's suffrage came in 1915, he records of Ella: '800 women in this city have votes. My wife took the matter in hand and every Alderman lost his seat, but she worked above board, and the other day four of the defeated men were standing at a street corner when she passed them. They lifted their hats and said, "You did it"—no ill will.' In the summer of 1919 two years before he died there was a royal visit:

Ella and I were presented to the Prince at Governor Grant's and Mrs Grant's official residence. Prince George with two midshipmen went into the free lunch for soldiers and sailors and sat at my wife's table, and said to her, 'What would my mother say if she saw me here? I wish she was looking at me now.' He recognized Ella when introduced by Grant, at least as much as was possible or allowable; also made some remark about me which I did not hear as my deafness has increased.

My cannon was mounted [with] ammunition on the spot the three ships with the Prince for Prince Edward Island and Quebec passed within half a mile, and they had not the spark to salute them. The same guns 20 years ago I myself loaded and fired when his father passed. I had written explaining everything, and the whole crowd were like drunk dogs—no bark in them.

From your affectionate father, Henry N. Paint

Henry Paint visits Wightwick, c. 1904
with Mary (sitting), Geoffrey (standing), and Geoffrey's children Mervyn and Mavis

Mary's portrait by A. Jonniaux, 1927

Mary Le Mesurier Mander, Henry's younger daughter, reigned at The Mount for sixty years as a formidable and elegant figure; by all accounts a great character and lively entertainer. She presided over a well-run country house in her Edwardian heyday, with a staff by then of some twenty indoor servants, the footmen dressed in the family livery of dark blue with yellow silk facings and striped waistcoats, processing from the kitchens. The bull terriers were trained to leap up at the bell pulls, so she didn't have to stir from her chair to summon the butler. He, in a ritual recording the nursery jingle *The Queen asks the parlour maid,* summoned the footman who summoned an under-footman to put a log on the waning fire. She had a fondness for extravagant hats, which she trimmed herself; for bright and striking clothes in scarlet; and fashionable shoes which she sported on dainty Cinderella feet.

Mary won prizes for golf (a game played also by Daisy); and croquet, taken seriously at The Mount and to competition standard at Trysull, the Howard Manders' house. In June 1894, whilst mayoress, she laid the foundation stone for the Grand Theatre in Wolverhampton. Six months later, the theatre, a neo-Renaissance effort with a splendid auditorium by C.J. Phipps, was up and running, just in time for the first pantomime season.

Croquet at The Mount, after the alterations of 1891

Her grandchildren recall taking tea at The Mount in the Thirties at the lovely long refectory table when Mary, as was her custom, was sitting with her back to the door. 'In came the footman with a huge tray of Chelsea china cups, etc., but hit the door and there was an almighty crash. Mary didn't turn round but said "Just that" (she used this a lot), "I always knew it would go one day". The rest of us were in minor shock. Not to mention the poor footman when Armer, the butler, got hold of him!'

Her pre-first world war letters to her daughter, Daisy, show the resilience of Jane Austen's England, in the provinces at least, with its solaces of visiting and news. In a generous, sprawling hand, she gives breathless, conversational accounts of visits to her dressmaker, attending the Meets of hounds—describing who was out (and who was not), what they wore, and following in the motor—a stifling round of calling books, carefully written up, family gossip, formal dining and petty snobberies. These are interspersed with regular visits to London and Paris, again to visit dressmakers and milliners, the Edwardian hotels, the theatre, make social calls. Arthur describes how in April 1909 in Paris his mother and sister characteristically spent the morning (or what little remained of it after they got up) trying on dresses, and 'when the trying on had finished, they had to agree about the price, which had previously been agreed upon, but which both had forgotten'.

She was remembered in the village for her good works; anecdotally recorded by a local in the *Tettenhall History*:[14]

The family exercised a good deal of influence in the village and had an enduring reputation for deeds of charity. There is a tale of ... Lady Mander who towards the end of the nineteenth century made regular visits to her tenants to see how they were getting on. One such family living at Tettenhall Wood always aroused her pity and this invariably led to her sending her maid down with some food for them. On one occasion, however, so the story goes, the family had a boiling fowl in the stew pot when Lady Mander was seen approaching. There was a mad scramble to get the fowl out of the pot and into an out house. Lady Mander commented on the appetising smell. 'Oh, it's just a few vegetables boiling up', they said, raising the lid of the pot to show her. 'Oh dear', she said, 'No meat? Send your child up to the House and I'll find something for you'. As soon as she was out of sight there was a rush to the out house to retrieve the fowl. Alas, the dog had beaten them to it!

Mary continued an intrepid traveller into her old age. Between the wars she is recorded as taking early summer cruises to such places as West Africa, Morocco, Syria, Jordan, the West Indies and Cuba. She had a collection of over 200 fans which she had gathered fitfully on her travels, mainly in Italy, Spain and France. She lent choice examples to the Baldwins for a charity exhibition at 10 Downing Street, to which another contributor was Queen Mary.

When the Queen visited The Mount on 27 July 1939, she took a 'special interest' in these—although the prize ones had been surreptitiously removed beforehand by Gerald Mander, 'as Her Majesty had a good eye for the best when politely offered to choose one'. She was presented with an obligatory white tortoiseshell fan, bearing the name *Mary* on the shaft and, by Gerald, with an enamel needle-case from his own collection. 'When presented to her, I was impressed by her firm handshake which helped me up from my curtsey', recalls Hilary. Queen Mary had already visited as Duchess of York, and the two Marys seem to have had a formal friendship, exchanging telegrams of greetings. The Princess Royal visited to see her collection in 1945. Mary attended the Royal Wedding in 1947, aged 88.

She had her quiverful of humorous parlour tricks and house party games. She was often asked to chant nonsense jingles learnt in her youth; 'the counties of Nova Scotia' or, more remarkably, 'all the prepositions in the English language' in order, declaimed in an express, uninflected monotone, which she did without hesitation on her ninetieth birthday:

about, above, according to, across, after, against, amid, amidst, among, amongst, around, at, athwart, BATING [the archaism with emphasis], *before, besides, behind, beneath, between, betwixt, beyond, by, concerning, down, during, for, from, in, into, out of, past, regarding, respecting, round, since, through, throughout, till, to, touching, towards, under, underneath, upon, with, within, without.*

The Family at The Mount on the occasion of Mary Lady Mander's ninetieth birthday, 12 March 1949

(Front row) Emily Mander, Lady Mander, Charles Marcus Mander, Jill Ramsden, Marietta Stirling, Sir Charles Arthur Mander, Mary Lady Mander (*centre*), Gerald Mander, Daphne Mander, Philip Mander, Hilary Purslow, Nancy Mander, Margaret Cardew
(Centre row) Elizabeth Neve, Hilda Vaughan, Irene Neve, Dolores Mander, James Ramsden, Rosalie Lady Mander, Sir Geoffrey Mander, Daisy Mander, Margery Nevile, Peter Nevile, Priscilla Mander, William Purslow, Amy Stokes, Mary Kettle
(Back row) Mary Vaughan, Edmund Vaughan, Margaret Neve, John Neve, Sir Louis Knuthsen, Mary Lena and Patrick Hickman, Cecily Phillips, Mary Amphlett, Mrs Amphlett, Reginald and Bridget Bailey, Violet Hargreaves

Mary with Arthur and Gerald, c. 1890

[1] He was born 10 April 1830, the son of Nicholas Paint (m. 17 Dec. 1814 Marie Le Mes[s]urier, both born at St Peter's Port, Guernsey); he married on 17 March 1856 in Halifax Christiana St Clair McVean (b. 1824 Islay [?or Colonsay], Argyllshire; d. ca 1890), by whom he had five children: Louisa (b. ca 1852), Flora St Clair (b. ca 1857; m. Theodore Mander of Wightwick; d. 1905), Mary LeMesurier (b. 1859; m. Charles Tertius Mander of The Mount), Arthur (b. ca 1864; d. 1877) and Laura G. (b. ca 1866). He married secondly Ella Maria Cowdray of New York (b. 1868; d. 1930), and died in Halifax on 29 September 1921, having by her had further issue.
(For Henry Paint, see *Canadian parliamentary Companion, 1883*, 1885; *Census of Canada*, Halifax City, 1871, 1881; obituary of Henry Paint in *Halifax Mail*, 30 September 1921, p. 6, and John Sarre and Lorena Forbrigger, 'Some Guernsey Connections with Cape Breton Island', *Nova Scotia Historical Review*, vol. xiv, no. 1 (1994), 68-78. I am grateful to them and to Rosemary V. Barbour and Garry Shutlak of Nova Scotia Archives for supplying photocopies and transcripts of archive material and references.)

[2] The name of 'Guillaume de Guernezé' is recorded in a St Malo roll of 1535, accompanying Jacques Cartier on his second great voyage of exploration to Canada (May 1535-July 1536).

[3] John T. Mellish, *History of Methodism in Charlottetown, P.E.I.*

[4] Henry's mother was Marie Le Messurier (b. Guernsey 1786; d. Canada 1864). The Le Mesuriers, demonstrating a line of unbroken descent from Michel Le Mesurier born about 1375 in St Pierre du Bois, are another old Guernsey family, who intermarried several times with the Paints over the generations. Marie's father was James Le Messurier (1743-93) of La Madelaine du Bois who m. 1 Feb 1779 another Marie Paint.

Sir Geoffrey Le Mesurier Mander tried in 1946 to buy the Le Mesurier ancestral property at La Madelaine. 'As this did not come off, he turned his attention to the Paint ancestral property at Les Fontaines, also at St Peter's, and nearly got his wish' (letter of T.F. Priaulx to C.J. Wallis, 11 Jan 1971). The genealogy was researched by Gerald Mander with T.F.P.

[5] Peter (or Patrick) McVean was born in Perthshire in 1738 and settled in Prince Edward Island at the end of the 18th century with his third wife, where he died in 1818. Many of the Prince Edward Island McVeans stem from him. He was born c. 1738 at Easter Drumcharry; baptised April 1762 Fortingall in Perthshire, ten miles northwest of Glen Lochy. He married (1) 24 Feb 1759 in Fortingall, Janet Stewart (born Milntown, Kaltney; baptised April 1762 Fortingall); married (2) 7 December 1769 in Drumhaig, Catherine (or Christian) Robertson (born Ovar Blarish, Perthshire); married (3) 23 June 1792 in Tonguil, Dull, Girsel (Grace or Isobella) Walker (born Tonguil; settled in Bothwell, Prince Edward Island, where she died [buried Kingsboro in the East Point Baptist Church Cemetery]). Peter had by his first wife (with other issue) a son, Donald McVean, baptized Fortingall, Perthshire, 4 October 1774.

The McVean family, 'a sept of the clan McNab', were settled in Glen Lochay, Breadalbane, Perthshire, where we find Donald McVean, son of Donald, at a croft named Batavernie, c. 1550. Many of his descendants in the region were forced out with the beginning of the Clearances in the late 18th century. John McVean (1768-1867), a deacon, wrote an account of the family up to his times. (Other McVeans came from Kilmartin, Argyll, Lochgilphead and Glasgow.) Christiana is a family name. (See David McVean, 'History of the McVean Family', Manuscripts and Special Collections Department, New York State Library.)

[6] Charlotte, dau. of William Dockendorff of P.E.I. married there in 1841 Rev. John Shaw of Colonsay (1796-1879), who left for Pictou, Nova Scotia, in 1815.

[7] Jacob Dockendorf[f] was born about 1732 in Bad Kreuznach-Winzenheim, on the Lower Nahe in the Rhineland, and was baptized there 1 Feb 1732/33. He died 12 Mar 1812 in Bristol (buried Bremen; will proved 13 Aug 1816), near Lincoln, Maine. (He was dubiously forced to leave home because he would neither speak to nor of his father's second wife by

her noble title, but insisted on calling her 'Nancy'.) He is recorded as a 'butcher' sailing by the ship *Elizabeth* from Rotterdam to Maine in June 1753, aged 20, arriving St George's River, Maine, in October (see Brigitte Burkett, *Emigrants from Baden and Württemberg in the Eighteenth Century*). 'He was taken prisoner by the Indians, carried off and left by them in a dying condition; but after they were gone, he crawled on his hands and knees seven miles to a place of safety, and was rescued after much suffering.' He acquired a large tract of land in Bristol, later owned by Thomas Johnston. His daughter, Isabella (b. 1765), settled in Prince Edward Island about 1790 with her husband, John Peter Cramer (from Darmstadt), two daughters, and her brother William, a member of the Legislative Assembly (who m. and had 9 children, and died there 24 June 1839). Many early P.E.I. settlers from the U.S.A. were Empire loyalists.

[8] John Salusbury records anchoring 19 April 1750 off 'cape Porcupique—Port Epicque ... and between the Pisquid River and Petit Riviers is the Cape Feundu call'd by the inhabitants where there is Copper—and a little island near shore call'd paint Island'. (Ronald Rampey, ed., *Expeditions of Honour: The Journal of John Salusbury in Halifax, Nova Scotia, 1749-53*, Newark, 1982, p. 87.) The editor suggests the island is probably that called today 'Partridge Island'.

[9] He is buried at the Pioneer Cemetery, Embrée Island, outside Port Hawkesbury: 'Nicholas D. Paint, born in Guernsey 1790, died of cholera at Philadelphia, U.S. 1832, A merchant in foreign trade & shipping. Eliza Paint, youngest daughter of Nicholas, d. 1864, 39 yrs. John Paint, b. Guernsey 1822—d. 1832, 10 yrs., 2nd son of Nicholas, died a few days before his father of cholera at Philadelphia.' (Transcribed 1998, Nancy MacDonnell.)

[10] See the Cartaret Priaulx papers, Priaulx Library, Guernsey, for the correspondence.

[11] The name, contrary to what is often claimed, has nothing to do with paint. It is said to be Norman French, the family tracing their descent from one William Paen, apparently granted lands in Guernsey by William the Conqueror; they are recorded as 'prominent in the time of Edward III'. The name was 'subsequently anglicised to 'Pain', the 't' being added in the seventeenth century'. The form 'Le Pent' also occurs on Guernsey (1742). Sir John Gaspard Le Marchant, Governor of Nova Scotia in 1852, was a connection. An account of the Paint family, detailing the contribution to trade, shipping, religion and education of 'one of Port Hawkesbury's most famous families', is given in J. L. MacDougall, *History of Inverness County, Nova Scotia* (Truro, 1922; April 1923), pp. 135-8. See also: Sarre and Forbrigger, 'Some Guernsey Connections with Cape Breton Island', op. cit.; J.L. Embrée, *Boats Built at Ship Harbour, Port Hawkesbury, by the Embrée family and others 1823-1948*, 1987; *Methodist Church Records*; *Belcher's Farmers' Almanac*, 1874; *Annual Report for the Town of Port Hawkesbury (incorporated 1889)*, 1954; and L. Forbrigger (ed.), *Port Hawkesbury, Nova Scotia: A Glimpse of the Past*, Sydney, 1988.

[12] Henry writes: 'He was second in command at the battle of Aboukir. He was a native of Guernsey. He died in 1835. He is buried in the Catal Parish. I stood on his grave in 1842 when a boy at school.'

[13] T.F. Priaulx, 'Guernsey at Cape Breton', *Review of the Guernsey Historical Society*, vol. xxxi, no. 2, (Summer 1975), 50. For Guernsey connections with Cape Breton, see generally John Sarre and Lorena Forbrigger, 'Some Guernsey Connections with Cape Breton Island', op. cit.; Marion Turk, *The Quiet Adventurers in Canada*, Detroit, 1979; and Gregory Stevens-Cox, *Canadian Connections*, Royal Bank of Canada, 1990.

[14] G. Hancock, *A Tettenhall History*, 1991, pp. 55-6.

14

AMY AND THE IRISH CAUSE

1851-1919

Amy Matilda Mander, elder sister of CTM, always known as 'Miss Mander' ('Aunt Bee' in the family), is one female of the talented mid-Victorian generation who emerges as a personality. Born on 9 February 1851, she was well educated, intellectual—in family terms a 'bluestocking', translating dull books assiduously from the German—and a confirmed spinster.[1] She was independent, a keen traveller, progressive. She lived at a time when a growing number of educated middle class women, excluded from universities and the professions, was aspiring to worthy occupations outside the domestic sphere.

The outlet she found for her immense energy was the Irish Cause. She was a suffragist liberal in politics and became one of the most committed members of an inner circle of English women activists on behalf of the Irish nationalists, 'as faithful an ally as the cause can have', wrote Sophie O'Brien, the wife of one of their leading figures.[2] She was part of a sorority of gentlewomen whose mission was to relieve by practical means the plight of the Irish poor towards the end of the last century, also to support their political leaders in adversity. As part of this sorority, she often found herself a bystander on the edge of historic events.

She took up liberal causes with enthusiasm early in life, particularly locally in education, where she used her influence as a member of the School Board in Wolverhampton. On 11 February 1882, when she was 30, the local paper published a few lines of doggerel referring to her good works, which had already made a mark on the community:

A lady this, who's added much to fame,
To her sterling virtues and her honoured name

Amy became passionate about the Irish Question. She had been taken to Ireland as a child to visit her Weaver aunt, married to the Rev. George Shaw of Portrush, co. Derry.[3] She was connected by marriage somehow to the Healy brothers of Bantry, the nationalist leaders, described as her 'nephews' in contemporary accounts. Timothy Michael Healy (1855-1931), Charles Stewart Parnell's (1846-91) assistant, was to become first Governor General of the Irish Free State.[4] His talented younger brother, Maurice Healy (1859-1923), a solicitor, was Amy's close friend and correspondent throughout her life. Timothy Healy married Erina, the daughter of T.D. Sullivan,[5] of another noted nationalist family from Bantry. Through these circles she met the rising young Parnellites early in life.

She befriended the nationalist leaders in Parliament, like John Dillon,[6] William O'Brien,[7] Michael Davitt[8] and Alfred Webb,[9] who all write to her from the House of Commons and their various prisons and places of refuge. Her numerous correspondents also included John Morley, the statesman, biographer and chief secretary for Ireland,[10] Timothy Harrington[11] and Charles Conybeare.[12] She was on terms of particular intimacy with the women of the movement, like Mary Davitt and Anne Deane, as well as Sophie O'Brien, with whom she shared ideals and aspirations through times of unprecedented historic struggle. Their mission combined the personal and the political, the practical and the ideal. Above all, Amy was active as an organiser and campaigner of ability on behalf of the various charities and fund-raising initiatives for the relief of the distressed people of Ireland, lecturing, travelling, pamphleteering, lobbying, wherever an audience would listen, until she wore herself out to exhaustion.

The background is of interest. The Irish Question loomed the most intractable in British politics after the 1880 election of a strong group of more than 60 nationalists, including many homerulers, under the leadership of Charles Stewart Parnell. This developed from irritation to crisis when, after the fall of Gladstone on the defeat of his first Home Rule Bill of 1885, they controlled the balance between the parties in Parliament and were in a position to hold the Empire to ransom.

Dillon was the most prominent of Parnell's followers in the 1880s and an engaging personality; though an advocate of physical force at this time, he had never joined the more extreme Fenian agitators. Like Parnell, he saw hope for an effective constitutional movement through vigorous support of the Land League—which sought fixed tenure, fair rents and the free sale of Irish land—in an attempt to secure Home Rule by legitimate parliamentary means.

O'Brien started working as a journalist from 1869, achieving prominence when in 1881 Parnell appointed him editor of the newspaper, *United Ireland.* In 1886 he and Dillon marked out an independent challenge when they stirred things up as advocates of political-agrarian agitation by jointly promulgating, in defiance of Parnell, their famous 'Plan of Campaign' for land reform; under this tenants were encouraged to withhold their rents from absentee landlords and instead pay what they considered 'fair' rents to trustees of a common fund for mutual defence and support in case of eviction.

In 1887 under A.J. Balfour, the new and uncompromising Tory chief secretary (1887-91), the government passed a new Coercion Act in order to suppress the movement: its harsh terms ensured that political prisoners were to be treated as ordinary criminals. It was soon strictly enforced against both Dillon and O'Brien.

In April 1887 Amy is trying to canvas support for John Dillon, who was about to be imprisoned for his role in the Plan of Campaign, by gathering distinguished women to sign a petition. She wrote to the veteran activist, Josephine Elizabeth Butler (1828-1906), a kindred spirit as another liberal, suffragist and social reformer of the elder generation, agitator (like Gladstone) for 'fallen women' and higher education for women (and author of a life of Catherine of Siena). Josephine Butler writes back on 17 April suggesting names who could sign the 'address': Mrs Vanderbil[t], staying at the Hotel du Louvre in Paris, Miss Chapman, secretary of the Women's Liberal Federation, and Mrs Kitchin ('but her father and mother are so terribly opposed'), amongst others. Dillon's health was not robust, and she writes expressing concern for saving 'dear Mr Dillon from the misery of imprisonment. What a vile thing it seems that these men should be deprived of books and writing materials and treated as common felons.'

By May, Amy had secured the support of a dozen influential English women, including Lady Anne Blunt,[13] Miss Jane Cobden,[14] Countess Tolstoi, Mrs Rowntree and Miss Chapman, all signing her presentation on Dillon's trial in co. Louth. Amy drafted the address in token of Dillon's 'self-sacrificing devotion to his Country and heroic labours in the Irish cause', asking that 'God may give him the happiness of seeing the speedy establishment of a Parliament in College Green and the regeneration of the Irish People'.

After a visit to Canada, O'Brien was imprisoned. On 9 September 1887, Dillon was prosecuted after addressing a huge crowd at Mitchelstown where the police had been driven back and fired on the crowd, killing three people. The situation was only saved by the courage and calm of Dillon himself. Amy stood in the witness box at the trial and appeals such as hers had some effect on the public and the authorities in London. Patrick Callinagh wrote in October 1887: 'You, an amiable charitable educated Lady, came over to our shores and you stood up in the witness box in Mitchelstown and defended our country'. John Morley writes to her on 22 April the following year: 'I entirely concur with your view of the scandal of the Mitchelstown case'. T. Harrington writes: 'Gladstone's speech which I have just read, is a great vindication of our position and will put fresh heart into the people who are carrying on the struggle here.' Gladstone's was so horrorstruck he used the election cry 'Remember Mitchelstown!' and compared the event to Peterloo.

At the end of 1887 Amy is again writing to a number of liberal authorities to whip up support for the Irish cause. Elizabeth Butler writes back to her on 19 December:

> I follow your active life with deep sympathy, and eagerly read every report concerning the action of women in the right direction. That split in the women's suffrage movement was inevitable, I think. Vital principles, like this of justice to Ireland, must divide women as well as men.

Elizabeth records a moving scene recalling the chorus of prisoners in Beethoven's *Fidelio*:

> My sister, Madame Meuricoffe, of Naples, has been helping to prepare the Villa Rocca for Mr Gladstone. She and her husband, the Chevalier Meuricoffe, have a great affection for him. They witnessed that most touching sight of the release of the political prisoners from the dungeons of St Elmo. Some were quite blind—others found not one person who knew them, after so many years of living death.
>
> I am grieved to hear that dear Mr Dillon is still so much out of health. I hope his voyage may restore him.

Peter Murphy, a parish priest in County Clare, writes to her on 27 December 1887:

My dear Miss Mander,
Thank you most sincerely for your kind remembrance of myself and my poor people at this holy season. I am sure we can never return you sufficient thanks for all you have done for us and for your determined resolve to do all you can for our unhappy, persecuted country in this hour of her sore and bitter affliction.

Were it not that providence has raised up so many and such true friends for us in England who like yourself sympathise in our sorrows I know not how we could have patience to suffer so silently and bravely as we do.

My poor people are still as you left them unsettled and unhappy, but God is good and, I trust, that in his own appointed time He'll extend his mercy to us and bring things to a happy and peaceful issue.

Wishing you—and joined in the wish by my poor people—a bright and happy New-year and many such returning, I remain my dear Miss Mander very sincerely and gratefully,
Yours, Peter Murphy P.P.

Another of Amy's correspondents was George Ketchin,[15] a senior churchman and a noted liberal who even supported the Boers in Africa. He wrote to her on 13 January 1888:

The Deanery, Winchester

Our cause is too just and strong to take any harm from the weapons of our opponents. It is a pity that they don't see that stupidity is never helped forward by its kinsman, brutality.

I have been a Home Ruler ever since—perhaps 20 years ago—I had to lecture at Oxford on the relations of States, federations, etc. The more one studies the past and present, or forecasts the future, the stronger becomes one's assurance that we are on the right path. Indeed, I will go further, and say that nothing in my lifetime has so acted as a touchstone of political genuineness as the Irish Question. It is a question which must be dealt with on its own merits, without any cross-bewilderments from 'interests'; it is too essentially a people's question. In this it differs vastly from the old free trade agitation.

I am in high spirits as to the future of political life in England and the improvement which the new electorate will eventually bring about. Meanwhile if Lord Salisbury's Consolidation means anything, there is mischief for us in the immediate future.

But Amy could be irritating to her brother at home, the autocratic CTM, for her progressive views as a 'rad' in politics. He was not only unsympathetic to the cause of the Irish, whose leading agitators were 'outlaws' as far as he was concerned, but what angered him most was that Amy was hopelessly improvident in money matters. CTM was clearly head of the family, looking after his indigent relations, his duty to upbraid them for their extravagances when necessary. Always practical and down to earth, he could have no truck with this, and is stern with his elder sister, known to him as 'Bones', writing to her on 18 February 1888:

My dear Bones,
What can I say to you? You're hopeless. Why spend £53 on a black frock and frippery when at the time you have not money to meet your liabilities? Mary fitted herself out in black for under a fiver and I will guarantee looked just as well.

To review matters over again. I started you on my birthday in 1887 with a balance in the bank of £111 & an income of £240. In less than 13 months from that date you had spent that £350 and were in debt to the tune of £190. On Aug. 25th last you promised reformation & I gave you £140, leaving you a balance in the bank of over £50 after as *you assured me all your debts were paid*... for my part I don't see where the reformation comes in.

Now really Bones, have you the faintest notion how many shillings go to the £?... Have you the least intention of living within your income? or do you intend to spend 50%, or more, over your income? Because, if so, I am wasting money that I could readily spend to more advantage. You don't seem to appreciate that it is I (C.T.M.) who is fooling money away, through you, in agitation against *my own party. You* have spent £10 of my money buying flowers for O'Brien or some other outlaw. If you had denied yourself some new frock or other frippery, I could not well complain, but as it is I do, bitterly.

You may say I am unkind, but what am I to say, to make you see your folly & amend your ways? I must speak home truths...

Let me hear what you have to say & believe me to be

always your most affectionate brother, C.T.M.

Clearly none of this activity pleased CTM. Besides, she never mended her ways financially, as he is writing again on 15 July 1889:

My dear Amy,
... you spend £62 in 6 weeks or £350% more than your income. It is about the worst show you have made yet.

You then write me a ridiculous letter in excuse about "things calculated to last some time". I should think so indeed; you spend £4 right off for gloves, giving 8/6 a pair for "hard wearing" gloves. Lucy S... gives 2/6 for one pair which last one year or more. You buy 6 at a time, which is rank folly. Why in the name of common sense do you buy a plush mantle at £5:5:0 or spend £5:19:6 in altering an old dress, especially when plush has gone out of fashion? Why give 10/6 for Russell's Parnellite speech?—you cannot afford such follies.

It is too ridiculous talking or writing you. Possibly you don't realize that you have an available income (after paying bills) of nine shillings and one penny to last you till Jan. 1 1890?

You had better make an appointment to meet me and talk over matters on some day between Saturday next and Aug. 1, otherwise you may expect a cheque to close a/c on that day.

The only course I see open is to close your a/c at the bank and allow you £1 a week to throw about and pay the mater for your board and lodging myself. Also advertise in the papers that no one is responsible for your bills.

Let me hear from you soon.

He did not approve of the Plan of Campaign either, writing on 11 May 1889:

... I hear some nonsense from Louie [their sister, Louise] that you are going over to Ireland again on eviction business. I hope it is untrue; but if not, remember you do so at your peril.

The Irish people though did appreciate her good works. Daniel Stephens writes to her in March 1889 from his rural parish in Falcarragh:

Dear Miss Mander

I am very grateful for your most kind letter of sympathy with me and my people in our present suffering and persecution. As for the people they are—thank God—brave and true to the traditions of courage of 'dauntless Donegal'. I myself gladly undergo my share of the sufferings and sacrifice without which no victory was ever won. Let me thank you, which I do from my heart, for the practical interest which you show towards the evicted. Not content with devoting your leisure hours to working to provide clothing for them, you are besides it would seem advocating their cause with the English public. Whilst there are hearts in England such as yours—and, thank God, their number is increasing every day—there is hope for poor persecuted Ireland.

At the time of my arrest all my papers were hidden away by the people I am lodging with lest a raid should be made on them similar to that made on Father McFaddens' [?]. Not that there was anything treasonable or seditious in them but that my friends did not want my private correspondence and other matters to come under the prying eyes of the police. On this account my papers are all in confusion and I cannot just now find the figures in connection with the recent eviction cases. However when I find them I shall forward them to you.

I sent today a pamphlet written by Mr Byles of the *Bradford Observer*... You will find a lot of useful information for your lectures. One fact of great importance is omitted. It is that the landlord of the [?]Ockfurt estate could never by any possible means be induced to give a site for a national school on his whole estate and when questioned as to the motive of his refusal, he used to reply: 'If the people got educated I would not be able to keep them down'. He would not even give half an acre of ground in which to bury the remains of the dead!

The photographs of the evictions came out so badly that it was thought useless to have them copied. I am sending you one of my own as you desire and a print accompanying one of our local papers.

Again thanking you, I remain, dear Miss Mander,
Yours very faithfully,
Daniel Stephens

I haven't as yet received your parcel but it is sure to reach me safely. When I retire into private life, for six months my successor here will be Father Boyle to whom you may address any further consignment of clothing. My appeal does not however come on till April 12th. D.S.

But Father Stephens lost his appeal and was soon in prison, where he was poorly treated. In August, Charles Connybeare writes to her from Derry jail:

What might be the effect on my moral nature were I treated in the same spirit of Balfourian brutality as poor father Stephens, debarred from writing or study almost entirely, I will not undertake to say.

In September, Connybeare writes again from prison, thanking her for her offer to send food and asking her to act as messenger:

And now I want to ask you to be so kind as to post the enclosed by first post to my friend & alter ego in London. The letter is so surcharged with treason that I fear to send it to him direct... I hope that its effect may become apparent in the world in the shape of an explosion in the *Star* on or about Thursday next.

William O'Brien attended the grand opening of New Tipperary on 12 April 1890. He writes Amy a hurried note from London (where he was involved with the passage of Balfour's Land Purchase Bill) on 18 April, enclosing an inscribed copy of his new nationalist novel, *When we were Boys*, about the Fenian movement:

I must write you a line to tell you how really *delighted* I was to see your welcome handwriting again. Believe me, I do not forget how often I have seen it in hours of trouble, and how splendid a fidelity your friendship has evinced to our cause through good and ill. I do hope we may have a chance of a chat in London next week—possibly with Mr Dillon on the premises. He goes well—so well that I *do* feel free to relax the frightful strain of the last few years as you will hear—but there is a long tug before us yet.

You are responsible for the dedication—I do hope you may like the book

With all best wishes, ever your remembered, William O'Brien

The marriage of William O'Brien and Sophie Raffalovich took place on 11 June 1890 when, Sophie wrote, 'the Irish cause was at its brightest'. Amy was present among the guests, with Parnell (who made a speech), the Irish Party and English friends. A month earlier, O'Brien had written to Amy to thank her for her congratulations:

House of Commons, 12 May 1890

My dear Miss Mander

From my heart of hearts I thank you for your delicious note, which John Dillon has just handed me. I cannot possibly express to you how deeply it touched and gladdened me, and how very largely you have added to the happiness of my future wife and of myself. You are indeed a true, true friend—not content with brightening my hours of misery, but sympathising still more generously with what has really been my first glimpse of worldly happiness. May God bless and reward you with all that can make your noble life an honoured and happy one! Miss

Raffalovich will be so charmed with your most beautiful words of friendship. She and her mother will reach town tomorrow night, and will be staying at the Alexandra Hotel, Knightsbridge…

It is so, so good of you to think of sending a wedding present, though you have sent me the present both my future wife and myself value most in sending her and me your delightful messages of congratulation. What will give us most pleasure is that you should send either Browning of whatever else you think a lady would most like to Miss Raffalovich herself … rather than to me.

Believe me I will never forget your extraordinary goodness to me and to Ireland ever and always. May God always bless and brighten your life, is the earnest prayer of

your grateful friend, William O'Brien

In early 1890, O'Brien and Dillon had been attending rallies in Tipperary and Cashel for the Evicted Tenants, where they stirred up agitation and their welcome was fêted as they travelled; 'the whole of the mountains in Tipperary along the road were in a blaze with bonfires', remarks O'Brien. But in the autumn, on 18 September, when they were again touring Ireland, they were arrested on a charge of criminal conspiracy in connection with these rallies.

Sophie O'Brien and Amy were among a number of liberal women who attended the trial in Tipperary. The trial was a fiasco, of course, marked by a struggle between the crowd and the police, when the doors of the court house had been closed to the public, during which O'Brien was covered with blood from his wounded friends. Sophie, Amy, and the other ladies attending (Lady Robinson and Miss Borthwick, an artist and leader in the Gaelic revival) 'were most unpleasantly struck by the wife of the keeper, who refused to provide water'.

It seemed the authorities were trying to draw out the proceedings, to prevent Dillon and O'Brien departing to America, where they sought to rally the support of the Irish Americans for the Evicted Tenants. They were granted bail on high sureties and evaded the authorities during an adjournment, escaping in a sailing boat to France, and thence to the United States. There the fund-raising was a success, but the strain took a toll on O'Brien's health, and the news reached them that both he and Dillon had been sentenced in their absence to six months' imprisonment, again under the Coercion Act of 1887.

In November, the O'Shea divorce proceedings, in which Parnell was named as a correspondent, took Ireland by surprise. Events took an unexpected turn for the worse and the Irish Party was split on the question of Parnell's leadership. Anne Deane, Dillon's aunt—'the best, the ablest, the most thoroughly Irish woman I ever met', according to Sophie—writes to Amy on 6 December at 'the unhappy turn the affairs of our poor country have taken':

One can only pray that God will lead us safely through the dreadful crisis... a cruel situation for Mr Dillon and Mr O'Brien with the responsibility of the evicted tenants on their minds—I feel too for Mr Parnell, but the country before all. I have not had a line from Mr Dillon since the trouble began. His latest address is c/o A.D. Gill Esq, Fifth Avenue Hotel, New York.

O'Brien and Dillon realized it was useless to continue their campaign in America when their presence was needed at home in the leadership crisis, and immediately returned to France. They arrived at Boulogne in a thick fog at Christmas. O'Brien conducted protracted negotiations, trying as peacemaker to restore unity to the Party by deferring to Dillon as leader until the feeling of Catholic Ireland against Parnell had subsided. Dillon repudiated Parnell as a liability, and the Party split. Nothing came of efforts to conciliate between Parnell and his opponents, while Parnell insisted he would only retire on condition that O'Brien took over as leader. 'The Boulogne negotiations belong to Irish history', wrote Sophie O'Brien.

In the following year, 1891, there was a succession of reversals for Amy's 'dear friends' William O'Brien and John Dillon and the Cause of the nationalist movement. When the talks collapsed in February, the two leaders travelled to London to surrender themselves to the police, so that their prison sentences could commence. Sophie O'Brien relates the way events unfolded in a letter to Amy:

72 South Audley Street, Wednesday February 18[91]

Dear Amy, dear friend,
We had so often spoken about you, dear Amy, and I was so anxious to hear...

We have been at Boulogne all these weeks. It was a sad, anxious time, full of care and torment to them—but it was happy too—for me—and now it has come to an end, and they failed to make peace, and yet somehow one cannot bear to think that all the trouble they took was vain and some good may come yet. But the present is dark and sad and perhaps they will be happier in jail than those who are in the midst of the struggle.

As you will see, they were arrested on landing. They were well treated, Mrs Deane and I were allowed to come in the same train, and what is a great comfort they are not going on to night—the journey tomorrow will be long enough. They are going on to Calomel and then, who knows?

However, they are both well and strong, thank God, better in health than they have been for years, and that makes one hope they will get through the ordeal. The stay in Boulogne was very beneficial, as in spite of anxiety and sorrow, they had the benefit of good air and rest.

Dear Amy, what a hard, noble work you are doing! You are a true friend, and so *they* both said.

Let me hear from you again. And as soon as I have news of them, I will let you know...

Willie often said he knew with what sympathy you were watching what was going on, and your letter was a great pleasure to him.

Things are very sad now, and the struggle is going to break out afresh, but somehow one cannot help hoping that the interval of truce—or half truce—will have done something to soothe the bitterness.

Men of the two parties crowded in the room in Scotland Yard, where the criminals [were] received. Did I tell you?, I was allowed in too and we three had our dinner together—and it was so sad to think of those old friends being divided, and seeing them all, one felt they were such a splendid party. However, time is a great healer. We must not lose heart, dear Amy.

You are doing real good work and getting real though terribly sad experience and you will know how to make good use of it.

Mrs Deane sends her love to you and best regards from them. In the train from Folkestone Willie reminded me to write to you, dear, and so I do, the very first thing after leaving him.

your friend, Sophie O'Brien

...Whatever happens we must keep friends with all sides, don't you think so?

In March 1891, Dillon and O'Brien were summoned as witnesses to the trial of Harrison and the Tipperary prisoners in Cork. Anne Deane writes to Amy of arrangements for the trial from Ballaghadereen, Roscommon, on 20 March:

Mrs O'Brien ... is to stay with Mrs Healy during the trial. I am not going, so I shall not see Mr Dillon until the first three months are ended. I see by the evening paper that you are to be one of the witnesses.

Amy indeed acted as witness at the trial, as she was now used to doing—where her presence, with Lady Robinson and Miss Borthwick, writes Sophie, 'had a soothing effect'. On Good Friday, she went to the Catholic church with Sophie, who commented 'our petition for prisoners was specially fervent'. Amy writes on Easter Sunday from Cork describing her role as mediator at the 'dramatic' events which culminated in a fire in the court room during the trial:

My dear Friend,
This had been a very exciting, eventful and exhausting week...

I found 'Sophie' [here at 8.15 on Tuesday] in very good spirits.

My role has been to be friendly with both sides and to put suitable remarks whenever I could. Of course I think P. [?Parnell] is impossible, but I can't [take] violent sides in Ireland, or indeed anywhere. I am trying to make peace wherever and whenever I can. It is not for us women to call our brothers and comrades in the fight *names.* I think, indeed I know, that Sophie & I have made very belligerent parties *friends*, who might have remained estranged for long. I was in Court all day on Wednesday and saw the Prisoners depart under the cheers of a great crowd. I had no opportunity of speaking to Mr. D[illon] that day, tho' I had and used it of navigating a letter of yours to S. and another cheering one with interesting enclosures. On Thursday I gave him some delicious violets & he thanked me in his beautiful way for them and afterwards when the Court adjourned we had a talk across Miss Cullinane [O'Brien's sister] about *books.*

Friday was indeed a memorable day. I managed to navigate some violets c/o Col. ?Choe and a silver pen and pencil combined. Then came the fire and I was with them right through, except in the Grand Jury Room for a quarter of an hour. For 10 minutes I was standing in a dark passage by his side and we had a real little talk, though we were in considerable danger of suffocation. Then afterwards in the Vestibule whilst waiting for their departure I had another.

The scene was most dramatic. They and we escaped only *just in time* and when they came outside the building the multitude cheered enthusiastically. The streets were thronged and they received a great oration. It was one of the finest receptions I ever saw I think—bless them. You will have seen the accounts in the papers. But I am sending you a set.

On Saturday during the rest of the Judge's charge, he was sitting just in front of me, and from time to time we had great little talks. I showed him your telegram to me; also two from Mrs Rae and E. D. He was in great form—in good spirits, smiled and made fun as at Tipperary when, as you know, he was very happy. He looked ever so much better each day and really I do think you may be quite easy about him. They were *delighted* at the result of the Trial. In fact it was a great fiasco for the Government. They had excellent luncheons every day sent by Mrs Wilson who is awfully good. So they had on Saturday.

We—Mrs A.M. Sullivan,[16] Mrs M. Healy, Sophie, Lady R[obinson], Mrs Barry, Miss Borthwick and I—were especially allowed to see them depart from the Model School—at the *back*, and say goodbye.

Amy sent Sophie a note to say that the Governor of Cork jail had invited Sophie from the hotel to call on her husband before his departure for Galway, where both he and Dillon were serving their sentences of six months' imprisonment. But Sophie had already left. At least Amy was able to see the prisoners off at the station.

In June 1891 Amy writes to O'Brien in prison on their wedding anniversary; 'such a pretty message', he writes to Sophie, '[she] is a most ardent admirer of yours and a true friend'. He replies to Amy from his 'place of confinement':

I have received your beautiful flowers and still more beautiful words of congratulation on the anniversary of my wedding day. It was so like you to think of it. I suppose no wife was ever tested by so many anxieties and calamities in the first year of married life as my wife, but, thank God, there was never wife better qualified by love and courage to come through the ordeal without being apparently even conscious that she has endured suffering. She is indeed the greatest miracle of tender-hearted devotion and nobleness that ever a man was blessed with, and the best prayer I can form for myself is that I may be worthy of her.

I have news of you occasionally from the wild place you have done so much to brighten. May God reward you with the blessings that never fail to follow noble and unselfish toil for others' happiness! I enclose a little daisy. It is the nearest approach to a bouquet our prison resources will afford. Accept it, my dear Miss

Mander, in testimony of the pride and admiration with which I shall always treasure your friendship and your wonderful work for Ireland.

I hear that Mr Dillon gains in weight & was never in better form. So unlovely is the strife outside, one is little to be pitied for having prison walls around to keep out the din. Unfortunately, one's thoughts are apt to fly over prison walls.

He had sent a letter to Sophie on their wedding anniversary, also enclosing a daisy in similar words, 'the nearest approach to a bouquet that I can offer you this day'.

When Dillon and O'Brien came out after six months, they declared unconditionally for the anti-Parnellites.[17] But the condition of the people was dire, and as well as being an activist for the tenants' rights movements, Amy was always working for social justice behind the scenes. On 31 July 1891, Anne Deane writes from her house at Ballaghaderreen in Roscommon of the case of Gallagher family, evicted from their cabin on Lord Dillon's estate:

It is a cruel case of eviction... They have offered two years' rent; money subscribed at home and some earned in England, but the agents vow that they shall never get back to their home because the man took an active part in the Plan of Campaign. John [Dillon] sympathises very strongly with the poor family. The little wife was twice in prison for going back into her little cabin, while her husband was in England...

You are working hard indeed—I fear too hard—to help our poor people. This is a dreadfully poor place, but you know what Irish poverty is.

She asks Amy to send them clothing for their three girls 'and if you have any bed covering it is much needed'. On 10 September Anne Deane writes again:

your parcel of clothes for the Gallagher family has arrived, and I had the pleasure of reading your letter for poor Mrs Gallagher and giving her the postal order for 10/-... The poor woman is most grateful and indeed she well may for she sorely needed the clothing for herself and her children. She has offered her bad land and two years rent which he refuses to take. Her husband was prominent in the Plan of Campaign and they say they mean to make an example of him. They are very woeful, and it was gratifying to be the medium of sympathy and comfort to them. I have written to let John [Dillon] know how well you have provided for them, and I feel most grateful for your assistance to the poor persecuted creatures.

Fr O'Hara was a parish priest in Mayo, attempting to do his bit for the poverty in his poor parish in the West. He writes to Amy, who had sent parcels of food and clothing for the worst cases, referring to the arguments raging between Dillon, now in France, and Parnell:

Private

Parochial House, Biltemagh, co. Mayo, 18th January

I succeeded in inducing Mrs Deane to go to Paris. She is on her way. She thinks Mr Dillon will assent to nothing less than Parnell's retirement. He has always said in his letters, 'Parnell must go'.

I agree thoroughly with what your friend says about going to prison. I think one of them should go. But one of them must try to raise money for the united tenants. Tipperary has been a source of great trouble to them, and Mr O'Brien particularly feels intensely about them, as it was on his advice they first acted...

Yours sincerely, D. O'Hara

I got a small parcel of clothes from Mrs March Phillips

Fr O'Hara's describes one of the poorest parishes in Ireland at that time in his first letter to Amy on 26 December:

Your name is quite familiar to me, though I never had a letter from you before. My parish is unfortunately the most congested in the Swinford Union, which according to the *Forger* correspondent 'is the poorest inland union in Ireland'.

We have a population of 5000 in this parish—over 900 families. Most of these are all very poor, a good many of them expect work on the railway, which is expected to be commenced here soon, but there will be close on 100 families who, for one reason or another, will not be able to avail themselves of work of this description.

Mrs Home Payne—who is probably known to you—stopped with me for nine or ten days in October last. She promised, and fully expected, that she would get employment for a lot of the women of this parish, but nothing has been done in that direction yet.

...Would there be any use in expecting you to come and see for yourself the state of this district? I fear that many will be in want of food and clothing, and *almost* all in need of seed potatoes. I am sorry Ireland is not showing more gratitude than it is at present to English men and women.

Wishing you every blessing... D. O'Hara PP

Another nationalist leader whom she knew well was Michael Davitt, the militant labour agitator who was himself evicted as the child of a poor labourer during the clearances after the potato famine in 1852. His letters to her are more mellow, bemoaning in December 1891 'the injury which is done to our Cause and the character of our poor old Country by violence & rowdyism. The men who are encouraging proceedings of that kind are becoming the deadliest enemies of Ireland.' He writes to her fondly as a 'ministering angel' to 'our poor Irish people in their trials'. For Amy was active in humanitarian initiatives for the relief of the distress of the Irish people, appeals through the Evicted Tenants' Fund, The Irish Distress Fund and The Connaught Relief Fund. She was indefatigable, gathering clothes, parcels and blankets for the poor, particularly the children, and helping also in organizing political meetings and addresses, speeches (inviting John Dillon to visit Wolverhampton), campaigning for human rights, the rights of political prisoners. In the winter of 1892 John Dillon sends her lists of cases of 'exceptional hardship', such as tenants of his namesake, Lord Dillon: 'Two families evicted recently by Lord Dillon near Charleston [co. Mayo]—in one case the house was burned down & all the bedding burned.'

Amy relates an anecdote, patronizing in its sentimentality, of a friend of hers, a Mrs Cole, encountering 'a dirty, untidy, miserable Irishwoman':

The friend asks, ' How are you serving your country? You love Ireland, don't you?' 'Shure, and I do.' 'Well, do you think you are *now* an *honour* to your country? Won't English people think from your ways that perhaps there is something in what the Unionists say, that the Irish are a low, degraded set, and it's no use giving them Home Rule?' 'Ah, ma'am, d'ye think *I* could do something for the cause?' 'Of course you can! Just tidy yourself up, and keep yourself respectable. Although you are poor, you may be clean. Just think what the English Liberals, what our Prime Minister, are trying to do for Ireland.' 'What, ma'am, I will'. That woman went away, got her apron out of pawn, washed it, and having no irons or mangle, sat upon it to serve the same purpose, and generally straightened herself, and came back again to my friend in two hours with a beaming face, saying, 'Will I hurt the cause *now*, ma'am?'

This shows the intense love of country which lives in every Irish heart.

At one time she is working trying to get nurses, although 'surrounded by a fever plague', as Anne Deane writes: 'You can see how the poor law system works in this unfortunate country. I hope you are not exposing yourself to danger.' Amy appears ever thoughtful, and her charity and concern did not just extend to the indigent. Mary Davitt writes to thank her for her gift of a 'frock' on the birth of a son, Cahir, explaining why she cannot make her godmother to the child:

Bally brack, Oct. 24, 1894

Mr Davitt and myself are thankful to you for your congratulations. Yes, the little fellow will be a companion for Michael and we hope that both will grow up to love and serve their country.

Cahir was born the 15th of August and was christened the following Sunday. You could not anyhow, I am sorry to say, be his godmother owing to the difference in our religion. Those who act as godmothers and godfathers of Catholic children have to accept all the articles of Catholic belief at the Christening and undertake to bring the child up in that creed if anything should happen to the parents.

Mr Davitt says that political godmothers are a new invention, and he does not know how you could be invested with that responsibility except by making a rebellious speech over the wee thing's head at a mass meeting on some green hillside in Connaught.

Her Irish experiences were taking their inevitable toll on her health. She spent twenty years—frail, worn out and ill—in and out of clinics, and her correspondence tails off. She wrote home to CTM from the Sanatorium Quisisana in Baden-Baden on 27 February 1901:

By degrees I have found out that I nearly died on Feb. 7 from sudden heart failure. The operation was successfully performed—but my heart gave way & the Doctors & Nurses had all they could do to get me round. They used artificial respiration and pinched and rubbed me black and blue...

I made a Codicil to my will under date Feb 6 1901 ... directed to my Executors, Lord Alverstone[18] & Uncle Fred [?Weaver] & made a Disposition of my effects. It was horribly near to being carried out. Not that I minded, or mind, for myself, but I am glad my family did not have the shock.

She spent some of the war years with the Mander women helping in the war effort in Staffordshire. Daisy complains of her company over the long winter evenings: 'Aunt B. is very prosy and rather a bore, talking over people all the time: makes Mother and I so sleepy.' Maurice Healy thought otherwise, writing to her: 'I am very proud to be fighting on the side of England in a war in which she has behaved so nobly and so well'.

When she finally died on 27 July 1919, there were generous tributes from the nationalist leaders. Maurice Healy wrote of her letters in her declining years as 'a regular and unfailing source of comfort and sympathy. I think her heart was large enough to contain pity for all the sorrows of the world. In days when high ideals tottered and were sustained with difficulty, new courage sprang from every line she wrote. Her love of Ireland burned true and constant. Those who knew her in the old days still vividly remember the kindly lady who came to minister to our poor people in their time of sorrow.'

William and Sophie O'Brien sent a telegram: 'The Irish people feel they owe a deep debt of gratitude for her noble and unselfish life'. Her coffin had a breastplate inscribed with a traditional prayer for Ireland: 'May God win for ye'. But the Irish cause, with its invective and suffering, was to outlive her longer than she could have guessed.

Amy (standing center) at the Giants' Causeway, near Portrush, 1880s

[1] For Amy Mander's papers in public collections, see inter alia National Library of Ireland, Ms 24,507-24,536. For her translations, see e.g., Dr Julius Baumgärtner, *Appendicitis: when should one operate?*, T. Fisher Unwin. (The author was directing physician of the Hospital at Baden-Baden.)

[2] *Golden Memories*, 1929-30, I, p. 106. Sophie was the daughter of Herman Raffalovich of Paris, a Russian Jewish banker (who did a good deal of business with Schroders, see second volume), and married William O'Brien in June 1890.

[3] Her youngest sister, Laura Louisa, married Dr George Reginald Leeper, of Dublin, in 1881. A cousin of his, Alexander Leeper (1848-1934), was a controversialist and opponent of Home Rule who founded Trinity College at Melbourne University, Australia. (See: John Poynter, *A Life of Alexander Leeper*, 1997.)

[4] Healy helped to organize Parnell's public duties (it was said he had the only political head among his followers); he would describe Parnell as the 'uncrowned king of Ireland', the political heir of O'Connell, but he was never as close to him as he was to William O'Brien. He made a volte-face after the divorce case of 1890, capturing North Louth for the Anti-Parnellites in 1892, but he was a constant thorn in the flesh for their leaders like John Dillon, whom he accused of subservience to English liberalism. He contributed a weekly letter to *The Nation*, owned by T.D. Sullivan, who had married his father's sister. See Frank Callanan, *T.M. Healy*, Cork, 1997.

[5] He was one of the six sons of Daniel Sullivan of Dublin who all gained distinction, including Alexander Martin Sullivan (see below).

[6] John Dillon (1851-1927) was the son of a rebel and an M.P., a supporter of Parnell in the constitutional movement for reform. Imprisoned in 1881 in Kilmainan jail, he was released on grounds of ill health, for the second time just before the Phoenix Park Murders. He

formed an alliance with O'Brien and was, from 1878 to 1918, with O'Brien and Davitt, the most important figure in Irish nationalist politics. Dozens of letters from him to Amy are preserved, mostly dealing with the day-to-day business of the movement.

[7] William O'Brien (1852-1928), the Irish nationalist leader second only to Charles Stewart Parnell, was editor of *United Ireland*.

[8] Michael Davitt (1846-1906), the son of an evicted tenant farmer, was the founder of the Irish Land League in 1879, with the aim of organizing resistance to landlordism, and M.P. for co. Meath. He lost his right arm in a machinery accident; joined the Fenian Brotherhood in 1865; was imprisoned in 1870 for sending firearms to Ireland and then for his seditious speeches in 1881-2 and 1883.

[9] Alfred Webb (1834-1908) was a Quaker and early home ruler who owned a printing shop. He became an anti-Parnellite M.P. for Waterford 1890-5, and wrote *A Compendium of Irish Biography* (1877) and a number of travel sketches.

[10] John Morley, viscount Morley of Blackburn (1838-1923), statesman and man of letters, M.P. and chief secretary of state for Ireland 1886 and 1892-5. He was a Cobdenite liberal, against coercion in Ireland, famous for his biographies of Gladstone, Burke and Cobden, editor of the *Fortnightly Review*, and friend of J.S. Mill, George Eliot, George Meredith and Joseph Chamberlain.

[11] Timothy Charles Harrington (1851-1910) was editor of *Kerry Sentinel*; secretary of Parnell's Land League; imprisoned under the Coercion Acts; acted as Parnell's counsel in the Parnell Commission; largely devised the Plan of Campaign; and was three times mayor of Dublin.

[12] Charles Conybeare (b. 1853), barrister and M.P. 1885-95.

[13] Lady Anne Isabella Blunt, née (King-) Noel (1837-1917), baroness Wentworth, was daughter of the first earl of Lovelace by Hon. Augusta Byron, the poet's daughter. She was a Catholic of high principles, horsewoman, traveller, and breeder of purebred Arab horses, who wrote two Middle East travel books and died in Cairo. She married the traveller, Arabist, politician, publicist, poet, diarist and 'amorist', Wilfrid Scawen Blunt (1840-1922). He contested Kidderminster for the Liberals and was an Irish Home Ruler, as an early anti-Imperialist and campaigner on behalf of weak nations (the Sudan, Egypt, etc). He was an active supporter of the Plan of Campaign and imprisoned in Ireland in 1887 in connection with agitation on Lord Clanricarde's estate. (Both were friends of Sir Emery Walker and often visited him at his Cotswold house, Daneway.) (See Elizabeth Longford, *A Pilgrimage of Passion: The Life of Wilfed Scawen Blunt*, 1979.)

[14] Sophie Raffalovich wrote a life of John Cobden.

[15] George William Kitchin (1827-1912), successively dean of Winchester and Durham, teacher and lecturer, he was responsible for the first Clarendon Press editions of the English classics, and was also a historian and archaeologist, particularly at this period in Winchester.

[16] Frances Genevieve, only surviving daughter of John Donovan of New Orleans, married in 1861 Alexander Martin Sullivan (1830-1884). He was deeply influenced by the distress he witnessed during the great famine of 1846-7; he was a barrister, who preceded his brother as editor, then owner, of *The Nation*, which favoured constitutional agitation as the principal opponent of the Fenian movement; he was returned to Parliament as a Home Ruler for county Louth in 1874.

[17] O'Brien founded the All-For-Ireland League in 1910 after control of the United Irish League had passed into the hands of the Parnellites under John Redmond, but most of his following had joined Arthur Griffith's Sinn Féin party by 1918.

[18] Richard Everard Webster, Viscount Alverstone (1842-1915), Lord Chief Justice 1900; Attorney-General three times from 1885 in Lord Salisbury's ministry; MP for the Isle of Wight 1885-; leading counsel for the *Times* at the Parnell commission; Master of the Rolls; PC. He was famous for his immense industry and 'boisterous geniality ... which his detractors sometimes regarded as artificial'.

Wightwick: the drawing room

Wightwick: hall and corridor leading to the great parlour

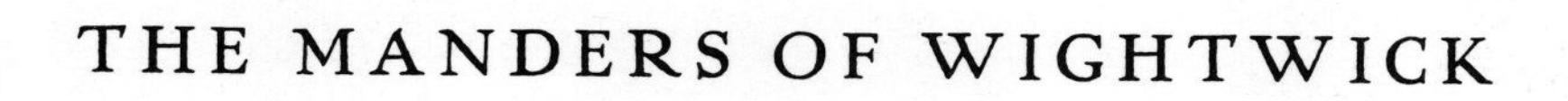

THE MANDERS OF WIGHTWICK

15

THE MANDERS OF WIGHTWICK

Samuel Small Mander
1822-1881

The Wightwick cadet branch descends from Samuel Small Mander. He was the younger brother of Charles Benjamin and co-founder with him of the Mander Brothers firm in 1845.

He was described by contemporaries as 'a person of high Christian character and attainments ... kind hearted and generous, [who] did much to assist the poor and needy' and 'took great interest in the cause of education, temperance and religion'. He settled at Glen Bank, Tettenhall, so that his side of the family were known as *Glen Bankers* to his cousins long after they moved from there. He was a strong Congregationalist, involved in the building of the Queen Street chapel in Wolverhampton. Then, at his own cost, he built a mission chapel at Horsely Fields to relieve the 'spiritual destitution of the working people in the neighbourhood'.

With a group of other leading local nonconformists, he promoted the company which built Tettenhall College, at a cost of about £23,000, designed for the education of the sons of commercial men in Free Church principles and to prepare them for University. He was a member of the School Board. He married Mary Wilkes in 1850, by whom he had three sons and four daughters. Many of his letters and papers survive at Wightwick Manor.

He had a brother-in-law who was a wine merchant. But he was a teetotaller and sternly promoted temperance principals, becoming chairman of the Good Templar's Lodge. As a temperance enthusiast, he wrote an earnest tract attacking the British government's monopoly of the opium trade: *Our Opium Trade with China* (1871). He quotes with evident opprobrium the saying of a mandarin: 'It is not the man that eats the opium, but the opium that eats the man'.

Samuel Small represented a blend of pious non-conformity, public-spirited liberalism, strict teetotalism and intellectualism which was to characterize the Wightwick branch of the family for the generations to come.

Samuel Theodore Mander
1853-1900

Theodore was the eldest of the three sons of Samuel Small Mander, 'good, stalwart and true'.[1] He, too, was given a strict Congregationalist upbringing, attending Tettenhall Proprietary School (which later became the College), studying at Dijon in France at the age of 16, when we find him contemplating becoming a minister. He writes home from Dijon, 13 September 1869: 'My desire and I think my duty is to prepare to enter Papa's business as you say, and I think I can be quite as useful in that way as if I became a minister.'

He went on to read natural sciences at London University (where nonconformity was encouraged), finally taking his B.A. at Clare College, Cambridge. In 1874 he spent a useful period researching into the organic chemistry of gums, drying oils and resins in various universities in Germany (notably under Dr Hofmann in Berlin), which was then in the forefront of the science. Then, in 1879, he joined Mander Brothers, where he could apply his knowledge practically in the industry. In the same year he married Flora St Clair Paint in Halifax, Nova Scotia (the elder sister of Mary, who we shall see was to marry his cousin, Charles Tertius, five years later).

Alfred Parsons (1847-1920), the garden designer and artist, describes him when he later came to re-order the garden at Wightwick (19 July 1899) as not the usual manufacturer 'of the self-made type' at all, but

> a University man and very pleasant. So is his wife, also is a Canadian and much easier to deal with than he is. I should think [from] his evident anxiety about money that he was very rich, & don't think you will find him an easy subject to tackle.[2]

Theodore continued the family tradition of combining sound business sense with a strong social conscience. He followed his father as a lay preacher and a deacon of the Queen Street chapel, and in the temperance movement. He became involved in many local charities and organizations. In public life he pursued interests in the arts and education and followed Charles Benjamin in his work for a local Wolverhampton School of Art, becoming 'chief moving spirit' in the campaign. Other cultural activities included acting as chairman of the School Board, a governor of the Grammar School, of Tettenhall College and of Birmingham University (where he endowed a scholarship), a member of the Royal Commission of the British Section of the Paris Exhibition and one of the founding benefactors of Mansfield College, Oxford, which was the first nonconformist college in the University. In politics he was a 'Gladstonian Liberal' (in contrast to his cousin, Charles Tertius, who was 'a staunch Conservative') and was chairman of the election committee of Sir Henry Fowler,[3] whom he described as his 'political mentor'.

Like Charles Tertius, he served on the Council (elected in 1881), was an alderman (from 1891) and magistrate, and followed CTM three years later as a successful mayor of Wolverhampton (1899-1900). He was chairman of the Art Committee (1885-1900). On 27 April 1900 he and Flora were presented to Queen Victoria at Wolverhampton's Low Level Station, during a halt while changing engines:

> Her Majesty, having previously intimated that she would receive a bouquet from the Mayoress, invited her into the carriage, and the Mayoress having presented a basket of roses, her Majesty graciously accepted them, and said, 'I thank you. You are very kind', and shook hands with the Mayoress. The Mayor was then invited into the carriage and presented to her Majesty.

In May, the Chinese ambassador, Sir Chih Chen Lofengluh, came to Wolverhampton with his retinue, including his two sons, wearing their Chinese costumes of black silk, and two of them with 'red spreading tassels on the tops of their hats'. CTM, as chairman, showed the party round the Thomas Parker factory: 'a far cry from the Celestial Empire to the smoke and stir of this district, with its ceaseless crash, rattle and roar of machinery'. They stayed the night in 'the peaceful shelter of Wightwick Manor and its rural beauties'. The Ambassador made his 'open door' speech in the Council Chamber: 'You know', said his Excellency, 'that China is now quite open to you for trade, and that you have always the open door of hospitality and instruction.' The reporter added: 'That is an announcement which elicited ... a ringing cheer.'

In July Theodore entertained the Duke and Duchess of York (later King George V and Queen Mary) at Wightwick, when they planted two trees in the grounds, visiting Wolverhampton to open the new Royal orphanage and lay the foundation stone of the building of the Free Library, with which he and Charles Tertius had been so much involved.[4]

It was to be one of his last public acts. He died seven weeks later, still in office as mayor, aged just 47. His final words to his colleagues of the Town Council, before leaving on a fishing and shooting holiday with CTM at Llangollen, were: 'I hope you will all enjoy your holidays, gentlemen'. He 'caught a severe chill' while fishing there, 'recruiting after a tiring period of official work', at the end of August. An official announcement was published on 3 September, and he was brought home 'in a critical condition' by special carriage to Wightwick on 6 September, where he underwent an operation—reputedly on his kitchen table—for an abscess of the liver. Percy Dean, the surgeon from London, met Dr Deanesley in consultation, and performed a second operation: 'It was decided, in view of the continuance of the symptoms of blood poisoning, as a last resource to search for a possible deep-seated abscess in the substance of the liver. After a most difficult and prolonged operation, Mr Dean succeeded in reaching and evacuating the abscess. Unfortunately, the patient's strength failed, and he succumbed soon after the completion of the operation.'

The Town Hall blinds were drawn as soon as the news was announced, and messages of condolence were received from 'all over the Empire', including the Lord Mayor of London. The papers printed florid descriptions of his civic funeral amid the general public sorrow for the 'departed Chief Magistrate'. As the procession of coaches and the open hearse drawn by four black horses led from Wightwick:

> The morning broke cool and dull, and Nature ... seemed to set the seal of a great peace upon the proceedings... The peaceful beauty of an autumn landscape seemed symbolical, as though trying to express the thought that all the pain, the worry and the weariness were gone, and only peace remained... Little groups of bareheaded spectators sorrowfully watched the passing of their dead friend, and all the blinds of the houses en route were drawn... The flags on all buildings were at

half mast, and the places of business were closed. All the neighbouring coigns of vantage occupied ... the footpaths being lined with a silent crowd ... the procession passed through a vast and orderly throng, whose sympathetic bearing was most marked.

Flora's tribute on his bier read:

Revered, beloved, who camest to thy goal
So early, leaving me behind.
I would the great world grew like thee,
Who grewest not alone in power,
In knowledge, but by years and hours, in reverence and charity.

The obituary notices describing 'A useful career cut short' followed over the next few days:

The deceased gentleman belonged to one of the oldest Wolverhampton families, which for several generations has held a deservedly high position in the town and commanded the respect of the inhabitants for their generous spirit and for the prominent part they have always taken in its progress and development. It may be mentioned in this connection that for the last four generations, two members of the [Mander] family have in succession taken an active part in the good government of the town...

Flora Mander, née Paint

Mr Samuel Theodore Mander, with greater opportunities for good which an advanced education gave him, and the experience he gained by extensive travels on the Continent ... entered Mander Brothers with his cousin, Alderman C.T. Mander... United in family and in business life, the two cousins have worked together ever since in further developing the high reputation which, under the management of their respective parents, the firm of Mander Brothers had already attained. By the united efforts of the later representatives of the firm, branches and connections have been established not only in every part of Great Britain and Ireland, in France, Germany, and America, but also nearly every other country in Europe.

Theodore is revealed in his diaries and letters as a man of refined tastes and sympathies. His life is well documented: scores of notebooks, photographs and press-cuttings record foreign travels, botanical expeditions in the Alps, manufacturing processes, visits to factories, jottings of lectures and sermons attended, scientific notes, informed architectural observations and judgments. These span his relatively short life, forming an exceptionally complete portrait of the activities and enthusiasms of a cultivated and progressive manufacturer in late Victorian England, and helping to explain the social background, the processes by which such houses as Wightwick were commissioned, built and lived in.[5]

Family group, c. 1898: Marjorie, Theodore, Lionel, Flora, Alan, Geoffrey

Wightwick Manor, 1887 and 1893

Theodore Mander's lasting memorial today is the House Beautiful he built. He bought the Wightwick Manor estate in 1887 and immediately set about planning and building a new house on the site. It was the beginning of an inspired project of artistic patronage which would last for six years.

As Mark Girouard writes, the Manders were part of 'a large body of cultivated upper middle-class families who read their Ruskin and Morris and expressed their artistic tastes in their houses.'

Wolverhampton was one of many lively, growing manufacturing towns where an educated middle class was beginning to take a keen interest in the arts. The young Philip Webb, William Morris's own architect, had trained there, before becoming assistant to G.E. Street in 1852. Compton Hall, a stone's throw from Wightwick, was home of Laurence Hodson, a Midlands brewer. It was decorated by William Morris & Co. and gave its name to one of the Firm's best-known wallpapers of 1896.[6] Edward Burne-Jones himself married Georgiana, companion and soulmate of Morris, and one of the three beautiful and talented daughters of the local Methodist minister, George Browne Macdonald. Her sister, Agnes, married the artist Sir Edward Poynter and she was the aunt of both Rudyard Kipling and Stanley Baldwin (another Midlander).[7]

The background is recorded in Theodore's own diaries. His notes of his attendance of an Oscar Wilde lecture in 1884 on 'The House Beautiful', one of many Wilde was giving on decorating and furnishing the aesthetic house, paraphrasing the ideals of Ruskin and Morris for a wider public, record Wilde's 'Rules in Art', with their emphasis on seeking inspiration from the past and the importance of hand craftsmanship. This is not the Wilde of the Decadence, with its delight in the perverse and the artificial, craving for new and complex sensations, with its 'analysis of the sensual and cerebral pleasures of refined and neurotic creatures',[8] but Wilde the performer, lecturing in America on *Art and the Handicraftsman*, or *House Decoration*, and asking for designs which will make modern life beautiful, with graduated colours and exotic Eastern flourishes, for the beauty which is no mere adornment, but 'a positive necessity of life if we are to live as nature intended us to do'. For the ideal of the house beautiful, in its buildings, its interior spaces and its objects, was a means of reforming architecture and society, the moral focus of family life and domestic values pursued in its rural setting, an enterprise to counteract rising industry and towns, what the architect Charles Wilson called the 'element of decay' in society.

At Wightwick, Theodore soon had a context where he could exhibit his progressive aesthetic ideals in complement to the successful business at Mander Brothers. First he put into repair the Tudor 'old manor' and then he commissioned the Liverpool architect, Edward Augustus Lyle Ould (1852-1909), as the result of a limited architectural competition, to build a new house on the site adjoining, which they called Wightwick Manor.

Edward Ould studied in York in the early 1870s and became a pupil of John Douglas (1829-1911) of Chester, the most successful of the Chester architects who had followed Thomas Mainwaring Penson (1818-64) and James Harrison. Their historicist revival of half-timbered architecture was based on the study of all the fine Tudor timbered vernacular buildings exemplified by Speke Hall and Little Moreton Hall in Cheshire and Lancashire, and Ockwells in Berkshire. Douglas had a practice producing country houses and their dependencies, including work for the Duke of Westminster (a founder of the National Trust in 1894) such as the Flemish Gateway at Eaton Hall of 1882, and churches all over the North West, into Wales and the Midlands.[9]

Ould followed this pattern and set up in practice in 1882, still working for the Duke of Westminster, and after 1886 with the older George Enoch Grayson (1834-1912) in Liverpool and Chester; mainly building villas, smaller houses, rectories. Their better known work included additions to the model Utopian village of Port Sunlight (1888-1914) on Merseyside for the philanthropic soap manufacturer, William Lever,[10] with housing, cottagy schools, a social club, an inn, and a post office and shops. They built Uffington House at Dee Hills, outside Chester, for Judge Thomas Hughes, author of *Tom Brown's Schooldays.*

Architects like George Devey and Philip Webb, and Norman Shaw and W. Eden Nesfield (acting in partnership in the 1860s), had successfully established their Old English revival by the 1870s as a pervasive orthodoxy; a mood and approach, national and cultivated, as much as a style. Edward Ould's deliberate and strict historicism offers the pun which describes his work at Wightwick: 'Ould English'. It looks back, particularly in the 1893 wing, to the Ruskinian aesthetic of the Gothic Revival, so instinctive at Wightwick: organic planning, structural truth, exemplary craftsmanship, sound building, 'fitness for purpose'. And the encyclopaedia of features is precisely what the Ruskinian language demanded: the nuanced accent, Webb's 'sign manual of instinct and imagination', Ruskin's 'architecture, dependent on the warmth of the true life—workmanship'.

Ould's approach was more eclectic. He was less interested in Ruskin's universal French gothic, than the charm of organic growth in the old Bavarian towns, say, with their 'medieval streets, the quaint simplicity, the glowing colour laid on by time'. His careful analysis of the half-timbered vernacular culminated with the publication in 1904 of the study on which he collaborated with James W. Parkinson: *Old Cottages, Farm-Houses and other Half-Timber Buildings in Shropshire, Herefordshire and Cheshire.*

Ould's half-timber vernacular is a provincial, accented variant, with the limitations, robustness and specialized knowledge implied; more scholarly, but also more felt and rooted. He was interested in the 'constructive details', using load-bearing beams, posts and trusses. This of course looks forward to Lethaby's emphasis on rational function, truth and efficiency; his insistence that even Gothic was basically an engineering solution to mechanical problems. But at Wightwick the core is self evidently brick, and the timber decoration does not accord with Arts and Crafts principles of 'truth to materials'. It is a surface treatment, visually convincing, but a structural sham, an overlay of evocative decoration, an imitation of style but not intention.

Functionally, Wightwick was not the traditional country house at the centre of an agricultural estate but, like The Mount, the country base—it is three miles from the town centre—of a manufacturer active in public affairs and municipal and social life. Other buildings on the estate he rebuilt along model village principles: the Mermaid Inn, run on temperance grounds, a village institute and reading room, the usual picturesque cottages. The press wrote in one of his obituaries:

Improvements at Wightwick. When he went there the house was surrounded by a scattered village of unhealthy and miserable cottages, but Mr Mander soon brought about a great change, a considerable sum being expended by him in practically re-modelling the whole village. The old decayed buildings were removed, and new and picturesque cottages, with pretty gardens, took their place, while even the village inn—the well-known Mermaid—was revolutionised.

He had the building, both exterior and interior, to a large extent reconstructed; attached to it a reading room and village institute; and re-opened it as a temperance public house on the lines laid down by the bishop of Chester. The sale of intoxicants was not prohibited, but limited in quantity; and here the wayfarer of visitor might obtain such other refreshments—in the shape of tea and coffee, and a well-cooked chop or steak—as they might desire.

Wightwick was built in two distinct phases. Substantially Phase I of 1887-8 was relatively modest, still the suburban villa in scale, in the Shaw-Nesfield tradition, but with exquisite craftsmanship and detailing which were further developed in a remoter key in the Phase II additions of 1893. Then the Great Parlour/Dining Room/Billiard Room wing was added to the east, as large again as the original house, and grander, richer, more delicate and lyrical, establishing Wightwick as a triumph of the aesthetic house.

The exterior is sixteenth century, a riot of carefully-crafted half timbering, jettied stories with rhythmic chimney stacks, in contorted barley-twists or capped with over-sailing courses; contrasting textures in unyielding Ruarbon brick, tile hanging of Madeley tiles, or local red sandstone with Tudor windows; a roofscape of gables with deep fretted barge boards and Perpendicular crocketed finials, or hipped roofs and dormers; a synopsis of vernacular detailing which is, at first sight at least, convincing because faithful. At worst it leads to baroque hyperbole, more mechanical than the originals, the timber theme exhausting itself in every variation; cusps in trefoils and quatrefoils, and skeletal herringbones and wishbones, ogival curves and panels, diapers, little oriels and bays, coved and jettied overhangs.

The cranked Jubilee porch (1887) of welcome proclaims homeliness and ease, carved with nocturnal owl and bat. A conceit allows the house to develop, visually and in its planning, from a pele tower kernel, with its battlements suggesting to the outside world that the house has evolved by a slow process of organic accretion from feudal times. The 1893 east wing is the apotheosis of the half-timber style, without the bright red brick; oak craftsmanship 'touched with emotion', all the timber 'cut from the solid', articulated with mouldings, corbels, splices, dowelled joints; chiselled, turned, carved, fretted—all set on a 'Straits' sandstone plinth course. It has acquired creepers and weathered to an ashen grey, confirming Ould's preference of half-timbering because 'no style of building will harmonize so quickly and so completely with its surroundings and so soon pass through the crude and brand-new period'. Pevsner describes it as 'eminently picturesque, but conventional', for this is the picturesque without frivolity, an earnest nineteenth-century taxonomy of timber styles and features, reverently executed.

If the outside is 'conventional', it is the interior which continues to delight and instruct, with its teasing accumulation of detail, its didactic show of contrasts. Janus turns a different face to the household gods. Ruskin reminds his disciples: 'Our God is a household god, as well as a heavenly one; He has an altar in every man's dwelling'. The interior is rich and more evolved, distanced from folk vernacular. The mood is later, more patrician, the context austerely late Jacobean, and everything is delightfully textured; oak emblazoned with telling blazons of colour, busy and frenetic, light playing on, penetrating, textures of wood and wool, tile, plaster and stained glass, establishing a late Victorian aestheticism of gloomy tranquillity. There are subtleties of planning which can seem to us quirky and tiresome; rooms disposed at angles to one another, so you must cross passages by what the family describe as a succession of knights' moves, with sudden shifts of view.

The Great Parlour, with its gallery and open timbers modelled on the Tudor hall and inglenook and hearth, its Ovidian plasterwork, is the focus of the house, the apotheosis of its decorative scheme. This exemplifies the Shaw-Nesfield 'Old English' of inglenooks and cosy dens, bays and screens of turned balusters, steps, internal screens and little windows in the chimney breasts, as described by the Arts and Crafts architect, John Dando Sedding, with its

> sparkling fires, radiant inglenooks, cheerful company, good fare, merry children, bright flowers, open windows and vistas of well polished furniture, mirrors, delft plates and rows of shining pewter dishes, jugs, tankards and braziers to make it seem joyous.[11]

Ould himself had praised the ideal in a photographer's house in Rothenburg

> Delightfully quaint panelling on the walls, relieved with little cunning recessed cupboards encrusted with the spreading wrought iron hinges and latches... On the shelf terminating the panelling was a rare collection of old bits of china, glass, pewter, and copperwork, and lovely old German heraldic glass had been worked up with the roundels of the leaded casements... Up in the roof was his own sanctum and studio, a little woodlined ark, the purlins of which formed shelves for further treasures. Nothing but genuine old furniture was here, and from this eyrie he looked upon the purple roofs and blue skies.[12]

Wightwick is a frame for the client's connoisseurship, here contrived by the man of taste who had 'read his Ruskin', to be 'rich of human pleasantness', in its Ruskinian 'colour, texture, ornament, delight'; suggesting a slow accumulation of possessions and interests, washed by the passing waves of humanity, a setting for the moral family life, lived on pious Christian principles, and the temple of the muses. The house here has successfully evolved in this direction, as a living, evolving museum of nineteenth-century art and architecture.

With its elaborate interiors of William Morris furnishings—tiles and lustreware pottery by William de Morgan (potter and novelist), plaster ceilings and friezes by Leonard A. Shuffrey, and stained glass and painted plaster reliefs by Charles Eamer Kempe (1837-1907)—it is often said to be the ideal of the William Morris interior, and a period piece. Neither is true, of course, in the sense that the complex of influences ranges way beyond Morris, and he never advised or came near Wightwick—here the owner was always the animating spirit and ensemblier—and the furnishings and collections have been systematically augmented since Theodore's death, with increasing quality and correctness. But the result is a happy example of what Morris described as 'the most important production of Art and the thing most to be longed for ... [The House] Beautiful.'

The retrospective creation we have forms a convincing illusion of the Morris style, which, as Rosalie Mander never tired of reminding visitors, both as a style and commercial venture was dependent on the successful manipulation and interpretation of the ideas of others. It is the integrated house beautiful, expressing the ideals of an entrepreneurial class committed to moral, social and aesthetic improvement rather than organized display. At many points Wightwick's interior scheme, with its romanticism, its surface articulation and historical references, departs from the anti-aesthetic austerity of the later Arts and Crafts. It reflects a personal and developed variant of artistic taste that related to a grander, more literary style; in sympathy, for instance, with the superadded sensualism of Swinburne and Rossetti.

This is partly because it has not stood still, of course, and Wightwick illustrates the whole gamut of late Victorian design. From the beginning much was supplied by Morris & Co., but much has been added, improved or renewed, illustrating all aspects of 'The Firm's' interests. It now contains some 400 items of Morris work; the Morris and de Morgan collections are 'perhaps among the largest in existence'.[13] Morris wallpapers include 'Pimpernel', 'Tulip and Rose', 'Peacock and Dragon', 'Bird and Vine'. There is embroidery, silk and wool textiles—including many of the woven woollens—hand-knotted carpets, and books of the Kelmscott Press. Kempe often visited the house, dressing for dinner in Elizabethan costume, and is said to be responsible for the medievalizing polychrome decoration in the Great Parlour, recalling Hardwick Hall. There are also two panels of the Seasons brought in 1937 from his own house at Lindfield, Sussex, with characteristic saffron colouring, signed with his wheatsheaf badge. Today the leading names are all here: there are light fittings and metalwork by William A.S. Benson (including candelabra designed for Holman Hunt) and also in the Great Parlour by George Jack (1855-1932), Philip Webb's pupil and then successor to his practice; a Japanese-style sideboard by E.W. Godwin, an early advocate of Eastern colour and delicacy; Morris glassware designed by T.G. Jackson; a settle by the great G.F. Bodley, painted by Kempe; and a folding bed like a cupboard, carved and painted, from Swinburne's house in Putney, bought for six guineas in 1939.

The Great Parlour

Geoffrey Le Mesurier Mander

[1] Candida Lycett Green, *Country Life: 100 Favourite Houses*, 1999. The other sons were (Benjamin) Howard, of Trysull Manor, and Martin Bertram.

[2] Walter Partridge, Parsons' partner, confirms his opinion, describing Theodore (26 July) as 'the most awful difficult man I ever tackled'. (See N. Milette, *Parsons–Partridge–Tudway, an unsuspected garden design partnership*, York, 1995.)

[3] Henry Hartley Fowler (1830-1911), first Viscount Wolverhampton, was also a nonconformist Gladstonian Liberal who opposed the introduction of politics into the municipal affairs of Wolverhampton. He was Liberal MP for the eastern division of Wolverhampton. He m. Ellen Thorneycroft and was connected by marriage to the Manders (his daughter, the novelist Ellen Thorneycroft Fowler married Alfred Felkin in 1903). (See E.H. Fowler, *The Life of Henry Hartley Fowler*, 1912.)

[4] By E.T. Hare. N. Pevsner notes it is 'a delightful little building'. STM's commemorative plaque is, appropriately enough, on the outside. Charles Tertius gave £500 to the subscription, of the total cost of about £10,000.

[5] Patricia Pegg (ed.), *A Very Private Heritage: the family papers of Samuel Theodore Mander of Wolverhampton 1853-1900*, 1996.

[6] The cabinet designed by Webb in 1861, now in the V.&A., was at Compton House. It has a front painted by Morris with scenes from the legend of St. George.

[7] See Judith Flanders, *A Circle of Sisters*, Viking, 2001

[8] Letter from Joris-Karl Huysmans to Edmond de Goncourt of 1882.

[9] Stephen Nicholas Keightley, 'Edward Ould and the late nineteenth-century picturesque movement', unpublished thesis, 1976. I am grateful to Monty Smith, former property manager of Wightwick, for making this and other material available to me.

[10] Lever was given his baronetcy at the same time as Charles Tertius.

[11] *Art and Handicraft*, 1893

[12] 'Liverpool Architectural Society: President's Inaugural Address', *The Builder*, 11 Nov. 1899, 440.

[13] Stephen Ponder, 'The Morris and de Morgan Collections at Wightwick Manor, *Journal of the William Morris Society*, vol. VIII, no. 2, Spring 1987, 1 and 7.

16

COUSIN GEOFFREY

1882-1962

When Theodore died aged just 47, much at Wightwick was left undone. But the sequel has been fortunate, for Wightwick is the creation of two generations. Theodore's heir, Geoffrey Le Mesurier (the second name after Guernsey forebears), was a man of vision and ability whose own contribution was decisive, and shows evolving attitudes at work in the interpretation of the nineteenth century.[1]

Geoffrey was the eldest of the three sons of Samuel Theodore Mander. He was educated at Summer Fields, Harrow and Trinity College, Cambridge, where he followed family tradition by reading Natural Sciences. His father died when he was still an undergraduate and his mother Flora died in 1905. Although the family spent a great deal of time with their cousins at The Mount, Geoffrey assumed family responsibilities of his father's estate early, under the guardianship of a cousin, Aldwin Soames.

He developed a precocious interest in radical politics and public life, joining the Cambridge Union and the University Liberal League, and founding a dining and debating club called 'The Dabblers'. But he was not all earnestness. Shortly after his father's death, he writes home to his mother on 25 November 1900:

> I have joined a thing called the Cambridge University Association for promoting Social Settlements. I have not the remotest idea what it's about, but I hope it's not socialism.

He married first in 1906, Florence Caverhill, a Canadian like his mother. The couple were treated 'like Royalty' by the Canadian crowds. But Geoffrey was not an easy bridegroom to organise, according to Charles Tertius, writing in September:

> Geoffrey arranged with Arthur two or three days ago to sail on the 28th, and changed from the 21st which he had originally settled. Last night he came up after dinner and arranged to go on the 21st, which is next Friday. So Arthur is in a complete muddle.

Geoffrey has had his kit bag (!) tied up at the Works with string and sealed, and his opera hat was tumbling about on the floor of the railway carriage out of his hat box. Arthur will have hard work to fix him up properly for the Wedding and if Florence does not mislay him, or he her, on their Wedding tour, I shall be surprised.

He started working for Mander Brothers in 1904, riding in on horseback from Wightwick. Like his cousin Arthur, he had joined the officers' training corps at Cambridge. After ill health in the early part of the war, he continued at Mander Brothers until he managed to get accepted by the Flying Corps in late 1917. He served in Egypt for a while towards the end of the war, while Charles Arthur returned to run things at the Works.

He soon continued in the mould of public service, with a radical slant. Stephen Ponder writes:

From an early age he had a strong sense of social responsibility and interest in public life... He was typical of a particular sort of English radical, a man of wealth and position who devoted himself to public service, supporting and proposing measures at odds with his background and private interests.[2]

Like many members of the family, he became a magistrate, in his case at the age of 24, and in due course Chairman of the Bench, serving for 50 years. By the time of the Kingswinford by-election in 1905, the press is describing him as 'a Liberal member of a distinguished local Conservative family'. He supported the Labour candidate in West Wolverhampton in the 1906 election against The Mount friend, Sir Alfred Hickman. He wrote later: 'My action caused great indignation in Conservative circles in the neighbourhood and I found myself cut in the hunting field by some of them.' His second wife Rosalie described how, like many radicals who refused to conform to the conventions of the 'County' pattern, he was looked upon askance by many families. This attitude only changed after the second world war, 'both because party bitterness in general had died out and because Geoffrey Mander's sincerity and his devotion to the causes in which he believed won respect all round': 'A tolerant "man of goodwill" himself, who never spoke or acted out of malice or spite, he was glad of this development and appreciated being invited to social functions in the neighbourhood—more perhaps than he enjoyed attending them.'

He cut his teeth as a Liberal member of the Wolverhampton Borough Council (1911-20). In 1911, CTM prominently campaigned against him in St Peter's ward for the Conservative candidate.[3] He shocked the Councillors, showing a foretaste of later interests, when he proposed a minimum wage of 23*s.* for all municipal employees. He came out in favour of his cousin Gerald's campaign to save the Old Deanery, an historic landmark in Wolverhampton attributed to Christopher Wren.

This initiative was frustrated by the onset of war and the building where Dickens is said to have stayed was demolished in 1921.

He was High Sheriff of Staffordshire in 1921. He again created a stir when he proposed a woman as his successor, Lady Joan Legge, daughter of Lord Dartmouth. The Privy Council wrote to her father to inquire whether she had the necessary property qualifications, and she was not appointed. But he did secure the selection of the first woman to serve on the grand jury, Mrs Kempthorne, the wife of the bishop of Lichfield.

He could not stand for the Liberals in the 1906 and 1910 elections as, with the fracas over his prolonged honeymoon, he was not granted leave of absence from Mander Brothers. He stood unsuccessfully as a Liberal candidate for the Midland constituencies of Cannock and Stourbridge and then Leominster in 1920. In 1929 he finally realized his early ambition by entering Parliament as Liberal MP for East Wolverhampton, a seat which had always been represented by Liberals since the Reform Bill of 1832. He held the seat until the Labour landslide of 1945.

He soon made a reputation as a parliamentarian by his skilful use of 'awkward' Parliamentary Questions, cornering the government of the day with his determined invigilation. The journalist Percy Cater recorded his memories of

> the pinkly pugnacious Mr Mander waving above the battle of question-time like the banner of some cause or another, accompanied by orchestral splurges of derisive laughter or 'Sit down'... one of the hornets or gadflies who animate the political scene, infuriating the stung and keeping the unstung in a lively state of tension. Baldwin once said, in one of those shrewd epigrams which come from him as easily as blowing the smoke from his pipe, that Mr Mander would 'tread honestly and conscientiously on every corn from China to Peru.'
>
> Mr Mander ... is not pompous. A mild and benevolent eye darts from sandy brows in a face which is conspicuously equable and good humoured. He is a good, if not a great man. He is a sort of pocket edition of noble indignation. See him pouncing up to ask a question. There you see fire, purpose, an inextinguishable soul.
>
> No good a Baldwin bobbing up and answering Mr Mander briefly and completely, 'No, sir,' and rousing shocking laughter. No good a Chamberlain using the iron hand from Birmingham. Sharp as a game-cock and as perky, Mr Mander dashes in for some more of the fight.

His special interests in Parliament were industrial relations, on which he spoke with authority as a manufacturer, and foreign affairs. Geoffrey became the Liberal expert on international relations, peace and disarmament, between the wars and the most ardent defender of the League of Nations system of collective security; 'the most persistent speaker and questioner on foreign affairs in the 1930s and altogether a zealot for the League'.[4]

He was one of the first to foresee the consequences of not taking a firm stand against the Japanese invasion of Manchuria in 1931. Into a House of Commons debate devoted to currency, commerce, industry and tariffs, typically he intruded Manchuria and put forward the League position:

> It is a test question. We have to decide whether war is to be permitted... We have the whole of the League plus America on the one side and Japan on the other... We have to take a bold and courageous view and, without using any physical force—that will not be necessary—mobilise all the different methods of economic, financial and moral pressure which are available to force Japan to realise that war is not going to be permitted to break out again... There is no doubt that, if we fail in this issue, we are abandoning all the hope that arose out of the war, and the sacrifice of a million Englishmen, to say nothing of nine million others, who gave their lives for a great ideal will very largely have been in vain.'

As war again threatened in the Thirties, he was one of the first to speak out against the Dictators. He tabled the International Economic Sanctions (Enabling) Bill of 17 May 1933, which made him 'one of the first to call attention to the German danger publicly in Parliament and at the same time make definite proposals for dealing with it'; supporters included Sir Austen Chamberlain whose 'death in 1937 was a heavy blow to peace'. The Peace Bill of 23 May 1935 (and subsequently) incorporated machinery embodied in the Covenant of the League of Nations for the settlement of international disputes, and was supported by Harold Macmillan, P. Noel-Baker, Sir Richard Acland and Lovat Fraser, inter alia.

He became a vehement, articulate critic of Neville Chamberlain's policy of Appeasement, and his 'inability to see what was going on in the world'. He was an ally of Churchill, Eden and Sinclair, whose polemical jabs were a wake-up call against a deep-rooted national will to self-deception. He said that it would remain 'one of the regrets of my life that I did not make some sort of speech ... when Mr Chamberlain announced his intention of flying to Munich... If the Debate had been kept up, the spell would have been broken... Others would have followed and the dangers inherent in what was happening would have been exposed.'[5]

His apology was set forth in his book, *We were* not *all Wrong* (1938), arguing that many people and parties foresaw the disaster to which errors of policy in dealing with 'the Nazi menace' would inevitably lead:

> Municheers should never again be allowed to control our destinies. It is too ghastly to think of the same unimaginative, isolationist, naïve, complacent attitude, however well meant, being adopted after the war. Absolute national sovereignty has outlived its usefulness in the world in which we now live, just as has the Divine Right of Kings internally. Old loyalties, deep-rooted, historic and admirable, remain... It is our responsibility as it is in our power in the great adventure we must lead: England cannot afford to be little, she must be what she is—or nothing.

A generation later, his son, John described the origins of Appeasement. Ironically, he wrote, in its intellectual perspective it was largely the creation of liberals of nonconformist background like his father:

Evidently ... the roots of Appeasement lie deep: they lie in the English penchant for wishful thinking, they lie in the English easy-goingness and tolerance, they lie in that insularity which for the greatest part of our history has been our greatest boon, but which, over the past century has proved, arguably, our greatest curse.[6]

When Geoffrey spoke up in the House of Commons in support of sanctions against Italy after the invasion of Abyssinia, Mussolini fired off a personal diatribe against him in his paper, the *Popolo d'Italia*. In 1938, in a climate of international tension, *il duce* took reprisals against the Milan branch of 'Fratelli Mander' and asked customers to boycott their goods.

He was far sighted in many of his peace campaigns. He was one of a handful of MPs who inveighed against Hitler's territorial ambitions in the Ukraine in 1935. As war broke out in 1939, he pleaded the Jewish cause, telling Parliament in July that Government immigration policy was leaving Jews with no escape from Germany 'other than by illegal immigration into Palestine'. In April 1941, he wrote in the *Jewish Standard*: 'The cause of the Jews throughout the world is the cause for which Great Britain and her allies are fighting'.

During the war, when, 'to sounds more strident than words', the Liberals were asked to join the government coalition under Churchill, Geoffrey became Parliamentary Private Secretary (1942-5) to their leader, Sir Archibald Sinclair (later Lord Thurso), the Minister for Air.[7] Mander Brothers' Heath Town works was marked with a red ring on a Luftwaffe plan, found after the war, as '*Chemikalien*', indicated as a strategic target for bombing. He rescued various bomb-damaged fragments of the House of Commons from the Blitz, installing two stone crowns from the pinnacles of Big Ben as ornaments about the garden at Wightwick. He kept the archives of the League of Nations Union when they were forced by financial difficulties to move to smaller premises in the early 1940s.

Wolverhampton East was one of the last urban constituencies that the Liberals managed to hold against both Labour and Conservative opposition up to 1945. But he lost his seat in the Labour landslide of that General Election and was knighted in the same year (K.B.). His was a great loss to Parliament. Thurso regretted the 'massacre' of so many 'able, experienced and popular' candidates as he.[8] In politics he was above all an oppositionist, with a tendency to pose as the Joycean 'Meandertale man'. There was rumour for a time of his being given a peerage, and the Press proposed he be gazetted with the equivocal title 'Lord Meander', in commemoration of his tireless crusades, tiresome, pertinacious questions, seamless diatribes and string of private member's bills in the House.[9] Apparently, there was some doubt, before the age of life peerages, that his heir, Mervyn, who had a dishevelled appearance and a stutter, would have the gravitas to succeed him in the Lords.

In 1948 he at last joined the Labour Party, arguing that it had become the logical successor of the liberal tradition in his pamphlet *To Liberals*, written for the Labour Party in 1950. In due course he became a Labour member of the County Council. To many members of a family whose traditions stretched to radical Whiggery, this was beyond the pale.

He had widespread contacts among the smiling public men and causes of his time and his letters to his circle of correspondents, from John Maynard Keynes to David Low, the political cartoonist, crop up in archives at the great libraries of the Anglo-Saxon world.

Lord Longford (then Frank Pakenham) wrote in his *Times* obituary that he was an 'issue man':

> There was never a more selfless politician... Perhaps he should not be thought of as a politician at all, for all his love of the House of Commons and the political life. He was supremely a man of causes. Abyssinia, Czechoslovakia, anti-Fascism, Collective Security—he preached them indefatigably and inflexibly, though with unfailing good humour, and what he preached he practised.
>
> He was the most modest of men and would have disclaimed the slightest comparison with Lord Cecil; yet even Lord Cecil did not embody more completely the idealism of the League of Nations and all it stood for. His horror of the whole policy of appeasement culminating in Munich led him to harry the Government with an endless stream of questions in the House of Commons, to the irritation of his opponents and the admiration of his friends.
>
> In all the developments leading up to the establishment of the United Nations and throughout the years that followed, his staunchness and energy in the struggle for peace never flagged. It was the greatest of pities that he was without a seat in either House during the post-war years. But whether in his own Midlands or in the national and international politics he continued to find ways of rendering service that counted.

Wightwick: postcard from Geoffrey, 1932

Geoffrey and Wightwick

Geoffrey's contributions to Wightwick have outlasted his politics, and were decisive in creating the ensemble we see today; improving and deepening the collections, but also the garden. One of his first acts was in 1910, when, still in his twenties, he was already commissioning Thomas Mawson to design the garden terrace on the south side of the house. The earlier part of the garden had been designed by Alfred Parsons in 1899. Parsons found the garden at that time uninspiring, describing the house to his partner, Charles Tudway, as 'a very elaborate modern oak timbered house, the best of its kind that I have seen—large rambling grounds with no coherence & no leading ideas, & the immediate surrounding of the house about as bad as it could be.'[10]

But the main impetus was to come after his second marriage in 1930 to Rosalie Glynn Grylls (1905-1988).[11] She was an early female graduate of Oxford; elegant and gifted. Elizabeth Longford was one of the last to remember this exceptional 'Cornish' girl as at Lady Margaret Hall reading Modern Greats, 'brown eyed, dark haired, with teeth really like pearls ... who went on from strength to strength'. She described her as amusing and amused, full of anecdotes, a vivacious speaker, quick thinking and always exquisitely dressed; she was also 'the last of the militant atheists'. Her husband, Frank, who took schools on the desk beside her, was taken by 'the exceptionally pretty young girl whose arrival was always heralded by a the tap of elegant shoes'.

Like Geoffrey, Rosalie also entered politics, as a prospective Liberal candidate for Reading, when the Party was enjoying a revival. She became secretary to the Liberal MP, Edgar Granville. But before the time came for her to face the electors, she married Geoffrey. She was eyed with suspicion as a bluestocking in the wider family. She soon became known to Geoffrey's relations, who tended to pious disapproval of divorce and remained wary of radical politics, as 'The Secretary'.

Rosalie never lost her interest in progressive politics. But she went on to pursue her literary interests as a highly-regarded biographer and scholar, particularly of the Shelley/Godwin circle and the 'Pre-Raphaeladies'. With her knowledge and encouragement, Geoffrey began in the 1930s to develop and extend the collections at Wightwick and they became pioneers and authorities in the overdue re-assessment of Victorian art. Norman Jewson, architect of Owlpen's revival and redemption, commends Rosalie's book on Rossetti in a letter to Nina Griggs in 1966, 'to my mind, a really good and sympathetic biography'. They were among the first collectors to take a serious interest in the art and literary manuscripts associated with this late Romantic flowering, coming to know the survivors and successors, the heirs and assigns, of the circle of artists, designers and writers themselves. Many of them now visited Wightwick, like May Morris in 1938, or contributed to the collection, like Helen Rossetti Angeli, daughter of W.M. Rossetti and Lucy Maddox Brown, enriching its associations.

She had an infections enthusiasm for her period and all it represented at Wightwick. She was an assiduous founder of the Byron Society. The diarist Jim Lees-Milne describes being seized by her as a 'predator' at a presentation of an edition of Shelley to the Queen Mother in 1981: 'wearing a horrible pink knitted dress and grey felt hat covered with stains and dust. She transfixes one like a butterfly on a board'. Then a few months later: 'Liked Rosalie and take back disagreeable things I may have said about her pretensions. She is good in her own house, relaxed. [Flat in Buckingham Gate] bright and agreeable.'[12]

Again, Jim Lees-Milne describes the flavour of a gathering of Pre-Raphaelite survivors in her house in 1948:

> To tea with Lady Mander. A Pre-Raphaelite tea party: Sir Sydney Cockerell with whom I had a long talk about Ruskin whom he knew intimately; Miss Lushington about Rossetti (she has his willow pattern dinner service to sell); Mrs Angeli, William Rossetti's daughter; and Mrs Joseph (Holman Hunt's daughter). It was fun.[13]

This Pre-Raphaelite and studiously biographical emphasis which emerged at Wightwick was appropriate in its late Romantic synergy of the pictorial and the literary, exemplified by Rossettism. Acquisition was informed by such literary predilections, where associations with the Victorian titans of the arts are reinforced by inscriptions from poems painted about the rooms. Geoffrey's favourite poet was Robert Browning:

Hold on, hope hard in the subtle thing that's spirit:
Though cloistered fast, soar free.

Here, within the fitting context of Arts and Crafts interiors and Ould's architectural setting, of which so much of quality was still in situ, Geoffrey and Rosalie created a many-layered ensemble which was seen as outstanding in its richness and completeness, acting out the associative memory.

The Pre-Raphaelite paintings and drawings were a new addition to the house. The three material founder-members (of the seven) of the Brotherhood in 1848 are represented: Dante Gabriel Rossetti, William Holman Hunt and John Everett Millais. Then there is an impressive array of works by artists in their circle: Frederick, Lord Leighton, G.F. Watts (his portraits of Jane, the sister of Thomas Hughes of *Tom Brown's Schooldays*, and of Effie Gray, who married successively Ruskin and Millais), Ford Maddox Brown (a fine painting of William Michael Rossetti, painted by lamplight in 1856), James Smetham, Walter Crane, Marie Stillman, Elizabeth Siddal, the muse and wife of Dante Gabriel Rossetti (including her self portrait and 'St Agnes Eve') and Ruskin himself, whose support of the Movement through the 'fifties helped to establish their reputations. There is the celebrated portrait of Janey Morris, begun by Rossetti, but completed by Maddox Brown.

Morris was never among the Pre-Raphaelites, of course (although he had an early ambition to become a painter), but his designs are displayed, as he intended, alongside Jacobean and early eighteenth-century furniture, Chinese porcelain, Flemish verdure tapestries, Persian rugs, again suggesting an organic process of accumulation and aggregation. At Wightwick, Morris's decoration is not seen as an eccentric or precious reaction to Victorian commercial design, but itself a commercial project responding to, part of, a widespread eclectic attitude to the past, shored up by a mosaic of objects, memories and reciprocal influences. Wightwick came to epitomise what C.L. Eastlake described as 'the picturesque element which has become conspicuous in the appointment of many English homes [which] may be traced to the early efforts of William Morris and Burne-Jones'.[14] It was recognised that, apart from the Green Dining Room at the V.&A., few of the larger-scale Morris & Co. interior schemes for the Ionides, Bell, Wyndham, Howard and d'Arcy families, even St James's Palace itself, had survived.

The National Trust, 1937

In December 1937 the future of house and collection was finally secured when Geoffrey presented it to the National Trust, with an endowment of 20,000 Manders shares. He was encouraged by the Trevelyans (of another Liberal family, who gave Wallington shortly afterwards) and Professor W.G. Constable.[15] But it was a courageous acquisition at a time when Victorian art and architecture in all their forms were little esteemed. This was the first country house to be presented during the lifetime of its donor and arguably the first presented under the Country Houses Scheme itself. Rosalie Mander wrote: 'He never regretted it, for he liked to think that the public should enjoy what had been his private property.'[16] He delighted in showing visitors round the house, and insisted on keeping no quarters barred from public view.

Geoffrey and Rosalie continued to add to the collections, in association with the Trust buying good examples of Pre-Raphaelite art and William Morris furnishings in the period when they were least popular in the '50s and '60s. Their vision was prophetic; they were ahead of their time in their recognition of the importance of the house and its collections. The house has since acquired more by loan, gift and bequest: early Rossetti drawings on loan from Mrs Katherine Macdonald, a walnut rosewood piano made by Hopkinson for the Crystal Palace Exhibition of 1851.

Set prominently at the end of the Great Parlour is Edward Burne-Jones's *Love Among the Ruins* (1894), a late version of one his most evocative works from the Samuel collection at Upton House (National Trust). Browning's poem of the same title, with its transient narrative of young lovers meeting to extinguish sight and speech 'each on each' in the last turret of a city once great and gay, now overspread with the briar rose, dramatises a powerful moral: 'Love is Best'. Here Gerard Manley Hopkins noted a stranger 'instress of expression', referring to the neo-Platonic *Hypnerotomachia*, a dream world of neurosis, of mental strife in the pursuit of love. The lover sits with his Polia among the broken pillars and enigmatic inscriptions of the temple of a bygone age, both unsated on their journey to Cytherea, where they will find not fulfilment, but separation. Its classical architectural capriccio could be taken as a symbol of Wightwick and of Ruskin's romantic associationist aesthetics which posited architecture as embodied memory, which rises out of the 'contrast of the beautiful past with the ... monotonous present [and] depends on the existence of ruins and traditions, on the remains of architecture, the precursorship of eventful history'.[17]

Under Geoffrey and Rosalie's guardianship, Wightwick was both a living house in renewal with a growing collection, but also a remarkably intact survivor of the previous generation, and a richly nuanced expression of Victorian liberal culture. It is appropriate that they fostered links with the romantic Utopian socialism preached by Morris, and many of the radical politicians and thinkers of the day visited.

Geoffrey had installed a squash court at Wightwick in 1928 and continued to play tennis there until just shortly before he died aged eighty in 1962. But his widow, Rosalie, was much younger, and presided for another quarter of a century as a welcoming if capricious chatelaine, continuing to write and to lecture until her death in 1988.

Since then, much has been discovered about the house in its re-ordered archives, and there has been increasing interest in the life of the back rooms: the tiled kitchen with its range made by the Eagle Range and Gas Company of Birmingham; the servants' rooms which, exceptionally for the time, had central heating; and the cloakroom and Turkish bath (the only other known is at Cragside). Muthesius suggests that in such rooms we experience the first stirrings of functional modernism.[18] The nursery, redecorated in the Thirties, is evocative, with its toys and Cecil Aldin frieze and Minton tiles, described today by Candida Lycett Green as

> possibly one of the nicest rooms in Britain—light and happy, with distempered green walls, yellowy cream woodwork and green linoleum. The curtain materials depict 'The House that Jack Built' and 'Alice in Wonderland' and are designed by Voysey. The smell of hot buttered toast is almost in the air.

The family maintain a flat and, after a fruitful 65-year partnership with the National Trust, often remark that house and particularly garden have never looked better than they do today. Wightwick has become one of the National Trust's, and the nation's, paradigmatic late nineteenth-century houses, complementary to Webb's Standen and Shaw's Cragside. Like Owlpen, it attracts superlatives: 'the most complete example of late nineteenth-century artistic taste' and 'one of the two or three places in the world you must visit if you are interested in William Morris and the Arts and Crafts movement'.[19] Candida Lycett Green sums it up as 'in its way, one of the wonders of the world'.

Miles Mander and the Indian Princesses

Martin Bertram Mander (1869-1946), Geoffrey's uncle (third and youngest son of Samuel Small Mander), settled at Horoeka in the Waimata valley near Gisbourne, New Zealand, in about 1890. There he established a 2,000-acre sheep station and prospered in time, to become active as a philanthropist.[20]

Geoffrey had a beautiful younger sister, Marjorie, who went out to work for Uncle Martin. There she met and in due course married Gervas Nevile—a Trinity, Cambridge, friend of Charles Arthur's—who was employed by Martin on the sheep station at the time.[21] The young couple had little interest in children. Their son, Peter, born in Auckland in 1912, was sent back to England to be raised by the Wightwick governess, Miss Drew. She had run the Wightwick home school (another progressive project organised on PNEU principles[22]), and married Watson Caldicott, headmaster of the Wolverhampton Grammar School. Despite being directly descended from Gilbert de Nevill, mentioned in Domesday Book, he is proudest of having the professions of his parents entered on his birth certificate as 'shepherd' and 'domestic duties'.

Then Geoffrey had two younger brothers, Lionel and Alan. Lionel Henry (1884-1946) also spent his twenties in New Zealand farming sheep. He was a restless, colourful personality, breaking from the predictable family mould of business and public service. He made several false starts, with an youthful interest in aviation, horses and fast cars. He turned disastrously to drink under the pressure of the War, but eventually established a successful career as the film actor, producer and novelist 'Miles' Mander. He is remembered as a charmer to women, the epitome of the English gentleman, with a monocle.

He was billed as 'Luther Miles' in his earliest film appearances, reserving his real name for his screenwriting credits. He became well known as a character actor, typically as the gentleman cad or the conspiring, oily villain, in the early cinema. He made his screen bow as an extra in 1918 and went on to appear in over 100 films. One of the first was an early Hitchcock classic, *The Pleasure Garden*, in 1925. He played his Hollywood debut as Louis XIII in the 1935 version of *The Three Musketeers*, and then played Richelieu in a musicalised comedy version in 1939, where the musketeers are played by the Ritz brothers. His best-known Hollywood roles included those of Lockwood in *Wuthering Heights* (1939) with Laurence Olivier and Merle Oberon, and Ginger Roger's father in *The Primrose Path* (1940). He was never more unsavory than when he portrayed the master criminal Giles Conover in the Sherlock Holmes adventure *The Pearl of Death* in 1945. He starred in Noel Coward's operetta *Bitter Sweet* (1933). He directed nine films and wrote the screenplay for another eight. One of these was a comedy, *The Morals of Marcus* (1935), from a play by 'Stella Maris' author W.J. Locke.[23] *The First Born* (1928), which he directed and acted in, was based on his own novel and play.

As an author, he was foremost a novelist. But he wrote some forgotten plays, two of which were produced in London in 1927 and 1930, and a collection of essays on current affairs, conduct and character, religion, politics and sexual morality, called *To my Son—in Confidence* (Faber, 1934). This he dedicated to 'the legion of devoted fathers who, through doing the "decent thing" in divorce or estrangement, are now anxious for their sons'. Whereas he sees his father, Theodore's, life as a steady progression to affluence and success, his own was marked by a lack of parental guidance and 'a weakness for the vapidities of life... If a man's life has been crammed with vicissitudes like mine, then it seems a wicked thing that he should not give his son the benefit of his experience'. The son to whom he pertinently addresses that benefit was his 'greatest friend', Theo (1926-1990), his son by his second wife, Kathleen French of Sydney.

This is no smug collection of conventional platitudes. Lionel is brief but entertaining about his antecedents, the Manders:

My father was Samuel Theodore Mander, an excessively good man of puritanical yeoman stock. He was a member of a large and prolific family which is localized in the region of Wolverhampton, where they manufacture varnish. That they have been doing this for 150 years only goes to prove that insanity and integrity are very closely allied. The only justification for an occupation so prosaic, and an existence so provincial, must be the accumulation of wealth. This being so, the Manders have nobly vindicated themselves. In addition, at the time of writing, they have produced one baronet, one Member of Parliament, High Sheriffs, Deputy Lieutenants and several of the lesser municipal dignitaries such as Mayors, Magistrates and Councillors. In fact, we are quite obviously worthy people.

He confesses to the temperance of his side of the family—his father, grandfather, Geoffrey and himself—with descriptions of the pious ways at the Congregationalist Wightwick of his childhood:

My father was an extremely religious man. What is more, he practised what he preached. He did not conform to the Church of England, being Congregational by denomination. His children as a result were brought up in a strictly religious atmosphere. Every morning before breakfast all the indoor servants would troop into the morning room where the members of the family were already gathered. Father would then read an extract from the Bible and this would be followed by prayers when everyone would kneel down. On Sundays, Father and Mother would drive into Wolverhampton in the morning, accompanied by us children. In those days there were no motor-cars, so the drive in the brougham took a long time. On arrival at the chapel we would sit through a two-hour service, half of which consisted of a sermon. After lunch Father would take us in a scripture lesson. After tea we would all foregather in the drawing-room and sing Moody and Sankey hymns with mother at the piano. Father would then go out somewhere and do duty as a lay preacher. When he returned we would have supper and then, at ten o'clock, all the servants would line up in the drawing-room and we would go through the same prayerful procedure as on week-days before breakfast. It is almost incredible, looking back now, to think what we children must have suffered. The household of a bishop could not have been more devout. And when one remembers that my father was at other times a fine shot, an enthusiastic fisherman and a keen rider to hounds, one is left groping in a forest of irreconcilability.

But that is not the end of it. At the age of five I was christened in the morning-room by Father's great friend, Dr. Robert Horton. I remember the blue vase which held the water and the sprinkling of my hair. What it meant I had no idea. Neither do I know why, at the age of fifteen, I was confirmed by the Bishop of Edinburgh. It is true that Father was then dead, but how Mother was persuaded to hand me over to the Church of England, I cannot imagine.

In politics he professes himself a socialist, declaring an interest:

Your Canadian great-grandfather was in the Ottawa Parliament, your grandfather, Theodore, was one of the most prominent Liberals of his day, your Uncle Geoffrey is at present a Liberal Member, and I am hoping to be in the House shortly myself.

Lionel's first wife was an Indian princess: Prativa Devee—or 'Pretty'—known after their marriage as Princess Prativa Mander. Born in 1891, she was the daughter of Sir Nripendra Narayan Bhup Bahadur, the Maharajah of Cooch Behar, by his wife, Sunity Devee.[24] The Maharajah was a model ruler of his princely state in West Bengal, who from infancy had been brought up as a ward of the British government. His race had been founded by the love of a god and a maiden, wrote the Maharani, 'and through successive ages strife and love have been associated with the dynasty of Cooch Behar, whose chiefs have always been great rulers, great lovers, and great fighters'.[25] The Maharajah died suddenly at Bexhill-on-Sea 'in the prime of life' in September 1911. His Maharani describes Pretty at the time of her wedding aged 20 at Woodlands, Calcutta, in February 1912, as 'a gorgeous damask rose just unfolding into loveliness, but perfectly simple and sweet':

Pretty's wedding lightened a little of our sadness at this time. My second girl was engaged to Lionel Mander, a young Englishman who appeared devoted to her. She was just like an English girl, although at home she lived as an Indian Princess. I gave my consent to the marriage, as I had long ago determined to let each of my girls marry the man she loved, and I quite realized that, owing to caste and creed, there would be many difficulties in the way of marriage with any of our princes.

The marriage was not a success, and they divorced in 1926, when Lionel married again, dying twenty years later in Hollywood in February 1946, aged 57.

His younger brother, Alan Jocelyn (1891-1967), was indulged as a youth, and described by staider members of the family as 'a bit of a card', forever badgering them for money after he had dissipated his inheritance. This was eked out by the dowry of jewels which were said to arrive in caskets from India after his marriage. For he had accompanied his sister-in-law, Pretty, on a visit to her sister, Sudhira Sundari Devee, known as 'Baby' (1894-1968), when she was ill at a nursing home in London in 1913. A tempestuous courtship ensued and they were married in Calcutta the following year, when she became known as 'Princess Sudhira Mander'.[26] The Maharani writes of her youngest daughter's marriage:

> Baby has married Allen Mander, the younger brother of Lionel. I did not wish her to marry so soon, especially as it is only six months after I had lost my [son] Rajey, but now my life has come to that stage that I must not be heard, my love must pray silently for the happiness of my children. They are very precious and their happiness is my happiness. Baby wished to marry this boy; he is fine looking, and has travelled a good deal, and as he was anxious to have the wedding soon I did not stand in their way, and they were married in Woodlands on 25th February, 1914. During the War he was in the Army [he spent two years in the trenches with the King's Own Cameron Highlanders] and now they are in England. Allen has been a very good son-in-law; I don't think I could have had a better, even in fancy.[27]

Despite the Maharani's rather forced acknowledgement of another cross-cultural match as something of a fait accompli, the marriage was strongly disapproved of by both families. Their grandfather Henry Paint remarked of both 'the lads who married the Indian ladies': 'a youth of follies, an old age of cares'. But it was by all accounts a happy one, with three children, and they died within three weeks of each other over Christmas and New Year 1967-8.

John Mander

Geoffrey had five children: Mervyn, Mavis and Elizabeth by his first marriage to the Canadian Florence Caverhill, and Anthea and John by his second, to Rosalie Glynn Grylls. Mervyn entered Mander Brothers for a while, but was always hopeless in business. He was sacked by Charles Arthur, and ended up dairy farming in Jersey. But his dismissal set up a sour note within the Company, as increasingly fractious and distant relations sat on the Board together.

Geoffrey at Wightwick with Anthea, John and Rosalie (at typewriter), c. 1948

Anthea married an American, John Lahr. He is a brilliant author, theatre critic, biographer and editor, notably of the playwright Joe Orton and the critic Kenneth Tynan, and son of Bert Lahr, the American actor best remembered as the Cowardly Lion in *The Wizard of Oz.* Writing of her childhood at Wightwick in the post-war years, she recalls a cheerless house without heating (except on Open Days), a family who 'discarded people but not things', 'emotional scars' and 'painful memories'. Today she ensures the house is bright and welcoming, and reigns there as an inspired and tactful tenant-in-chief on behalf of the family.

Her brother and Geoffrey's younger son, John Geoffrey Grylls Mander (1932-1978), was educated at Eton, where he had an early interest in studio pottery in the Leach manner,[28] his hands in clay. He went on to Trinity College, Cambridge where, despite a precocious interest in literature and ideas, he said he read Medicine. A younger contemporary there of Tom Gunn, he was described as 'one of the best undergraduate poets of his generation'.[29]

He spent four years in Munich and Berlin in his early twenties, studying German language, politics and contemporary literature, of which he became an authoritative interpreter. He went on to establish a career as an author, editor and translator (from the German),[30] a professional intellectual in literary London, settling in Islington and contributing to publications in Britain, the United States and Germany. He was on the staff of *The New Statesman* as assistant literary editor, and was assistant editor of *Encounter*.

He published a number of 'provocative' books, mainly thematic politico-philosophical studies on current affairs and cultural criticism, variously described by reviewers as 'lucid', 'sane' and 'well written', and always informed, as Bernard Levin wrote, by an impeccable sense of history and omnivorous reading. *Berlin: the Eagle and the Bear* (1959), published when he was 27, was described by the *Times* in 1972 as 'still one of the best books on Berlin'. It was followed, three years later, by a Penguin Special, *Berlin: Hostage for the West* (1962); 'a brilliant book', wrote David Marquand. *The Writer and Commitment* (1961) compares the New Left and the Old, examining the theme of moral and political commitment in the work of various contemporary authors from Auden and Orwell to Tom Gunn. Some of its themes he developed in *Great Britain or Little England?* (1963), also a Penguin Special; 'his diagnosis faultless', wrote Levin, of a subject that remains prophetically topical. *Static Society: The Paradox of Latin America* (1969) was acclaimed by *The Guardian* as 'by far the best and most readable introduction to the continent's history, literature and civilization'. His last book was *Our German Cousins: Anglo-German Relations in the 19th and 20th Centuries* (1974).

He never took much interest in the family business, and for long periods claimed to be hardly on speaking terms with his mother. But he was proud of his Mander connections, describing the family without affectation or snobbery as 'the Kings of Wolverhampton'.

In later life, he went back to poetry writing, some of which appeared in *The New Review*. He published two much-praised collections of poetry: *A Calvary* a few months before he died and *Elegiacs* in 1972. The final poem of the latter, *In Patris Memoriam*, 'in memory of his fathers', describes the commonplace Mander virtue of *Noblesse Oblige*; by which, he writes, 'Cincinnatus in time of dire invasion [laid] down the plough'

> Did not once to great Mr Gladstone, cutting down trees,
> A rain-coated messenger come
> Begging his pardon, but if the old gentleman kindly
> Could form a new government, some-
> Time today or tomorrow, the Queen would be much obliged?...
>
> He believed in his household gods, shall we say, too devoutly...
> And we are obliged, doubtless, to go on cutting down trees,
> (Without being Mr Gladstone, of course).
> A useful task, clearing dead wood, creating some order:
> Not doubting that also to us,
> Through the wet bracken a messenger's coming,
> who brings us good tidings.

[1] R.G.G. Mander published a pamphlet life of *Geoffrey le Mesurier Mander (1882-1962), Donor of the house*, Oxford [n.d.], mainly for sale at Wightwick.
[2] *Wightwick Manor*, National Trust guide, 1993
[3] *Express & Star*, 31 November 1911
[4] R.A.C. Parker, *Chamberlain and Appeasement*, 1993, pp. 40, 52 and 54.
[5] Geoffrey Mander, *We were* not *all Wrong*, 1938, pp. 87-9.
[6] John Mander, *Our German Cousins*, 1974, p. 247.
[7] Archibald Sinclair (1890-1970), first Viscount Thurso (1951).
[8] G.J. de Groot, *Liberal Crusader: The Life of Sir Archibald Sinclair*, 1993, p. 227.
[9] *We were* not *all Wrong*, pp. 87-9.
[10] N. Milette, *Parsons–Partridge–Tudway, an unsuspected garden design partnership*, York, 1995
[11] See obituaries in *The Times* (4 Nov. 1988); *The Daily Telegraph* (in part by Elizabeth Longford, 4 Nov. 1988); and Martin Drury (*National Trust Magazine*, Summer 1989).
[12] *Deep Romantic Chasm; Diaries 1979-81*, 2000, pp. 130, 152.
[13] *Midway on the Waves*, 1985, p. 53; 20 May 1948.
[14] *Magazine of Art*, 1903, p. 37.
[15] Director of the Courtauld Institute, London, and Slade Professor of Fine Art at Cambridge. Another kindred spirit in the League of Nations, connected (distantly) by marriage through the Turnbull family, was Roger, ninth Lord Stamford; the tenth earl presented Dunham Massey to the National Trust in 1976.
[16] *The Country House Remembered*, edited by M. Waterson, 1985
[17] *The Seven Lamps of Architecture*, V. 369.
[18] He calls for a new aesthetic based on 'spiritualized practical intention'. 'There are signs of this in those parts of the house that have to do with hygene.' *The English House*, 1904-5, trans. J. Seligman, 1979, p. 163.
[19] J. Orbach, *Victorian Architecture in Britain*, 1987, p. 440; Martin Drury, 'Address to the 1999 AGM', *Historic House*, Spring 2000, p. 13.
[20] Martin Mander gifted the Anzac Park to the town of Gisbourne in 1916; a YMCA building in France for New Zealand troops on leave behind the Front in World War I in 1917; and money to buy a Spitfire during the Battle of Britain. (Ex inf. his great-grandson, Andrew Davy, 2002. For his development of the Waitangihiia station on Cape Runaway, see J. Hindmarsh, *Come be a Pioneer*, Gisbourne, [n.d.], pp. 140-1, 144-5.)
[21] The Neviles (of Skellingthorpe Manor, Lincs.), formerly of Thorney, descend in the male line from Gilbert de Nevill, mentioned in Domesday Book, an ancestor of the Nevilles, earls of Westmoreland.
[22] Theodore and Flora Mander established a school in the old malthouse at Wightwick, attended by their cousins at The Mount and other relations. In 1890 Flora wrote to Charlotte Mason, founder of the PNEU (Parents National Educational Union), expressing an interest in home schooling and the PNEU. Another correspondent and early supporter was Mrs Mander Smythe, married to Theodore's cousin, several of whose many daughters actually attended the PNEU teacher training college in Ambleside as students.
[23] Other film credits include: Murder, My Sweet (1945), The Brighton Strangler (1945), The Pearl of Death (1944), Sherlock Holmes and The Pearl of Death (1944), Return of the Vampire (1943), Mrs. Miniver (1942), Fingers at the Window (1942), Babies for Sale (1940), The House of the Seven Gables (1940), Tower of London (1939), and The Private Life of Henry VIII (1933).
[24] H.H. Sri Sri Maharaja Sir Nripendra Narayan Bhup Bahadur, Maharaja of Cooch Behar (b. at the Royal Palace, Cooch-Behar, 4th Oct. 1862—d. Sussex, 18th Sept. 1911); m. 1878 H.H. Maharani Siniti Devi Sahiba (b. at Sen's House, Calcutta, 1864—d. at Ranchi, November 1932), sometime Regent of Cooch-Behar and Presdt. State Council, eldest daughter of Babu Keshab Chandra Sen. They had four sons and three daughters.

The Narayan dynasty founded the principality on the ruins of the ancient Hindu kingdom of Kamarupa. The first Raja, Chandan Narayan, of Koch and Mech descent, established himself on Mount Chikna in 1510. His half-brother and successor, Maharaja Vishnu Narayan, greatly expanded his domains and established his capital in the plains. Vishnu's son, Maharaja Nara Narayan, conquered vast territories and subjugated most of the surrounding principalities. Their successors maintained their independence until the late seventeenth century, when Maharaja Mahendra Narayan faced repeated attacks by the Mughal Nawab-Nazims of Bengal. His successor ceded half his principality and became their tributary in 1711. The state came under British protection after the acquisition of the Diwani of Bengal, Bihar and Orissa, by Lord Clive of Plassey in 1765. Bhutanese intervention in succession disputes prompted a formal treaty between the rightful heir and the British in 1775. The family, belonging to the Rajbhansi and Sudra caste, was highly cultured and of modern outlook, championing education, Hindu reform and Indian literature. Maharaja Sir Nripendra Narayan, and his wife Maharani Siniti Devi, were court favourites of the Queen-Empress Victoria, attending the Imperial Durbar at Delhi and the Golden Jubilee in London in 1887, as well as the Coronations of Edward VII in 1902 and George V in 1911. The state acceded to the Dominion of India in 1947 and merged with the state of West Bengal in 1950.

[25] Sunity Devee, Maharani of Cooch Behar, *The Autobiography of an Indian Princess*, 1921, pp. 43, 203-4.

[26] The two sisters were styled before their marriages Sri Sri Maharaj Kumari Prativa Sundari Devi and Sri Sri Maharaj Kumari Sudhira Sundari Devi. A third sister, Sukriti, married The Hon. Sir Josna Nath Ghosal (son of Janaki Nath Ghosal, Zamindar, and Srimati Svarna Kumari Devi, poetess and author, daughter of Maharshi Devendra Nath Tagore, and sister of Maharaja Sir Rabindra Nath Tagore, the famous Nobel Prize winner and Bengali man of letters). Two of their brothers, Rajendra (briefly) and Jitendra, followed as Maharajahs.

[27] *Autobiography*, p. 230

[28] The 'Mander [Pottery] Prize', endowed after his death by Rosalie, commemorates his youthful efforts in the Art Schools.

[29] *Times* obituary, 8 September 1978

[30] His translations (with his first wife, Necke) include the notable work by Görgy Lukács, *The Meaning of Contemporary Realism* (1963); also Klaus Roehler, *The Dignity of Night* (1960) and Carl Zuckmayer, *Carnival Confession* (1961). He said he declined the opportunity to translate Günther Grass.

Charles Arthur Mander
1884-1951

CHARLES ARTHUR

17

BUSINESS HABITS

Charles Arthur, 1884 - 1951

Charles Arthur was the eldest son of Charles Tertius and Mary. He was educated at Eton, which he loved, and Trinity College, Cambridge, where, in Mander tradition, he read Natural Sciences.[1]

From an early age, he learnt, like his father, to ride well and to shoot well. He was in the Cambridge University Royal Volunteers mounted infantry team at the Royal Military Tournament in 1904. He became a first-rate rifle shot. He shot for Eton, where he was captain of the shooting Eight which won the Ashburton Shield, the premier public-school trophy, at Bisley in 1901. Shooting was an important part of officers' training and the medal was given to him with much celebration 'at the hands of Field Marshall Lord Roberts'—himself an Old Etonian.

English VIII at Bisley 1905
Back row: P.K. Whitehead, CAM, AE Rogers, Col. Hopton, Hon. T. Freemantle, Col. Gibbs
Front row: A.P. Humphry, Maj. Edge, H. Whitehead, Sir Edmund Loder, Col. Mellish

'VARSITY TEAMS' CONTEST.

The 'Varsity teams had a fine contest for the Humphry Cup on the long ranges. The Light Blues drew away at 1,000 yards, and won by 801 points against 784 scored by Oxford. The best score was 208 by Private Mander, for the winners.

Private Mander shooting, Inter-Varsity Contest
Daily Graphic, July 14 1904

He followed up shooting for Cambridge University, where he was in the Varsity team three years running (1904-6) against Oxford, Cambridge gaining the highest score ever recorded in 1904; for the Queen's Yeomanry; and finally for England, for the first time just aged 21. In the Elcho Shield at Bisley in 1906 he again made a record score.[2] He thus achieved a modest fame, at a time when the sport was followed closely by a wide public, and Bisley meetings were social occasions, their antics described blow by blow with detailed scores and dramatic commentaries in the London papers. And in the run-up to 1914 there was an earnest purpose when the British Army had attained a standard of rifle shooting, according to Liddel Hart, 'unique among the armies of the world'.

Cambridge Pitt Club, coming of age dinner party, 1903
of LW Huntington, AW Berg and HNS Wilson (in effigy) (CAM 2nd from right)

Dr Dootson's Reading Party, Isle of Wight, Easter 1905
?A, Oke, Cooke, Guy Cobbold, Ramsay, Wilkins, John Christie and The Dr (sitting in ye old car), Longman, CAM, Dotteridge (sitting on mudguard), Landerman, Michell, Stivite

He said he trained for business life by going to Canada, Berlin (in both places Mander Brothers had branches) and Norway, 'in other words by taking a holiday, which was a good idea'. He visited other agencies and branches of the Mander firm in Paris and Milan, learning idiomatic French and German, always spoken with an uncompromising English accent. His main interest in Norway seems to have been salmon fishing with John Phillimore (who caught an 22.5-pounder).

His early life of louche and gilded youth is recorded in the diaries which describe these travels, focusing on the cosmopolitan social life of the *belle époque* of Edwardian summers, the sports and diversions in the great capitals, tourist cities and playgrounds of Europe and eastern North America, the grand new hotels, liners and clubs, the country house weekends with hunting and shooting, race meetings, rather than any apparent business grind.

One of these describes an early visit to Canada from September to November 1906, when he was 22, in order to be best man at the wedding of cousin 'Geoff' Mander to Florence Caverhill in Montreal. His father wished him to spend a week or so 'in our Montreal House' after the wedding, and then 'play about America', escorting his sister Daisy, travelling independently with her lady's maid, home in November.

Evocative today is the flavour of the life travelling first-class on the transatlantic liners. Returning from New York on the Cunarder, *Carmania*, he summoned up courage to introduce himself to Nora Langhorne and her sister, Phyllis ('Mrs Reggie Brooks'), two of the famous five Langhorne belles of Richmond, Virginia: 'Dick Derby had told her I was going to be on board, so it was all right... It is her sister [Irene] who is the original Gibson girl'. He was struck by Nora's undoubted charms. She was very funny, played the guitar, sang, tap-danced and was always getting engaged. Her family described her as having 'a heart like a hotel'. He joined in impromptu concerts with her and the others, or sang 'until turned out by the sailors

who had come to swab down the decks'. As the boat rocks and shudders, and the spray is blown right over it, he notes: 'Miss Langhorne has not appeared today, and I have consequently found the time hang heavy on my hands'.[3]

He exchanged yarns with the 'amusing and not a bit assuming' tea planter, Sir Tommy Lipton 'with yachting cap',[4] who 'was always coming out with "and that reminds me of a story..." One about the Scotch purser provisioning a yacht with 16 bottles of whisky and two loaves was most amusing'. 'The king's grocer' described his making butter into pats behind the counter in his early days, and talked about Balmoral and his tea estates in Ceylon with equal ease. Meanwhile Lady Cunard, travelling with Nancy, her small girl of ten, 'played rather delightfully and is a keen Wagnerian' who 'paints, powders and smells of scents'.[5]

On the Sunday, 'the extraordinary passenger who took the service' gave a sort of Salvation Army oration for a sermon, 'with an impossible story of Queen Victoria saying "Good morning, Duke" to the Minister who brought a young man's death warrant to her on a Sunday morning, whereupon she wrote "Pardoned" on it using a rose stalk instead of a pen.'

Another diary which he titles 'Business Habits' deals with the musical world of Imperial Berlin the following spring, in 1907, attending 20 operas and 20 concerts. He found himself sharing lodgings with the musicologist from Trinity, Donald Tovey (1873-1940), who entertained the guests with about twenty Chopin *mazurkas* and the Brahms Intermezzo, op. 119, no. 4 (*Klavierstücke*); 'delightful'. He befriends Edward Dent, another old Etonian and aspiring music critic (who in 1913 published his acclaimed study of Mozart's operas). They go together to legendary performances of Mahler's third symphony conducted by Himself: 'interesting, but dull and disjointed. Dent had the full score'.[6] There are recitals by Eugen d'Albert, and by Ferruccio Busoni: 'Some of the notes he produced at the end of the *Papillons* of Schumann were like small explosions. At the end he was recalled about 10 times... I was introduced, and we sat at the same table.' He heard the virtuoso violinists, Fritz Kreisler and Pablo de Sarasate. In Bayreuth, he saw Isidora Duncan, who 'went about in a weird sort of Grecian costume and bare feet with sandals. Her dancing was extremely tame, and as comme il faut as you could want. She sort of glided round slowly and flopped her arms about'.

He escorts the attractive young baroness Roth von Schreckenstein 'with the blue eyes', who takes him about and eases his way into society. Clearly smitten, his notes concerning her are written cryptically in German gothic script. She dances well, and her eventual departure is mournfully *schade.* Throughout, the critical banter of a talented musician is interspersed with descriptions of soirées 'in a sort of an attempted fancy dress', masked balls 'with singing stunts', skating, embassy life, and more accountable lessons in German and singing.

He was supposed to be learning business, of course, but his attendance at the offices of the Manders' branch under Herr Külm was dilatory: 'Father is not satisfied with the hours I spend at the office', he notes guiltlessly. But on a tour arranged for him of German cities, he visits various clients in Dresden, manufacturers of sewing machines and 'Ideal' typewriters; and 'the court coach builder who employs 160 men; he was rather grumpy and only gets flatting varnish from us'. At Magdeburg, the first thing that fretted them on arrival was a wagonload of Blume's varnish, twenty barrels, going to London. A manufacturer told him that he would only allow that England was superior to Germany in varnish and jams (possibly). He discovers that, although Voigtlanders (opticians) now buy nothing, 'as the master is bribed by a Brunswick firm, ... we do all the trade with Zeiss'.

He returns home via Paris, diverting for a family party playing golf with CTM in Biarritz. Here, on his way back from Merrimans, he met Edward VII just outside his window, 'and was greeted affectionately by his terrier Jock, though I have not had the pleasure of making his acquaintance yet'. Also staying were Lord Curzon and the young Winston Churchill, and a baroness de Rothschild, who 'so far has worn eleven different outfits in four days'. In Paris the following year he sees the aged Sarah Bernhardt (1845-1923) in one of her greatest triumphs, as *L'Aiglon* in the play by Rostand: 'Poor old Sarah's voice was very weak and suffering from age, and she was talking nearly the whole time. But she was wonderful all the same.'

A hunting expedition in the autumn of 1911 is a contrast. He sets out from The Mount with Guy Cobbold[7] to sail on the *Virginian*, delayed by violent scenes of dockers' and railway strikes. Storrar, the chauffeur, 'who drove us up to the High Level Station in the new Rolls Royce, must needs stop the 40-50 engine outside Hinde's shop in trying to start on the slope'. At Liverpool there is industrial unrest. They find 'St George's Hall opposite is still occupied by "the military", and the stars and holes generally in the hotel windows show what happened on last Sunday week. The streets are still full of refuse.'

The journey takes him to the 'Smoky River District' of the Canadian Rockies above the Yellowhead Pass (Tête Jaune), where he explored the high peaks, valleys and glaciers with a small party of Eton and Trinity, Cambridge, friends, including Perry Osborne, Cobbold, and at one point 23 horses. First, he stays with the Osbornes at Castle Rock, Garrison, above the Hudson River, 'on the top of an 800-foot hill; you can see 80 miles from the dining room windows... They are going to introduce me to the President, probably'. [8]

Then, in quest of wild sheep, caribou and moose, they 'discovered' uncharted mountains and lakes at the backbone of the Continent, along the Divide. One lake, deep in 'country absolutely unmapped and almost trackless', he was informed by a letter from the Department of the Interior in Ottawa of 20 April 1912, would be named henceforth 'Mander Lake' after him, but it is not known whether the name stuck. The area, within striking distance of the railway since 1886, was being explored by Dr J. Norman Collie and A.L. Mumm of the Royal Geographical Society at the same time. Arthur's party met the astonished explorers at the bottom of Twin Tree Lake, climbing a 9,000-foot mountain north east of Mount Robinson, which they had just christened 'Mount Hoodoo' in honour of a bulldog 'who, much against his will, was taken up the mountain'.

The 1911 trip to the wilderness was intended to give him mental space to contemplate the prospect of his proposed marriage to Monica (1888-1964), youngest daughter of George Harding Neame (1855-1928), of Sevenoaks and Kensington, which went ahead in April 1913. The festivities were much curtailed, and the ball had to be cancelled, as the bride's grandfather, George Friday Neame (sometime mayor of Canterbury), had died suddenly just before.

The Kentish Neames have a long if dull pedigree given in Burke's *Landed Gentry* (1952) showing the descent from one Thomas of Woodnesborough and John Neame of St Mildred's, Canterbury, tanner, who died *c.* 1450.[9] Monica was descended from the branch of Thomas Neame (1746-1817) of Selling Court by a succession of three sons, all called George.[10] These Neames were large farmers, already considered the most extensive hop growers in East Kent. Thomas's descendants have an old-established family business, Shepherd Neame, founded in Faversham in 1698, which claims to be the oldest brewery in England— although the first Neame, Percy Beale (1836-1913), only joined the firm in 1864.

Not all the family could join the brewery, of course, and Monica's father, known to us as 'Humpah', had his own business as a timber broker with Boyson Neame in the City, doing a big trade with Imperial Russia, Finland and the Baltic States. At the Revolution, the butt ends with the firm's mark were sneaked off millions of trees by the Bolshevik officials, and he lost a fortune, never quite recovered, through honouring his contracts.[11]

Monica had a cousin, Lt-General Sir Philip Neame of Selling, who was awarded a V.C. in the first world war, at Neuve Chappelle.[12] Her mother, born Anne Ellen ('Nellie') Cotterill, was descended from an eighteenth-century Admiral Cotterill, of Arlington Street.[13] He was supposed to be related (?collaterally) to the historian, Edward Gibbon—who is candid about his impassioned sighs as a lover in his *Autobiography*, but died childless and unmarried.[14] The contradictions of oral family history are perverse, but Nellie would tell her Magill grandsons, Desmond and Shamus, both clever—as 'tugs', or King's Scholars—in College at Eton: 'You know where you got your brains from, d' ye boy? The great Gibbon was an ancestor or yours!'[15]

Arthur and Monica welcomed home to Kingslow from their honeymoon by his Staffordshire Yeomanry troop, 1913

George and Nellie Neame had one much younger son, Lionel, and four noisy daughters, of whom three became 'ladies'. The eldest, Winnie married Sir Ernest Fass (b. 1881), finance secretary to the Sudan government in Khartoum, and later the public trustee. The second, Doris ('Dordor'), married Major Patrick Magill (1871-1949) of Churchtown, co. Kerry, a remount officer who spent his life in Ireland buying horses for the Cavalry. The third, Gwen, like Monica, married a baronet; Sir Thomas ('Guy') Wrightson (1871-1950), of Neasham Hall, Darlington. His family business was Head, Wrightson & Co., of Thornaby on Tees; engineers, iron founders, bridge builders and metal roof manufacturers, who exported their railway equipment all over the Empire.

By this connection much nonce jargon entered the family, adopting a private and merry idiolect amongst themselves. This patois lasted into my youth, when Sir John Wrightson (1911-1983) continued to utter Sitwellian obiter dicta on the usage and abusage of the family lexis. For instance, was it an 'exception to the Kyloop Rule' (a rule which only existed by virtue of its exceptions) when my father, the third baronet, was asked by a tripper in the piazza S. Marco to photograph him eating a banana? The answer was, no, but *it would have been* if *the third baronet* had asked the *tripper* to photograph *the baronet* eating the banana. Another admissible Exception involved my grandmother, Monica, dropping her snood in St James's, where it was picked up half an hour later by one of her brothers-in-law passing outside his Club, who promptly impaled it on the railings. She would only demand of him curtly, *why he never gave it back?*

Wedding of Lt. Charles Arthur Mander and Monica Neame, April 1913

[1] His Turnbull cousins (by marriage) of the previous generation were educated at Trinity, including Peveril, of Sandybrooke Hall, Ashbourne, Derbyshire, sometime agent to the Sitwells at Renishaw, and his younger brother, William Peveril (1841-1917), of Stockwell End, Wolverhampton, who was a fellow. (Two sisters were early Newnham students.)
[2] One of the other shots, all much older than he, was Sir Edmund Loder, whose great nephew, Simon Loder, married CAM's granddaughter, Penelope.
[3] Nora, the youngest of the sisters, married Paul Phipps, and was the mother *inter alios* of Joyce Grenfell. She was legendary for her promiscuity; she 'appears to have been a nymphomaniac and fell in love with virtually every man she met and tried to marry most of them' (Philip Ziegler). Irene married Charles Dana Gibson (1867-1944), the popular illustrator whose facile pen-and-ink drawings delineated the slender-waisted, richly busted Amazonian who epitomized the American ideal of feminine beauty and charm at the turn of the century. Another sister, Nancy Witcher Langhorne (1879-1964), had married (secondly) Waldorf Astor in May of the same year. (James Fox, *The Langhorne Sisters*, 1998.)
[4] A recent biography is James Mackay, *The Man who invented himself: A Life of Sir Thomas Lupton*, 1998.
[5] She was Maud Alice, born in New York. The Cunards (more successfully than the Paints) had been a merchant family from Halifax, Nova Scotia.
[6] Theodore writes from Vienna on 10 June 1875 to say 'Heard Strauss play and conduct his band last night'.
[7] Guy Freemantle Cobbold (1885-1969) was a major in the Yorks and Lancashire Regt., gaining an MC at the same time as cousin Arthur Turnbull in 1916.
[8] The Osbornes of Castle Rock were magnates in Illinois railways and Philippine shipping from Salem, Massachusetts, and old family friends. The Castle Rock estate was bought by William Henry Osborne in 1855, who built the granite castle like a picturesque Schloss on the Rhine in 1881. Osborne was an early conservationist, and married into the Sturges family, like his friend J.P. Morgan.

His son, Fairfield Sr., known in the family as the 'Prof' (1857-1935), was a distinguished vertebrate palaeontologist and biologist, who worked under T.H. Huxley. He was President of the American Museum of Natural History, New York, where he is commemorated as interpreter of one of the world's finest fossil collections (beside Roosevelt) by a life-sized seated statue. He extended Castle Rock at the time of Arthur's visit in 1906.

His sons were Perry and Fairfield Jr. The first was a lawyer in New York. His brother, Fairfield, was one of the first eco-activists, author of *Our Plundered Planet*, praised by Einstein and Aldous Huxley, and President of the New York Zoological Society.
[9] He may have worked with cousins in Neamestown, co. Wexford, exporting hides, where Thomas Neame, son of John, was born ante 1435.
[10] According to Catholic author Alan Neame (d. 2000) of Selling, this branch were (like the Manders) well-off farmers, not freeholders; for many years land agents and reeves to greater men. These included James II's Catholic courtier Sir Edward Hales, titular earl of Tenterden (d. 1695), and in the C19 Lord Sondes, at his Lees Court estate. Frank Dilnot's popular novel, *Neame of Kent* (1928), is a vivid romance based on one of these 17th-century yeomen, who challenges sour-faced Puritans and overbearing Cavaliers in a welter of adventure and intrigue. (For the brewery, see Theo Barker, *Shepherd Neame,* Cambridge: Granta Eds, 1998.)
[11] The Neames also managed timber concessions in the Caucasus, based at Odessa, where George Austen Neame was working at the time of the 1918 Revolution. Gebhard Blücher mentions meeting Neame there while visiting with the landowner de Boursac in 1911 (see *Memoirs of Prince Blücher*, 1932, p. 216).
[12] Lt Philip Neame, KBE, CB, DSO, etc., on 19 December 1914 'in the face of very heavy fire, engaged the Germans in a single-handed bombing attack, killing and wounding a number of them. He was able to check the enemy advance for three-quarters of an hour and

to rescue all of the wounded whom it was possible to move'. He was the only VC recipient to win an Olympic Gold Medal, when he competed in Paris in 1924 as a member of the Running Deer Team. See his *Playing with Strife: the Autobiography of a Soldier,* 1947.

[13] *The Navy List* gives a Charles Cotterel (sic), rear admiral, who died 28 July 1754. By the following century, the Cotterills were prosperous distillers in Northamptonshire.

[14] Edward Gibbon (1737-94), the great historian of the decline of Rome, written in augustan cadences, was himself a family historian. He writes in his posthumous *Autobiography* (a minor classic):

Could I draw my pedigree from a general, a statesman, or a celebrated author, I should study their lives with the diligence of filial love. In the investigation of past events our curiosity is stimulated by the immediate or indirect reference to ourselves... The nobility of the Spencers has been illustrated and enriched by the trophies of Marlborough, but I exhort them to consider the *Faery Queen* as the most precious jewel of their coronet.

The Gibbons are described as a 'good' family, established in Kent: 'In [the Weald], and in the hundred and parish of Rolvenden, the Gibbons were possessed of lands in the year 1326; and the elder branch of the family, without much increase or diminution of property, still adheres to its native soil.' Gibbon, born in Putney, was descended from a younger branch who set up as merchants in the City in the early seventeenth century:

Our most respectable families have not disdained the counting-house, or even the shop; their names are enrolled in the Livery and Companies of London; and in England, as well as in the Italian commonwealths, heralds have been compelled to declare that gentility is not degraded by the exercise of trade.

[15] Desmond won an impressive number of caps at Eton, but was killed on exercise on the Yorkshire coast 4 Sept 1940 at the outbreak of the War. Shamus (1911-2000) continued with Lionel Neame a while in the timber business, where he met and married Gunvor Hjelt of Helsinki in 1939. He was distinguished as a scholar and linguist, a sportsman, colonel in the Coldstream Guards, and then as a diplomat and intelligence specialist, close to Field Marshall Mannerheim and to the leaders of Cold War Finland, Paasikivi and Kekkonen. (For Magill of Churchtown, see Burke's *Irish Family Records.*)

CAM on parade at camp in front of Yeomanry lines

18

THE FIRST WORLD WAR

The Staffordshire Yeomanry in Egypt and Palestine, 1916–19

Charles Arthur had joined the Staffordshire Yeomanry in 1906, when his father was Colonel in command. He describes the badinage, tent-pegging, snap-shooting at cocoa-nuts, at the officers' training camp at Netheravon on Salisbury Plain, listing all the Old Etonians and Trinity men he met up with. On the first day, 29 April, he reports:

> They have drugged a cock which they bought from an old woman for five shillings by giving it port, and have put it in Caruso's room in the hope it will wake him up in the morning... We held a court marshal on Knollys,[1] and the jury after deliberating found him guilty and sentenced him to bed. However he appeared later in his pyjamas and bowler, and we upset Crudall's tent at last, fortified by steak and kidney pie...

A gilded youth of Edwardian summers could not last for ever. Soon he is describing 'everything outside the walls of home—Europe, and even England—in a state of chaos'. Things grew more earnest as the Yeomanry was mobilised when war broke out on 4 August 1914, and he immediately volunteered for active service. He was just thirty years old, and married a year, when he went with them on training exercises in Bishops Stortford and then at Diss in Norfolk.

Machine Gun Section fishing competition, training at Diss

Arthur (2nd from right) with Machine Gun Section, Staffordshire Yeomanry

The Regiment was eventually sent to Egypt in 1915. He served in Egypt and Palestine in conditions contrasting with his life of slippered ease, initially in command of their First Machine-Gun Corps until 1916, when he became second-in-command of 'C' squadron.

He was soon gazetted a major, taking part in the three battles—or 'stunts', as he prefers to call them lightheartedly—of Gaza. This was stoutly defended by the Turks, in a line stretching to Beersheba, guarding the southerly approaches to Palestine. Lieutenant-General Sir Archibald Murray, in command of the Egyptian Expeditionary Force, launched his attack on 26 March 1917. The fighting was tough, under heavy shell fire, then shrapnel, 'like rain on a pond'.

Charles Arthur's journal letters home of the Egyptian and Palestine campaigns, scribbled hastily in the field with blunt pencils and sent with numerous photographs and sketches, give a spirited cavalry officer's account of life on the front line in one of the last great cavalry campaigns. They communicate a sense of futility and despair as a spectator as much as an officer participant in the stirring events of military history: 'All is shadowed by this damnable war—most damnably disturbing and senseless.'

Gaza stunts, March 1917

About six miles NE of Gaza

I am sitting in the middle of a green amphitheatre, about two miles in diameter, and there are also with me about 2000 men and horses—men lying about, horses grazing contentedly. On both sides of us—that is towards Gaza and Beersheba—the most earsplitting *ccrrumps* are going off; shrapnel and every other kind of shell. It has really been a very dull day and tiring, but we may yet have some closer experience of fighting, as if the Infantry do not take Gaza, we are to be slipped in from the side this evening.

The more troops are multiplied, the slower things become, so that yesterday morning up to Belah, it took us from two in the morning till seven; about twelve miles. Then we had a reconnaissance to do in this direction: this meant an outpost line, while the staff officers made up their minds where we should cross the Wadi Guzze to Gaza—this morning. This Wadi is an odd feature—a sort of canyon about 50 feet deep and 100 yards wide, with terribly difficult banks all cut away by the rain. When it does rain, it rises rapidly and is often impassible. In fact, the other day some Lincoln patrols had to swim for it, practically. We got back to Belah just getting dark and found thousands of troops everywhere—camels, guns, every conceivable thing.

It was dark when we got in, and in the chaos I got into a 'diddy' encampment, instead of HQ. One flea at least got up each leg, and in the four days that have ensued they (or he) has caused considerable havoc; just above the left sock I have a circular ring of 65 flee bites. I caught him yesterday. Not the least of the discomforts we had to contend with!

Bazaar at Khan Yunnis, Gaza strip—'Napoleon was here in March 1799'

27th March 1917 We had scarcely got down, when orders came to move at two —which meant a rise at 12.30—pitch dark and much time wasted; very cold and later on a thick fog arose, so that delays were inevitable. Everyone lost themselves, and it was not till 7.30 that the two mounted Divisions, Cavalry, Infantry, guns, etc., got over the Wadi Guzze.

It was a thrilling site to see in the rolling plain among the rising mist as a hot sun struggled through; thousands of horses, men, guns, ambulance wagons. The whole place seemed alive—and I waited anxiously for a first shell. We were four or five miles from Gaza. A hostile aeroplane came over, and later *ccrump*—a high explosive in a plume of brown sand, very wide; later still one much nearer, which made us all flinch.

We moved very slowly with frequent halts, for the Australians had various detachments of enemy to drive in. At about 2 p.m. we were at the place I first mentioned with the Australians well round to the sea, and the Imperial Division joining up with the Infantry, preventing the enemy escaping, and reinforcements arriving up to the town. We watered the horses and waited, and it was very hot. As we didn't know when we should get drinking water again, I only took a sip now and then, and next morning when we were once more in Belah, I had a drop over.

About four we were told to move, and later learnt we were to make an attack from the rear, as the Infantry were not advancing quite as quickly as had been hoped. We rode further behind Gaza, to a slope beyond which the positions could be seen. Our batteries were already bursting shrapnel over it. The Regiment was very split up at this time; 'C' Squadron having gone as escort to the guns, 'B' Squad as flank guard, and the remainder were kept in reserve. Practically the rest of the division in Brigades rode extended over the intervening crops and dunes, until quite down to the trenches, then dismounted and advanced up the slope. The Brigadier and Staff rode with the East Riding and Lincolnshire Yeomanry at a steady trot into the setting sun, very thrilling to watch—and successful to boot, very few casualties resulting. (E.R.Y: one killed, five wounded all evening.)

I sat on the hill next the divisional people whose headquarters were there, and watched. Shrapnel, men advancing in rushes, gaining trenches; a white flag here, the crest gained there; on the right the dunes and the sea; on the right front the sun setting, but still light, crops intervening—combined to form a spectacle that I only want to see once. Resistance was gradually overcome on our side, and firing almost ceased, and at 5.30 we were told to ride up and report to the General. There were a certain number of stray bullets, but I don't think any arrived, mostly coming from the further side. As far as we could see, Gaza was captured. But would the light hold sufficiently to round up the Turks, and prevent them getting away? We could see that the chief position was ours, but heard the firing making for the sea.

Crossing Wadi Guzze at Goz Mabruk

Yeomanry crossing Wadi near Belah

At Marakib, divisions by the sea

It got dark, and we prepared to spend the night, when we got orders to go back to the hill we started from. A different matter in the dark from the daylight, for the ground although it looked gently sloping was cut up into small water-courses; and having crossed one, the men had to gallop to keep those in front in view, who never waited! Result: riderless horses wildly galloping, and no doubt casualties.

A long wait in the dark. Eight, nine, ten. Then I got orders to escort 130 prisoners and two captured guns back to Belah, our starting point—perhaps a matter of 20 miles—and the Staff were evidently in a great hurry that this should be done with the greatest dispatch. Firing could be heard in the distance from the relieving column who were being held off by the Imperial Mounted Division.

It was a rotten job. Pitch dark. Prisoners to be woken up and collected. Guns to be collected. Guide to be found. And it was 45 minutes before we all started, with the General fuming and saying he could not be responsible if the worst happened if we did not leave at once.

At last we got off with the prisoners in a hollow square, the guns behind and the guide (who was running the signal wire cable through a crook to see it was not cut) ahead. Every now and then we came to ravines which the guns crossed with great difficulty, and in which if there was a drop of filthy water to be found the prisoners did there best to lag behind and scoop it out. I had to threaten to prod them with bayonets, which had a salutary effect, for they really walked splendidly, and no men dropped out at all.

We kept on plodding, and later on met returning columns of mounted troops. About half an hour before dawn we halted, as it was impossible to know exactly where the crossing of the Wadi was… I went to examine the guns more closely and was not a little startled to find a dead man tied reclining at full length on the front seat. He was explained as being concerned in the capture of the guns and the New Zealanders wanted to give him a good burial. Rather gruesome he looked though in the starlight.

We got in very dusty and tired at 7.30, and no sooner had we off-saddled, than we were ordered to move in fifteen minutes. A considerable scramble ensued, especially as the prisoners had to be handed over and it was essential that all water bottles should be filled. There was no water except from a deep well, with men crowding round to get a bucket full.

Our job was to relieve a Regiment of Gloucester Yeomanry who were protecting the Infantry's left flank, south of Gaza, so evidently we had *not* captured it. We marched down along the beach, in which there were beastly quicksands which quaked and, from the last I saw of two maxim gun horses, it looked as if they were bogged.

The Squadron was in reserve, and I had time for a wash and a shave. Just as I was stripped to the waist, the Colonel sent for the Squadron, but I finished my wash! We rode forward a mile, and the Colonel pointed out a position which he wanted us to hold, joining up with the Infantry. It was about a mile on or more, and as we rode forward extended, the shots 'phutted' unpleasantly near.

In fact, I didn't care about it at all, especially over the last rise which unexpectedly on the far side sloped away into a sand fall, and made us pull up. I didn't go further because I could see that the position we had been pointed out was on the same ridge and beyond the Turkish trenches, and we had orders not to become involved in a fight. We were under cover, but the bullets came hammering over, and we could see where they hit on the sand slope behind. We crawled up behind some bushes, located their trenches, and could see them dodging about and firing. We gave them later some cause to dodge, for we got our Hotchkiss gun on, and plastered the three redoubts (about 800 yards away) at one time or another with bullets.

As the afternoon latered, I didn't feel at all comfortable, for we were too far on and our right was in the air. At dusk we withdrew our line for three quarters of a mile and prepared to spend the night linking up with the Lincolns on our right, and still in touch with 'C' Squadron on our left.

I also sent the horses to water under [Captain G.H.] Anson—about two and a half miles—and arranged with him to have the signal lamp flashing to guide him back. But he didn't come back! Hour after hour passed; it was obvious he had lost himself. It seemed almost impossible to get a message through to HQ by lamp. Everyone was mythered with tiredness, and no one could understand anything which was said unless repeated three times. About this time firing commenced on our left, and I received orders that we were to withdraw our line back over the Wadi, at twelve. Obviously Anson didn't know this and, lost and waiting for daylight, would be captured on the wrong side of the Wadi in the morning, with all our horses and half our men.

However, things were not so bad as I thought. I tried to get to HQ myself, stumbling for about half an hour, and nearly losing myself, found Ronald, but not HQ, and returned, dead beat. But in a few minutes we heard the neighing of horses, and Anson turned up having been lost and eventually found, and been detained at Brigade HQ to take a message.

It was now after eleven and we had to move at 12.15, so what chance of sleep was there? However, everyone was half asleep, or wholly, having turned in again after the firing had finished on our left. At midnight we turned out and moved away and found Brigade headquarters about one o'clock. Tudor fell off his horse asleep, and it was very difficult to think clearly. Another long wait until scattered parties had collected, and by three we had got back over the Wadi and were wandering and wondering where our positions were. I saw the General and soon a Scotch Infantry colonel looking for him, but could never find both together. Eventually we got somewhere and off-saddled, stand to at four, and then we all got two hours' sleep, some kind of breakfast, and then orders to move again.

Convoy going over dunes to the sea

The odd thing was that none of us was over hungry, and personally for the whole of the second day I only ate one biscuit, although my pockets were full of good things. We moved this time to reconnoitre the enemy's front-line trenches towards Gaza, which was still less than ever occupied by us, though we heard that the Queen's and other of the 53rd Division had captured it on two consecutive days, having had to march back each time. On the way over our aeroplane dropped a message to say that the trenches were strongly held. The Lincolns and E.R. were in front and after playing about a bit Dobell[2] rode up and told us to return to camp.

We had done 61 hours, and for 51 the saddles had been on the horses' backs for all but half an hour. Nor had we had any sleep, practically; except of the kind that makes one wake sore and stiff. No wonder that the flea had been so restive that he had bitten me 63 times; or was it 64? A record number of bites, if not of jumps and hunting!

Since then, in two days we have changed camps twice, but otherwise been resting. Gaza still is in the hands of the enemy, and it is more on the cards that we shall retire further than advance at the moment. We had a glorious bathe yesterday and the beach was covered with troops glorying in the wash. Ships were lying off the coast, and two 'monitors' landing shells, we were told.

We had 14 out of 140 horses done up when we got in, but most of these have recovered now. We have two men in hospital—a touch of sun and the fall from the horse. Four horses are now permanently out of use. In the Regiment we have had three horses hit, one in the Squadron and one mare hit in the bottom—but not badly.

So ends my experience of the battle of Gaza, probably hardly mentioned in the English papers, except incidentally as a further success falling to the British arms in Palestine. But all the same really a nasty knock in which we lost 5000 casualties.

RAMC 22nd Mounted Brigade, en route near Beersheba

At the time the battle was indeed reported as a British victory. But although General Dobell's cavalry had secured ground to the rear of the town, the infantry follow-through failed to break the Turkish line. The British withdrew after a Turkish counter-attack at the very moment the German garrison commander was considering surrender. On the west bank of Wadi Guzze, Arthur's squadron settled down in the following months to trench warfare; all in tatters, almost bootless from the heat and sweat. But Arthur reported positively that he was awfully well, and besides they had plenty of water.

Squadron wagon team: L. to R.: Cpl Thraves, ?, Roger Manley, Colonel, Bullock, CAM, Sgt-Maj. Asbury, ?

Staffs Yeomanry officers in Palestine: John Godfrey, Spinney, Charles Wiggin, Lord (Will) Lewisham, CAM, H.E. Nash, Wood, Niven, Bullock, Brough (sitting)

Second Gaza Fight, April 1917

16th April 1917 We moved out at dusk and had an interminable ride to Shellal, parading at seven. It is damnably dusty, and we were covered from head to foot with yellow glue long before we arrived. By daylight our faces looked like those seen by sodium flash, from which bloodshot eyes gleamed. It was good to see the sun rise and imposing to see the divisions stretching out like a mammoth worm stretching over the barley fields with the Guzze.

We watered there and ate a frugal breakfast, for when one may be hurried off at a moment's notice, it is not worth while trying to be elaborate. A biscuit can always be eaten on the march, plus dried fruit and chocolate, keeps one going indefinitely.

Soon I was called up and detailed as advance guard squadron to the division. Perfectly flat open country, gently sloping barley fields, and in the distance steeper ground. Considerable confusion occurred after we had started, as the New Zealanders all came across our front in a slantindicular direction, and the point we were marching on, which in any case was impossible to indicate, was altered twice.

We had many stops and eventually got about five miles; clouds of dust behind, guns away on our right had been booming since dawn, and before. A message came to push on to a further wadi, and report on the crossings.[3] A definite order which admitted only one construction—the hill beyond was obviously strongly held, and also a ridge away on our left.

On we went without being shot at. I wondered vaguely when they would begin, but they were much too cunning to start while we were at any distance. Eventually, we got the horses under cover up to the wadi, and then the fun began. At first only a few shots, and while our troop held the further edge, I rode up and down the dry bed of the wadi to see what crossings could be effected. Gradually the shooting brisked up, and I wrote my report and went back to the centre troops who were lining the near side. Found Ronald there with three troops, one of whom had been sent to guard our right flank. Shrapnel burst too short, and then too far, and *then* they got the range!

'A. watching Mander Bros clerks preparing dinner'

At first we sat tight, thinking the bank would protect us, and it did more or less, but not the poor horses. Over they came, four at a time, angrily screaming, a shattering burst, and then dust churned all around. Blower was killed at once, another exploded among the horses, wounding Morris and Houghton; fortunately not all came into our little valley, or none would have been alive today. Rifle fire is child's play, for against shrapnel one feels so helpless; firing is no good, even if the position of the guns was known...

I looked back and saw that the division were evidently not going to assist us, and had actually retired and decided it was time to quit. We were, you see, only making a 'demonstration', but how could I know that such an unconvincing demonstration would be sufficient as that of the pillory of a miserable squadron? Almost this time, the doc who had turned up was hit in the back, and others wounded. Roger Manley, he and I were carrying Morris away and it burst right over us; a piece missed my jugular vein by an inch, and I can hear it now. I felt quite deafened and dithery.

It was obviously time and more than time to quit. Ronald [?Ratcliff] at the same moment came to the same conclusion. I took the Squadron away in none too orderly a formation, under shell fire, and rallied them about a mile back to come on quietly. Meanwhile, the first troop under Bullock, and some of 'C' Squadron with Ratcliff and Anson, collected those remaining. Led horses had to be sent up for those who could be mounted, and three charges were made by half a dozen men at advancing tanks, cavalry and snipers.

But before these horses could be collected and got back, Sergeant Asbury and two others who had been lying very doggo and had not got the order to retire, by some mischance were surrounded and taken prisoners by ten or a dozen mounted Turks. They were at the time trying to move the doc, and did not fire—though one man, Bowyer, fired six shots (by another account at the same Turk, and missed him!) Fortunately for them, the hostile captors did no more than take all their equipment and, leaving them with their water bottles, sent them back to our lines. Meanwhile, we had secured the stray horses, and a sledge, and with more difficulty the services of a doctor and an RMAC sand cart. It was with great difficulty and risk that Harvey, Morris and Palmer were brought in, and Anson was splendid, giving up his own horse on two or three occasions to a wounded man. We had seven men wounded and one killed in the squadron, and I hope our demonstration was considered worth while.

After we had retired, our guns came into action and we had to protect them, occasionally under shrapnel fire, during the afternoon. We retired at seven, and withdrew over the Guzze.

Four men of 'B' Squadron could not be found on an advance observation post, and during the night, were attacked; two wounded and one killed. We got into our bivouac area at 1.30, and to bed at 2.30, for we had to feed man and beast.

18th April 1917 The next day, we rested, except for the excitement of two bombs dropped as soon as it was daylight.

19th April 1917 The day we were to take Gaza, we held an outpost line which we occupied the previous evening. Tremendous thundering of guns. Our division was practically out of the battle; we lazed about and waited for information which either did not come or was not available. In the afternoon, we were hurried north to reinforce a portion of the Imperial Mounted Division which had bulged badly. However, we were not wanted. Orders and counter-orders resulted in our getting somewhere by 1.30 in the morning, with a stand-to at four. So not too much sleep.

20th April 1917 We moved south, and occupied a flank outpost line at Wadi Sheikh Nuran. We were horribly bombed twice during the day; each time they dropped six to eight bombs, and many horses were killed, though none in the Regiment. Two men, however, had to go to hospital suffering from shell shock. Bombing is, I think, the most horrible form of warfare, because every bomb, as it drops and the ominous hiss gets louder, seems to be dropping straight on one's devoted head. Then follows a deafening crash, which we will hope results in a harmless cloud of dust several hundred yards away. If the bomb drops near, the only chance is to lie flat; to be caught bending is better than to be caught standing. In this way, in one troop of Australian Light Horse, twelve horses were killed, and only one man touched. He was standing, and all the rest lying down. We withdrew in the evening to bivouac in very snug dugouts.

General Murray was sacked after the repulse of the second battle, which ended with heavy British casualties. The main attack against the Turks was the decisive third battle of Gaza the following October and November 1917, this time under General Sir Edmund Allenby as commander of the British Eastern Expeditionary force: two corps of 40,000 men.[4] On 31 October the first phase of attack culminated in the charge of the Australian General Sir Harry Chauvel's Fourth Light Horse Brigade on the stronghold of Beersheba, in a shallow saucer of the Judean hills. The vigorous onslaught of 800 troopers gallop-ing in line formed the last great cavalry charge in history and a heroic victory for the 'diggers', as they were known, which overwhelmed the line of Turkish rifles and machine-guns stoutly defending the city.

'Competing 'bints' (but in Arabic = girl). The centre one, Timmins of my squadron, won the costume prize.'

The mounted troops of the Staffordshire Yeomanry were engaged in the follow-up main attack on 6 November, on the flanks of the infantry who occupied Tel-el-Khuweilfeh, ten miles north of Beersheba, 'and assisted in repulsing repeated counter-attacks made by strong enemy forces'. The system of Turkish defences was at last crumbling, leaving the field open for the final advance on Jerusalem.

Heavy fighting followed in the Judean hills, where the Turks attempted holding actions. As the Turkish retreated northwards from their eight miles of trenches, Arthur was 'struck' by shrapnel in the ankle. He was taken away from the battle field slung precariously in a 'cakaley' on the side of a camel—'an invention for torturing the wounded'. A fellow soldier who happened to be quite close to him ran back to see him being taken away. He asked him rather anxiously how he felt, and received the unexpected reply, 'I feel very happy'.

His wound meant he wrote no journal of the battle. He cabled home: 'Wounded in left ankle, going on famously, nearly well.' He was soon invalided near Cairo, as the wound would not heal, writing by 15 November: 'It is going to be a slower process than I thought at first. Except for an occasional twinge, perhaps due to an odd bit of sock not quite disgorged yet, I have no discomfort. Both holes are as big as 18*d.*, that is, rather bigger than a shilling!'

'Some methods of progressing'

Jerusalem, 4 June 1918

He made a slow recovery, one of 18,000 allied casualties in the battle, while the British forces entered Jerusalem on 9 December without him. There was a lull in the fighting and the sequel was more relaxed. An Old Etonian dinner was held in Jerusalem on 4 June 1918 to celebrate the capture of the holy city.[5] The venue was the German Hotel, now HQ of the 20th Corps, 'a really improving building founded by the Hun emperor in 1907, with a statue advertising the fact that Wilhelm gave it, and that everyone on earth should be thankful'. The company of 84 included no less than five others of Brinton's (double from any other house, and one of them, Graham, a VC), as well as eight generals and many senior, highly-decorated officers. As the guests gradually put a name to a strangely familiar face, drinking champagne out of beer mugs, things became progressively merrier:

Sir Philip Chetwode[6] proposed 'The King' and '*Floreat Etona*'. At the crisis of our Empire, nay civilisation, the toast was drunk solemnly, even devoutly, with as much of the *carmen* as everyone could remember, which was only the chorus. And then the fun began...

A general was produced who could play by sight and not by ear, and tried the 'Boating Song'. We all turned towards the high table and, holding onto the shoulders of whoever was in front, swung back and forth in time to the song, like a gaiety chorus (male). Of course, by the end of the second verse, nearly everyone was over-swinging, and trying to upset his neighbour, and at this everyone became very successful, and many collapsed.

Then we called on Major Hole for a speech, who left Eton in 1879 and was the senior O.E. present. He had evidently been warned what might happen, and made a very amusing speech of how the privileges of his day had gradually been filched away and how he had attended the last matinée performance at Windsor Theatre to which the school was officially allowed. It was 'Hamlet', and in the grave scene they tried to 'tice the grave-diggers out of the grave by throwing coppers on the stage. They proved obdurate till the sum reached 18/7, when the greed of one overcame his artistic scruples. He clambered out of the grave, only to be bitten in the leg by the other digger, while Hamlet boned the coppery harvest...

But by this time, someone had produced a football and oranges were being thrown about, and although Pardoe[7] tried to preach a sermon on the text of 'Three Blind Mice'—'A mystic number, my friends' and 'The blindness of those I see around me...' were the only two sentences I could catch—he had to dodge oranges, and made some excellent shots himself, which all hit *someone.*

At this point, General Howard-Vyse[8] came down to speak to his old fag-master, who was a full-blown captain, and anxious to chastise him now as he had done some 20 years before; a friendly free fight ensued, and several tables were smashed. At this point, I earned a mention from the General by going down into the mêlée and rescuing twenty whole glasses and three bottles of brandy.

By this time, many bullies were occurring in various points of the room and rams were forcing goats, defended by tables and chairs; oranges and napkins rolled tight. It looks as if much damage would be done, if not to Hun property, then certainly to the persons of his British Majesty's subjects, for the floor was covered with broken glasses and was itself composed of corrugated tiles, and many parties hit the earth. The most uproarious of the lot was Dalmeny,[9] horrible man, who had three teeth knocked out, I am glad to say; but I suspect they were false ones, alack.

Eventually most of us split up into groups in safer places, while the super-diners tried to get others to pull down the Kaiser's statue, which would have taken a very sober conspiracy to undermine, as it is 30 feet up in a snug niche. Well, I got to bed at 11.15 and was asleep in two minutes, conscious of hunting noises fading away into the night as motors bore the revellers away.

The advance on Damascus, Autumn 1918

Arthur had eventually rejoined his regiment at the crusader city of Ascalon, just north of Gaza. Then his squadron was sent for a month's rest in the Valley of the Jordan, after acting as escort to General Chauvel's Desert Mounted Corps. CTM writes: 'They had not been there a week, when General Allenby collared them, and they were instructed to join the Fourth Cavalry Division at Sorona, where he had a force of three Cavalry Divisions, about 15,000 strong.'

From there Charles Arthur took part in the aftermath of the great battle of Megiddo—the site of the biblical 'Armageddon'. According to the Revelations of St John, this patch of the Levant, by then a pile of rubble in the desert, was where the world would end in a last battle between God and the AntiChrist. It now marked the final push which annihilated the three Turkish armies in Palestine for ever. It was the British blitzkrieg; according to Liddell Hart, 'one of the most completely decisive battles in all history'.

Arthur's part in it was to follow the Fourth Cavalry Division in Allenby's strategic cavalry 'bound' from the desert through Beisan in September 1918, a forced march which covered an epic 87 miles in 33Q hours—a record in Cavalry history. The Regiment, after resting four days during which they took 5,800 prisoners, finally marched on Damascus, where they were one of the first to converge with the Allied advance, making their triumphal entry with Allenby on 1 October.

The enterprise was seen by the sporting Australians, wrote T.E. Lawrence, 'like a point-to-point, with Damascus the post'. It was a symbolic prize, with the endgame in sight. Lawrence prophesied: 'Damascus meant the end of this war in the East, and, I believed, the end of the general war, too; because the Central Powers being interdependent, the breaking of their weakest link—Turkey—would swing the whole cluster loose'. Arthur knew Colonel Lawrence quite well. His narrative as a rank-and-file participant in the advance on Damascus, harrying the retreating Turk in the follow-up of Megiddo, is evocative, if more prosaic than that of *The Seven Pillars*:

26th September 1918 We got orders to pack up and move overnight, which were countermanded several times, so that by 8 o'clock I did not know whether I was saddled up or not. This new venture is a bigger one than before—the general scheme being, now that the main Turk army has been annihilated, to push on rapidly to Damascus with the three cavalry divisions, and capture it before they have time to organize resistance. Our role is to deal with the remaining army on the east of Jordan, which is supposed to be retiring from Es Salt with all speed. We shall get to Damascus too, no doubt, but shall not have the kudos of being there first. However, we shall have got the most prisoners.

We marched about ten miles to the Rey bridge over the Jordan, and crossed by a saddle-backed prehistoric bridge with arches again on each side. I made a hurried sketch of it, which does less than justice to its picturesqueness. It was a frightfully hot day and several fellows went sick partly from the heat, and partly I think in one case to a surfeit of figs; in another to eating too much lamb, for the last batch of prisoners had some sheep with them, and two of these we commandeered. The mutton was excellent, and as tender as the best Welsh well-hung.

We camped about three miles on the further (east) side of the river, which here is about 20 feet across, and rather reminiscent of a highland trout stream. I never felt less inclined to do anything in my life—the mugginess and the low altitude affected everyone the same way. But the mosquitoes were not quite as bad as they were at Beisan. Really there they kept me awake at night; but fortunately the doctor found a parcel of German quinine tablets which he handed round and with which every evening I dose the subalterns—they are about three times as efficacious as the English ones, as they are much more soluble.

27th September 1918 We started off the 40-odd-mile trek for Deraa which is the junction of the Palestine and Hedjaz railways. It was half an excellent ride through the hills up which we had to climb 2,000 feet, and looked in many places as if it was engineered with the idea of building a railway—except the gradients were too stiff. When we got on the top table land, it became very stony. The Turks were evidently intending to repair it, but hadn't had the time, for there were great worked blocks of stone for culverts lying about. The plateau itself is most wild and dismal: grey lichenous rocks and stunted oak trees are the only things that meet the eye, except here and there a grey mud village.

We watered after going about 25 miles at a place called Erbid, from cisterns just outside the village. The water has to last from rainy season to rainy season, so the inhabitants presumably were not very keen on our taking their supply—at least I found a cairn and, underneath when I shucked the rocks away, a most excellent supply of icy water.

We waited a couple of hours and marched on very wearily to a place called Er Remte, just six miles from our objective. Here we had to water again from cisterns. This takes an awful time, for many are 20-30 feet deep and only one bucket can be let down at a time. We got in in the pitch dark, and found that all our wood, and all our dixies [iron cooking pots] and cooking utensils had fallen off the mess pack. Sheer carelessness and I was *frightfully* angry, and threatened to make the wretch walk back eight miles to where he'd last seen them. However that didn't bring any wood, so we had to go to bed without a hot drink. Our new cook, Gander, is almost slower than Tudor, and his horse always escapes off the line in the night, so that instead of getting breakfast, he has to wander about looking for it.

During the night, we had 'made' a horse which had stayed from the 6th Cavalry, only unfortunately, just as he had saddled up, its rightful owner turned up and claimed it in a terrible state of excitement, so I had to hand it over.

28th September 1918 The sun rose in a whole rainbow of glorious colouring, and just next to us were some shepherds' shacks and some thousands of sheep who had been collected there for the night. As dawn broke, they blew, each shepherd, a different tune on his pipe, and the sheep sorted themselves into flocks and stood patiently waiting for their shepherd to lead them off. I am not surprised that they felt it hopeless to find pasture by themselves unaided!

I am writing this halted while the situation round Deraa is being cleared up by two brigadiers, and then we move onto Mezerib, which is the nearest place at which we can water. Meanwhile, 2,000 men are moving south from the same place, which we believe to be Hejaz troops ... I hope so. (They turned out to be the supply train of the king of the Hejaz. Deraa was found to be full of dead Germans and Turks killed by the Arabs for murdering one of their women in a revolting fashion—but this I only heard today [1st October] as I write under the trees at Damascus. This rather spoils the story—but you will have seen a month ago that we captured it, and so there is no use pretending that there will be many excitements in my narrative. However, there were possibilities in every situation at the time.)

We had only been going an hour for Mezerib, which was supposed to be held, when the Colonel sent for me, & pointing out that 'B' squadron had gone a bit wide, asked me to carry on with advance guard. It is a job I always dislike very much, for it practically means riding on until the advance men are shot at. I had hardly any time to explain the situation either, as the Gun was in such a hurry—but it worked very well, and when we got there we found the Divisional staff ahead there! There was a big pool and the ruins of a square castle, of quite possible crusader origin.

'What a calamity for a self-respecting L&SWR engine!'

Prisoners disinfected—'like sheep through Coopers' dip'

29th September 1918 I did a sketch the next morning and had a lovely bathe in the rocky stream running out of the lake. Roger said it was exactly like a trout lake in Ireland, so perhaps this describes it to you, but the country round is absolutely flat, and featureless and nary a tree to be seen. As we went on after spending much time waiting for precious rations, the road became more stony than there is sand on the sea shore, and one felt miserable for the poor horses' hoofs after doing 150 miles. We did progress, but very slowly; and all the way along the roadside lay dead Turks—I mean every few hundred yards—bombed by us, or killed by Arabs or Bedouins, until at last we began to feel desperately sorry for them. I don't suppose they wanted to fight any more than I did. We were intending to go further than we could actually do owing to the bad roads, and stayed at a village called Delli, reminiscent of ducks! And every mile Mount Hermon became more immense on our left front, and fainter as the sun rose in the morning, and more sombre and forbidding as the sun set. There was a white patch of snow snuggled away near its topmost peak.

30th September 1918 The next day the road was worse, and we were on our last day's forage, and last but one of rations; but I don't think that, in spite of the strong range of hills to be crossed, anyone thought for a moment that any serious resistance would be offered —the Turks were too demoralized and our advance too well co-ordinated and rapid... We halted short of the hills, on which Turkish rearguards were reported. During the evening, red glows lit up the sky to the north, and we climbed the near ridge to see more clearly. Evidently the Turks were burning military buildings in the city. We were all in bed at eight, for we had an early start—three o'clock—and "bitter chill it was". Pitch dark, or only the merest slip of a waning moon, and the road full of stones still. We were leading Regiment, so it wasn't quite so bad, but even so we were going in fits and starts, trotting and then pulling up suddenly in the dust.

1st October 1918 When it became light, I was detailed for entrance guard, with 'B' Squadron, and on our right we could see hundreds of Bedouins ready to fire their rifles at everyone and everything. We got about thirty Turks who were only too glad to surrender to British troops, as the Arabs were literally murdering them. In fact, one wretched man walking back to the troop after surrendering to the 'advance mount', was shot by a band of eight Bedouins and robbed of his equipment before we could get to him. We had a horribly rocky ridge to climb, and there in front of us lay Damascus, robed in white mist and surrounded by green gardens; a fair and fruitful city indeed (from the distance). On we went, for our objective was still ten miles off, and now we began to meet bands of prisoners who had been captured by the other two divisions, who had cut across our advance.

The other two divisions were moving along a shorter road from Tiberias and the south west, and were confidently expected to be in ahead of us. However, as it turned out, we all arrived the same moment, which showed the skilful handling our generals displayed. I ran into Jacko Watson, now commanding the Gloucesters, who had left Haifa only five nights before. We had orders not to go into the town, and so laid an outpost line just short of the town, which resolved itself into piquetting the road. Everyone had an eye for foraging, and it wasn't long before someone spotted a field of potatoes—King Edward VII, I should think —and they proved as good as any I've ever tasted. It was about 3 p.m., and from then until next morning we were all in a state of semi somnolence or complete repleteness.

2nd October 1918 We went into Damascus and I was filmed with the rest of the procession. In the night, we got orders that there was to be a ceremonial march through the town, in which each regiment was represented by a squadron—and of course I, as senior squadron leader, went with it. Colonel Newnham of the 6th Cavalry commanded the composite regiment from the brigade, and there was a brigade from each division, so that we were in all one division strong and about three miles long. Of course we were late in starting and, when we did get under way, we were some six hours moving with only about half an hour's rest in all, so that the whole performance was most tiring for horses and men, and most trying to our tempers, for I should think that we went quite two hours' ride out of our way after the procession, because some incompetent S.O. who was leading lost his way.

My first impression of the town was that it was the filthiest and most uninteresting and disappointing place I had been in. I still think it the filthiest, but that is only an incidental annoyance which our arrival will alter, but I have since discovered some fine buildings and Roman remains, and even its eastern squalor and rags has its attractions, when seen from a sufficient distance.

Our route lay along a double tram line which certainly had not been used since the War, for the lines were bent, and the granite setts were in some parts a foot above the road, in others removed with gaps a foot below—the cables for electricity were broken and hanging about—and every now and then the crust of the road had caved in six feet and more, showing a stream of clear water beneath. I do not know the derivation of the name 'Damascus', or the Arabic *Es Sham*, but I should have thought it ought to mean 'city of running waters' for, at every turn, the water squirts out of pipes and fountains, and runnels course in the gutters and beneath the roads—lovely, clear, cool water, for all the garbage thrown in it.

We went through the usual crowded bazaars, but the population seemed quite indifferent to our arrival, and only in one place was there any clapping. But of course over a mile of the procession had already passed before I came along, and the Spanish consul has since told me that everyone was overjoyed at our arrival, and particularly impressed by the beautiful horses we rode, and the size of the motor lorries which began to turn up as the procession passed the main square. They were also amazed that we should harness four horses to lumbers loaded with what they said *one* horse could easily draw!

Old well at Belah, near Beersheba

In the 38 days since the start of the battle of Megiddo, the Desert Mounted Corps, supported by Lawrence and his Arab irregulars, had swept spectacularly across the Turkish rear destroying three of their armies in the process, advanced 350 miles and captured 76,000 prisoners, 360 guns and 89 locomotives. The days of the tottering Ottoman empire were numbered. Allenby was created Viscount Allenby of Megiddo and virtual ruler of Egypt until its independence, and Chauvel of the Light Horse was described as the greatest Cavalry commander of the twentieth century.

True to Lawrence's prophesy, Turkey had signed the Armistice before the month was out, on 31 October. At this point, the combined squadron of the Staffordshire Yeomanry was under Arthur's command. CTM takes up the story in his letter to Colonel Sewell:

After a week, the Regiment started on a 200-mile trek to Aleppo, and my son shortly after assumed command; Colonel (then Major) Sir Charles Wiggin[10] was ill, and Lord Lewisham[11] had left for England to contest West Bromwich for which he was member, the Regiment having been reduced to 75 men, 200 of them becoming casualties from malignant malaria, etc., caught in the Jordan valley. At this point the Brigade became immobilized through sickness and, shortly after, the Armistice was signed with Turkey, and the Brigade were sent to Beyrut. As soon as the War was over, I 'raised Cain' to get him home, and he left Beyrut in a drifter for Haifa, and arrived home in February 1919.

He had taken his own hunters from England to the war. As the army provided no way of repatriating them, like many officers he preferred to have them put down before embarking for home, rather than see them maltreated—as he thought—by an Arab master.

When he arrived home, he wrote up his Game Book of the war years. With habitual irony, he records the Turkish prisoners under 'Various'; the Guns '1/1 Staffordshire Yeomanry':

1916	*Fayoum, Egypt*	*Duck of many kinds, poor bag of Senussi*		
1917	*Sinai, Palestine*	*Turks difficult to circumvent*		
		March 27	Gaza	147
		April 19	Wadi Imlih	?
		Oct 30	Beersheba	
			Jerusalem	
1918	*Syria, Lebanon*	*Turks strong on wing*		
		Sep 19, 23	Beisan	5,900
		Oct 1	Damascus	80,000

Years later, Charles Arthur related an anecdote in his speech on retiring from his second term as mayor of Wolverhampton. He recalled how, stationed in the Lebanon waiting for his drifter home, he had set out to find what the 'far-famed' cedars looked like, involving a climb to 10,000 feet on horseback. Late in the evening, down a mountain path, the party stumbled on the village of Bserreh, and he was the next day prevailed upon by the innkeeper who had provided them mattresses on the floor, one

Joseph Tuma, to make him mayor. There was lawlessness in the liberated Syrian village of 20,000 people, which had been left without a leader after the Turkish retreat.

'There had been great arguments, resulting in free fights, and there was no one to administer the affairs of the town.' Charles Arthur pointed out that he was there simply as a visitor and that it was not his job to make mayors in Syria. The innkeeper convinced him that, unless he took some action in the matter, there would probably be bloodshed, as there was a rival claimant. 'So, with the help of an interpreter, Sir Charles drew up a very formidable document in which "whereas", "aforesaid", "herein before mentioned", and so on made frequent appearance.' [12]

Another time he shared a meal with a Bedouin in a manner which seemed stranger to the reporting journalist than it would have done to CAM, who was a good mixer, a quality which helped him as a traveller:[13]

He partook of a friendly repast with a Bedouin in his camel-hair tent. They sat on their haunches and helped themselves from a communal hot-pot in the centre. The Bedouin, to emphasise his feelings towards the British nation as exemplified by Sir Charles, thrust his finger into the pot and drew out a goat cutlet. From this the Bedouin bit a mouthful and handed the rest to Sir Charles, with the words, 'We eat together.'

Arthur surveys the Promised Land from a hillock.

He won several decorations 'on which matter no-one can make him talk' and was known as 'Lightning' by his comrades owing to his dislike of 'hustle': 'he will tell you that he possesses none of the characteristics of this destructive element'. When his sergeant asked him for orders as to when the troops should march, he would retort unhelpfully, 'When they're ready'. He was not a natural soldier. But he ended the war as second-in-command of his Regiment. His father, CTM, wrote defiantly to Colonel Sewell to complain when he was passed over to command the Regiment, on 14 November 1924:

My son, Major Mander, is being invited to resign in favour of Major Vaughan Williams for reasons which, in my opinion, are ridiculously inadequate. Major Vaughan Williams is a Welshman who left the Regiment in 1916 for Staff duties, and was only six or nine months in Egypt, and never served with them in Palestine, whereas my son is a Staffordshire man, and was with the Regiment all through the War. He is a sound business man, and the one on whom I depend most in the conduct of the important business of which I am Chairman.

---

[1] Frederick Knollys, City of London Yeo., b. 1884—died of wounds received in action, Sept. 1915.

[2] General Dobell was Commander of the Eastern Forces.

[3] The message reads: 'You are to advance to the Wadi Imleih. Examine all crossings over Wadi on your front and see if there are any not marked on the map. Report also what country on the other side looks like. 5th Inf^{y} B^{d} hold Khirbit Ekk to El Munkheileh...'

[4] Charles Arthur's brother-in-law, Colonel Lionel George Cotterill Neame, married Daisy Bendix, née Hancox (as her second husband). She married (thirdly) the General's nephew, becoming in due course the second Lady Allenby.

[5] The official report of the capture of the city on 9 December 1917 ran: 'Thus, at 12.30, the Holy City was surrendered for the twenty-third time, and for the first time to British arms, and on this occasion without bloodshed among the inhabitants, or damage to the buildings of the City itself.'

[6] Lt-Gen. Sir Philip Chetwode, Bt, KCB, KCMG, DSO (b. 1869—d. 1950). He commanded the British 20th Corps in Palestine and Syria. He was later Field Marshal, CGS, OM, and first Baron Chetwode. His daughter, Penelope, married the laureate and architectural critic, Sir John Betjeman.

[7] Lt-Col. Frank Pardoe (b. 1880), King's Royal Rifle Corps, of Leyton Manor, Essex.

[8] Brig.-Gen. Richard G.H. Howard-Vyse, CMG, DSO (b. 1883), Royal Horse Guards, son of Howard Henry Howard-Vyse, of Stoke Place, Bucks.

[9] Lt.-Col. Albert Edward, Lord Dalmeny, MC (b. 1882), Gren. Gds., heir of Lord 'Primrose' Rosebery, foreign secretary and first lord of the Treasury in the 1880s-90s.

[10] Sir Charles Wiggin, TD, DL, JP, 3rd Bt. (b. 1885—d. 1972) was at Eton and Trinity with C.A.M., and Lt.-Col. and then brevet Col. commanding the Staffs Yeo. 1921-25.

[11] William Legge, later 7th Earl of Dartmouth (b. 1881—d. 1958) was Lt.-Col. of the Staffs. Yeomanry and MP for West Bromwich 1910-18.

[12] *The Express and Star,* 10 November 1933

[13] 'Quaestor' (W. Byford-Jones), *I Met them in the Midlands*, Midland News Assn., 1937 [with portrait by Arrowsmith], p. 42.

19

MANDER BROTHERS
LIMITED, 1924

Between the Wars

Charles Arthur joined the partnership in 1909. He was groomed to succeed CTM as governing director of Mander Brothers; but 'by the caprices of human destiny', Geoffrey Mander wrote, with a younger brother, Gerald, in the firm, he had a smaller share in its capital, and was anyway two years younger than Geoffrey. When CTM finally died in 1929, Charles Arthur became managing director, while Geoffrey was chairman. But Charles Arthur was a man of stature, who would not naturally play second fiddle to Geoffrey (or anyone else). And Geoffrey, after winning his seat in Parliament the same year, spent much of the time in Westminster, while the firm continued to be run by the heads of department, as it had been for at least 50 years.

Charles Inman Smyth, son of Mander John Smyth, was general manager of the colour works; Noah Butler was assistant works manager in charge of dry colours at the Townwell works; Tom Carrier was foreman of the paint department in John Street; William Weaver was foreman of the enamel department, also in John Street; Edward Shale was foreman of the ink department; William Kiteley was assistant works manager at Wednesfield; Dr Reginald Mander Smyth was works manager of the varnish department; an accountant, Richard Archer, came from Sissons Brothers of Hull, to take charge of the accounts and 'propaganda' department; sales were in the hands of and Arthur King (foreign) and H.L. Mallandine (home), who became company secretary when the company was set up in 1924. Geoffrey and Charles Arthur set up the first sales committee to formulate a constructive marketing programme, and appointed Charles I. Smyth and Archer as joint general managers under Mallandine.

War in 1914 had marked the beginning of the end of the 'boiling oil' school of varnish making which had served the company so well since its earliest days. Mander John Smyth, whose career as chief research chemist was in terms of copal and kauri, retired in 1905, and died in 1911. Two years later, a new era was marked by the launching of an entirely new kind of water-based paint called 'Vernasca'. Of the new 'Olsina' washable water paints made in 100 different shades, Manders claimed: 'nothing like them has yet been introduced, and we have received from all quarters of the decorating world intimations of their wide acceptance and exact suitability to modern requirements.'

Dedication of Mander Brothers' war memorial, 1923.[1]
Centre: Geoffrey, Charles Tertius, Charles Arthur, Howard Vivian, Gerald

Natural resins were versatile, but their technical limitations were legion. Oil paint needed a coat of copal varnish to keep it from peeling. It took two days to dry and in two years could start to fail. Inside, it developed cracks on ageing. Outside, it relied on the natural tendency of pigments to adhere by mechanical means. Techniques were rough and ready: in the memory of Ted Salter who retired from Heath Town as works' engineer in 1972 after 40 years, the gauging of how much each vat of varnish held was made by lowering a 'lead mouse' over the side on a piece of string.

With the coming of war in 1914, many traditional commodities suddenly became unobtainable, and the new chief research chemist in the varnish department, Dr Robert Morrell, began to set in train the process of freeing Manders from dependence on natural gums and resins from far away corners of the Empire. The old crafts of gum running and tanking of varnishes were in decline. He made a lasting contribution to Manders' development when he started to develop the synthetic resins, producing paints adapted with great chemical precision to specific end uses and formed in a huge variety of suspending media. These were the condensation polymers, like the alkyds, phenolics and polyurethanes, and the addition polymers, like PVA. He was not alone here, but Manders as ever was in the vanguard.

From the 1930s, Manders' research and development team was led for a generation by their brilliant chief chemist, William Wornum (1897-1969). He kept the firm at the forefront of the advances in organic chemistry, formulating and—to the frequent irritation of the directors—reformulating new synthetic resins. They were stronger and more durable, more flexible and, most importantly, more quickly drying, than the resins laboriously dug from swamps and bled from trees in Africa and New Zealand. These benefits added greatly to the popularity and acceptance of the 'ready-mixed' paints which no one had thought of marketing before 1912—though Manders had been offering the next best thing since 1895. Their development constituted a revolution, second in importance only to the development of the 'Manderlac' emulsions and 'fleck' paints. With their own resin plant, which made them independent of the gum shops of London, Manders were able to produce quality products at a lower raw material cost than the competitors who still had to buy them in.

Innovations in organic chemistry, with the synthetic resins of the plastics industry, led to better extenders, toners and thinners. This was matched by developments in the dye industry, with new dyes and tint bases, to upgrade and evaluate pigments; in thermodynamics, controlling the reactions of paint compounds; and rheology, a new science concerned with the flow characteristics and deformation of polymers. In Bell Street a Swiss chemist called Erni began making cellulose from waste cinematic film. The proliferation in packaging and the articles requiring coatings continued, with more industrial uses, and increasingly Manders' corporate clients began to sell the coating as part of the finished product. Dispersion systems were improved, becoming central to the process, involving major investment in dispersion mills to bring the new pigments and binders together.

MANDERS OFFSET INKS
Manders Printing Inks Limited, Wolverhampton.

In September 1920 the partners agreed that the firm's Welfare Committee should produce a monthly house journal—one of the very earliest in Britain—which they launched as *The Green Can.* George Deacon was editor, beginning his first editorial:

Today dear reader we stand on the threshold of the second great era in industrial history. The first era as you all know was when factories were instituted in the early part of the last century and workpeople no longer performed their tasks in their own homes. This second era is intimately connected with the principle of welfare work or the 'Resuscitation of the Personal Relationship between Master and Man'.

Deacon carefully pointed out that the magazine was not run by the management, but by the employees' own committee. Each issue, however, carried a page clearly headed: *Communicated by the Firm*, in which the management could deliver any message it wished. A new spirit of efficiency, with business school methodology, was abroad. Geoffrey let it be known through this column: 'there have been times when regular meetings of the partners have been sporadic and on no ... systematic basis; the minutes, though entertaining and expressive as inscribed, were not always a crystal clear official record. Nowadays all this is changed.'

The directors took new, expansive initiatives in marketing. In December 1927 the firm bought a controlling interest in the wholesale distributing and merchanting business of W.S. Low Limited of Preston, Lancashire, paint and wallpaper merchants. They had been customers for years, with a branch network and some 50 depots selling home decorative finishes throughout the north west. Manders were brought into direct contact with their principal customers, the decorating contractors, and set in motion a new activity, the factoring of paint's principal competitive material—wallpaper.

The economic crisis of 1930-1 brought an unprecedented worldwide trade depression to almost every branch of economic activity and created 2.5 million unemployed in Britain. It called for decisive action at Manders. Geoffrey Mander wrote in *The Green Can* that it might take the form of short-time working and, perhaps, sackings. If the Company were to survive, overheads and stocks had to be controlled. The position of the business was fundamentally sound, but the operations of the Foreign Department would have to be scaled down and there would be no room for mistakes.

The crisis brought home to the management the importance of productivity. Geoffrey sought to introduce the Bedaux System, which appraised workers' aptitudes for their jobs and established norms so that bonuses could be awarded for improvements in output. A team of 'experts' was engaged to carry out time-and-motion studies. But the trades unions distrusted a science which seemed to reduce people to automatons whose performance never varied and could be computed in statistics and graphs. The unions refused to co-operate.

But Geoffrey and Charles Arthur on the Board saw in the system a chance at last to create a realistic correlation between wages and output, and were determined to give it a trial. In return for the co-operation of the unions, they offered a forty-hour week without reduction in pay—five days a week of eight hours per day each, in place of the previous 47 hours a week. The basic wage was set at 55*s*.6*d* (£2.77a) for men and £1.40 for women.

It was an offer too good to refuse, and Manders became the first company in the country to introduce the forty-hour week. The new model agreement, the first of its kind in Britain, was signed by Ernest Bevin, general secretary of the Transport and General Workers' Union, in September 1932.[2] 'Bevin was very proud of signing that agreement', said Geoffrey later: 'He used often to refer to it when were both in the House of Commons.' Manders found that they were able to offer their workpeople 'either an increase in earnings or an increase in leisure'. Geoffrey Mander told the press: they had decided on the first 'and given themselves a free Saturday and Sunday, and thereby retained a number of people who would otherwise have inevitably gone to swell the ranks of the unemployed'.

Other progressive initiatives between the wars included a joint works' council providing a workable system of joint consultation (1920), a welfare club (1920), profit-sharing schemes for employees, holiday schemes, suggestion schemes (1925), works pensions (1928), staff pensions (1935), and a 'contributory co-partnership scheme' setting aside shares for employees, with provisions to pay for shares by installments. *The Express and Star* wrote: 'In the history of industrial welfare, Manders may claim a high place', where welfare had been 'part and parcel of the outlook of Manders as employers almost since the company's foundation in [1773]'. Geoffrey was reported summarizing:

> My ancestors were very religious people. They always used to open the day's work with prayers and lead hymn-singing at the end of the day. Those religious principles which coloured their dealings with the then small number of workpeople were the forerunners of welfare principles as we know them today. In the history of industrial welfare Manders may lay claim to a great deal of pioneering work.

Manders expanded steadily between the wars. The manufacturing division moved out of town to the new Heath Town works, where the can, ink and paint making divisions were in operation after a three-year process of equipping ready for the Duke of Kent's visit in October 1931. Manders had just taken out a patent for the first modern paint tin.[3] Plans had been made to consolidate the offices there too, but what had been the Colour Side in John Street was redeveloped as new offices in the town centre, which were opened in a grand ceremony on 24 July 1933. These were the offices, with their panelled Board room hung with sombre portraits of whiskered forebears, and a working scale model of a railway engine by Philip in the entrance hall, where I played as a small boy.

After thirteen years operating as a private company, in 1937 Manders 'went public' when a holding company, Manders Holdings Limited, was formed, incorporating the various interests, with 25 per cent of the shares being offered for subscription to the public—the first non-Mander shareholders.

Visit of Duke of Kent to Mander Brothers, October 1931

The printing ink operation run as 'Mander Printing Inks Limited' was becoming a major division, with new machines, materials and processes. It was consolidated under one roof at Heath Town by 1934, with new ink mills, colour precipitation plant, filter presses, pigment mixers, drying ovens, grinding mills, can works, a production department for matching and a 'tank farm' for storing the vegetable and other oils, and more storage tanks for the finished product. It became one of the largest and most modern printing ink works in the country.[4] A specialist product was the fugitive ink used against forgery and tampering on bank notes, cheques and postage stamps.[5]

Another old-established ink business, John Kidd & Co. Limited, was acquired in 1937. They had London offices and a laboratory in Wine Office Court, off Fleet Street, and works and another lab at Old Ford, Bow. It had been established probably before 1765 by one Benjamin Smith, and taken over by John Kidd in 1862. John Kidd & Co. continued to make and market their own brands in competition with Manders, with their own sales force, for some time. The joint printing division, rebranded as 'Mander-Kidd', claimed to be the largest printing ink manufacturers in the U.K., with a London factory and nine branches. Eventually it acquired a number of factories abroad, with three in the Union of South Africa, and one each in Rhodesia and Australia.

Opening of the new offices at John Street, 1933

With Rearmament after the Munich Agreement of 1938, government orders came again for varnishes and rust-resistant coatings for munitions, while the home decoration trade withered away. With the coming of war, colour making was consolidated at Heath Town, as the works were made more secure with trenches and air-raid shelters. The Wednesfield works were closed, except for a small unit making camouflage paint and aeroplane 'dope'. The Townwell works were evacuated in 1944. With paper rationing, the demand for printing ink fell off, but there was a call for white line paint for blacked-out roads, and paint and varnish for ships and aircraft and munitions factories.

Charles Beaumont, seeking ways of making pigments when raw materials were scarce, secured valuable chromic acid which he heard was being thrown away by aluminium anodysers and converted it into lead chrome for the camouflage paint which the works were now making at a rate of 10,000 gallons a day, seven days a week. He refined scrap lead thrown out by plumbers and devised a paint which prevented limpet mines cleaving to the sides of tanks.

Another successful anti-magnetic tank coating was based on the suggestions of Manfred Hess.[6] He claimed to have been 'weaned on black enamel', as his father had built up a chemicals and paints business based at Pirna, outside Dresden, of which he was managing director from the age of

24. But the family was Jewish, and the business was extorted by wicked Nazis on the outbreak of war. After a spell in Buchenwald concentration camp, he fled to England as war broke out, only to find himself interned on the Isle of Wight as an enemy alien. But he was taken on by Manders in 1940 as a paints' chemist (*c.* 1940-63), where in due course he became head of industrial research.

Hess soon began research on nitrocellulose lacquers and alkyd resin-based surface coatings, and under him Manders became pioneers in the use of ball mills for paint grinding and introduced the first steel mills designed for this purpose in the country. Hess's special subject was paint adhesion, oxidation and gelation, and he went on to publish the definitive monograph on *Paint Film Defects: their causes and cure* (1951, 1965).

Richard Archer became managing director in 1944—the first manager outside the family to have a seat on the Board. But he was ever an outsider. Monica joked to her husband, 'If he calls you Arthur, I shall divorce you'. (For *nobody* then—beyond the realms of family, close friends, 'social equals'—*ever* called him by his Christian name.)

After the end of the war, materials remained in short supply. The price of linseed oil rose from £62 to £130 a ton. Manders stopped making pigments in 1945, and started buying them in again for the first time in 65 years, as developments in the coal tar industry made synthetic colours and extenders universally available, but expensive to produce in smaller quantities. (A minimal amount of cochineal was still being produced at Heath Town in 1973 for fugitive inks.)

The rebuilding of houses, factories and infrastructure bombed in the war was a national priority, and Manders had a prior call when it came to allocation of jobs on demobilisation. The 40-hour week returned, and Heath Town and John Street restored production as colour came back into the drab Britain left by the years of austerity and global war. Sales of the pre-war 'Aqualine' water paint soared. Manders revived pre-war plans to concentrate again on industrial coatings—the paint applied in factories by spray rather than by brush to the new products—cookers, refrigerators and cars—of the post-war affluent society. VE day was followed by a five-year boom, a sellers' market when every product was sold as soon as produced.

Charles Arthur, twenty-first birthday,
Mander Brothers' works party outing, June 1906

[1] The names on the WWI and WWII Memorials are as follows (transcribed by Peter Hickman, 'We Will Remember Them', *The Blackcountryman*, vol. 32, issue 1): Albert E Beresford, Frederick Bradley, Joseph Butler, James R Colley, Alfred E Collins, Albert E Darby, Sidney C Davis, Arthur G Day, Thomas Devereux, Harry Eggington, Samuel Hadock, Alfred J Hadfield, Thomas Hanstock, William Hayward, W Rowland Johnson, Albert Lee, William Lloyd, Reginald Martin, Herbert Mattox, Charles Miles, Edward Millington, John B Morris, Charles H Pearson, Frederick Reynolds, Thomas Richards, Harry Savage, James E Sproson, Frederick Swatman, Thomas Tomkinson, Arthur Turner, Laurence Vitty, William Westwood, John H Davies, HAN Mander [Howard Anthony], William Wilson.

[2] The agreement is quoted verbatim in *The History of Mander Brothers.*

[3] The patent was taken out with an employee, Frederick Cox, who also devised the machine to make the 'channel lip' on paint tins (*ex inf.* his grandson, David Reynolds, 8 April 2004).

[4] *How Printing Ink is Made*, Mander-Kidd Ltd., Wolverhampton and London, n.d. [circa 1955]

[5] Manders inks were used on the postage stamps of the Republic of Ireland, eg., the 6*d.* value of Ireland's first definitives (first issued in 1923, but the fugitive inks were first used in the mid-1930s) and the 6*d.* Thomas Davis stamp of 1945 (*ex inf.* Paul Baines, 2002).

[6] *Paint Technology*, vol. XXV, no. 4, April 1965, 26-7

20

'GREAT-HEART'

Arthur devoted his energies early to follow the strong family tradition of public service. He stated in a speech on his twenty-first birthday at a works' party in Tewkesbury: 'I have been advised to follow in Father's footsteps. (*Applause and Laughter.*) I hope I shall not trip, for it is no easy task set before me to follow in those great strides.'

He served from his twenties (with various members of the family) as a county magistrate (1912), as High Sheriff of Staffordshire (1926), as a Deputy Lieutenant, twice as mayor of Wolverhampton and finally as an alderman (1938). He was the outstanding chairman of the Council's Finance Committee (1936-50), where his acumen and experience were so much appreciated that he continued to preside through the post-War period of a Labour majority. He was the 'guide, philosopher and friend' of the Boys' Club Movement in the region. In October 1945, the greatest honour of the borough of Wolverhampton was conferred on him when he was elected Honorary Freeman, as his father (and Lloyd George) had been, and he became one of the two living freemen.

He entered the Wolverhampton Borough Council as a Conservative member in 1925 and made a public career there parallel to his industrial one. He was first elected mayor in 1933, the third Mander to hold the civic chair. It was a period of unprecedented economic depression worldwide.

The theme of his first mayoralty was the plight of the unemployed. As mayor, his interests 'extended into all types of social and philanthropic activity' in the Wolverhamton region. He took a number of creative initiatives for relief programmes to help the poor and unemployed. He was active on behalf of boys' clubs and allotments, 'where about £7 worth of vegetables could be grown on an average allotment cultivated by an unemployed man'. He set up the 'Good Companions Club' movement to provide social centres in derelict buildings where the unemployed would meet and 'engage in useful and congenial hobbies and recreations'. It was a successful initiative which caught on rapidly, and his suggestion that the example could be followed not only in the Midlands, but throughout the country, 'was taken up in many quarters'.

Dab hand in his 'Good Companions' movement

As the crisis deepened, he appealed typically 'not so much for money [but] for personal service', where 'everybody would be doing a little bit' to help the cause of the unemployed. Meanwhile, Monica's special appeal as Mayoress was 'for blankets and bed linen for the families of the unemployed'. 'Sheets were a forgotten luxury for many of the unemployed', she wrote to the press, and blankets replaced by

> threadbare odds and ends, a species of miserable patchwork of cotton and serge ... the clothes worn during the day piled on the beds. Some families are covered ingeniously with paper stitched together. Quite an amount can be done with a few old newspapers. But the rustling and crackling keeps sleep away... I have seen a child with pneumonia lying on an old straw mattress covered with father's jacket (the father went about in his vest as he had no shirt sleeves to show), and mother's skirt, and oddments of woollen caps and the like belonging to the younger children. It was freezing outside, and there was no fire in the room.

Christmas was the bleakest moment of the Depression. He asked the townspeople to show their sympathy in a practical way by providing 10,000 parcels of groceries—containing sugar, cocoa, milk, tea and seedless raisins—to all the unemployed of Wolverhampton. The first batch he himself handed out from the nave of St Peter's Collegiate Church to 'a gradually-increasing queue of 400 to 500 men'. Lord Bradford provided a Christmas tree 20 feet high as 'a kind of rallying place'. Fearing a riot, police were on hand, and F.H. Houldershaw, the organist, played solemn strains to relieve the impending tension. But in the event, all was orderly.

At the end of his term of office in April 1934, the Council made a presentation to him, with the usual resolution of appreciation engrossed on vellum, as they had done for his father. The new mayor, Bertram Kidson, recalled that 'the name of Mander had been associated with Wolverhampton for at least 150 years', contributing considerably to the public life of the town. He was 'one of their best ambassadors... His ability, charm of manner, and probity ... did much to add to the prestige of Wolverhampton, not only in the borough, but the country, and abroad also'.

He was asked to serve a second term as mayor in 1936-7 when it was known that it would be the Coronation Year of King George VI. It was felt that he would be a more dignified representative of the town than a butcher who was next on the list for the office.[1] He had met the new king officially as Duke of York when in April 1932 he was called upon to present a Rotary badge to him. His 'baby' Rolls Royce 25/30 Laudalette, bought for the Coronation, with a folding hood so he could be seen and speak on public occasions, survives in pristine condition. (Jack Barclays, the dealers, gave his chauffeur, Turley, a tip of £20 when it was returned on his death in 1952, stating they had never seen a car so immaculately kept.) The chosen theme of his second mayoralty was the plight of youth. He opened the Odeon 'super-cinema', at the time Wolverhampton's ultimate art deco building in tiles with a neon-lit tower, and plans were put in hand for a new Civic Hall. He declined a further term, claiming the job involved 'so much more than it had done in his father's day'.

In business and at Mander Brothers his particular passion was everything that touched the human side of industry—social welfare and employment conditions—as well as financial matters, savings and pensions. In these fields Manders continued to lead the field between the wars under the liberal tutelage of Geoffrey and Charles Arthur. Arthur commended the idea of a shorter working week as a solution to the problem of unemployment and was an early supporter of the five-day and 40-hour week. Mander Brothers had never had a strike: he

spoke in 1941 'as an employer of labour, associated with some 600 human beings with whom during 140 years we, as a firm, have never had a cross word'. He prophesied a 30-hour week for all working people in his lifetime.

Manders were among the first to introduce pension schemes, setting a precedent locally. In the borough, campaigning at elections in 1930, he proposed the extension of pension schemes to all manual workers in the employ of the Wolverhampton Corporation, as 'the best in the town', and a model for businesses there. The Corporation had been 'cogitating the matter for six years' under his vice-chairmanship of the finance committee. The plan was that workers would pay in 1*s.* 3*d.* a week so that they could 'spend their retirement in reasonable comfort and happiness', earning a pension—after 40 years—of a pound a week. The press wrote that 'he claimed that the business of which he had the honour to be managing director was one which was up-to-date and progressive'. He discovered that people voted for him not because of any political faith, but 'because one of their relations was employed by his firm. Because the firm gave their people a straight deal, the voters thought it was worth while trusting the affairs of the town in his hands in so far as he had an opportunity to help the town.'

In everything he did, he was guided by a strong commitment to Christian principles. With an Anglo-American perspective and a Canadian mother, he was involved at the heart of the Rotary movement, the civilian club founded in Chicago in 1905 to foster ideals of service and high ethical standards in business, and to promote an international fellowship among business leaders and professional men. He founded and became president of the Wolverhampton club and in due course became president of Rotary International for Britain and Ireland (1929-30), travelling extensively in the United States and Canada, as well as all over western Europe. He formed a wide circle of friends among business leaders and the so-called 'merchant princes' of America, like the Roth shipping family in San Francisco, senators and state governors.

In May 1932, he set out on an 18,000-mile tour of the North American continent as a director of Rotary International. Among the public duties he most enjoyed, he gave the dedication address when the Waterton Lakes National Park in Alberta, Canada, and the Glacier National Park in north-western Montana, U.S.A., were united as a result of the efforts of Rotarians as the 'Waterton-Glacier International Peace Park'. The huge Rocky Mountain wilderness above the big skies of Montana straddles the Continental Divide and was dedicated as a monument to the enduring friendship between the two countries under the authority of acts of U.S. Congress and the Canadian Parliament.

He was proud of being 'half Canadian' and had been made an honorary chief, *Me-tas-to*, Chief 'Red Crow', of the Blackfoot tribe of Indians during a previous visit to Montana in 1928, an honour given to other Englishmen in public life at the time, like John Buchan. Press photographs show him as the epitome of the patrician Englishman admired by Americans; his suit, Churchillian bow tie and wing collar contrast like fustian with the exotic headdress of eagle feathers, wampum and tribal mantle of the Indians. His squaw Monica was adopted into the tribe on the 1932 visit as 'princess' Shining Star. The profile of his old friend 'Two Guns'—'as I can familiarly call him'—who performed the ceremony, appeared on the five-cent piece.

The initiation ceremony is quite informal ... and consists chiefly in hand shaking and a short complimentary speech. This finishes with the recitation of the name by which the candidate will be known when visiting his brothers (and sisters) in future, if he ever does. When this point arrives, the chief pauses and looks dreamily into the sky for inspiration. Sometimes the name he utters is a happy choice, but not always. The dictates of an inspired mind are wayward, and I felt that one of the ladies who was given the title of 'Little Weasel Woman' was not altogether gratified.

'Chief Red Crow' of the Blackfoot tribe, Montana, 1928

His account of their privileged journeys was published (August 1932-October 1933) in the Mander's house magazine as *American Notes*:

Perhaps our most thrilling experience was being conveyed through Seattle with a police patrol clearing away the traffic ahead of us. On this occasion we arrived at the landing-stage from Victoria at the precise moment when our train should have been leaving the 'depot' three miles away. We were met at the quay, hurried through the customs formalities, conveyed to a throbbing car (with our thirteen pieces of luggage) and sped away into the brilliantly lit streets—ahead and by our sides were police on motorbikes with sirens (which they used incessantly), blocking the side streets and forcing the traffic metaphorically to its haunches. Without a check at a steady 40 we completed the course, and reached the station where an army of porters was ready to seize our impedimenta. The train steamed out only nine minutes behind time, while the passengers who had been craning their necks from the coaches racked their brains in pondering who on earth we were, and in what 'flicker' they had perhaps last seen us!

He was in demand as a public speaker of authority and charm. A supporter of the League of Nations and a veteran of the first world war, he spoke out with foresight at public speeches at international conferences and congresses against the terms the Versailles treaty had imposed on Germany and in favour of international co-operation. Other recurrent themes of his American speeches in the Thirties are tariff reform, something of a family cause, strongly backed at the time by Geoffrey Mander in Parliament, and against the interest on war debt and reparations by Germany and Britain. (He was, of course, a contemporary at Eton and Cambridge of John Maynard Keynes, although he confessed to failing to recognise his genius at the time.)

The various organisations in which he was interested gave him a platform at international conferences attended by 'many important people, and others whose importance was exaggerated', where he 'tried to create better understanding between countries'. As an industrialist and, as far as the Americans were concerned, a British aristocrat, he was a popular speaker with transatlantic audiences and a natural ambassador for the causes he supported. At a Rotary congress in San Francisco in May 1932, for example, he gave one of his standard speeches advocating compromise over war debts and the hoarding of gold by America and, drawing attention to the 'fear and suspicion' which European nations like Germany and France held of each other, arguing for a strengthening of the League of Nations. His delivery warmed the hearts of delegates. The papers wrote: 'The British industrialist's address proved the highlight of yesterday's sessions, as it brought to the delegates a straight-from-the-shoulder view on international affairs, from a man who is an acknowledged leader in the field... Sir Charles was received with deafening applause, the great crowd of delegates upstanding and waving their arms about frantically.'

In turn, he genuinely loved the American West: 'There is a wide spaciousness about the country', he wrote, 'and an open-handed hospitality and friendliness among the people—a scorn of pettiness and an innate love of fair play and manliness which endeared them to us.'

In England, in the Thirties he appeared regularly on the early radio, chairing in Birmingham a successful programme called the 'Midland Parliament', a 'chat show' *avant la lettre*, more closely scripted than such programmes would be today, where public figures debated topical industrial and social issues. He also espoused the cause of the National Savings Movement, which had been started in 1916, rooted in nineteenth-century philanthropy, to encourage working men in habits of thrift and good housekeeping: 'not to create a nation of misers, but to enable people to help one another in a time of need'. He became vice-chairman of the National Savings Committee, working closely with Lord Mottistone.[2] One speech made in Croydon in January 1940 was quoted by Hitler's propagandist, the treacherous broadcaster 'Lord Haw-Haw', who claimed it had resulted in the wholesale flight of capital from London. 'Yet another example of the confusion of British economic policy', the press commented: 'like many other "facts" we learn from Hamburg and Bremen, this is real news to us.'[3] The Trustee Savings Bank, of which he was a director, was another of his national interests in this area, which 'owed much to his wisdom and energy'.

An enterprise he supported in the dark days from the Thirties onwards was Moral Re-armament, a non-denominational, revivalist movement founded by the earnest U.S. churchman, Frank Buchman (1878-1961). He attended and spoke at congresses and meetings in many countries, seeing much that was sincere and useful in the ideals of a movement which hoped to avoid another world war through a moral and spiritual awakening. His commitment, with an Englishman's disdain of cant and what he called 'blah', was light hearted and suspicious, even critical. He said of Buchman's ardent friends and followers, who insisted on 'a spot of 'G', as they called divine 'guidance', that, 'like the children of Israel, they seem to regard him as a Moses and certainly drink in his words as if they were divinely inspired ... and allow them to override their own judgment'. Although the movement primarily cultivated the rich and influential, zealously opposing Communism, he always enjoyed meeting and arguing about industry and the future of industrial relations, among his special interests, on equal terms with radical Trade Unionists and miners' leaders from Wales and Staffordshire, like Jack Jones, the communist from Ebbw Vale.

During the second world war, he led a home guard fire-watching unit. He wrote that he had 'no near shaves' with a doodlebug, which were much more wearing than the bombs in 1940-1, 'because one was never free of them in day time, and people went about with one ear cocked':

One passed over the train as we were drawing into Euston, and later in the same day we all took refuge under the board-room table at a meeting of the National Savings Committee. The secretary, who was only half listening to the chairman's remarks, heard the doodlebug engine cut out, and called out, "Under the table!"—whither we all dived in anxious disarray. A few seconds later, there was a tremendous crash somewhere 'off', and we then unscrambled ourselves looking somewhat sheepish (better safe than sorry), and the chairman unperturbed proceeded: 'As I was saying, gentlemen, in the post-was period, I think we should consider...'

He was 'wet' as a Tory, who tended like his father to be 'above' politics locally, with a strong social conscience guided rather by his humanity and Christian principles than 'party'. In 1946 he dropped a bombshell when he came out in agreement with local Labour housing policy, which resulted in him resigning from the local Conservative party presidency. A *Herald* headline stated that he 'shocked the party':

Tories throughout the Midlands are shocked by the news that Sir Charles A. Mander has thrown up the presidency of the South-West Wolverhampton Conservative Association. Last year his cousin, Sir Geoffrey Mander, left the Liberals to join the Labour Party. A week before the municipal elections, Sir Charles made a speech praising the work of the Labour-sponsored building department of Wolverhampton Corporation. This prompted the Labour agent, Mr Justin Jones, to distribute 50,000 leaflets on election morning stating: "Sir Charles Mander, Conservative leader in the council chamber, said the Labour party was right." The speech was severely criticized by Tories on the council.

Tall—at 6'2"—in photographs when inspecting troops and taking salutes on official occasions, he appears to tower loftily over the ranks. He was good looking, with clear blue eyes and classical features, a patrician bearing and 'engaging personality'; always, according to the press, 'with a cigarette and a smile'. He was painted in dashing hunting pink striding diminished fields by Jonniaux, and then in bow tie and ill-fitting suit by Arthur Pan, who famously painted Churchill at the same time, with their faces looking like lard. (Monica so hated her own portrait, that she burnt it; ever frugal, she kept the frame, in case it should come in useful some day.) As a speaker he had gravitas and presence as well as wit, who could silence hecklers at a public meeting (with the rather ineffectual local M.P., Sir Robert Bird, for example) just by rising unruffled to his feet. He was known to his children, family and friends with mingled admiration and affection as 'The Duke'; to us grandchildren as 'Grand-duke'.

John Ryder, fifth Earl of Harrowby (1864-1956), the Lord Lieutenant, had written to the prime minister, Clement Attlee, in 1946 to recommend him for 'a substantial honour'. In 1948, Harrowby's own term of office came to an end. Charles Arthur's secretary cabled him at his Montreal office to the effect that Attlee had written on 5 July to say 'it would give him great pleasure to submit his name to The King' for appointment as Lord Lieutenant for Staffordshire to succeed Harrowby. Attlee, recognising all he stood for as a popular candidate of stature in the community, and one acceptable to the Labour interest, was evidently anxious for him to accede. But Charles Arthur was hesitant, feeling other county figures of the diminishing band of landowning grandees 'in the traditional sense' would be more suitable. He asked Attlee, when he discussed the appointment at Downing Street, 'Have you considered the point that I am a manufacturer?' To which Attlee, brushing aside an objection whose premises were already outdated in the post-war world, replied, 'Why not?'

In the event, he felt Lord Harrowby would criticize him for accepting a Labour prime minister's nomination and he wanted to keep on with the humbler duties of Council work, which he felt was 'of greater value to the community'. He was anyway easily bored by stuffy uniforms, the pretence and protocol of ceremonial and military inspections and parades, indicated by a half-completed *Times* crossword concealed in the lining of his cocked hat, and he refused.

He describes an occasion when he had to make an impromptu military inspection in America:

> At Marfa, Texas, near the Mexican border, we met Colonel Austin of the First Cavalry Regiment, U.S. Army, whose Regiment was there quartered. He asked me whether I would like to look round his 'outfit', to which I naturally assented.
>
> My time was crowded, but he promised to have them on parade and a quiet horse for me the following morning at 7.30. On my arrival, clad in ancient jodhpurs, which had seen service during most of the war, and an older shooting jacket, I found the whole regiment drawn up in Review order, anxiously awaiting my inquisitional Inspection. After this they marched and galloped past the saluting post while the band played martial tunes and the dust rose in clouds. The possibility of a casual American arriving in Aldershot and having the 14/20th Hussars paraded for his benefit cannot be conceived! Not only, however, did I inspect them with what gravity I could muster, but they subsequently admitted me into the inner circles of their crack squadron, 'The Black Eagles'. Beneath their extended swords I pledged myself to maintain and cultivate various soldierly virtues in which I am sadly deficient.

In general, his dedication to public causes was insatiable; selfless to the point of neglecting his own, Mander Brothers and family interests. The press reported that his New Year's resolution in January 1939 was to spend more time with his family: 'having spent so many evenings away from my family—it has averaged five a week when I have been Mayor—I am not going out so much as I have done. I shall reduce my evenings out to two a week.'

But he could never resist an appeal. He was present at virtually every public gathering in the region. His secretary calculated that he served at one point on 67 committees and organisations, 'for many of them as chairman, vice-chairman or treasurer'. Then there were the industry and business organisations, like the Paint Federation, on several of which he served his term as president. When his health suffered and his doctor ordered him to reduce his workload late in life, he grudgingly resigned from 35 of them. They were concerned with every aspect of the public life of Wolverhampton and the county, from the bells of the village church at Tong to Rotary, school governorships, and the county Bench.

In turn, his movements were recorded like royalty today by the local press, as in 1934: 'Sir Charles Mander ... who was injured on Saturday while hunting with the Albrighton Hounds, was yesterday reported to have had a rather good night.' He was President of 'Wolves', the Wolverhampton Wanderers football club for many years, often attending matches on Saturday afternoons muffled in a great-coat worn over his hunting clothes.

He was an active fundraiser for Lichfield diocese, raising over £150,000. One of his appeals as mayor in 1937 was for the restoration of St Peter's Church, Wolverhampton, when he was responsible for raising £10,000 in fourteen days, using his civic hat, 'probably for the first time in the history of the borough', to collect the first contributions. He approached Stanley Baldwin (1867-1947), who had resigned the previous year as prime minister, for public support. Baldwin, recently created earl Baldwin of Bewdley, responded warmly from Eaton Square on 30 October, declaring his personal interest:

CAM as Mayor, civic procession, 1937

I cannot forget that it was in that church that my parents were married, now more than seventy years ago.

We did have business associations with your district. When my great grandfather moved from Shropshire to Stourport, his brother went to Bilston (about 1790) and started blast furnaces. I think St Martin's church in Bilston was built by Martin Baldwin... The last of that branch died in 1870. About 1848 we took a small works at Horseley Fields and worked it for about a generation.[4]

The Chamberlains were another public service family of a liberal nonconformist background rooted in Midland industry; dominant for two generations in local and then national politics, they were always close to the Manders as theatre- and concert-going companions. On the fringes of national politics as a prominent Midland personality, Charles Arthur's extensive correspondence includes letters from a host of public figures. Many stayed at Kilsall on their travels, where he continued The Mount tradition of official hospitality to all parties. There are letters from Anthony Eden, and from Clement Attlee and Herbert Morrison in the Labour government; Sir John Anderson, Chancellor of the Exchequer, who stayed at Kilsall in July 1945 when he was acting Prime Minister after the fall of Churchill;[5] Field-Marshall Sir Claude 'The Auch' Auchinleck (who also stayed at Kilsall);[6] and his personal friend William Jowitt, the Lord Chancellor. Evelyn Waugh described the latter as a man of striking looks, 'as a great officer of state should be cast in Hollywood, [with] a doggy droop in his eyebrows and all the sensibility of a painting by Landseer'.[7]

Many of these are perfunctory. But more poignantly he preserved warm and touching letters from lonely, humble people, the destitute and distressed, school children, the unemployed, veterans of the war, laying before him their problems, asking for small favours—sometimes for him to find a 'sweetheart'—or offering him praise, suggesting he should be prime minister, to which he always replied personally. To an extent, he became a sainted figure in the county.

A youth writes asking 'if you could find me a nice young orphan girl for a wife as I should like to get married and settle down with her... I should like to get a nice homely girl as I am rather on the affectionate side'. A female writes in 1937, wanting to get in touch with 'some lonely soldier, perhaps, returning home from abroad... I am very lonesome, I am 29 years of age and am in domestic service... (P.S. Excuse the several mistakes, I am only a servant girl.)'

Monica and the children at Kilsall, 1933—
Marcus, Jill, Bumble, Monica, Marietta—by Compton Collier

He found lasting content in family life, in marriage and home. Arthur and Monica had three children: Marietta, Jill and Marcus. He notes in a journal, looking back on his family as 'quite ideal ... it is wonderful to think that we have enjoyed such an idyllically happy married life for 32½ years.'

He was like his father a sportsman who enjoyed golf and racing; competing at point-to-points in earlier life; hunting and shooting from childhood. He said, in a remark worthy of the old squire of Wilfred Scawen Blunt, 'I prefer a good day's hunting to a good day's shooting'. But he had none of the bluff, bumptious manner of his father. He was rounded, talented intellectually, artistically, musically, socially.

He sketched, particularly whenever he travelled, and wrote two episodic children's adventure novels sent to his children, Jill and Marcus, aged just six and eight at the time, with his comical pen-and-ink illustrations.

These he posted instead of the usual weekly letter when they were recovering from tuberculosis contracted from drinking milk from the home farm near Kilsall. The children were sent—alone, except for their personal nurses—to 'Home des Esserts', near Leysin in the Swiss Alps, where they learnt child French while undergoing a course of 'heliotherapy', Alfred Rollier's progressive nature cure which involved exposing their bodies to the high altitude sunshine. The tone is set by the opening of *But Why Ferdinand?*, dated 10 October 1927:

Ferdinand Herbert Bunkum was in many ways a lucky boy, or unlucky, depending on how you look at things. For instance, when he was a baby, some petrol was mixed in his milk in mistake for water. You see, Sarah went to the petrol tank instead of the radiator, but he only rumbled and frothed a bit, and didn't go off, which he certainly would have done if any one had come near him with a lighted match…

His mother was naturally very annoyed, because petrol is so much more expensive than water, and Sarah did ought to have knowed better.

The novel soon leaves the character of Ferdinand behind, of course, *Lucus a non lucendo,* with its tale of stock villains like 'Bill Deadly', of Indian braves, prisons, escapes and secret passages.

He was a musician, always happy making music, whether singing —from madrigals and glees at the Trinity Madrigal Society or the Noblemen's and Gentlemen's Catch Club, to large-scale choral works like *The Apostles* of Elgar at May Week in Cambridge, and music hall and folk songs, rewritten for family occasions with his own Kiplingesque jingles. He played his mouth organ merrily with the troops in Palestine. He was an Eton friend of John Christie, the eccentric founder of Glyndebourne. He played ensembles on the piano with Bishop Wood's wife at the Palace, or with Monica accompanying him in a duo on the violin. She had perfect pitch, and would shriek menacingly through the house if she heard a less competent performer play a false note.

Sir Malcolm Sargent, the conductor, was one of the guests who regularly stayed at Kilsall when he visited the Midlands to conduct, signing the visitors' book with musical quotations. He had his batons painted in Manders paints, which, Sargent wrote, added *un peu de je ne sais quoi* to his conducting. He sends a new batch of batons on 16 January 1950:

I am taking you at your word, and daring to send you some more batons to be lightly coated with the Mander superlative white paint, 'Than which there is no better.' … the quality of sound resulting from the orchestras I direct will be immediately enhanced.

Kilsall Hall, by the Shropshire village of Tong, was a 'comfortable, cheerful house, neither an old house nor modern', unpretentious with barge-boarded gables, old sundial, and an acre of walled kitchen garden, and with plenty of bedrooms up and down flights of stairs for family gatherings and house parties. Daisy describes her first sight of it in January 1917: 'See over Kilsall Hall, Tong. Horrid day. Most charming place, so much white panelling, large drawing room, square smoke room, square panelled hall, oblong dining room and quaint wee room off hall; three stair-case[s]... So cold inside seemed quite warm when we came out again; wanted a lot of work doing to it.'

They spent nearly all their married life there. But it was rented from Daniel Jones, another paint manufacturer. He writes in 1917: 'My grandfather bought the place from the Bishton family about 80 years ago. The Bishtons held it for about 300 years'. Arthur's brother, Gerald, the scholar with an interest in toponyms, objected to this as a pleonasm:

> The word means 'Cylle's hall'; therefore to call it 'Cylle's hall's hall' takes us no further—is mere tautology in fact. Who old Cylle, the Anglo-Saxon, was I cannot tell you, but he lived before 1006 (not 1066!), when, in the will of Wulfgate, the place is first mentioned. Anciently the place is known as Kylshall simply: 1593 (being then a farmhouse) and 1605.
>
> This is correct, but as 'hall' does *not* mean house or mansion or suchlike (although people unacquainted with our language may think so), you would be quite in order in calling the place Kilsall *House*, by which name it is already to be found on some maps.
>
> You will forgive me for pointing this out to you, but unless you informed Harrods of the right nomenclature (good old English word!), I feel sure they will fall into the common pit when printing your choice vellum bond.

Gerald may have been wrong. Eckwall prefers the meaning 'Cylle's halh or valley'.[8] In any event, CAM does not seem to have taken any notice, and the name was engraved for his writing paper, and has stayed.

Gerald remarked on his fondness for children: 'He has, I observe, a liking or a benevolent manner with young children of the pram age, chucking them under the chin or pressing their cheeks (and then withdrawing his hand covered with slobber); but to great pleasure of gaping parent.' The journalist, 'Quaestor', writes:[9] 'With all his ability, he is an absolute child in spirit; he is very fond of children and on his birthday throws a children's party in the garden, near the lovely avenue of lime trees'.

Quaestor's account is deferential, emphasising a man of 'easy distinction and charm', whose devotion to public service was 'absolute':

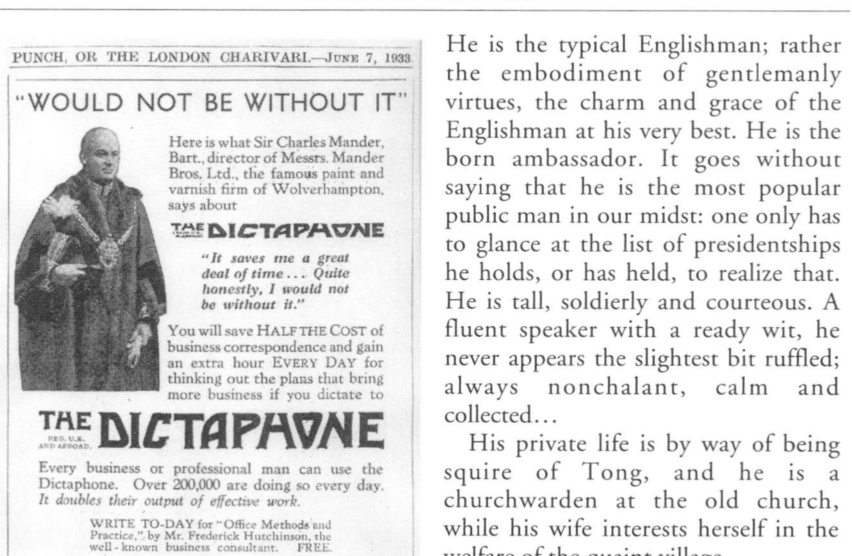

He is the typical Englishman; rather the embodiment of gentlemanly virtues, the charm and grace of the Englishman at his very best. He is the born ambassador. It goes without saying that he is the most popular public man in our midst: one only has to glance at the list of presidentships he holds, or has held, to realize that. He is tall, soldierly and courteous. A fluent speaker with a ready wit, he never appears the slightest bit ruffled; always nonchalant, calm and collected...

His private life is by way of being squire of Tong, and he is a churchwarden at the old church, while his wife interests herself in the welfare of the quaint village.

CAM as Mayor, 1932, advertisement

Hunt ball at The Mount circa 1934. Centre: Mary, Daisy, Monica, Arthur.

He died suddenly, aged 66, in January 1951, collapsing with a cerebral haemorrhage while taking the chair at an acrimonious meeting of the Albrighton Hunt committee. His friend and supporter, Edward Woods, the Bishop of Lichfield (and formerly Coventry), was a hunting prelate, who gave the oration at his memorial service, later printed by the Curwen Press. It strikes the same panegyrizing tone, emphasising the gentlemanly Englishness that he exemplified to his generation: 'the English ideal of those who are endowed with exceptional benefits of education, breeding and culture and freely use such gifts in the service of their fellow men.'

'A vast and representative congregation' gathered at the service as some token of 'the immense respect, regard and affection' in which he was held 'as a man widely beloved, who lived a full and many-sided life, covering an immense field of varied activities'. He filled life's cup to the brim, said Woods. His natural impulses of kindness and generosity, accompanied always by a charm of manner, were always finding outlets in many kinds of activities. 'The most unselfish of men', he quoted from one who had known him for many years,

> he brought into the lives of all who knew him the sunshine which emanated from a heart of gold; a man who was the soul of honour and truth, a hater of intrigue and underhand dealing; he was always courteous, kind, tolerant and sympathetic, seeing the best in everything and everybody.

But 'the spirit and temper he imparted to his labours' and many personal contacts with all kinds of company is what made him 'outstanding', and impressed all who had contact with him. The Bishop declared that what impressed others above all was 'his serenity and happiness, as a humble, sincere, believing Christian':

> remarkably like Mr Greatheart in *Pilgrim's Progress*, that intrepid, cheerful conductor of convoys of pilgrims to the heavenly city ... never afraid to stand up boldly for truth and righteousness, and to let men see that the great object of his life was to do anything he possibly could to forward the interests of Christ's Kingdom. [This was] the hidden mainspring operating in the depth of his personality.

The hagiography of the funeral oration makes hollow and mawkish biography. But, like Woods himself,[10] he had the qualities of a good-tempered, gregarious nature, personal magnetism, organising powers; these were qualities of greatness. His selfless drive, 'upright in the service of God and his fellow men', saw local and international politics, industrial relations, family life itself, in terms of strongly-held religious and moral values, questing, asking like John Bunyan's pilgrim, 'What shall I do to be saved?' But it was combined with reserves of warm humanity, an impish

Mander wit, a self-deprecating sense of irony and the absurd, and an utter lack of vanity, indifferent to personal ambition. He treated all men as equals, finding it natural to mix without affectation with all sorts and conditions of people, from the very old to children, from ministers to miners with 'no instinct to seek for perquisites for himself'; his friends numbered Bedouins, sheikhs, Red Indians, unionists, troopers, magnates and merchant industrialists; his chauffeur, Turley, and his private secretary, Miss Barton. His magnanimity and friendliness were qualities which marked him out for contemporaries who came across him in public and private life as a paragon of that ideal of service of his generation, 'displayed in the English gentleman at his very best'.

He was much loved as a family man, drawing strength from his Midland roots. His memorial tablet in Tong Church[11] records his dates 'after a full and generous life' and bears the inscription: 'Many waters cannot quench love'.

---

[1] G.W. Jones, *Borough Politics*, 1969, p. 251

[2] John Seely, first baron Mottistone (1868-1947), sometime MP for the Isle of Wight and Secretary of State for War, was chairman of the National Savings Committee 1926-43.

[3] *The Express and Star*, 12 January 1940

[4] Baldwin's father, Alfred, was from a family of Shropshire yeomen and ironmasters who also ran 'an old-fashioned business of the patriarchal type' (*DNB.*). His mother, Louisa, was the daughter of the Rev. George Browne Macdonald of Wolverhampton.

[5] John Anderson, first Viscount Waverley (1882-1958), was a talented administrator, independent university MP, Home Secretary and minister of home security (1939), and Chancellor of the Exchequer (1943); appointed by Churchill to succeed him in 1945 should he and Eden perish at Yalta.

[6] Sir Claude Auchinleck (1884-1981) served in Egypt, Aden and Mesopotamia in W.W.I; in W.W.II he was the Comdr in the Middle East (1941-3) who halted the German advance into Egypt, but was forced back to El Alamein (1943); he was C.-in-C. India (1943-7) and Supreme Comdr India and Pakistan.

[7] William, Earl Jowitt (1885-1957), advocate, Liberal, then Labour, MP, was Attorney and then Solicitor General, and Lord Chancellor (1945-51); also Minister of National Insurance.

[8] E. Ekwall, *Concise Oxford Dictionary of English Place Names*, Oxford, 1960, p. 276. For an account of the house, see Betty Wilson, 'Beautiful Midland Homes No. 16', *Sunday Mercury*, 12 Sept 1937.

[9] 'Quaestor' (W. Byford-Jones), *I Met them in the Midlands*, Midland News Assn., 1937, p. 46.

[10] Woods died just two years later. See the appreciations collected by his daughter, Janet Stone, *Edward Sydney Woods, 94th Bishop of Lichfield*, Gollancz, 1954, in which the Queen Mother's treasurer wrote, 'He was, as you know, one of Her Majesty's oldest and most trusted friends...' Janet married Reynolds Stone (who cut the datestone and her initials 'MPS' on Marietta Stirling's house in Bembridge, IOW).

[11] Made by Panchieri of Birmingham. For his life, see notices in *The Express and Star* dated 25 January 1951 (obituary) and 3 February 1951 (Memorial Service).

21

GERALD AND DAISY

Gerald Poynton Mander
1885-1951

Gerald Poynton[1] was the younger son of Charles Tertius and Mary Mander. He was educated like Charles Arthur at Eton and Trinity College, Cambridge, where he read history and law. He was up at Trinity with his elder brother. Arthur remarked that, if only he had done any work, 'he would be really very good: he has been working most nights, and one night he did not go to bed at all, and his landlady brought him coffee at 6 a.m. when she came in to do up the rooms'.

He made friends with his tutor, called Lapsley. Gerald described him as 'an American, though quite anglicised; he clears his throat while lecturing by snorting from time to time. When I went to see him he said, "How are you?" I said, "Still alive". He upped and said, "You seem very pleased at your continued existence".'

Arthur told Lapsley, 'I am afraid he is not working at History as hard as he might.' Lapsley replied: 'I am sure he isn't.' 'What he does I don't know, but the man who lives the other side of the street told me the other day, without knowing that he was talking of my brother, that there was an extraordinary man who never did anything but work, and was always to be seen pouring over his books at all hours of day and night.'

The academic world was congenial. He matured into a donnish antiquarian (elected F.S.A. in 1929) known as 'Donny', an aesthete and gentleman scholar steeped in erudition; a Midland historian and bibliophile; an asthmatic dilettante who turned night into day with his lucubrations as he applied himself without much discipline to his books and papers, habitually rising for afternoon tea. He was a genial eccentric, who remained a diffident Edwardian figure, a picture of elegant emaciation in his spats, pince-nez and winged collar, bubbling with a disarming and facetious humour all of his own. 'What a beautiful *garnet*!' he would say to my young mother, as she proudly displayed her ring, mounted with one of the limpid Longueville rubies. At his worst, his habits and his barbed and unpredictable witticisms could be trying to his family and disconcerting to strangers; his father described the wayward angularity of his manner as 'three-cornered'. Arthur shared rooms with him at Eton, as brothers did in those days, and bore a scar on his brow for the rest of his days, after Gerald had hurled an oil lamp at him in a fit of temper.

The flavour of an endless fund of erudite and amusing stories and anecdotes is preserved in a few of his surviving letters to Arthur:

8 June 1938
The anecdote I delivered with success, to Fothergill[2] the inn-keeper (now at Market Harboro') when having tea there the other day. "Do married men live longer?" I asked. "Now, let me see," said he, "do they?" and he pondered. (The answer is "No, but it seems longer".) I was surprised he hadn't heard of it. He said he "wasn't exactly married" though he mentioned his "wife doing a cross word below." Actually I think he is a bigamist: but that is "neither here nor there", as S.J. Lubbock said when a stink-bomb secreted under the cushion of his chair exploded, when Philip was up to him.

6 Sept 1933
It is related that when closing-time came at a certain village inn, the angling club moved off with dignity to the bridge from which they were to angle that night.

They seated themselves, cast their lines over the parapet, and "fished" steadily till the grey dawn was breaking.

Then with a roar the first down train passed under the bridge!

One of the last days of 1948
I rather think Geo. Bobey than Clement Attlee is "the Prime Minister of mirth".

"Sorry Doc., it slipped" was when Jones "bowled through Grace's beard". The ball whizzed over the wicket keeper and broke to pieces on a distant boundary. Meanwhile W.G. walked threateningly up the pitch saying "what's this, what's this?" I seem almost to have been there. Or was it spoken by Holmes to Dr Watson when Prof. Moriarty fell over the cliff?

He entered Mander Brothers in 1907 where he was a director from 1910. But never enjoyed robust health. He went before the Medical Board in 1917, and was in the last class to be called up; in fact 'he is practically an invalid now', wrote Daisy at the time. 'My father was *delicate*,' his daughter Hilary recalls, suffering most of his life with asthma and eczema; the unlikely beginning of the asthma being put down by my grandmother to having allowed him to 'play outside in the snow with measles'. Asthmatics find it easier to breathe at night, so if he had no meetings, he did sometimes catch up on sleep and reappear at tea time. His shyness and bad temper at times were understandable.

With all this, he was a brave rider to hounds, and raced in point-to-points, wearing a pure silk shirt and cap in mauve and emerald, and one time won a wager of £5 (a large sum in those days) by turning his horse away from running hounds and jumping a five-bar iron fence. He never missed Henley; local shows (of which Wolverhampton used to have a splendid one on the Park, including a circus); the Wall Game at Eton; Eton and Harrow cricket at Lord's; holidays abroad from Greece to Scandinavia.

He never took his medicines for his asthma; or he drank a tipple straight from the bottle, not in the prescribed measures. He had a leather-covered travelling chest made to house six medicine decanters, with a long strap so it should not be lost, therefore known in the family as 'the dog'.

His lifelong interests, however, were antiquarian and artistic. He was always most at home in the his library, occupying the best room of his house in Tettenhall Wood, where, to the despair of his wife, an appalling clutter of books, manuscripts and Roman pots multiplied in piles and boxes. He was author of monographs and articles on many recondite aspects of Wolverhampton and Midland history, the scholarly editor of its antiquarian journals, including his own pet project, *The Wolverhampton Antiquary,* begun as an 'antidote to war' in 1915.[3]

He joined the William Salt Archaeological Society in 1906 while still an undergraduate and was elected to the editorial committee in 1916. For a generation (1922-46), he saw through the press the publications of the Society, known from 1936 as the Staffordshire Record Society—notably its on-going 'Collections for a History of Staffordshire'. He was fastidious as an editor and is described as one of the three great names in the history of the Society's first century (with Colonel Wedgwood and its founder, Major-General George Wrottesley). He published his first work for the Society in 1920, an edition of Gregory King's notebook of 1679-80, and his last and most notable was his catalogue of the *Staffordshire Views* in the William Salt library (1946), 3116 items, 'giving ample scope for his artistic and antiquarian interests'.

He was a versatile scholar. He had a special interest in subjects such as heraldry and genealogy, medieval Latin, palaeography, seals, ceramics and chart pedigrees, books of reference. This he deployed as a distinguished archivist in the patient transcription, editing and translation of charters, muniments, pipe and muster rolls, and parish records, as well as many less ordered documents, and line sketches of seals and pots, making public the raw material by which Staffordshire county history has been studied ever since.[4] He would lose himself copying out dusty charters in the libraries of his cousins and relations, like the Vaughans of Blackladies and the Wolseleys of Wolseley Hall, or descrying the inscriptions on tombstones in upside-down postures. As a field archaeologist, 'he was in charge of excavating several Roman camps, mostly on Watling Street or the Viroconium Way,' his daughter adds, 'most of which had to be filled in after photographing and searching for pots, which he stayed up all night mending.'

His publications, always produced and printed to his exacting standards, are not typically definitive or sustained; rather notes towards a definition of the many subjects he tackled, where the journal article, or editorial snippets under headings such as 'Notes and News', were an eloquent medium: 'A grave error has been pointed out, in that the abbreviation W.R.V.C. should have been written W.V.R.C. This is very disturbing: one cannot be too exact in matters antiquarian.' He expresses mordant wit as well as urbanity in the most scholarly writing: 'even the most dry-as-dust antiquary may be allowed some moments of grim humour, if it be impossible for him to rise to the heights of sparkling wit'.

By 1906 he had collected 'all the information then available' regarding the history of the Mander firm and family, much of which is assembled in *The History of Mander Brothers*, edited from his miscellaneous articles and notes after his death by his cousin Geoffrey. He toiled like Casaubon on his works in progress, notably the monumental and ever-unfinished history of Wolverhampton. It was completed posthumously and published in 1960 by Norman Tildesley—when his family, it was feared, with an obsession for 'tidying', had burned the final version of his manuscript.

Towards the end of his life, in 1946, he was instrumental in the revival of the Staffordshire volumes of the Victoria County History, a project which had been in abeyance for 40 years. He wrote to the William Salt librarian, Miss L.M. Midgley, foreseeing difficulty in finding authors: 'so many more people have to earn a living these days that the leisured worker is dying out (and the parsons are not what they were, e.g. Eyton, Canon Foster).' By November 1948 he was writing to the general editor, L.F. Salzman:[5]

> I write to you about the sad state (almost a corpse-like appearance) of V.C.H. Staffs. The galvanic battery which will set things going is I believe £10,000. Would £5,000 be of any use? I.e. would it produce two more volumes? How are these to come out? Do we have to have vol. ii with abbeys, industries, schools, etc. before getting on to the topography? (I feel the topography is wanted first.) The prospect of rescuing Miss Midgley from her pilgrimage [she was undertaking the Pilgrim Trust survey of ecclesiastical archives] for work which none can do better encourages me to take this matter up.

Gerald enlisted the support of the clerk of the Staffordshire county council, and particularly of his brother, Charles Arthur, chairman of the finance committee of the Wolverhampton borough council. In due course he raised the necessary funds when the county council voted £500 a year for five years and, with the six county boroughs more or less on side, the project was re-launched.

In a tribute after his death, Sir Frank Stenton claimed that English medieval studies owed much more to him than was generally recognized. Ill health and meticulous scholarship limited his output, but as Stenton wrote, 'his published work may be small in volume, but it is a model of its kind'.

He lived for a short time when he was first married (from 1913 to 1915) at Ludstone Hall, a moated Jacobean house 'of great charm' (Pevsner) near Claverley, with shaped gables and a central bay window. From here he bicycled into the Works during the war. But seventeenth-century austerity did not suit his wife, Nancy, and they went on to rebuild The Dippons, on family land opposite The Mount. It reflects his artistic tastes, with a romantic garden of box-edged borders, gazebos with ogive roofs, and pergolas. Hilary recalls:

> He was always improving The Dippons with architecture and various types of gardens. He owned two farms and kept and eye on them, and called into 'the Works' most days.
>
> My mother was very kind to young people starting out, and The Dippons was open house. Some of the orchestra visiting to play at the Civic Hall also stayed with us, as they were too badly paid to pay for digs. Many friends walked in to the Dippons to 'borrow the telephone'.
>
> My father was no snob. He had strange friends from all walks of life, especially a Yorkshire sweet shop owner in Chapel Ash, who turned up regularly on a bicycle with an assortment of boxes of chocolates for him, and stayed for tea and chat. On one occasion, as a joke, he brought a fake box of 'Black Magic' chocolates designed for window dressing. It amused my father until, a few days later, aunt Daisy, who frequently just walked into our ever-open front door, helped herself to a chocolate and broke a front tooth. She later sent in the dentist's bill. My father said to her; 'Daisy, you are so greedy!' I don't think he did pay.

He collected with taste and discrimination from undergraduate days: incunabula, books by Caxton, Sixtus Riessinger and the rare Wolverhampton printers on which he wrote a standard monograph,[6] miniatures and enamels by local Midland makers (on which he was the foremost authority), and prints—including, behind the dining room door, the Griggs etching of Owlpen. I once found on a stall his bookplate in a black-letter *Aeneid* (1562), englished by 'Thos. Phaer, Docteur of Phisike', a translation dismissed as 'tenebrous' by Ezra Pound. Odd volumes of his today ornament the rare book collections of the great institutional libraries.

When Queen Mary visited The Mount, he as put in charge of showing her over the collections. He came over attired in his tail coat (as was his custom on such occasions), bringing choice examples of his famous collection of enamels. But in his anxiety he had one of his asthma attacks. 'Won't you sit down, young man?' said the Queen.

He gave numerous paintings, mainly of local interest—like a collection of early portraits of the Bagot family, bought at the Blithfield sale—to the Wolverhampton Museum and Art Gallery during his lifetime. Many items, including his research notes and manuscripts, have found their way to public collections since he died. Largely under his inspiration as the local connoisseur-in-chief, the Wolverhampton Museum now has, as it deserves, one of the best collections of Midland enamels in the country.[7]

In public life, he was chairman of the governors of Wolverhampton Grammar School for fourteen years (from 1934). He had written already in his twenties an exemplary monograph, *The History of Wolverhampton Grammar School* (1913), and became a governor for 37 years the year after. His speeches at the annual prize-giving, a grand occasion when he introduced the Master of the Merchant Taylors' Company to the assembled School, were 'excellent examples of his ready wit'. 'My father's *History of Wolverhampton Grammar School* was presented to the Queen (Elizabeth) on her visit to the School', Hilary recalls, 'and we teased him that she would sleep well in the train on a siding in Tipton, trying to read the book that night.' The 'Mander Common Room', with his portrait by Louise Sanders, was named after him. He presented the *lampa honoris* cup. His style could be humorously lapidary, and he delighted in presenting Caroline silver to members of the family inscribed with pithy and ambiguous Latin epigraphs.

He married in 1913 Nancy Steward Hargreaves, daughter of Lieutenant -Colonel Robert Hargreaves, who served with CTM in the Yeomanry. He went through the Boer War, only to die following a chill caught at camp in 1906. He lived at Knightley Grange, a 'free Elizabethan' pile of 1860-8, with tower and spirelet, near Newport. Hilary, writes:

> I spent much of my young life at Knightley Grange. My cousin, Robert Wolseley lived there, his mother Ruth [sister of Nancy] having refused to live in Birmingham with her husband, Captain William Wolseley. They all used to live in style with a coach with a crest on the door. There were skating parties by candlelight on a mere, and the next estate was Aqualate, where my godmother lived, which has the largest private mere in England.
>
> My mother and her two sisters were taught by a governess: arithmetic, French and the violin. They all did well on this start.

The Hargreaves were another early industrial family, in Lancashire cotton—rather earlier than the Manders. The most noted of them, James (d. 1778), had patented his miracle device, the 'spinning jenny', in 1770. Whereas the traditional spinning wheel turned only a single spindle, his innovation was to carry several spindles on a framework, so that multiple threads could be spun all at once. It was a timely invention and a major impetus towards the factory system in the textile industry. It led to one of the first industrial riots, when his house and loom were gutted by a Blackburn mob of traditional spinners, fearing unemployment and destitution. On her mother's side, Nancy could trace her line back to Walter Steward of Dundevale, Seneschal of Scotland 'about the twelfth century'.

Gerald and Nancy had three children: Philip, Daphne and Hilary. Philip in due course was the last family member to be chairman of Manders. Gerald writes of him in 1946:

> He is very quiet, and seldom speaks. I was told the other day (in fact, yesterday) that he was lively at the club, but, on checking this up, found he did not speak there either. Perhaps, like the parrot, he 'thinks the more'. In the Aston Cantlow parish register today, I saw the baptism of Philip Mander in 1652.

---

[1] After his great uncle, Frederick Poynton Weaver (from Cheshire, though the village is in Shropshire).

[2] John Rowland Fothergill (1876-1957), who 'looked like a golliwog with bow tie', was at Brinton's house at Eton, and came from a family of early Birmingham industrialists. Another of Fothergill's bons mots referred to the 'marriage of inconvenience'. He was author of *The Innkeeper's Diary* (new edition by the Folio Society, 2000) about the Spread Eagle Inn at Thame and collaborated in forming the Boston Museum of Fine Arts collection of classical antiquities.

[3] Volume One (of twelve numbers which appeared irregularly 1915-32) was collected in 1933 as *The Wolverhampton Antiquary, being collections for a history of the town gathered by Gerald Poynton Mander.*

[4] M.W. Greenslade, *The Staffordshire Historians*, Staffordshire Record Society, 4th Series, vol. XI, 1982

[5] Quoted in Greenslade, *The Staffordshire Historians*, p. 157.

[6] *Early Wolverhampton Books and Printers, with a note on some playbills*, 1922.

[7] Mary S. Morris, *English Painted Enamels 18th and 19th Century in the Wolverhampton and Bilston Collections*, 1973.

Mary and Daisy Mander, Empire Day celebrations, Girl Guides, 1931

Daisy, early 1890s

Daisy St Clair Mander
1887-1968

If thou follow but thy star, thou shalt not fail of a glorious haven—Dante[1]

Daisy Mander was the successor 'Miss Mander' to her aunt Amy, as a cultivated and independent spinster. All her life she was interested in places as much as people. Always on the move, she read and travelled widely, returning with entertaining traveller's tales of her incessant trips and cruises as she trotted all over the world.

Aged eleven, she is already telling a local paper (July 1899):

I am always going away somewhere. I have been to Spain twice, once to France, twice to Scotland, and four or five times to Wales, and heaps of times in England in different places... I love London.

In early life she was keen on riding and reckless hunting, and her diaries record the meets attended, with the press-cuttings carefully preserved of her exploits with the Albrighton Hunt: 'We have a very big house, stables, and garden. I have two ponies of my own; one in harness, the other for riding... I am always with our horses.'

Her private education was finished in Paris, Dresden and Berlin. In Berlin in 1905, Miss Dr Luce, the lady principal of the Willard School, possessed 'a refined and sympathetic personality', and prepared young English and American ladies for 'intelligent travel': 'a feature are the tours made to places of historical or literary associations and to the various art centres.' She visited Prague, Warsow, St Petersburg and Moscow.

By now she had the travel bug. In the autumn of 1906 she travelled round north America for 15 weeks with her lady's maid, Watson, and 28 pieces of luggage, on her way to cousin Geoffrey's wedding in Montreal. They crossed on HMS *Caronia*, where the biscuits tasted like bath towels and the first-class passengers were mostly Americans. 'Everyone either drawls or twangs', except her cousins Marjorie and Lionel; the latter 'so irresponsible', and says nothing but 'it's a bit off' all the time.

She stayed with a succession of her rich and glamorous American friends of the East Coast. The Mathesons had made a charming place out of an old fort at Lloyd's Neck on Long Island, where each room was panelled in a different wood, and the bedrooms had bathrooms attached to each one, 'so daintily papered and furnished'. She visits the Osbornes, railway magnates, at Castle Rock on the Hudson, and takes a private train to the Helliers at Fairhaven. She stays with the Turnbulls at Arkledun in Hamilton, Ontario, the most important historic house in the town, red sandstone in a pretty garden; 'where the king and the Prince of Wales have both slept, in fact in the room I have which overlooks the Lake'. But Mr Turnbull 'is so Scotch I can only just make out what he says, and must give

my full attention always'. They gave an 'at home' for her, 'and I really did nothing all afternoon but shake hands'; every paper in Hamilton had an account of it later, 'and each one had my name spelled differently, the nearest being "Manders"'. The wedding itself felt 'unlike a wedding and more of a show'.

The first ball in the big room at The Mount was her twenty-first birthday party in January 1909. She continued to reign there most of her adult life, latterly as a companion to her mother for nearly a quarter of a century after her father's death, retiring to her 'spinster's boudoir', which had an internal oriel window on the first floor.

A stray surviving 1933-4 diary is typical of the between-the-war years. During the depths of the Depression she records an endless round of hunting ('very twisting fox, but quite fun'; 'run of the season from Knightley: 2hrs 30mins, 6 mile point, 15 as hounds ran') and long dinners in the winter, often playing bridge till 2 or 3 a.m.—noting, 'as usual, lose'—but satisfied when she gains a shilling or two. There are hunt balls, the Albrighton one being held at The Mount in 1934. Servant problems are noted: 'Household upheaval, four maids gave notice owing to Armer' [the butler]. She had an interest in motoring, where excursions are frequent: 'went in huge new Humber to try it, and ordered one, rather than Lord Derby's second-hand Rolls. It can go 90 m.p.h. and over'; 'Sir W. Middlemore[2] came in, and made me go in his racing Riley, but under 60 m.p.h.' Trips to London and (occasionally) Paris ('got some dark flying glasses'), visiting friends and dressmakers, punctuate the year. Concerts in those two years starred Horowitz, Beecham, Furtwängler, the young Menhuin ('a genius, such ease') and Solomon ('went to hear Solomon play at the Palladium. He looks like Mussolini'). The theatre, with sometimes two performances a day, includes Fred Astaire in *Gay Divorcee* and Sybil

Thorndyke in *Distaff Side.* In Paris, she sees three plays by Pirandello, Zandola and Coraggio after the Ambassador's garden party, admitting candidly: 'very interesting, without understanding a word'. On her travels, she always records shopping for hats ('M. bought three hats'), and bibelots.

After the hunting season is over, there are annual cruises with her mother. One (a 'huge success') on MV *Britannic* in the early spring 1933 took her 12,056 miles via Barbados, Trinidad, Venezuela, Panama, Jamaica, Havana, Nassau and Madeira. She writes off the Azores on 30 January: 'Blue sea, with white caps, but very calm, tho' rather cold. The odd-looking man is Aldous Huxley and wife, *very* tall. Lot of dancing.'[3] Another cruise with a party of 650 Boy Scout and Girl Guide officers for a 'floating camp' holiday round the Baltic in August 1933 is a highlight that year; later she lectures, rather diffidently, on her adventures and writes them up for *The Green Can.* There were rallies and 'lots of banners', with flag waving and presentations of troops. Off Pomerania 'Miss Acland gave a lantern lecture on birds. Too long.' Her mother dined with Count Bernadotte in Stockholm, but failed to recognise King Haaken in Oslo. The following year they took the *Britannic* again on their spring cruise to the Mediterranean and Palestine.

The summer in England is a 'hectic' social round of soirées, bridge evenings, the 'season' of royal garden parties, Henley, the Fourth of June, the Eton and Harrow match at Lord's, classic race meetings. She and her mother forgot their vouchers for Ascot (in 1934), 'devastating', and, after driving 31 miles back home to get them, Mary found the butler 'utterly bewildered, so I said to him, "we haven't got German measles!"' Once at Ascot, 'it was very windy, and the paddock was half full of hats rolling about. I studied the people there—so much older since last year—some of them quite *dilapidated*!' Then there are late summer visits to Scotland for grouse shooting parties, with a side-trip to Glasgow (September 1934) to attend the launching of the '534', as the code name was, an event which later commentators said marked the end of the Depression: 'Queen in bright blue and looked stunning. [The King] made a good speech. All surprised at the name, *Queen Mary.*'

She faithfully attends the big Wolverhampton Wanderers matches: 'saw a very thrilling cup tie at Molyneaux grounds, for which A. had given me tickets. Wolves v. Newcastle. Right at the end Wolves got one goal. Wild enthusiasm'. 'Wolves v. Arsenal [November 1933] *ought* to have been a draw, game all in our favour, but one goal against us; some 40,000 spectators'.

Her visit with the Wolves football team to the Soviet Union in August 1955, aged 67, as one of the first groups of visitors after the Cold War, caused something of a stir and was widely reported in the press at the time. Clips of her cheering grandly in hat and veil, 'looking after' her nephew, Marcus, on the *Pathé* newsreels have been replayed many times. Wolves were to play Spartak and Dynamo in Moscow. The *Daily Express* reporter wrote that she had packed three hats at her Ritz Hotel suite for the occasion. She told the reporter: [4]

> I have not been to Russia since 1905—in the reign of Czar Nicholas II, when I chose a trip to St Petersburg instead of hunting in the Shires. And I never regretted the choice. I remember the ice tobogganing, the vodka, and the cotton wool in the windows which never opened... I have been a Wolves' fan since my [brother], the second baronet, became club president more than 20 years ago. [My] father started the club. But that's not why I follow the team almost everywhere; I like the science of the game so much that I get too absorbed even to cheer.

She performed her first public duty when she was six, on 17 October 1893. CTM had taken her with him to the Fire Station, invited to christen a new fire engine, and promptly announced that his little daughter would perform the ceremony instead. It seems to have been stage managed: 'She was handed a cord, which was attached to the engine, and also to a bottle of champagne, and after saying "I call this engine Daisy", she let go the cord, the result being that the bottle was smashed to atoms on the wheel of the engine.'

The first world war was spent at The Mount, doing war work, still hunting regularly, with trips back and forth to London. But she was frustrated: 'I do wish I could go off and do something for my country as I have absolutely nothing to do here but work, read a little and think.' She tried to persuade the family friend, Dr Louis Knuthsen,[5] to allow her to join him at Lady Hadfield's field hospital in northern France. But he gives her no hope, 'as all are paid workers and no ladies among them'. So the caption to her picture in *Tatler* reads: 'Daisy St Clair Mander is the daughter of Lady Mander and Sir Charles Mander, J.P. and Deputy-Lieutenant for Staffordshire, and is a worker for Queen Mary's Guild of Needlework, which has done so much good work during the war. She is also actively interested in the Duke of Portland's work for the Army Veterinary Society for the Prevention of Cruelty to Animals.' She is hard at work at her Depot, supervising the preparation of roller bandages: 'It takes four minutes to wind a bandage tight enough, and fifteen to pull and set a many-tailed abdominal bandage, and over one hour to sew it.'

She was accurate in observation to a fault. She once invited Nancy, her sister-in-law, to go on a little trip 'to admire a stallion' (pronounced by her with a long 'a') at Codsall Wood. When there, Daisy said, 'Lend me a fiver for the chap'. Nancy handed it over, but later asked for it to be returned. 'No', said Daisy, 'you had a good look too!'

In public life, she was 'a lady of great strength of character', writes Geoffrey Hancock in *A Tettenhall History* (1991). She was one of the first women to sit on the county council; she was one of several family magistrates at the time; she organised the Staffordshire branch of the

Women's Voluntary Service during the second world war (which gave her a petrol allowance, useful for Gerald's antiquarian researches); and took an active interest in the many local charities with which the family were involved. The Girl Guides were a cause close to her heart, and she was a county commissioner—and her mother the local President—as a personal friend of Lady Baden-Powell. She was a member of both its Overseas Association and its International Council, travelling to China, Siam and Hong Kong for the Guide movement.

She collected and hoarded compulsively. After lunch with her uncle Jack at his Country Club in Norfolk during the first war, she writes: 'Did old shops afterwards. Got an original drawing by Rembrandt, and another little Dutch head of an old man, three Empire fans, two little Mason jugs and a wee Rockingham cottage... Very pleased with little fans at 1/6 each; cheapest buy I have ever had.'

St. Peter's Ward.
MUNICIPAL BYE-ELECTION.
PLEASE SHOW THIS IN YOUR WINDOW.
YOUR WORK and VOTE are solicited by
MISS MANDER.
VOTE FOR MANDER
Economy, Efficiency and Enterprise.
Committee Room: 69, Red Cross Street.
Printed & Published by Whitehead Bros., King Street & St. John's Square, Wolverhampton.

Her specialities were china cats,[6] and dolls, 'which were numerous'. She picked them up on her travels about the world, mostly in the Edwardian era. There were folk dolls in regional and national dress, vigorous Javanese and Burmese puppets, play dolls, peg dolls, rag dolls, tassel dolls and 'Dutch' dolls, ranging from figures of harlequins, dervishes, golliwogs and piccaninnies to grand Italian or German examples in bisque porcelain, with sleeping eyes (that blink) and swivel heads. They are carved, cast, whittled and sewn in every material; malleable, durable, ephemeral. They are made of wax, composition, celluloid, papier mâché, gulls' feathers, and mud and fibre (from north Africa). They come from Lapland to Macedonia and Thuringia, from the Caucasus to Madeira and Sicily, from Brazil to Bechuanaland, from the Hopi Indians to the Pueblo Indians, from the Eskimos to the Santals of Bihar. They are rich in the regional inflections of traditions, or mirror fashionable taste; 'so à la mode', writes Mary Mitford in 1824, 'that a Parisian milliner might have sent her as a pattern to her fellow tradesman in London'.

Even during the first war they are being sent over to her from friends in America: 'Doll from Louise [Hellier] represents Empress Eugénie in cyclamen velvet & fur hat & greeny paisley shawl; too delightful, in wide crinoline flounced skirt and tight plain bodice. Had to have special Board of Trade permission to bring it into England. L. insured it for £6.'

She asked an obliging friend who was visiting Switzerland to get her a Bernese doll. After several weeks, a card came back saying 'I have looked everywhere for a doll with bare knees, and can't find one'. As a collection they express Daisy's boundless curiosity, acquisitiveness and energy. She bequeathed some 200 of them to the Borough to form the nucleus of a collection at the Bantock Museum,[7] which already had the quantities of baskets collected all over the world by Monica Mander.

She also amassed needlework and textiles on her travels, with good examples from Turkey, Palestine and the Greek islands, and tatting, which she practised assiduously herself. With ample leisure she covered long sets of chairs and cushions, petit point bell-pulls and pictures of family houses prepared for her by the Royal Needlework Society, worked during idle ocean voyages, or afternoons by the Library fire with her mother, waited on by footmen and cutseying parlour maids, at The Mount. Of living things, she adored her hunters and her French bull terriers; Joffre, Rhu and Fritz. I remember her in state in her Hepplewhite four-poster after she had moved to Kilsall in 1952, where she lay late, rattling the *Times*; or imperious in her elaborate feathered hats which she never removed—perhaps, like the Bishop of Lichfield's wife, she slept in them? She would read from her illustrated children's books in a slow drawling voice accompanied by shallow asthmatic wheezing; and dispense us Belgian chocolates and butterscotch, like giving tit-bits to puppies. They were confections to us quite unknown in the days of post-war austerity.

As a traveller, she expected and exacted comfort; always enjoying the best hotels, food and company. In September 1916, Louis Mander Stokes, a younger cousin, records receiving from her as he was deprived in the trenches of the Somme 'one huge and rich cake elaborately packed by a London firm called Gunter', a few weeks before he died.[8]

She writes in August 1915: 'In a year of war, 55 friends of ours have been killed, 53 wounded, 21 acquaintances killed, a few wounded two or three times... There will soon be no one left we know.' She was of the generation of maiden aunts brought about by the mass slaughter of that war. Grand, stately as a ship of the line in full sail, a sharp and witty conversationalist with a clear memory, she was courted by a succession of bachelor admirers. But she kept them at a respectable distance, dining with them at her favoured haunts—like the same Gunter's, the Carlton grill room, the Ritz or Claridge's.

During the First World War a flame was Count Enrico Serra, a Genoese diplomat who wrote her 'quaint' letters. Her diary records him looking 'flourishing' in his uniform and herself feeling 'restless; too introspective, *qu'est-ce qu'il y a*? ... He thinks I have changed a lot since 1906, more compressed; *pas de tout joie de vivre*, alas, and I know it.' But her father was *furious* when she stayed up late to talk to him into the small hours—'too absurd at my age'. (She was 28.) He capped it all when he was asked shooting over the Christmas house party of 1917. 'Much excitement because E.S. peppered Mr Lovatt (without being aware of it) and would have shot a fox if he hadn't been yelled at!' It seems he was never forgiven, or asked back. 'But very sorry to say goodbye to E.S.'

Her later 'young men' as suitors and always very proper escorts included Sir Roger Curtis ('lunched at Gunters with R. [sandwiches!!!] and Lady B[rady] there. Not at all the same thing!')[9] and, *years* younger, Willie Berington, like her brother Gerald an antiquarian and archivist, of Little Malvern Court. But she outlived them all and died unmarried, aged 81, asthmatic and lonely, in a nursing home in Droitwich. She has a doll pasted in her album for Russia in 1905, captioned: 'The baby Czarevitch's first toy; a multiplying manikin given to the future Czar of Russia by his mother'. Visiting in her dotage, her niece recalls, 'one present which was a success was a Russian doll with other dolls inside, such as a child would play with; full circle!'

---

[1] Quoted in a diary note, 1917.
[2] Sir William Middlemore, 2nd bt. (b. 1908), of Woodside, Worcester.
[3] Huxley, for his part, deplored the elderly haute bourgeoisie: spinsters and widows with incomes, enriched businessmen, interspersed incongruously with very *bien* people who kept themselves from the rest. *Beyond The Mexique Bay* (1934) was his resulting 'book of travels—really a book about everything' written at the time. (See N. Murray, *Aldous Huxley*, 2002, pp. 271-2.)
[4] *The Daily Express*, August 1955
[5] Sir Louis Francis Roebuck Knuthsen, OBE; b. Santa Cruz, W. Indies; dermatologist and Fellow of the Royal Society of Medicine; was decorated for his war work, and twice mentioned in dispatches. He lived at 33 Chesham Street.
[6] *Staffordshire Life*, January 1951.
[7] *English and Foreign Dolls and Toys, 1780-1950: A Catalogue of the Wolverhampton Art Gallery and Museums*, n.d. [*c.* 1985], Bantock House, 92 p.
[8] Louis Stokes, *A Dear and Noble Boy: The Life and Letters of Louis Mander Stokes 1897-1916*, ed. R.A. Barlow and H.V. Bowen, 1995, p. 165.
[9] Sir Roger Curtis, 4th bt. (b. 1886) was an inspector for the Board of Education. His mother, Sarah, dau. of Alexander Dalrymple, m. 2nd Sir R. Maziere Brady, 3rd bt.

MANDERS: EPILOGUE

'My leaves have drifted from me. All. But one clings still. I'll bear it on me.'
—James Joyce, *Finnegan's Wake*

Manders PLC, worthy scion of the company founded and nurtured by forebears with their varnished faces and brown-paper hats, and which nurtured them, remained based in the town where it was established into its third century, emerging as an international company, a 'mini-conglomerate', with a mix of businesses in coatings (as the paint and varnish Sides were now called), printing inks (where they were large players in the UK market), and commercial property.

The nonce derivation of varnish is from Berenice, queen of Palestine, Racine's queen of sparse silences and tragic refusal. At first, against the counsel of my housemaster, Salmon, I turned my back on Manders. When my cursory application to work for them was wisely rejected after I felt I had proven myself at other things, I inadvertently became the representative of the first generation of the senior branch of the family *not* to join the Mander management since it started in 1773, while an implicit birthright of vain expectation slipped away. That of my son, Charles Marcus Septimus, probably the first Mander to gain a double first at Cambridge, was stonewalled after me. The mill does not grind with water that is past. Whatever Whig or Wasp—or Catholic—humane values of literacy and manners we had been educated in and to some extent symbolised, and our broader connections with the company—genealogical, cultural, commercial, social—our horizon of European languages, our classical education, were by now evidently retrospective, marginalized, minority concerns, at least in a provincial manufacturing company. It was fashionable to look forward, rather than backward. There was no place for sentimentality in the hard-edged world of global corporations. The family had outgrown the business and the business no longer needed *them.*

Manders continued to display a diluted, facile version of the family crest as a trademark. But there was little understanding of the history underlying the business or the human side of industry, no evident commitment to the local community which had so distinguished the firm, or the patrician ideals of Christian public service epitomised by the family motto in its Epicurean/Hedonist ambiguity: *Vive Bene*, 'Live Well'. The liberal aesthetic of Ruskinian moralism, symbolized at Wightwick; the 'wet' paternalist ethic of guardianship and stewardship, through good times and ill, of the family firm and its jobs; not least the dedication of generations of employees, whose ties of loyalty and affection had developed and endured through several generations of a single family—had become redundant. The company archive, carefully garnered for two centuries, was relegated to a cupboard with scant respect after Hugh Barty-King's research, and much seemed to be needlessly threatened or lost. 'Now is the time for the burning of the leaves', Laurence Binyon had written.

But the business continued, and we remained shareholders, if with a diminished portion.[1] Towards the end of 1993, the Board decided, in their jargon-speak, on 'an effective realignment of the group's activities' by focusing on developing the Manders' speciality chemicals business globally, 'with particular emphasis on printing inks'.

A radical restructuring was sweeping through the paint industry in the 1990s. With slow organic growth in markets, there was a strong 'urge to merge' in the global economy, and many well-known brands were being bought up, to be concentrated in the hands of a few big multi-national players: in Europe, ICI, Akzo and Total. In 1992, the Manders Decorative Division successfully resisted a takeover attempt from an upstart northern rival, Kalon Group, who had made a cheeky, hostile bid for the whole company of £89 million.

Manders was forced to review its long-term strategy and the decision was taken to focus on the successful printing ink operations. The decorative division was sold to Johnstones Paints PLC, a division of Total, for £55 million in early 1994. In due course, Euridep, the paint subsidiary of Total, also took a controlling stake in Kalon in March 1995. So the paint businesses were in the end consolidated under the Kalon umbrella, where its Manders, Johnstone's and Leylands brands in the UK formed together one of the top three producers and 'one of Europe's leading decorative paint manufacturers'.

Also in 1994, the Wolverhampton property of The Mander Centre, part of which at least had been in family ownership for three hundred years or more, passed into alien hands when it was sold to the Prudential for £82 million. The 485,000 square foot Centre had been refurbished in 1987; it was then described as a 'covered, pedestrianized shopping complex at the centre of the principal shopping area of Wolverhampton' with more than 150 shops, and was making easy operating profits of £4.8 million on £5.3 million rent. It is again being refurbished and roofed in 2003.

The remaining company was to develop, following Benjamin and John Mander's prescriptions two hundred years earlier, 'the higher-technology activities of speciality chemicals and coatings', with particular emphasis on the 'more profitable' printing inks business. Here it became a major operator as the country's leading independent manufacturer and supplier of printing inks: 'a business requiring a high degree of technical competence and innovation. We specialize in the production and supply of inks for the food packaging sector, newspapers, magazines and general commercial printing.'

From 1994 Manders used part of the cash reserves from the sale of their decorative and property divisions to expand their ink operations in Europe through acquisitions in the Netherlands, Ireland, Italy and Sweden. They bought a number of coatings and inks businesses from Croda International for £27 million. They continued to develop the business aggressively with strategic overseas acquisitions in an attempt to become a multi-national force. These included the Dutch company Premier Inks, one of Europe's largest manufacturers of publishing inks; Morrison Printing Inks in Australia and New Zealand; the Klintens business, specialising in metal decorating coatings, from a Swedish company; and then a small United States company, Croda Inks, bought for £4.7 million (in August 1996).

Manders changed its brand name to 'Manders Premier' when they acquired Premier Inks in 1994. They set up six 'centres of excellence' in various European locations, where Wolverhampton became the centre for the manufacture of coldset inks, the fast-drying inks used in newspapers. Most of the national British papers by now used inks that were manufactured in Wolverhampton, and the company supplied many in Euope also. Manders Premier successfully began to create a world-wide market presence in a more focused international speciality chemicals business, based on the new high-tech inks: heatset web offset inks, coldset web offset (newspaper) inks, sheetfed inks, metal decorating inks, and water-based liquid packaging inks. They invested heavily in research and development.

But their strategy had been misconceived from the outset. The management were soon reporting that they found themselves in an 'extremely competitive' market, with declining profits in the face of huge international rivals, like Dai Nippon of Japan,[2] the market leader, rapaciously undercutting prices to gain market share, and strategically buying their way into European markets. With a strong pound, by April 1996 Manders were describing the UK ink market leaders, themselves and Sun Chemicals, as 'two wounded elephants lumbering around in the jungle'. Investors fought shy, as without the property there was no longer anything to 'go for', and the share price fell on the London Stock Exchange from a peak of 403 in 1994 to languish at a low of 130 after the Board had announced a profits warning in June 1997. Turnover in the inks division had grown from £40 million (1993) before the restructuring to £162.5 million (1996). About sixty countries worldwide were being supplied through 28 manufacturing and distribution centres. But it was still not enough, and profits before tax were unexciting at £5.5 million.

This was a management of commercial men (often with share options of their own) who never forgot their duty to add shareholder value, particularly for institutional shareholders. Just two institutional investors spoke for 34 per cent of the shares: British Steel Pension Fund (20.5%), and Schroders Investment Management (13.5%). With a few others, like Mercury Asset Management (5.2%), Britannic Assurance (4.4%), Prudential Assurance (3.2%), etc., they controlled the Company. The family holdings were by now much depleted, without a stake in the management and with horrendous and widely-reported Lloyd's underwriting losses affecting several family 'names' in the early 1990s.

The UK could not meet the challenge of the global economy. Finally, in late 1997, as they downsized towards oblivion and continued to achieve mediocre results, despite the huge windfall generated by the sale of the Mander Centre, the Board admitted that 'it could no longer compete with its larger international rivals'. The directors stripped the remaining assets of Manders and announced the sale of everything they had not destroyed, after 225 years, for £100 million. The controlling shareholders had jumped at an offer of £2.50 a share.

The purchaser was Flint Ink Corporation of Detroit, the second largest ink company in the United States of America, and the fifth largest in the world. The Manders acquisition would be a bridgehead, providing 'an excellent entrée to the European market'. The company publicity stated:

> Chances are, you touch our products—products touch your life—every day. From the bag that protects your morning bread, to the label on your afternoon soft drink, to the newspaper you read in the evening, Flint Ink is there, decorating, and communicating.

Founded by H. Howard Flint in Detroit, Michigan, in 1920, it had achieved a million-dollar turnover by 1936, and operated 70 factories in North and South America, South Africa and the Pacific Rim, with turnover sixty years later of £424 million (1996), and 2,500 employees. Its three main businesses were printing ink, colour pigments and printing blankets. Unlike Manders, it was still owned, either directly or through trusts, by approximately 30 descendants of its founder. H. Howard Flint II, chairman, wrote to me reassuringly on his purchase of Manders PLC: 'I can assure you that your family company will be cared for very well by my family in the coming years'.

On 20 December 1997 the *Financial Times*, announcing the news, wrote: 'More than 200 years of British chemicals history came to an end yesterday'. A few weeks later Manders had ceased to exist as an independent company.

'When he casts his leaves forth upon the wind, the author addresses, not the many who will fling aside his volume, or never take it up, but the few who will understand him, better than most of his schoolmates or lifemates'
—Nathaniel Hawthorne, *The Scarlet Letter*

All is not valedictory, as a millennial commemoration stirring up the ghosts of vanished leaves. At the time of writing, the Mander brands survive, just, as dominant players in the global coatings industry, moving into the fourth century in which they have traded. The Manders decorative paints' brand continues in the UK, and Manders Premier has established itself in Europe as 'one of the world's largest suppliers of coatings, colorants, inks and toners, as well as graphic arts products, consumables, and machinery'.[3]

This two hundred years of history and anecdote demonstrates no retrospective destiny. We locate the beginnings of modern technology and technical-industrial production in such firms of eighteenth-century Midland England as Manders, with their blend of materialistic practicality and moral idealism. The middling sort like them, who—with their kinsmen, their unsung employees and dependants, and their network of customers and friends—created recognisable mercantile capitalism and its liberal institutions, are in retreat, askew in irrelevance. An age of democratic urgency, of global corporatism, cultural displacement, of post-industrial 'high' technology, with its deterritorialising, multinational logic, has emerged and defined itself in my lifetime. The smell of varnish compounds at the Works in John Street, evoking early memories, has vanished from the city air.

Like Primo Levi, Italo Svevo and Sherwood Anderson, I write from a past rooted in the varnish trade. Primo Levi describes the beauty of the process of distillation, a masterpiece of rationality, like chemistry itself, 'an existential parable'. 'Varnish,' his story *Vanadium* begins, 'is an unstable substance by definition,' because at some point 'it must turn from a liquid into a solid'. The same can be said of memories and histories, though Levi says it by implication only: at a critical point they congeal.

The Manders, as cousin Lionel saw them in 1935, were 'good if not great men', vindicated in their wealth and philanthropy, in their 'prosaic and provincial' role as varnish kings. Like him, ejected from the firm, in my generation the family finds more catholic, expatriated interests, infused with their protestant and patrician liberalism. From outside the city limits, I seem to be again in a pre-industrial world, rooted in place and land. My professional interest in paints focuses on early glue temperas and earth pigments in raw umber, Venetian red, burnt sienna; all conservation work at Owlpen where I live is done in lime washes and renders, caseins and ox-hair, using sustainable pre-industrial technology.

The old values and signs and the stories they represent have never been more scrutinized—nor, I suspect, less understood. They shine, and become mythologised in the retelling. In the face of what Heidegger calls the essential homelessness of man, the future of old houses and estates, of old family companies, of commercial 'Houses'—the meaning of titles and philanthropy, of private lives, the leaves of papers and possessions, varnished or plain, that define and express them—is likely to remain contingent. The glory of dynasties is transient and attenuated in what seems like the twilight of an age.

'The owl of Minerva spreads her wings as the dusk gathers', Hegel reminds us. For it is only at the ending that we begin to make out the pattern. The patriachal proper name is ungrounded. An alien terror has swept out in the darkness and we Trojans are at an end, and Ilium itself has ended. As Homer speaks, like that of leaves is the generation of men (*Iliad*, vi, 146). Like Kathleen Raine, I have witnessed the showering down of leaves which were once—even within my own memory—quick with life.

But living at Owlpen, in this leafy valley the centuries overlooked, has brought deep joy in the making and the sharing. Something at least is saved. The house below its church and waking weathercock—and the garden they stand in, the springs and the environing woods—always refresh and adapt, making themselves acceptable, and something does not quite fade away into the shades of the indefinite. They gather together instead the paths and connections in which death and renewal, disaster and triumph, disgrace and victory, acquire the shape of a destiny. Like the sherds in the soil, the leaves themselves, they hold their ground against the storm raging in the western twilight, as they have done for a thousand years.

Owlpen Manor, etching by Joseph Webb (1908-62)

[1] The Company Secretary stated to the press the family share was about 6% in March 1993.
[2] Dai Nippon Printing, with a market capitalization of $9,888 million, turnover of $9,932 million and 14,309 employees in 1998.
[3] But on 18 May 2000, Flint Ink Corporation announced that Manders Premier had changed its name to 'Flint Ink Europe'; 'the name change is a natural part of our growth as a global company'. The Heath Town works has become the European headquarters of Flint Ink Europe. The remainder of the works has closed, and since become 'Manders Industrial Estate', home to a number of local companies.

Gum picking, English varnish factory, 1890s

APPENDIX I

Mander Family Booklist

(books by and about the Mander family)

General

Barty-King, Hugh, 'Mander Brothers of Wolverhampton, 1773-1973', 1972, 71p. [unpublished typescript]

———, 'Preliminary Survey for Mander Brothers of Wolverhampton', July 1971, 12p. [with chronology 1720-1937and family trees] [unpublished typescript]

Burke's *Peerage, Baronetage and Knightage* [various editions, of which 106th the fullest]

Green Can, The [Mander Brothers' house journal], September 1920–

Mander, Sir Geoffrey le Mesurier (ed.), *The History of Mander Brothers*, n.d. [Whitehead Brothers, 1955]

Pegg, Patricia (ed.), *A Very Private Heritage: The Family Papers of Samuel Theodore Mander of Wolverhampton, 1853-1900*, Malvern: Images Publishing, 1996

Eighteenth Century

DeVoe, S.S., *English Papier-Mâché of the Georgian and Victorian Periods*, Middletown, Conn.: Wesleyan University Press, 1971

Godden, G.A., 'English Paper Trays, 1790-1815', *The Connoisseur*, vol. 165, Aug., 1967, 250-4

Jones, William Highfield, *Story of the Japan, Tin-Plate Working, and Iron Braziers' Trades, Bicycle and Galvanising Trades, and Enamel Ware Manufacture in Wolverhampton and District*, London: Alexander and Shepheard, 1900

Jones, Yvonne, *Georgian and Victorian Japanned Wares of the West Midlands: Catalogue of the permanent collection and a temporary exhibition*, Wolverhampton Art Gallery and Museums, 1982

Mason, Frank, *Wolverhampton: the Town Commissioners 1777-1848*, Wolverhampton, 1976

Morris, Mary S., *English Painted Enamels 18th and 19th Century in the Wolverhampton and Bilston Collections*, 1973

Parsons, Harold, 'The Mander Story', *The Blackcountryman*, vol. vi, no. 1

Woodall, Joy, *Portrait of Lapworth in the 18th and 19th Centuries*, Solihull, 1986

John Street Chapel Case

Anon., *An Answer to the Calumnies contained in Mr C. Mander's Minute Detail*, [n.d.]

Anon., *Observations on the Nature and Results of the Legal Principles Asserted in the Lady Hewley and Wolverhampton Cases*, 1836

Anon., *Presbyterian Endowments: Report of the hearing of the case of the Wolverhampton Meeting House, Attorney General and Mander—v.—Pearson, before Lord Cottenham, Lord High Chancellor, at Westminster Hall*, January, 1836

Anon., *Proceedings on the Hearing of an Appeal from a Decree of the Vice-Chancellor, as to the Presbyterian Meeting House, Wolverhampton*, 1836

Anon., *Reports for the Charity Commissioners for the County of Stafford*, 1839

Anon., *Resolutions of the Board of Congregational Ministers in the Wolverhampton Case, July 7th 1818*, 1818

Anon., *The Case of the Old Dissenting Meeting House, Wolverhampton*, 1817

Anon., *The Wolverhampton Case: A Defence by the Editors of the Congregational Magazine of the Board's Resolution*, 1818

Anon., *The Wolverhampton Case. Vice-Chancellor's Judgment with Prefatory Remarks*, 1835

Anon., *To the Rev. John Humphrys relative to his Late Controversy with the Rev Benjamin Carpenter. By a Friend to Both*, 1783

Congregational Magazine, 1817-9 [passim]

Courier, The, 16 July 1817 [report of the case of Mander and Stewart—v.—Pearson].

Blazier, Stella M., 'The Wolverhampton Chapel Case', Polytechnic of Wolverhampton M.A. thesis, 1985

Bransby, James Hews, *Old Dissenting Meeting-House, Wolverhampton,* Dudley, 25 May 1818, 16p. [?reprinted 1819]

James, J.A., and others, *Concise Account of the Situation of the Old Meeting House, Wolverhampton,* 1818

———, *Religious Liberty not Infringed by the Proceedings in the Case of the Meeting House, John Street, Wolverhampton: An Appeal to the Public in Answer to the Remarks of the Rev. Joseph Robertson, by the Dissenting Ministers who Originally signed the case, with an Appendix, containing a Detail of Facts by Mr C. Mander* (December 16, 1818), London, 1819, 107p.

———, *Reply to Remarks (by J. Robertson) on the Wolverhampton Case,* 1818

James, Thomas Smith, *The History of the Litigation and Legislation respecting Presbyterian Chapels and Charities in England and Ireland, between 1816 and 1849,* 1867

Jones, W.H., *A History of the Congregational Churches of Wolverhampton, from 1662 to 1894,* 1894, pp. 43-

Kell, R., and others, *Case of the Old Dissenting Meeting House in Wolverhampton,* 1818

Lee, Thomas Eyre, *Reply to 'Verax' on the Case of the Old Meeting-House in Wolverhampton, in a letter to the editor of the Monthly Repository,* Birmingham, 16 May 1818

Mander, Charles, *An Appendix to an Appeal to the Public,* 1818

———, *A Minute Detail of Circumstances relative to the Old Meeting House in John Street, Wolverhampton, a case of great importance to orthodox dissenters,* Wolverhampton, 26 March 1819, 16p.

Mander, John, Linney, Joseph, and Hanbury, John, *A letter to Rev. John Cole,* Birmingham, 1780, 15p.

Matthews, A.G., *The Congregational Churches of Staffordshire,* 1924, pp. 152-64; 231-5

———, *Trans. Congregationalist History Society,* XII, no. 1, 9

May, Henry Arthur, *Queen Street Congregational Church, Wolverhampton, The Story of a Hundred Years, 1809-1909,* 1909

Merrivale, *Law Reports,* vol. III, pp. 353 ff., 390-2, 419

Monthly Repository, 1817, pp. 430, 441, 494-5, 512, 541, 666; 1818, pp. 95, 98, 531, 708, 717

Pearson, Joseph, *The Case of the Old Dissenting Meeting House, Wolverhampton,* 1817

———, *Remarks on an Appendix to An Appeal to the Public in the Case of the Old Meeting House, Wolverhampton,* London, 1819, 15p.

Pearson, Joseph, and others, *The Case of the Unitarian Society of Wolverhampton,* 1830

Robertson, The Rev. James, *Religious Liberty Applied to the case of the Old Meeting House, John Street, Wolverhampton, including remarks on the conduct of the editors of the Congregational Magazine; and the Resolution of the Congregational Board, July 7,* London, 1818, 63p.

———, *On the Wolverhampton Case,* 1818

———, *Infringements of Religious Liberty Exposed, in the case of the Meeting-House, John-Street, Wolverhampton, in Answer to the Appeal of the nine dissenting ministers who patronise that case,* London, 1819, 51p.

Steward, J., *Mr Steward's Vindication,* 1817

Taylor, E., *Proceedings in Chancery with Regard to the Meeting House at Wolverhampton, Deeply Affecting the Property of Unitarian Christians,* 1817

'Verax', *Facts connected with the Case of the Old Meeting House in Wolverhampton in reply to a statement which appeared in Monthly Repository for March 1818,* 1818

'Vigil', *On the Wolverhampton Case and the Necessity for an Association for the Protection of the Civil Rights of Anti-Trinitarians,* 1818

Nineteenth Century

Anon, *Our Contemporaries, a biographical repertoire of Men and Women of the day 1896-7*, London: Klene & Co., [n.d.]

Anon, *The County of Stafford and Many of its Family Records*, Exeter: Wm Pollard & Co., 1897

Burke, Peter, *The Romance of the Forum*, series 1, vol. II, 1854, pp. 18-34

Hancock, G., *A Tettenhall History*, 1991

Hickman, Peter, 'Advice for a Commercial Traveller', *The Blackcountryman*, vol. 31, issue 2 [C. Mander's 'Regulations for a Traveller']

———, 'The Wolverhampton Flour and Bread Co.', *The Blackcountryman*, vol. 31, issue 3

Jones, G.W., *Borough Politics: A Study of Wolverhampton Borough Council, 1888-1964*, London: Macmillan, 1969

Jones, J., *Historical Sketch of the Art and Literary Institutions of Wolverhampton, from the year 1794 to1897*, 1897

———, *The Mayors of Wolverhampton*, vol. I, 1848-80; vol. II, 1881-1909

Jones, J.P., *History of Tettenhall*, 1894

Jones, W.H., *Story of the Municipal Life of Wolverhampton*, 1903

Mander, Benjamin, *The King versus B. Mander and Eight Others: The Trial at Large of the Committee of the Flour and Bread Co. (of which Benjamin Mander was Chairman) at Stafford Summer Assizes,* 1814, 1956 (reprinted)

Mander, Samuel Small, 'Historical Sketch', *Queen Street Church Manual*, 1873

———, *Our Opium Trade with China*, London: Simpkin Marshall; Wolverhampton: J.M.'D. Roebuck, 1877, 72 p.

———, *The Relation of Children to the Church*, London, 1872

Measom, George, *The Official Illustrated Guide to the Great Western Railway*, London: Richard Griffin, n.d. [1860], pp. 505-508; 2nd ed., Griffin Bohn & Co., n.d. [1861], pp. 450-4 [both eds. with engraving of 'The Works of Messrs. Mander Brothers, Wolver'ton']; *The Official Advertiser* [supplement], p. 80 [Mander Bros' advertisement]

New Illustrated Directory Entitled Men and Things of Modern England, The, 1858 [trade advertisements for Mander Brothers and Mander, Weaver & Co.]

Parsons, Harold, 'The Mander Story', *The Blackcountryman*, vol. 6, issue 1

Reade, Thos, 'John Mander and Reade Brothers', *The Wolverhampton Journal*, June 1907

Smart, Joseph, *Directory of Wolverhampton, also Bilston, Willenhall and Wednesfield*, 1827

Upton, Chris, *A History of Wolverhampton*, Chichester: Phillimore, 1998

Wallis, George, 'Free Library and Practical School of Art', reprinted for Benjamin Mander, 18 May 1860

Ward, John, *Blood Money: an incident in Wolverhampton with national consequences*, Wolver-hampton Public Libraries, 1988

Warren, Samuel, *Now and Then*, 1848

Twentieth Century

Addenbrooke, P., *A History of Wolverhampton Transport*, vol. I, 1833-1930, Birmingham: Birmingham Transport Historical Group, 1989

Attwood, S.J., *Jarvis Mount Hotel: a brief history*, n.d., 6 p.

Bantock House, *English and Foreign Dolls and Toys, 1780-1950: A Catalogue of the Wolverhampton Art Gallery and Museums*, Wolverhampton, n.d.

British Printer, The, London: Raithby, Laurence & Co., 1888- [passim, for Manders trade advertisements and specimens]; 1893, vol. VI [all nos., including supplement]; 1901, vol. XIV [section reprinted in *Modern Letterpress Designs*, vol. IX, 52 p.]; 1908-9 (Dec.-Jan.) [with account of new works]; 1927 (Jan./Feb.); 1931 (Sept.); 1939 (Nov.); 1937 (Autumn); 1937-8 (Winter/ Spring); 1939 (Nov.)

Devee, Sunitee, Maharani of Cooch Behar, *The Autobiography of an Indian Princess*, 1921

Hickman, Peter, 'Men before their time: the Mander Brothers' Joint Works Council', *The Blackcountryman*, vol. 31, issue 1

Mander Brothers Ltd., *An Account of the Internal Organisation of the Business of Mander Brothers, Ltd., Wolverhampton, In its relationship to the Employee (Approved by the Joint Works Committee)*, 1925, revised 1934, 1939, 24 p.

Mander-Kidd Ltd., *How Printing Ink is Made*, Wolverhampton and London, n.d.

Mander, Sir Geoffrey le Mesurier, *We Were* Not *All Wrong*, Victor Gollancz, 1944

———, *What is patriotism? Answered by Lord Allen of Hurtwood, Geoffrey Le Mesurier Mander, Lady Cynthia Asquith, [etc.]*, ed. N.P. Macdonald, 1935

Mander, John Geoffrey Grylls, *Berlin: The Eagle and the Bear*, Barrier & Rockliff, 1959; *The Writer and Commitment*, Secker & Warburg, 1961—US ed., Dufour, 1962; *Berlin: Hostage for the West*, Harmondsworth (Penguin Special), 1962—US ed., Boston, Mass.: Houghton Mifflin Co., 1964; *Berlin. Unterpfand der Freiheit, aus dem Engl. v. G. Schönmann*, Bonn: Athenäum, 1962, 134p.; *Great Britain or Little England?*, Harmondsworth (Penguin Special), 1963—US ed., Boston, Mass.: Houghton Mifflin Co., 1964; *Static Society: The Paradox of Latin America*, 1969; *The Unrevolutionary Society: The Power of Latin American Conservatism in a Changing World*, New York: Knopf, 1969—Harper & Row, 1971; *Elegiacs*, Hatfield: The Stellar Press, 1972; *Our German Cousins: Anglo-German Relations in the 19th and 20th Centuries*, John Murray, 1974—US ed., Albuquerque, NM: Transatlantic Arts, 1975; *A Calvary*, 1978

Mander, John and Necke (trans.), *The Dignity of Night*, Lippincott, 1958 (Klaus Roehler, *Die Wuerde der Nacht*); *Carnival Confession*, 1961 (Carl Zuckmayer, *Die Fastnachtsbeichte*); *The Meaning of Contemporary Realism*, Merlin Press, 1963, 1972 (Geörg Lukács); *Realism in our time: literature and the class struggle*, NY: Harper & Row, 1964, 1971 (Geörg Lukács, with pref. by George Steiner).

Mander, 'Miles' [Lionel], *Oasis*, 1927; *Gentleman by Birth*, 1933; *To my Son—in Confidence*, Faber & Faber, 1934

Mander, [Charles] Nicholas, Verity, Simon, and Wynne-Jones, Davina, *Norman Jewson: Architect*, Cirencester, 1986

Mander, Nicholas, *Owlpen Manor: a short history and guide*, Owlpen, various eds, 1993-2000, 64p.

Mander, Rosalie, Lady [also as 'Rosalie Glynn Grylls'], *Mary Shelley: A Biography*, Oxford, 1938; *Claire Clairmont: Mother of Byron's Allegra*, John Murray, 1939; *Queen's College: 1848-1948*, Routledge, 1948; *Trelawny*, Constable, 1950; *William Godwin and his World*, Odham's Press, 1953; *Portrait of Rossetti*, Macdonald, 1964; *I. Compton-Burnett*, Longmans & Green, 1971; *Mrs Browning: The Story of Elizabeth Barrett*, Weidenfeld & Nicolson, 1980; *Categories, an Anthology About Cats, Arranged According to Their Characters, Chosen By*, Weidenfeld & Nicolson, 1981, 99 p.

'Quaestor' (W. Byford-Jones), *I Met them in the Midlands*, Midland News Assn., 1937 [contains biographical sketches of CAM, with portrait by A.Arrowsmith, and of GleMM], pp. 42-7, 108-111

Stokes, Louis Mander, *A dear and noble Boy: The Life and Letters of Louis Stokes 1897-1916*, edited with a biography and introductory material by R.A. Barlow and H.V. Bowen, Leo Cooper, 1995

The Studio, 46, 1909, vol. II, 140 [description of Library and Music Room at The Mount]

Woods, Edward Sydney, Lord Bishop of Lichfield, *Address delivered at the Memorial Service ... for Charles Arthur Mander, second baronet*, Curwen Press [privately printed], 1952

Gerald Poynton Mander

The History of the Wolverhampton Grammar School, Wolverhampton: Steens, 1913

The Wolverhampton Antiquary, being collections for a history of the town gathered by G.P.M., Wolverhampton: Whitehead Bros, vol. I, 1915-32 (12 nos); vol. II, 1933-45

Early Wolverhampton Books and Printers, with a note on some playbills, Wolverhampton: Whitehead Bros, 1922

Descriptive Catalogue of the Topographical Sketches and Prints forming the Staffordshire Views *Collection in the William Salt Library, Stafford,* Staffordshire Record Society: Collections for a History of Staffordshire (hereafter 'Staffs Record Society'), 1942-3, 257 p.
[ed.], Sketchley & Adams, *Wolverhampton Directory of 1770. Reprinted with an introduction as a supplement to The Wolverhampton Antiquary,* Wolverhampton, 192-
A History of Wolverhampton to the Early Nineteenth Century (ed. and completed by N.W. Tildesley), Wolverhampton: C.B. Corporation, 1960
Green Can, The [Mander Bros house journal] [contributions passim]
[ed. and intro.], *Notebook of Gregory King, 1679-80,* Staffs Record Society, 1919
[calendar], *Lichfield Diocesan Register of Wills, 1553-8, 1575-7,* Staffs Record Society, 1926
[calendar and intro.], *The Staffordshire Quarter Sessions Roll for 1586,* Staffs Record Society, 1927
[calendar], *Ancient deeds preserved at the Wodehouse, Wombourne,* Staffs Record Society, 1928
[text and intro.], *Walsall Churchwardens' Accounts, 1462-1531,* Staffs. Record Society, 1928
[ed.] (with A.T. Marston), *Index of Marriage Bonds: Wolverhampton Peculiar before 1846 and Tettenhall before 1858,* Staffs Record Society, 1931
[text and intro.], *The Walsall Ship Money Papers, 1635-1636,* Staffs. Record Society, 1931
[texts and notes], *Charters and Records of Black Ladies Priory, Brewood,* Staffs Record Society, 1939
[text and intro.], *Lord Aston's Letters, 1671-3,* Staffs Record Society, 1941
South Staffordshire Letters from the William Salt Collection, Staffs Record Society, 1941
[ed.], *Bilston Parish Register. 1684-1746,* Staffordshire Parish Record Society, 1937-8
[ed.], *Gnosall Parish Register. 1572-1699,* Staffordshire Parish Record Society, 1922
[ed.], *Pattingham Parish Register. 1559-1812,* Staffordshire Parish Record Society, 1934
[ed.], *Penn Parish Register. 1570-1754,* Staffordshire Parish Record Society, 1921
[ed.], *Wolverhampton Parish Register. 1539–* (transcribed by H.R. Thomas), pt. 1, Staffordshire Parish Record Society, 1932
'Queen Square, Wolverhampton, and its neighbourhood before the nineteenth century', *The Wolverhampton Journal,* March 1907, 69-71
'Feudal Essays. ii—The Buffaries of Penne-Buffare', *The Wolverhampton Journal,* September 1907, 239-43
[ed.] (with C.G.O. Bridgeman), 'The Stafford Hidation', *Staffs Record Society Collns,* 1919
(with T. Tape), 'Some Ridware armorial glass', *Staffs Record Society Collns,* 1923
'The Tomb of Richard Gorst at Lapley', *Staffs Record Society Collns,* 1925
'Forest of Secchehulle', *Staffs Record Society Collns,* 1925
'Report on the Roman Camp on Wall Heath, Kingswinford', *Staffs Record Soc. Collns,* 1927
'The Stafford Mint under Henry II, 1158-9', *Staffs Record Society Collns,* 1927
'Benolt's Visitation, 1533', *Staffs Record Society Collns,* 1928
'Staffordshire Deputy Lieutenants, 1689', *Staffs Record Society Collns,* 1931
'History from the Wolseley Charters', *Staffs Record Society Collns,* 1934
'Lows on Calf Heath', *Staffs Record Society Collns,* 1938
'An Audley Charter and its seals', *Staffs Record Society Collns,* 1941
'An Appendix to the same: charters of Gervase Paganel', *Staffs Record Society Collns,* 1942
N.W. Greenslade, *The Staffordshire Historians,* Staffs Record Society, 4th Series, vol. XI, 1982, pp. 148-9, 156-7 [with portrait illus., f.p. 144]
Wulfrunian, The, July 1952, pp. 454-8 [G.P.M. obituary notice]

Wightwick Manor

Builder, The, 24 May 1889, 420
Cornforth, John, 'Wightwick Manor—Staffordshire', *Country Life,* cxxxiii, 30 May and 6 June 1963, 1242, 1316
Girouard, Mark, *The Victorian Country House,* New Haven: Yale University Press, 1979
Keightley, S.N., 'Edward Ould and the late nineteenth-century picturesque movement', MA thesis, 1976

Lees-Milne, James, *Wightwick Manor, Staffordshire*, National Trust Guide, 1963, rev. 1972, 24p.
Lycett Green, Candida, *Country Life: 100 Favourite Houses*, 1999 [with chapter on Owlpen]
Mander, Nicholas, 'Wightwick Manor and the creation of the House Beautiful', *Architecture 1900*, ed. P. Burman, Shaftesbury: Donhead, 1998
Mander, R.G.G. Lady, *Geoffrey le Mesurier Mander (1882-1962), donor of the house*, Oxford: University Press, n.d.
————, 'Wightwick Manor', *The Antique Collector*, June 1975, 30-4
Ponder, Stephen, *Wightwick Manor*, National Trust Guide, 1993
————, 'The Morris and de Morgan Collections at Wightwick Manor', *The Journal of the William Morris Society*, vol. VII, no. 2, Spring, 1987
Tinniswood, Adrian, *The Arts and Crafts House*, Mitchell Beazley, 1999 [includes chapters on Wightwick and Owlpen]
Waterson, M., *The Country House Remembered*, 1985

Unpublished sources

Bristol University Library. DM668. Sir G. le M. Mander: correspondence (22 items) and incomplete autobiography, 1924-57 (NRA 33764 National Liberal).
Cambridge University Library, Department of Manuscripts and University Archives. Papers of H P Stokes. Add.MS8699/7/1/11 (including Amy Stokes papers and her memoir of H.P. Stokes).
Dr William's Library, Gordon Sq., London. P.P.3.12.27. Ms. headed 'The Wolverhampton Controversy: Tracts and Papers covering the Chapel in John Street, 1818-19'. P.P.3.12.26. (Mander birth registration records transferred to PRO.)
House of Lords Record Office. The Lloyd George Papers, 1922-1945: LG/G/1-271.
King's College, Cambridge. Modern archive collection, Keynes papers: PP/45/209. [Sir G. le M. Mander: correspondence,1904-6.]
London University, University College London (UCL) Manuscripts Room. The Gaitskell Papers correspondence with Geoffrey Mander, mainly Oct-Dec 1952, 1954, etc.
Manchester University, Labour History Archives and Study Centre. Labour Party Archives [LP/GS/PRE, LP/GS/DIN]
National Library of Ireland, Dublin. Amy M. Mander correspondence: MS 24,507-24,536.
Manders PLC. Mander Brothers business papers, minute books, etc., 1773–.
Nova Scotia Archives and Records Management, Halifax. Henry N. Paint, MP, papers.
Owlpen Manor.
Mander family: estate, business and legal papers, correspondence and publications, 1780s–.
B. Mander, C. Mander, C.B. Mander and families: correspondence and papers, 1780s–.
Sir C.T. Mander: correspondence, damp-press out-letter books, press-cuttings books, personal and business papers, misc. photographs, 1858-1929.
John Mander: Boer War correspondence, 1900.
Sir C.A. Mander: journals (including travel journals and first world war correspondence relating to the Palestine campaign 1916-18), press-cuttings books (relating to periods of mayoralty), speeches, personal papers (including letters from S. Baldwin, C. Attlee, A. Eden, etc.), sketch books, albums, 1880s-1952.
Sir C.M. Mander: letters and diaries of second world war, shrievalty, 1943-63.
Amy M. Mander: correspondence from Irish nationalist leaders, sketches and papers, 1887-1919.
Mary, Lady Mander and Henry Paint: correspondence and papers, 1880s-1939.
D.St.C. Mander: correspondence, diaries and papers, *c.* 1895-1965.
Public Record Office: court papers and affidavits covering the case of John Hall and Patrick Morrison, PRO: ASSI 5/137/17.
Wightwick Manor (National Register of Archives 32851 Mander).
S.S. Mander and S.T. Mander: correspondence, diaries, notebooks, press-cuttings, etc.

Sir G. le M. Mander: correspondence and papers, parliamentary papers, including correspondence from politicians, such as Chamberlain, Gaitskell, Sinclair, Macmillan, Attlee, etc., 1890s-1962.

Rosalie, Lady Mander: correspondence and papers, 1914-88, including letters from literary figures, such as John Betjeman, Walter de la Mare, Ivy Compton-Burnett, Edmund Blunden and A.L. Rowse.

William Salt Library, Stafford. Thos Mander, probate records, 1764.

West Sussex Record Office. The Cobden Papers: Cobden 971; 1065 (1887-8) [letters from Amy Mander to Emma Catherine Cobden].

Wolverhampton Central Library: archives and local studies collection.

Mander Collection (D/MAN; see NRA 22580 Mander): includes G.P. Mander's Staffordshire local history papers, research notes and manuscripts; 19th-century litigation (L28, L34).

Documents relating to John Street, D/JSR/33/1-2 [mortgage and conveyances, 1846-9]; DX119/4 [messuages in Victoria Street, 1876].

Crest from CTM's carriage hammercloth

APPENDIX II

The Mander Family Tree (abridged)

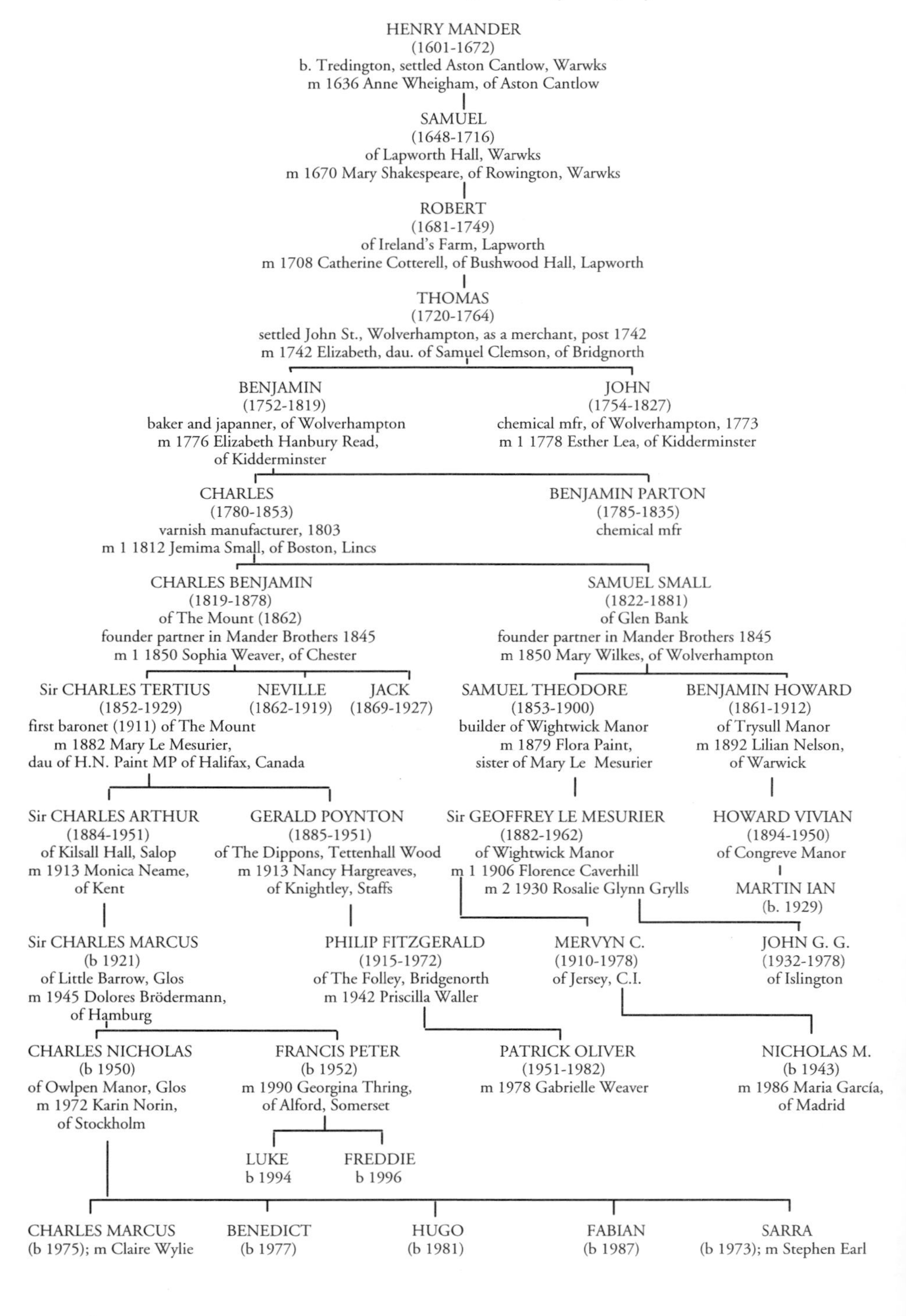

HENRY MANDER
(1601-1672)
b. Tredington, settled Aston Cantlow, Warwks
m 1636 Anne Wheigham, of Aston Cantlow
SAMUEL
(1648-1716)
of Lapworth Hall, Warwks
m 1670 Mary Shakespeare, of Rowington, Warwks
ROBERT
(1681-1749)
of Ireland's Farm, Lapworth
m 1708 Catherine Cotterell, of Bushwood Hall, Lapworth
THOMAS
(1720-1764)
settled John St., Wolverhampton, as a merchant, post 1742
m 1742 Elizabeth, dau. of Samuel Clemson, of Bridgnorth
BENJAMIN
(1752-1819)
baker and japanner, of Wolverhampton
m 1776 Elizabeth Hanbury Read,
of Kidderminster
JOHN
(1754-1827)
chemical mfr, of Wolverhampton, 1773
m 1 1778 Esther Lea, of Kidderminster
CHARLES
(1780-1853)
varnish manufacturer, 1803
m 1 1812 Jemima Small, of Boston, Lincs
BENJAMIN PARTON
(1785-1835)
chemical mfr
CHARLES BENJAMIN
(1819-1878)
of The Mount (1862)
founder partner in Mander Brothers 1845
m 1 1850 Sophia Weaver, of Chester
SAMUEL SMALL
(1822-1881)
of Glen Bank
founder partner in Mander Brothers 1845
m 1850 Mary Wilkes, of Wolverhampton
Sir CHARLES TERTIUS
(1852-1929)
first baronet (1911) of The Mount
m 1882 Mary Le Mesurier,
dau of H.N. Paint MP of Halifax, Canada
NEVILLE
(1862-1919)
JACK
(1869-1927)
SAMUEL THEODORE
(1853-1900)
builder of Wightwick Manor
m 1879 Flora Paint,
sister of Mary Le Mesurier
BENJAMIN HOWARD
(1861-1912)
of Trysull Manor
m 1892 Lilian Nelson,
of Warwick
Sir CHARLES ARTHUR
(1884-1951)
of Kilsall Hall, Salop
m 1913 Monica Neame,
of Kent
GERALD POYNTON
(1885-1951)
of The Dippons, Tettenhall Wood
m 1913 Nancy Hargreaves,
of Knightley, Staffs
Sir GEOFFREY LE MESURIER
(1882-1962)
of Wightwick Manor
m 1 1906 Florence Caverhill
m 2 1930 Rosalie Glynn Grylls
HOWARD VIVIAN
(1894-1950)
of Congreve Manor
MARTIN IAN
(b. 1929)
Sir CHARLES MARCUS
(b 1921)
of Little Barrow, Glos
m 1945 Dolores Brödermann,
of Hamburg
PHILIP FITZGERALD
(1915-1972)
of The Folley, Bridgenorth
m 1942 Priscilla Waller
MERVYN C.
(1910-1978)
of Jersey, C.I.
JOHN G. G.
(1932-1978)
of Islington
CHARLES NICHOLAS
(b 1950)
of Owlpen Manor, Glos
m 1972 Karin Norin,
of Stockholm
FRANCIS PETER
(b 1952)
m 1990 Georgina Thring,
of Alford, Somerset
PATRICK OLIVER
(1951-1982)
m 1978 Gabrielle Weaver
NICHOLAS M.
(b 1943)
m 1986 Maria García,
of Madrid
LUKE
b 1994
FREDDIE
b 1996
CHARLES MARCUS
(b 1975); m Claire Wylie
BENEDICT
(b 1977)
HUGO
(b 1981)
FABIAN
(b 1987)
SARRA
(b 1973); m Stephen Earl

APPENDIX III

THE FAMILY OF MANDER
or MAUNDER

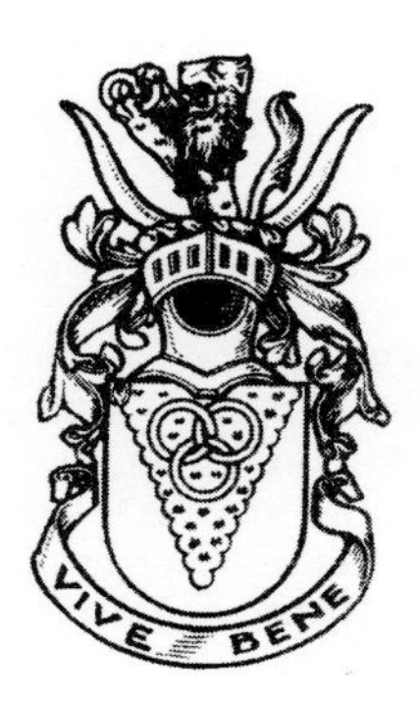

Arms:[1] *Gules, on a pile invected erminois, three annulets interlaced, two and one of the field.*
Crest: *On a wreath of the colours, a demi-lion couped ermine holding in the paws two annulets interlaced fessewise gules, between two buffalo horns of the last.*
Mantling: *Gules and or.* ***Motto:*** *Vive Bene.* ***Livery:*** *Blue, yellow facings, brass buttons.*

John MAUNDWER held half a virgate of land in the parish of Tredington, county Worcester, in the time of Pope Nicholas IV (c. 1288).

The Register of the Guild of the Holy Cross, the Blessed Mary and St John the Baptist of Stratford-upon-Avon, Warwicks., shows the entrance of William and Matilda MAUNDER of Armscote in the parish of Tredington, for the years 1494 and 1495.

First Generation

I.1 William MAUNDER was b. circa 1505 and d. 1566, leaving 4 sons and 3 daus.
I.2 **John MAUNDER**, of Blackwell, Tredington, Worcester, b. c. 1518; m. **Margery** — (who was buried Tredington 15 Sept 1593, and whose will dated 6 July 1588 was proved at Worcester on 10 Oct 1593); and he was bur. 4 June 1587, leaving four sons and one dau., of whom presently.

Second Generation

Issue of John and Margery MAUNDER, of Blackwell, Tredington (I.2):
II.1 John MAUNDER, b. Blackwell [?] 1540; m. 1st 21 Jun 1567 Isabella KECKE (bur. 1 May 1587), by whom he had issue, of whom presently; John m. 2nd in Tredington 25 Oct 1588, Jane HANNES, by whom he had 2 daus, Katherine and Margaret.
II.2 **William MAUNDER**, bapt. at Tredington, 27 Mar 1543; m. **Anna** —; and was bur. Sept. 1622, leaving 4 sons and 2 daus., of whom presently.
II.3 Thomas MAUNDER, bapt. Tredington 1 July 1546; m. there 21 June 1568 Joanne FULLER, and d. Blackwell 1587, bur. 26 June 1587, having by her had issue, of whom presently.

---

[1] Grant confirmed Heraldic College 30 May 1901 to descendants of Charles Benjamin Mander and Samuel Small Mander by Sir Arthur Wm. Woods, Garter, and George Edward Cockayne, Clarenceux.

II.4 Robert MAUNDER, bapt. 3 Sept. 1546; [?] m. 1st 1576 Joan HANCOCK, by whom he had William MAUNDER (b. 1581 and d. 1582); Robert [?] m. 2nd Frances BURNETT.

II.5 Jane, bapt. 23 Apr. 1550; d. [?] Armscote, bur. Tredington 6 Aug. 1611.

Third Generation

Issue of John and Isabella MAUNDER, of Tredington (II.1):

III.1.1 John MAUNDER, b. Blackwell; bapt. Tredington 3 Jun 1579; m. Tredington 24 Nov 1612 Anna HANNS, of Armscote (bur. Tredington 2 Mar 1668/9), by whom he had issue, in addition to 6 daus. and 2 sons (both d. young), 3 sons of whom presently.

Issue of William and Anna MAUNDER, of Tredington (II.2):

III.2.1 **Richard MAUNDER**, b. Blackwell; bapt. Tredington 9 Jan 1575/6; m. Tredington 13 June 1598 **Elizabeth TEALE** (d. Armscote; bur. Tredington 4 Feb. 1631/2); and was bur. 21 Mar 1629 (his Will dated 18 Mar 1628/9 was proved at £384 4*d.*), having by her had issue 2 sons and 2 daus., of whom presently.

III.2.2 Humphrey MAUNDER, bapt. Tredington Dec. 1580; bur. there 11 Mar 1581.

III.2.3 William MAUNDER, bapt. Tredington 20 May 1583.

III.2.4 Edmund MAUNDER, bapt. Tredington 18 Nov 1585; [?] m. 12 Sept 1619 Anna MILLES.

III.2.5 Marianne [?Maria], bapt. Tredington 2 Oct 1579.

III.2.6 Margery, bapt. Tredington 4 Mar 1593; [?] d. 1638.

Issue of Thomas and Joanne MAUNDER (II.3):

III.3.1 William MAUNDER, tallow chandler, of Blackwell; m. Katherine — (bur. Chacombe, Northants, 14 Oct 1644); tithingman and constable 1616-7; will dated May 1639; and bur. Banbury 1 Apr. 1639, having had issue 3 sons and 2 daus.

III.3.2 John MAUNDER, b. Blackwell; bapt. Tredington Jun 1577; m. Brailes 5 Aug. 1605 Joan, dau. of Edward RYLEY (bur. 25 Aug 1656 Chipping Warden, Northants),;and he d. Chipping Warden, Northants, bur 8 Sept. 1656, having had 2 sons and 1 dau.

III.3.3 George MAUNDER, b. Blackwell; bapt. Tredington 23 Nov. 1582; m. Shipston-on-Stour 26 Apr. 1607 Maria WILKINS, and d. 1639-49, having had 1 son and 2 daus.

III.3.4 Edmund MAUNDER, bapt. Tredington 6 Apr. 1585.

III.3.5 Margory, mentioned in will of her grandmother, Margery.

III.3.6 Emma, b. Oct. 1580; from Armscott m. Tredington 4 May 1607 Thos GARRETT.

Fourth Generation

Issue of John and Anna MAUNDER, of Blackwell, Tredington (III.1.1):

IV.1.1 Edward MAUNDER, bapt. Tredington 14 Aug. 1614; ?m. Ombersley, Worcs., ?14 Oct. 1639 ?Mary PATTYE, by whom he had 1 son and 1 dau.

IV.1.2 Bernard MAUNDER, clergyman; b. Blackwell ?1622; matric. Wadham Coll., Oxon, 9 Mar. 1637/8 (BA 1642; MA 1645); vicar of Copredy, Oxon, 1657; rector of Chipping Warden, Northants, 1657 to his death; m. 1st Drayton St Peter, nr Banbury, 13 Jan 1648 Sarah BIRD (bur. 14 Feb. 1649/50 Alston Chapel, Overbury); m. 2nd Mary — (d. 23 Oct. 1669); m. 3rd Newbottle 26 Oct. 1671 Margaret DELATTAY (d. 1698). Bernard d. Chipping Warden, where bur. 1 Jul. 1703, having had issue, 15 children.

IV.1.3 John MAUNDER, bapt. Tredington 25 Dec. 1629; m. there 1 Mar. 1651/2 Sarah (bur. Tredington 18 Feb. 1668/9), dau. of Simeon ROWNY; and d. having had issue, six children.

Issue of Richard and Elizabeth MAUNDER, of Tredington (III.2.1):

IV.2.1 **Henry** [Henricus] **MAUNDER**, settled at Aston Cantlow, Warwicks, where he was appointed constable 1646 and churchwarden 1640 and 1641; he was bapt. at Tredington 7 June 1601; m. at Exall, Alcester, 13 Feb. 1635/6, **Anne** (b. 1613 and was bur. at Aston Cantlow 2 Sept 1662), widow of Thomas (son of Richard) Ingham and dau. of Robert **WHEIGHAM** of Aston Cantlow (b. 1585; son of Thomas Wheigham and Darrita TIBBES). Henry was bur. at Aston Cantlow 18 May 1672 (Will dated 16 May and proved 8 June 1672 at £257 17s. 6d.), having by her had issue 8 sons, of whom presently.

IV.2.2 Samuel MAUNDER, b. Blackwell; bapt. Tredington 9 Oct 1608; m. 1634 Marie, dau. of Thos FIELD (see deed of marriage portion 27 Dec. 1634) of Blackwell; d. Tredington, and was bur. 6 Nov. 1669, having by her had issue 6 children, all b. and bur. Tredington.

IV.2.3 Mary, b. Darlingscott; bapt. Tredington 22 April 1599; m. MARKMAN and by him had 1 son, Edward MARKMAN.

IV.2.4 Anne, bapt. 10 Feb 1604/5; bur. at Darlingscott.

Fifth Generation

Issue of Henry and Anne MAUNDER, of Aston Cantlow (IV.2.1):

V.1 Henry MANDER (the Younger), yeoman; bapt. 13 June 1639; m. 1st Kinwarton, Warwks, 8 Feb. 1665/6 Elizabeth MANDER (bur. Aston Cantlow 3 Oct. 1670); m. 2nd Alcester, Warwcks, Mary (bapt. Honington [?]25 Nov. 1651; was bur. Aston Cantlow 25 Oct. 1681), dau. of Robert GIBBS. Henry d. and was bur. Aston Cantlow 8 Oct 1680 (having by his Will dated 5 Oct. [proved 20 Oct.] 1680 left his house in trust to his brothers Samuel and Robert; inventory value £146 9s.), and having by his 1st wife had issue, 2 sons (d. young) and by his 2nd wife 1 son, of whom presently.

V.2 Richard MANDER, bapt. Aston Cantlow 24 Jun; bur. 9 Sept, 1641.

V.3 Robert MANDER, bapt. 26 Oct 1642 Aston Cantlow; m. Joan MEASEY at Aston Cantlow 16 Jan 1667/8, and d. Aston Cantlow 1697, leaving issue of whom presently.

V.4 Thomas MANDER, bapt. 4 Nov 1644 at Wilmcote (?m. Jane CLARKSON).

V.5 **Samuel MANDER**, of Lapworth Hall, Henley-in-Arden, Warwicks; bapt. Aston Cantlow 6 Jan 1647/8; m. Feb. 1670 **Mary** (bapt. 14 Aug 1637 Rowington and bur. there 14 May 1694), dau. of Thomas and Elizabeth **SHAKESPEARE**; and he was bur. Lapworth 20 Nov 1716, leaving issue, of whom presently.

V.6 Job MANDER, bapt. 9 Feb 1649/50.

V.7 Philip MANDER, bapt. 2 Jun 1652.

V.8 Caleb MANDER, b. 1659.

Sixth Generation

Issue of Henry (the Younger) MAUNDER, of Aston Cantlow (V.1):

VI.1.1 Henry MAUNDER, bapt Tredington 23 Jan. 1667/8 and bur. there 24 Jan. 1667/8.

VI.1.2 Henry MAUNDER, b. Aston Cantlow, bapt. 14 Mar 1668/9; bur. there 16 Dec 1680.

VI.1.3 Thomas MAUNDER, b. [?]1673; m. Aston Cantlow 25 Jul. 1698 Mary, dau. of Thos BIDDLE of Sambourne by Winifred HAINES; and d. 1629-30, having had issue 6 sons and 1 dau. (of whom the 3rd son, Samuel, of Meadow Furlong Farm, had issue: ancestor of Jane Mander, the New Zealand novelist).

Issue of Robert and Joan MANDER, of Aston Cantlow (V.3):

VI.2.1 Henry MANDER, b. Aston Cantlow 1668; bapt. 21 Nov. 1668.

VI.2.2 Thomas MANDER, b. Aston Cantlow 1671; bapt. 31 Oct. 1671; m. 1698 Mary BIDDLE; d. 1729.

VI.2.3 Robert MANDER, b. Aston Cantlow, bapt. 12 Mar. 1675/6; d. 1688; bur. Lapworth 28 Oct. 1688.

VI.2.4 Samuel MANDER, bapt. Lapworth 4 Jan. 1679/80; [?] m. 1st Aston Cantlow 16 Jan. 1706/7 Elizabeth JONES; m. 2nd Kinwarton 9 Jan. 1721 Mary PRICE.
VI.2.5 Anne, b. Lapworth 1683; bapt. there 22 Apr. 1683; bur. there 20 Oct. 1687.

Issue of Samuel and Elizabeth MANDER, of Lapworth Hall (V.5):
VI.3.1 Henry MANDER, bapt. 15 Sept 1671; m. 26 Apr. 1696 in St Nicholas, Warwick, Mary MORTIBOYS (b. 1667), by whom he had issue, 3 children.
VI.3.2 Samuel MANDER, bur. Lapworth 21 Aug 1701.
VI.3.3 Thomas MANDER, bur. Lapworth 16 Sept. 1675.
VI.3.4 John MANDER, bapt. Lapworth 16 Mar 1676/7; [?]m. 7 May 1705 at Aston Cantlow, Rebecca (bapt. 20 July 1682), dau. of Thomas BATES, and was buried at Lapworth 29 Dec 1729, having by her had issue, 3 children.
VI.3.5 William MANDER, bapt. circa 1679.
VI.3.6 **Robert MANDER**, settled at Ireland's Farm, Lapworth, near Henley-in-Arden, Warwicks, after 1698; b. 1681; m. 1st 2 Mar 1708/9 at Lapworth, **Catherine** (bapt. 26 Jan 1683/4 at Tanworth-in-Arden; buried Lapworth 13 July 1724), dau. of John **COTTERELL** (bapt. 14 Jan. 1657, son of William and Katherine), of Bushwood Hall, Lapworth; he was buried at Lapworth 17 July 1749, having by her had issue 6 sons and 4 daus., of whom presently.

Seventh Generation

Issue of Robert and Catherine MANDER of Ireland's, Lapworth (VI.2.6):
VII.1 John MANDER, of Tanworth-in-Arden, Warwks; bapt. Lapworth17 Nov 1713; m. 1st at Sheldon, Warwks, 1 Feb. 1743 Ann WOLLERSTON (bur. 10 Aug. 1764 Tanworth); m. 2nd at Tanworth, Catherine GILES (?b. Solihull); he d. Tanworth, bur. 25 Aug. 1797, having by his first wife had 6 sons and 4 daus., all b. Tanworth, of whom the 4th dau. Mary m. her 1st cousin William MANDER, son of Robert of Finwood.
VII.2 Robert MANDER, of Ireland's Farm, Lapworth, and Finwood Green, Rowington, Warwicks; bapt. Lapworth 28 Jan 1714/15; m. 1st Lapworth Mary (bur. Lapworth, 2 Sept. 1745), dau. of John WEETMAN, of Rowington; ?m. 2nd Stratford-on-Avon 14 Sept. 1749 Christiana BYSSEL; Robert was bur. Lapworth 3 Feb. 1788 (his Will dated 10 Jan 1787 was proved at Worcester 17 May 1788), having by his first wife had 5 sons and 3 daus. (of whom the 2nd son, Thomas, held Ireland's Farm).
VII.3 William MANDER, bapt. Lapworth 29 Jan 1716/7; m. Wooton Wawen 27 May 1756 Mary ROGERS (?d. 1795); he d. ?1787 (his Will dated 9 Mar 1786 was proved at Worcester 12 May 1787), having had 4 sons and 1 dau.
VII.4 Nathaniel MANDER, bapt Lapworth 21 Oct 1718; buried there 5 Apr 1720.
VII.5 **Thomas MANDER**, of 48 John's Lane, Wolverhampton, where settled by circa 1743; maltster and baker; b. Lapworth; bapt. there 2 May 1720; m. 9 Sept 1742 in Bridgnorth, **Elizabeth** (who m. 2nd 23 Feb 1775 Charles Hunter of Scotland [d. 21 Aug 1788, aged 73], and d. 1804, buried at St Peter's, Wolverhampton), dau. and co-heir of Samuel **CLEMSON**, of John's Lane, Wolverhampton, currier; Thomas d. and was buried in family vault in St Peter's Collegiate churchyard 1764 (Will dated 12 Dec 1764 [in Wm Salt Library, Stafford] proved 3 Oct 1774 at Lichfield), having had 4 sons and 1 dau., of whom presently.
VII.6 Henry MANDER, a soldier; bapt. Lapworth 5 Jan 1721/2.
VII.7 Catherine, bapt. Lapworth 8 Apr 1721/2; m. at Stratford-upon-Avon 15 Sept 1735 George BLUN of Shirley Street.
VII.8 Rebecca, bapt. Lapworth 19 Nov 1723; m. at Wootton Wawen, Warwicks, 15 Nov 1745 John READING [?of Henley].
VII.9 Mary [?m. GREEN of Packwood].
VII.10 Elizabeth [?m. KEMP of Clarendon].

Eighth Generation

Issue of Thomas and Elizabeth MANDER, of Wolverhampton (VII.5):

VIII.1 Thomas MANDER, b. 10 Oct. 1750; bapt. St Peter's, Wolverhampton, 9 Nov. 1750; died an infant.

VIII.2 **Benjamin MANDER**, of John Street, Wolverhampton, japanner and baker; b. 10 May 1752; bapt. 29 May Wolverhampton; Town Commissioner 1777; japanner1792, with tin-plate works, known as 'Benjamin Mander & Co.'; chairman, Wolverhampton Union Flour & Bread Co. 1812 (for whom led trial Staffs Assizes, 1814); m. 5 Dec 1776 in Kidderminster, **Elizabeth** Hanbury (b. 22 Apr 1752 and d. 20 May 1828, bur. at St Peter's, Wolverhampton), dau. and co-heir of Samuel **READ** of Kidderminster; and he d. 30 Oct 1819, having by her had issue 5 sons and 6 daus., of whom presently.

VIII.3 John MANDER, of John Street, Wolverhampton, manufacturing chemist and druggist with 'one of the largest elaboratories in the kingdom' in 1828; b. 13 July 1754; partner in 'J. Mander & Co.' 1773 and 'Mander, Weaver & Co.' 1803; a noted local Nonconformist; Town Commissioner 1777; co-founder with B. Mander and others of Wolverhampton Library 1794; promoted Wolverhampton Gas Works 1820; m. 1st 20 Jan 1778, Esther (d. 1802), dau. of John & Elizabeth LEA, of Kidderminster; he m. 2nd 25 Aug 1803 at St John's Chapel, Wolverhampton, Hannah Johnson, widow (d. 1835); and he d. 22 Aug 1827 (Will proved £16,000), having by his first wife had 3 sons and 3 daus., of whom presently.

VIII.4 Thomas MANDER, settled in Birmingham; b. 7 June 1757; m. 1 July 1784, Elizabeth, dau. of Edward URWICK, of Felhampton Court, Wistanstow, Craven Arms, Salop, and died 26 April 1813, leaving issue a dau., Elizabeth.

VIII.5 Sarah, b. 22 Sept 1748; bapt. 21 Oct. 1748, St Peter's, Wolverhampton; died an infant.

Ninth Generation

Issue of Benjamin and Elizabeth MANDER of John's Lane, Wolverhampton (VIII.2):

IX.1.1 Benjamin MANDER, b. 2 May 1779, regd at John's Lane Presbyterian Chapel, Wolverhampton; died 7 Nov 1780.

IX.1.2 **Charles MANDER**, of John Street, Wolverhampton; b. 21 May 1780, regd at John's Lane Chapel; apprenticed to father 1795; travelled Ireland 1800; japanner and varnish manufacturer1803; Reprieve of John Hall and Patrick Morrison 1817; John Street Chapel Chancery suit 1816-39; Mander & Wiley 1835-6; resident Croydon and Brighton 1850; m.1st 17 Dec 1812, at St Botolph's, Boston, **Jemima** (b. 8 Nov 1791 and d. 1 Nov 1834), dau. of Thomas (son of Stephen) **SMALL** (d. 26 July 1803, aged 43) of Boston, Lincs. by Elizabeth (d. 2 May 1803, aged 45), dau. of Joseph Harpham. Charles Mander m. 2nd Mar 17 1840 at Aston, Warwks, his deceased wife's sister, Elizabeth (b. 22 Aug 1797), and d. 22 Dec 1853 (bur. at St Peter's, Wolverhampton), having by his first wife had issue 4 sons and 6 daus., of whom presently.

IX.1.3 Samuel Read MANDER, b. 21 Oct 1783, regd at Grey Pea Walk Independent Chapel 25 Nov; died 14, bur. 16 Apr 1785, at Wolverhampton.

IX.1.4 Benjamin Parton MANDER, b. 9 Jan 1785, regd at Grey Pea Walk Chapel 3 Feb; Town Commissioner; chemist in partnership with his uncle, John Mander, 1818; d.s.p. 24 May 1838; bur. at St Peter's, Wolverhampton.

IX.1.5 Isaac MANDER, b. 10 Feb 1791, regd at Grey Pea Walk Chapel 13 Mar 1791; m. 20 Jul 1817 at St Marylebone, London, Mary Anne MILLART, of Stratford, Essex; and d. at Clapham, Surrey, 28 Sept 1861, leaving issue.

IX.1.6 Rebecca, b. 17 June 1781, regd at Grey Pea Walk, Independent Chapel, Wolverhampton; m. at Wolverhampton 17 June 1802, James PEARSALL of Cheapside, London, silk mercer and member of London Common Council; she d. Nov 1848, leaving with 5 other sons and 5 daughters issue, James PEARSALL, and Ellen.

IX.1.7 Hannah, b. 26 Aug 1782, regd at Grey Pea Walk Chapel 12 Sept 1782; died 19 Feb 1783 (buried at Wolverhampton 21 same month).

IX.1.8 Elizabeth, b. 17 Aug 1787, regd at Grey Pea Walk Chapel; died 3 April 1790 (buried at Wolverhampton).
IX.1.9 Sarah, b. 2 Jul 1789; regd at Grey Pea Walk Chapel 25 July; died unmarried Dec 1870.
IX.1.10 Lucy.
IX.1.11 Jemima.

Issue of John and Esther MANDER, of Wolverhampton (VIII.3):
IX.2.1 John MANDER, Lt Invalid Corps of E. India Co; bapt. 10 Feb 1779; d. unm. Bombay 1821.
IX.2.2 Joseph MANDER, b. 1784; d. 1800.
IX.2.3 Thomas MANDER.
IX.2.4 Amelia, m. 20 Mar 1817, John WILLIAMSON of Boughton, Chester, wine merchant.
IX.2.5 Elizabeth.
IX.2.6 Esther.

Tenth generation

Issue of Charles and Jemima MANDER, of John Street, Wolverhampton (IX.1.2):
X.1 **Charles Benjamin MANDER**, JP Staffs, of The Mount, Tettenhall Wood (where settled 1862), varnish manufacturer; b. 9 July 1819 at Chapel Ash, regd at Dr Williams' Library; a founder partner with his brother Samuel in Mander Bros Feb 1845; Town Commissioner and (later) Councillor; m. 1st 14 April 1850 at Chester Cathedral, **Sophia** (d. 29 Oct 1869, aged 42, and is bur. at St Peter's, Wolverhampton), dau. of John **WEAVER** MRCS of Chester. Charles Benjamin Mander m. 2nd 1874 Harriet SPOONER (d. 27 Aug 1915, aged 80); and d. 18 Aug 1878 (bur. at St Peter's, Wolverhampton), leaving by his first wife issue, of whom presently.
X.2 Samuel Small MANDER, of Glen Bank, Tettenhall; b. 8 Feb 1822, regd at Dr Williams' Library; founder partner in Mander Bros, Feb. 1845; m. 26 Sept 1850 Mary (b. 7 Jun 1831; d. 7 Jul 1900; bur. Wolverhampton Cemetery), dau. of Paul WILKES, of Wolverhampton; and d. 5 Nov 1881 (bur. at Wolverhampton Cemetery), leaving issue, of whom presently.
X.3 Joseph MANDER, of Kalbadarie, Bombay; b. 10 June 1828, regd at Dr Williams' Library; served Crimean War; accountant Great Indian Peninsular Railway; m. Anne Caroline — (who m. 2nd Madras 25 Nov 1864 Robert Whalley), and d.s.p. accident Kurfet station, India, 9 Nov 1863.
X.4 Benjamin MANDER, b. 19 March 1830; d.s.p. 11 Feb 1842; bur. at St Peter's, Wolverhampton.
X.5 Jemima, b. 22 Nov 1813 at George St., Wolverhampton; m. there 23 May 1839, Henry Beecroft JACKSON (1810-1884) of Basford Ho., Whalley Range (formerly Jackson's Moss), Manchester, merchant, by whom she had with 6 other children a dau., Louisa, who m. Aldwin SOAMES (exctr to S. Theodore Mander), of ?Moor Park, Farnham.
X.6 Elizabeth, b. 27 July 1815 at George St., regd at Dr Williams' Library, Red Cross St., London; m. 21 Nov 1835 at Wolverhampton, John Field SMYTH of Boston, Lincs, and d. 1865 having had (?with other) issue:
1. Mander John SMYTH; chief research chemist Mander Brothers; m. Catherine Inman Oram, dau. of Rev. Henry Austin ORAM by Mary Inman, and d. 1911, having had issue:
   a. Dr Reginald Mander SMYTH, manager at Mander Bros Colour Works; b. Wolverhampton 11 Dec. 1867; m. (as her 2nd husband) Arnhem 15 Sept. 1914 Countess Cecilia Johanna van LIMBURG-STIRUM (b. Leeuwarden, Belgium, 26 Apr.1871; d. Arnhem 20 Jul. 1956); and d. Alassio, Genoa, 27 Oct. 1924.
   b. Charles Inman SMYTH, general manager at Mander Bros Colour Works.
2. Frederick William SMYTH; m. Harriet Joule FELLOWES, and had issue.

X.7 Janetta, b. 23 July 1823 at Queen St, Wolverhampton, regd at Dr Williams' Library; m. 4 July 1844 at St Peter's, Wolverhampton, Henry George HARPER (d. 10 Aug 1894), of Wightwick House, manager of Mander Bros (and formerly wine merchant of Ludlow); and she d.s.p. 1899.

X.8 Anna Maria, b. 16 May 1825 at Wolverhampton; and buried there 30 April 1826.
Two stillborn female children, b. 8 Apr 1818 and 1 Jan 1827.

Eleventh generation

Issue of Charles Benjamin and Sophia MANDER, of The Mount, Tettenhall (X.1):

XI.1.1 **Sir Charles Tertius MANDER**, first baronet (UK) of The Mount (cr. 8 July 1911), TD, JP (Wolverhampton and Staffs), DL (Staffs); b. at Wolverhampton 16 July 1852; educ. Rugby and Corpus Christi Coll., Camb (matric. 1870, BA 1876, MA 1880); 4 times Mayor of Wolverhampton1892-6; Hon. Freeman 1897; High Sheriff, Staffs 1903; Maj and Hon Lt-Col Staffs Imp. Yeomanry; 1st chairman and governing director of Mander Bros Ltd 1924; m. 25 May1882 at Halifax, Nova Scotia, **Mary** Le Mesurier (b. there 12 Mar 1859 and d. The Mount 10 [bur. 13] Sept 1951), yr dau. of Henry Nicholas **PAINT**, MP in Dominion Parliament 1882-87 by Christiana St Clair McVean; and he d. 8 (bur 11) Apr 1929, leaving issue 2 sons and 1 dau, of whom presently.

XI.1.2 Neville Hanbury MANDER, JP (Staffs), of The Woodlands, Penn, Staffs; b. at Wolverhampton 30 June 1862; m. 19 June 1890 at Compton Gifford, Devon, Emily Louise (b. 1871 and d. 9 Mar 1957), yst dau of Archibald Edwardes CAMPBELL, ISC, Maj-Gen Bengal Staff Corps; and d. (bur. Penn) 7 Jul 1919 leaving issue:

1. Hilda Winfred, b. 1893; m. 25 Jun 1914 Eugène Napoléon VAUGHAN, DSO, JP, Maj Grenadier Gds Boer War 1899 and WWI (b. 19 Nov 1878 [sponsors Empress Eugénie and The Prince Imperial]; d. 11 Mar 1934) (see Lisburn earldom); and she d. 1972, having had issue:
   a. Edmund Bernard Malet VAUGHAN, of Blackladies, Brewood, Staffs; b. 6 Jun 1920; Maj Grenadier Gds WWII; m. 27 Feb 1950 Jean Elizabeth, dau of Lt-Col G.W. Nelson, MC, of Sevenoaks; by whom he has 2 sons and 1 dau.
   b. Mary Christine, b. 18 May 1916.
2. Irene Hanbury b. 1898; m. 1928 John Cecil NEVE, solicitor, of Wolverhampton (b. 1902; d. 1993); and she d. 1977, leaving:
   a. Margaret Louise, b. 1929; m. 1955 James SUTTON, and has 2 sons: Tristram Sutton (b. 1956) and Mark Sutton (b. 1958).
   b. Elizabeth Anne Campbell, b. 1931; m. 1956 John Wallace DUNCAN, and has 3 daus: Emily (b. 1958), Lucy (b. 1960) and Katharine (b. 1963).
   c. Susan Rosalind, b. 1934; m. 1962 Michael Murray COOMBS, and has 2 sons: Richard Murray Coombs (b. 1963) and Edward Neve Coombs (b. 1966).

XI.1.3 John [Jack] Harold MANDER, OBE (1920), of Thorpe Hurst, Thorpe St Andrew, Norwich; b. at Wolverhampton 3 Aug 1869; ed Rugby and Trin Hall, Camb (MA); served S. African War as capt Dk of Cornwall's L. Inf 1899-1902; brig maj Durham Light Inf 1902-4; Chief Constable of Isle of Ely 1906-15, and of Norfolk 1915-27; m. 27 Sept 1894 at St Mary's, Bryanston Sq., London, Maria Elinor Lloyd (d. 31 Aug 1957), dau of John Philipps Allen Lloyd PHILIPPS, DL, of Dale Castle, Pembroke; and d. 9 Jan 1927 having had:

1. (Eileen) Cecily, OBE 1950; b. 1897; m. 4 Feb 1920 Capt Francis Randolph PHILLIPS MC (b. 1888; d. 24 Jun 1942), yr son of Sir Lionel Phillips, 1st baronet, of Tylney Hall, Hants, partner in Werhner Beit & Co.; and d.s.p. 15 Nov 1962.
2. Rosemary Dorothy Esther; b. 1902; m.1932 Robert L.D. BARNETT

XI.1.4 Amy Matilda, Irish nationalist; b. at Wolverhampton 9 Feb 1851; d. unm. 27 July 1919 (bur. with her brother Neville at Penn, Staffs).

XI.1.5 Janetta [Fan], landscape artist in oils and watercolours; born at Wolverhampton 27 Jan 1854; m. 23 Jun 1885 at St Peter's, Wolverhampton, Henry Sparke STABB, Col

Duke of Cornwall's L.I. 32 Regt (d. Pietermaritzburg, R.S.A., 22 Oct 1888), son of Nicholas Spark Stabb (b. 1835) of St John's, Newfoundland by Anna Rebecca Smith (and brother of Sir Newton John Stabb, K.B., OBE, of Farnham Hall, Saxmundham, Norfolk, who co-founded Hong Kong and Shanghai Bank); she settled South Africa and d. Liphook, Hants, Sept 1913, having had issue:

1. Margaret, m. Rev. Canon William MILLS, of Devon, and by him had:
   a. Hugh MILLS, k.a. Burma, WWII.
   b. Peter Cecil Mander MILLS, headmaster of Highfield School, Liphook, Hants; liveryman Fishmongers' Company; m. and d. 198-, leaving:
      i. William MILLS.
      ii. Mary, b. 1969.
      iii. Jane, twin, b. 1969.
      iv. Henrietta, b. 1971.
   c. Rosemary, d. unm. 1983, having founded Social Sciences' Faculties in three Universities.
2. Barbara, m. and had one son, Alan (b. 1917).

XI.1.6 Sophia Emmeline, b. at Wolverhampton 6 Sept 1855; m. 23 Jan 1894 at St Peter's, Wolverhampton, Rev Canon Henry Paine STOKES, BA, MA, LL.M., LL.D., Litt. D., FSA, rector of Little Wilbraham, Cambs., Hon Fellow Corpus Christi Coll., Cambs., antiquarian (b. Margate 17 May 1849; d. 6 Jun 1931); and she d. Cambridge 2 Jul 1937, having had issue:

1. Louis Mander STOKES; b. 19 July 1897; educ. Rugby; k.a. Somme with Royal Marine L.I., 13 Nov 1916 (his diaries published 1995).
2. Margaret Sophie, illustrator; m. Anstruther CARDEW, musician, of Paris (?son of Sir Alexander CARDEW, of Madras and Paris); and d.s.p. 1960.
3. Amy Kinton, of S. Harting, Hants; d. unm. 18 Jan 1981, aged 84.
4. Mary Marrat, d. unm.

XI.1.7 (Annie) Julia, born at Wolverhampton 25 Jan 1857; m. 17 July 1879 at St Peter's, Wolverhampton, Robert Edward TURNBULL, of Four Gables, Bampton, S. Yorks, land agent to Lord Carlisle; and d. at Whitby 7 Jul 1902 having had issue:

1. Margaret, m. Rev. S. FOX.
2. Doris.
3. Olive.
4. (Catherine) Beryl; b. 1894; m. Rev. John Brooke KIRKHAM and had issue:
   a. Robert Mander KIRKHAM, lecturer at Bristol University; m. Margaret PAYNE, and d. 1997.
5. Agnes, m. GRIST.

XI.1.8 (Laura) Louisa, born at Wolverhampton 31 Jan 1860; m. 9 Jun 1881, George Reginald LEEPER of Dublin, M.D. (d. 26 Jun 1904) (son of Rev. Canon Alexander LEEPER, DD, of St Patrick's, Dublin, by Catherine Porter); and had issue:

1. Neville [Neil] Dermot LEEPER; b. at The Mount 30 Mar 1882; educ. Portora Royal Sch., Enniskillen; res. Hawaii, USA and Canada; m. twice and d. 3 Apr 1947 Vancouver, B.C., having had issue:
   a. Marjorie Louisa (by 1st wife); m. and had issue, two sons.
   b. Helen H. (by 2nd wife), b. Seattle, USA, 28 Jan 1931; m. ROGERS.
2. Charles LEEPER, an artist; res. in Kent; m. and had issue:
   a. Bridget, m. Aug. 1949 Lance K. JAPHET of Sandhurst, Johannesburg, S. Africa, and by him has issue:
      i. Miles JAPHET, m. Jetje – and has 2 daus, Antoinette and Caitlin.
      ii. Garth JAPHET, m. Jayne – and has dau. Rebecca, b. 2001.
      iv. Deidre Janet; m. 1st 1973 (m. diss. 1980) Hon. (Ian) Colin ORR-EWING (b. 1942), yr son of Ian, first and last Baron Orr-Ewing (and a baronet), by whom she has a son and dau; she m. 2nd Robin –-.
      v. Xanthe, m. Kelvin WILLIAMS of USA, ed. Oxford (Rhodes Scholar).
3. Nora, m. and had issue, four children; res. Liphook, Sussex.

4. Dorothy, m. Paul ROUSELL.

Issue of Samuel Small and Mary MANDER, of Glen Bank (X.2):

XI.2.1 (Samuel) Theodore MANDER, JP (Staffs); builder of Wightwick Manor (purchased 1887); b. 25 Feb 1853; educ. London Univ. (BA 1876) and Clare Coll., Cambridge (BA); partner in Mander Bros; Mayor of Wolverhampton 1900; m. 29 May 1879 Flora St Clair (b. Halifax, N.S., 30 Dec 1857 and d. 15 Apr 1905), eldr dau of Henry Nicholas PAINT, of Halifax, Nova Scotia, a member of Dominion Parliament; d. Wighwick 14 Sept 1900, having by her had issue, of whom presently.

XI.2.2 Benjamin Howard MANDER, of Trysull Manor, Staffs; b. 1861; partner in Mander Bros; m. 1892, Lilian, dau. of G.H. NELSON of Warwick; and d. 1912, having by her had issue, of whom presently.

XI.2.3 Martin Bertram MANDER, sheep farmer settled at Horoeka, near Gisborne, New Zealand c. 1890; b. 1869; m. Matawhero, NZ, 10 Mar 1897 Stella (b. Manchester 1876), dau. of Hervey Dean DODS of Manchester, and d. 1946, having had:

1. Mary Dorothy, b. Gisborne 1899.
2. (Phyllis) Marjorie, b. Gisborne 1901; m. John Lloyd GRAHAM, by whom she had 2 sons and 2 daus.
3. Margaret Hope, b. Gisborne 1905.

XI.2.4 Mary Jane, b. 1853; m. Robert William FELKIN, MD, of Merridale Grove, Wolverhampton, and had issue.

XI.2.5 Jemima [Mima], b. 1857; d. unm.

XI.2.6 Ellen Beatrice [Nellie], b. 1858; m. Howard PEARSALL.

XI.2.7 Charlotte, b. 1860, m. PARKER.

Twelfth generation

Issue of Sir Charles Tertius and Mary MANDER, of The Mount, Tettenhall Wood (XI.1.1):

XII.1.1 **Sir Charles Arthur MANDER**, second baronet, TD, JP (Staffs), DL (Staffs); of Kilsall Hall, Shifnal, Salop; b. at The Laurels, Newbridge, Wolverhampton, 25 June 1884; ed Eton and Trinity Coll., Camb (BA); High Sheriff, Staffs 1926; Mayor of Wolverhampton 1932 and 1936; Hon. Freeman 1945; Major Staffs Yeo., served WWI Egypt and Palestine; Vice-Chmn National Savings Committee; President Rotary International for Britain and Ireland; managing director of Mander Bros Ltd; m. 29 Apr 1913, **Monica** Claire Cotterill (b. 12 Apr 1888 at Upper Norwood, Middlesex, and d. 28 Feb 1964), yst dau of George Harding **NEAME** of Kent (see Burke's *LG*, 1952 ed.); and he d. 25 Jan 1951, having had issue, of whom presently.

XII.1.2 Gerald Poynton MANDER, of The Dippons, Tettenhall Wood, Staffs; FSA; Midland historian and antiquarian; b. at Newbridge 13 Nov 1886; ed Eton and Trinity Coll, Camb (BA 1907, MA 1930); director Mander Bros Ltd; m. 5 June 1913 Nancy Steward (d. 20 Nov 1960), 2nd dau of Lt-Col Robert Halfield HARGREAVES, JP, DL, of Knightley Grange, Staffs., and of Barnside Manor, Lancs. (see Burke's *LG*) by Rose Harriet Steward, 3rd dau. of the Rev. Charles Holden Steward, JP, of Northway House, Gloucester; and he d. 10 Dec 1951, having had issue, of whom presently.

XII.1.3 Daisy St Clair, JP Staffs (1935), of Small Place, Pattingham; b. at Newbridge 27 Dec 1887; d. unm. 24 Jun 1968 (bur. vault at St Peter's, Wolverhampton).

Issue of Samuel Theodore and Flora MANDER, of Wightwick Manor (XI.2.1):

XII.2.1 Sir Geoffrey le Mesurier MANDER, Kt Bach (1945); JP Staffs (1906); of Wightwick Manor (which he donated to National Trust 1937); b. 6 March 1882; educ. Harrow and Trinity Coll., Cambridge (MA); served RFC and RFA WWI; barrister Inner Temple 1921; High Sheriff of Staffs 1921; MP East Div. Wolverhampton 1929-45; PPS Sec of State for Air (Sir A. Sinclair); CC Staffs; chairman of Mander Bros; m. 1st Montreal 10 Oct 1906 (m. diss. 1930) Rosalind Florence (b. 1886 and d. 1956), dau. of Col. Frank CAVERHILL, of Montreal, Canada; m. 2nd 18 Nov 1930 (Mary) Rosalie

Glynn (b. 30 Apr 1905 and d. 2 Apr 1988), MA Oxon; authoress and lecturer; only dau. of Archibald Campbell Glynn GRYLLS, MA, of Maidenhead. Sir Geoffrey d. 9 Sept 1962 (bur Pattingham), having had issue by his first and second wives, of whom presently.

XII.2.2 Lionel Henry MANDER, film actor, playwright and novelist as 'Miles Mander'; b. 14 May 1888; educ. Harrow, Loretto and McGill University; m. 1st (m. diss. without issue) Princess Sudhira Sundari Devi, dau. of H.H. Sri Sri Maharaja Sir Nripendra Narayan Bhup BAHADUR, Maharaja of COOCH BEHAR (b. Royal Palace, Cooch-Behar, 4 Oct 1862; d. Sussex, 18 Sept 1911) by H.H. Maharani Siniti Devi Sahiba, sometime Regent of Cooch-Behar and Presdt. State Council (b. Sen's House, Calcutta, 1864; d. Ranchi, November 1932), eldest dau. of Babu Keshab Chandra Sen. Lionel Henry m. 2nd (m. div.) Kathren Bernadette, dau. of W.G. FRENCH of Sydney, NSW, Australia; and d. 7 Feb 1946, having by his second wife had issue, of whom presently.

XII.2.3 Alan Jocelyn MANDER, b. 28 Jan 1891; educ. Trin College, Glenalmond; m. Princess Pretiva Devi (d. 7 Jan 1968), sister of above and dau. of H.H. Sri Sri Maharajah Sir Nripendra Narayan Bhup BAHADUR, Maharaja of COOCH BEHAR; and d. 21 Dec 1967, having by her had issue, of whom presently.

XII.2.4 Marjorie Mima, m. 6 Jan 1910 Gervas Clifton NEVILE (b. 2 Mar 1883; d. 20 Jun 1943) of Skellingthorpe Manor, Lincs (see Nevile of Thorney, Notts, Burke's *LG*); res. in New Zealand and at Liphook, Hants; and d. 4 Aug 1968 having had:

1. Peter NEVILE, of London and Midhurst, Sussex; b. Auckland, NZ, 5 Mar 1912; MBA.

XII.2.5 Gladys, d. an infant.

Issue of Benjamin Howard and Lilian MANDER, of Trysull Manor (XI.2.2):

XII.3.1 (Howard) Vivian MANDER, MC, of Congreve Manor, Penkridge, Staffs; b. 1894; educ. Wellington and Oxford; Lt-Col WWI; dir Mander Bros Ltd; m.1st (m. diss.) Molly – and by her had issue one son and two daus, of whom presently. He m. 2nd Clarence Margaret (Peggy), dau. of John Douglas GRAHAM, proprietor *Express & Star* newspaper (she m. 2nd Cowan SHANKLAND of Esher, Middlesex); and he d. Wolverhampton Easter 1950, having by her had further issue.

XII.3.2 Lilian Brenda, m. 16 Jan 1919 (m. diss. 1940) Major Sir Alfred Edward Howard HICKMAN, 2nd Baronet of Wightwick, Tettenhall (b. 8 May 1885; d. 11 Mar 1947) (who m. 2nd 5 Apr 1940 Nancy Beryl Morse-Evans); and d. 16 Aug 1969, having had:

1. Sir Howard Whitby HICKMAN, 3rd Baronet, AIBE, b. 29 Jan; m. 1948 Margaret (d. 1996), dau. of Leonard KEMPSON, of Potters Bar, Middx (and formerly wife of Sir Denis Thatcher Bt [who 1951 m. 2nd Margaret Hilda, née Roberts, Prime Minister UK 1979-1990]), and he d. 1979, having by her had issue:
   a. Sir (Richard) Glen HICKMAN, 4th Baronet, of Manor Farm, Liddington, Wilts; b. 12 Apr 1949; educ Eton; m. 1981, Heather Mary Elizabeth, dau. of Dr James MOFFET, of Westlecot Manor, Swindon, Wilts, and has issue:
      i. Charles Patrick Alfred HICKMAN, b. 5 May 1983.
      ii. Edward William George HICKMAN, b. 1990.
      iii. Elizabeth Margaret Ruth, b. 1985.
2. Patrick Nelson HICKMAN, of Hale Park, Fordingbridge, Hants; F/Lt RAFVR WWII; liveryman Fishmongers' Co; b. 13 Mar 1921; m. 1st 13 Apr 1944 (div. 1950) Marylena, yr dau of Capt James Allen Dyson PERRINS, MC and bar, JP, Welsh Gds, of Worcs, by whom he has 1 son living; m. 2nd 28 Dec 1953 Margaret Gail, dau. of Col. Cassell Ryan ST AUBYN, 60th Rifles, of Paris, by whom he has issue 1 son and 1 dau. living.

Thirteenth generation

Issue of Sir Charles Arthur and Monica MANDER, of Kilsall Hall (XII.1.1):

XIII.1.1 **Sir Charles Marcus MANDER**, third baronet, of Little Barrow, Moreton-in-Marsh, Glos; b. at Kilsall 22 Sept 1922; ed. Eton and Trinity Coll., Camb.; capt Coldstream Guards, served WWII (N. Africa, Italy and Germany); High Sheriff, Staffs, 1963; dir Mander Bros Ltd 1948-58; chmn Arlington Securities Ltd and London and Cambridge Investments Ltd; liveryman Fishmongers' Company; m. 24 Nov 1945 at St James's, Spanish Place, London, Maria **Dolores** Beatrice Evelyn (b. 8 Feb 1919), yr dau. of Alfred Edmund **BRÖDERMANN**, banker, of Gross Fontenay, Hamburg (b. Hamburg 12 Jun 1874 and d. there 3 May 1923) (see *Hamburger Geshlechterbuck*, Band 36, 1929), by his wife (Jeanne) Marie Thérèse (b. in Paris 17 May 1886; d. Molesey 9 Jan 1968), widow of Francis Edmund Lane Fox, of Bramham, Yorks (b. 28 Nov 1872; d. Ryde 29 Feb 1908) and dau. of Count Henri Nicolaieff [?], diplomat (b. circa 1856), by Mariquita Consuelo Haffenden (b. Huelva 1860; d. Southampton 18 Dec 1894), dau. of Charles Dalley Haffenden (b. Bloomsbury 3 Nov 1821; will pr. London, 10 Dec. 1910); and has issue living, of whom presently.

XIII.1.2 (Anne) Marietta Patience, JP (Glos), b. 16 Oct 1914; fellow of King's Coll., London; m. Tong Jan 7 1939 Hugh Patrick STIRLING of Farmington Old Rectory, Glos. (b. 25 Mar 1913 and d. Oxon 1 Jan 1991), ed. Eton and Oxon (MA), barrister, twice mayor of Westminster, son of Kenneth Stirling of 9 Boulevard Lannes, Paris; and she died Banbury, Oxon, 29 October 2002, having had issue by adoption:

1. (Nicholas) Charles STIRLING, of Corbridge, Northumberland; b. 3 Oct 1947; educ. Eton; 16th/5th Queen's Royal Lancers; FCA; AIIT: MFH; m. Apr 1975 at Farmington, Glos. (Elizabeth) Emma, dau. of Brig. V.W. BARLOW, DSO, OBE, and has issue:
   a. William Nelson STIRLING, b. 20 Feb 1979; educ Eton and Edinburgh U.
   b. Frances Constance, b. 20 June 1980.
   c. Patience Joan, b. 28 March 1983.
   d. Alexandra Emma, b. 30 Jun 1988.
2. Charlotte Amelia, b. 27 Jan 1950; ed. Cranbourne Chase and Bristol (BA); soltr; m. 1973 at Farmington, Glos, Paul Francis SANDILANDS, of Falcut Ho., Northants, barrister, yr son of Sir Francis Sandilands CBE, and has:
   a. Frederick James SANDILANDS, b. 1982.
   b. Marietta Minette, b. 1980.

XIII.1.3 (Carinthia) Jill, JP (IOW 1958); b. 16 Jan 1920; served WWII in WRNS; m. 1st 2 Dec 1944, James RAMSDEN (d. 22 Oct 1956) of Kings Manor, Freshwater, IOW, yst son of Henry Ramsden of Edinburgh; she m. 2nd 22 Feb 1964 as his 2nd wife Lt-Cdr James de Votier Grosvenor WALLIS, RN, res. in Guernsey, son of William Frederick Wallis, of Norwich; and by her 1st husband has issue:

1. (James) Tobit RAMSDEN, of Edmonton, Canada, accountant; b. 6 Oct 1948; educ. Radley and Sheffield (BA); FCA; m. 1st 1973 (m. diss 1983) Linda, dau. of Walter CRITCHLOW of P.Q., Canada (who m. 2nd), and by her has issue living:
   a. Sarah Jill, b. 1977.
   Tobit RAMSDEN m. 2nd Sussex 1985 Ann, dau. of M. MILLER WILLIAMS, and by her has further issue living:
   b. Edward Henry James RAMSDEN, b. 17 Oct 1988.
   c. Sîan Amelia, b. 24 May 1986.
   d. Daisy Katherine, b. 9 May 1990.
2. (Charles) Riordan RAMSDEN, of Southampton; b. 20 Dec 1949; m. 1974 Elizabeth Mary, only dau. of Stewart KILPATRICK, of Bury, Sussex, stockbroker.

Issue of Gerald and Nancy MANDER, of The Dippons, Tettenhall Wood (XII.1.2):

XIII.2.1 Philip FitzGerald MANDER, JP (Staffs), of Albrighton, Salop; b. 29 Sept 1915; ed Eton and Trinity Coll., Camb (BA); served WWII RAOC; chairman of Manders Holdings Ltd; m. 20 July 1942 Priscilla Patricia, eld. dau. of Lt-Col E. de Warrenne WALLER MC (see Burkes's *L.G.*); and d. 2 June 1972, having by her had issue 1 son and 1 dau., of whom presently.

XIII.2.3 (Catherine) Daphne, b. 12 Mar 1914; ATS, FANY WWII.

XIII.2.4 Hilary Nancy, b. 14 Apr 1924; RN VAD 1942-6; SEN; m. 1st 15 Oct 1946 (div. 1981) William Reginald PURSLOW, son of Charles Purslow, of Cheshire, director Manders Holdings Ltd (who m. 2nd and d. 1991); m. 2nd 1985 Anthony Michél JARREY, regimntl bandmstr, res. in Gers, France, and has had issue by her 1st husband:

1. Ian Gerald Steward PURSLOW, of Château St Maur, Mirande, France; b. 28 Jan 1949; 2nd Lt 16th/5th Queen's Roy Lancers; m. 1st 1971 (div. 1982) Sally Anne, only dau. of Gordon MATTHEWS of Milton House, Shipton-u-Wychwood, Oxon (who m. 2nd); he m. 2nd 1988 Susan Kathryn, dau of Capt Colin McKeand LITTLE, RN, of Queen Camel, Somerset, and by her has:
   a. Margaux Rose, b. at Auch, France, 2 Jan 1991.
   b. Flora Louise, b. 7 Sept 1994.
2. Hugh Charles PURSLOW, b. 28 Oct. 1950; educ Cheltenham and Keele Univ; d. unm. 1975.
3. Valerie Christine, b. 29 Aug 1947; d. unm. 23 Apr 1966.

Issue of Sir Geoffrey MANDER of Wightwick Manor, by his 1st wife Rosalind Florence, née CAVERHILL (XII.2.1):

XIII.3.1 Mervyn Caverhill MANDER, settled in Jersey; b. 14 Jan 1910; ed. Harrow, Chillon Coll., Trinity Coll., Camb. and Pennsylvania U.; dir. of Mander Bros; m. 1st 29 Oct 1935 Elisabeth Maria Dorothea, dau of Judge METTLICH of Cologne; he m. 2nd 27 Nov 1952 Janet Prangley, elder dau of Leslie PHILP of St John Road, Clifton, Bristol; and d. 28 Mar 1978, leaving by his first wife a son, of whom presently.

XIII.3.2 Mavis Flora Rosalind, b. 19 May 1909; m. 1st 1931 (div.) (Fitzroy) Roger PARTRIDGE, by whom she had:

1. Carl PARTRIDGE.
2. Anthony PARTRIDGE.

Mavis m. 2nd Fitzroy PHILLIPS, and d. 23 Jan 1953, leaving by her 2nd husband:

1. Carlotta, b. 10 Oct 1940; m. — JAYAPAL.
2. Caroline, b. 17 Aug 1941; m. John LITTLE.
3. Venetia, b. 6 Aug 1942.

XIII.3.3 Elizabeth Bréhaut, b. 19 July 1916, and has issue one dau., Tess.

Issue of Sir Geoffrey MANDER of Wightwick, by his 2nd wife Rosalie, née GRYLLS:

XIII.3.4 John Geoffrey Grylls MANDER, of Duncan Terr., Islington, London, author, poet and potter; b. 28 May 1932; educ. Eton and Trinity Coll., Cambridge (MA); m. 1st 1956 (div.) Gertrude [Necke] BRACHER of Germany; m. 2nd 1969 Penelope Loveday, est dau of Lt-Cdr James Dennis WILLIAMS RN; and he d.s.p. 2 Sept 1978.

XIII.3.5 Anthea Loveday Veronica, b. 16 Jan 1945; m. 1st 12 Aug 1965 (div.) John Henry LAHR, of New York, USA, biographer and playwright, son of Bert Lahr, American actor; she m. 2nd 2003 Barry Coles; and by her 1st husband has:

1. Christopher David LAHR, b. Jan 1976.

Issue of Lionel (Miles) Henry and Kathren MANDER (XII.2.2):

XIII.4.1 (Fabian Lionel) Theodore MANDER, CBE, of New York, USA; b. 31 May 1926; educ Sherborne, Milton Academy, Pace Coll and Columbia Univ., USA; US Merchant Marine 1942-45; with Standard Oil of New Jersey 1945-9; with Penn Mutual Life Insurance 1959-1962; Pres Balanced Pension and Profit Sharing Plans Inc. 1962-90; m. 1st May 1946 (div. 1952) Diantha F., dau. of Connor LAWRENCE of NY, by whom he had issue; he m. 2nd (div.) 1953 Elizabeth Stuart, dau. of Richmond BROWN of Greenwich, Conn., and by her had further issue; he m. 3rd Lois DOHERTY (b. 28 Mar. 1947); and he d. NY 24 June 1990.

Issue of Alan Jocelyn and Princess Pretiva Sudhira Sundari Devi MANDER (XII.2.3):

XIII.5.1 (Arjun) Derek MANDER, m. three times [?] and has issue 3 sons and 1 dau, of whom presently.

XIII.5.2 Gita, d.s.p. 196-.

XIII.5.3 Monisha, who m. and d. leaving issue, 3 daus.

Issue of (Howard) Vivian MANDER, of Congreve Manor, by his 1st wife, Molly (XII.3.1):

XIII.6.1 Howard Anthony MANDER, b. 1920; m. and was k.a. 1944, leaving two daus.

XIII.6.2 Aline, m. Gerry de BOINVILLE and had issue 2 children.

XIII.6.3 Pauline Vivien, m. 5 Nov 1953 James Edward Alexander Rundell GUINNESS, CBE (see Guinness Bt) (b. 23 Sept 1924), of Coldpiece Farm, Hound Green, Hants; son of Sir Arthur Guinness KCMG; dep chmn of Guinness Peat Grp 1977-84 and Guinness Mahon Hldgs 1968-72; and has issue:

1. Hugo Arthur Rundell GUINNESS, b. 12 Sept 1959.
2. Miranda Vivien, b. 9 Jan 1955; m. Keith PAYNE, set designer.
3. Sabrina Jane, b. 9 Jan 1955 (twin to Miranda Vivien).
4. Anita Patience, b. 7 Dec 1957; m. 1st 1981 Hon Amschel Mayer James ROTHSCHILD (b. 1955; d. 8 Jul 1996 by his own hand), of Rushbrook, Bury St Edmunds, Suffolk, yr son of Victor, 3rd Baron Rothschild; she m. 2nd 25 Jan. 2002 James A. WIGAN; and has issue by her 1st husband.
5. Julia Aline, b. 12 Sep 1959, m. 1980 Hon Michael SAMUEL (b. 1952), yr son of 4th Viscount BEARSTEAD, and has issue.

Issue of (Howard) Vivian MANDER by his 2nd wife Margaret, née Graham:

XIII.6.4 Martin Ian MANDER, b. 2 Feb 1929; educ. Winchester; RAC; 10th Royal Hussars; manager of Mander Bros; m. 1st 15 Jan 1952 (m. div.) Mary-Jane, dau. of Capt. Thomas FULLER, of Nawton, Yorks (who m. 2nd CADMAN), by whom he has one son and one dau., of whom presently; Martin MANDER m. 2nd 18 Oct 1969 Jean Margaret, dau. of J. HOWARTH, of Almondbury, Yorks.

XIII.6.6 Michael Graham MANDER, b. 1 Oct 1931; educ. Winchester; 2 Lt 10th Royal Hussars; capt. Shropshire Yeomanry; dir. Singer & Friedlander.

Fourteenth generation

Issue of Sir Charles Marcus and Maria Dolores MANDER, of Little Barrow (XIII.1.1):

XIV.1.1 **Charles Nicholas MANDER**, of Owlpen Manor, Glos; Knight of Grace and Devotion of SMO of Malta; liveryman Fishmongers' Company; b. Wolverhampton, 23 Mar 1950; ed Downside, Grenoble Univ. and Trin Coll., Camb. (MA); m. 24 Jun 1972 at Burford, Oxon, **Karin** Margareta (b. Stockholm 19 Jan 1946), yr dau of Gustav Arne **NORIN** (b. 21 Sept 1915; d. 20 Mar 1985; bur. Bromma), of Stockholm, Sweden, by Marianne Greta (b. 14 Aug 1916; d. 15 June 1998), yr dau of Olov Janson, of Stockholm; and has issue living, of whom presently.

XIV.1.2 Francis Peter MANDER, of Heath Barn, Donnington, Glos; b. 4 Dec 1952; ed Downside and RAC, Cirencester; m. 14 Jul 1990, at Rendcomb, Glos, Georgina Jane, elder dau. of Edward THRING, Cdr RN (see Thring extinct barony), of Alford House, Castle Cary, Somerset; and has issue living, of whom presently.

XIV.1.2 Penelope Anne Mary; b. London 22 Sept 1946; m. 1st 4 May 1965 (div.) Michael Rollo HOARE (see Hoare Bt and Burke's *LG*) of The Dower House, Dogmersfield, Hants; educ. Eton and New Coll., Oxford; a partner in C. Hoare & Co., bankers (b. 8 Mar 1944; he m 2nd [div.] Caroline Abele and m. 3rd Olivia Cox, and d. 25 Nov. 2001, having by his 2nd wife had further issue living); and by him she has issue:

1. Venetia Elizabeth, b. Melbourne, Australia, 3 Sept 1965; ed Wycombe Abbey and Trin Coll., Camb (BA); a ptnr in C. Hoare & Co.; m. 27 April 1996 (as his 2nd wife) Hamish Peter LENG, of 13 Kassala Road, London SW11, eldest son of Gen. Sir Peter LENG, KCB, MBE, MC, by his wife Virginia Rosemary, née Pearson, and has issue living:
   a. Harry Archie Peter LENG, b. 13 Sep 1997.
   b. Rosanna Elizabeth, b. 31 Jan 1999.
2. Fiona Mary, b. 15 Aug 1969; educ. St Mary's, Leweston; m. 14 June 1997 Charles Robert CROLE, with Schroders (son of Gerard CROLE, of Auchlunkart Ho., Banffs.), and has issue living:
   a. Oliver Lachlan Gerard CROLE, b. 21 July 1999.

b. Archie Harry Michael CROLE, b. 20 Nov 2003.

Penelope Hoare m. 2nd 1979 (as his 2nd wife) Capt. Simon John LODER (2nd son of Hubert Sydney Loder by Brenda McNeill; see Loder Bt) (b. 4 Apr. 1932; d. London 7 Sept. 2002; bur. Slaugham, Sussex), of Clapton Court, Somerset; capt. Grenadier Guards; stockbroker; and by him has:

1. James Robert LODER b. 22 July 1981; ed. Wellington Coll. and Newcastle Univ.

Issue of Philip Fitgerald MANDER by Priscilla, née WALLER (XIII.2.1):

XIV.2.1 (Patrick) Oliver MANDER, b. 24 Mar 1951; educ. Eton; m. 1978 Gabrielle Patricia, publisher (res. Bedchester, Dorset), only dau. of Geoffrey Terence WEAVER, of Hayling Island, Hants; he was k. motor accident 1982, having by her had issue.

XIV.2.2 Philippa Hazel Jeanetta, b. 18 Feb. 1944; educ. Cheltenham Ladies' Coll., Exeter Univ. (BA), and Queen's Theological Coll.; deacon 1988; ordained priest 1994; m. 16 Oct 1965 John Patrick THORNEYCROFT, of Kemberton Hall, Shifnal, Salop (b. 1939); solicitor; er son of Gerald Thorneycoft of Park House, Codsall Wood, Staffs, and has issue living:

1. Hugh Martin Sumner THORNEYCROFT, b. 26 Jun 1967; educ. Wellington, and Durham Univ; m. 3 Jun 1995, Caroline Alison, dau. of George RIDDINGTON, of Crowland, Lincs., and has issue living, Harry George Sumner, b. 1998; Olivia Sophie, b. 13 Dec 1996; Isabel Lucy, b. 2001.
2. Martin Philip THORNEYCROFT, b. 1977; ed. Winchester and St Edmund Hall, Oxford.
3. Veryan Ruth, b. 29 Jan 1971; ed. Cheltenham Ladies' Coll. and Exeter (BA) and Reading Univs. (MA); m. 3 May 1997 Paul David EVANS, son of John Evans of Caversham, Reading.
4. Naomi Priscilla, b. 1975; ed. Oakham Sch, and Brookes U., Oxford.

Issue of Mervyn and Eliza Maria MANDER, of Jersey (XIII.3.1):

XIV.3.1 (Mervyn) Nicholas MANDER, b. 22 Jan 1943; ed. Shrewsbury and Trin Coll., Cambridge (MA); m. 14 Mar 1986 in Hammersmith, Maria Prudencia GARCIA Sánchez, yst dau of Ulpiano García of Salamanca (d. Madrid 3 Nov 1958, bur. Ajalvir) and Emiliana Sánchez, by whom he has issue.

Issue of (Arjun) Derek MANDER (XIII.4.1):

XIV.4.1 Nigel Peter MANDER, b. 1952.

XIV.4.2 Alan MANDER.

XIV.4.3 Paul MANDER.

XIV.4.2 Marcus Nairendra MANDER, b. 1966; m. and has issue.

Issue of Theodore MANDER of New York by his 1st wife Diantha née LAWRENCE (XIII.4.1):

XIV.5.1 Richard C. MANDER, b. 26 Nov 1950; m. and resident in USA.

XIV.5.2 Melanie Reid, b. 8 June 1949; resident in USA.

Issue of Theodore MANDER by his 2nd wife Elizabeth née BROWN:

XIV.5.3 Fabienne H.B., b. 6 Aug 1956; m. and resident in USA.

Issue of Martin and Mary Jane MANDER (XIII.5.4):

XIV.6.1 Simon Vivian MANDER, of Liverpool, accountant; b. 1954; m. and has issue.

XIV.6.2 Taynith, m. CAMERON, and d. Brewood riding accident 1993.

Fifteenth generation

Issue of Charles Nicholas and Karin MANDER, of Owlpen Manor, Glos (XIV.1.1):

XV.1.1 **Charles Marcus Septimus Gustav MANDER**, b. Swindon 26 July 1975; ed. Eton and Peterhouse, Camb. (MA); solicitor advocate; m. at Owlpen 21 Feb. 2004 Claire (b. 16 Sept 1973), solicitor, dau. of Alan Robertson WYLIE (b. Beaconsfield 23 May 1939) by Marta Cecilia (b. Montevideo 23 Apr 1942), dau. of – GOLNIC of Montevideo, Uruguay.

XV.1.2 Benedict Edward Arthur MANDER, b. 6 Feb 1977; ed. Eton and St John's, Cambridge (BA); journalist.
XV.1.3 Hugo Richard Theodore MANDER, b. 3 Apr 1981; ed. Eton, and Edinburgh and Salamanca Universities.
XIV.1.4 Fabian Edmund Quintin MANDER, b. 3 May 1987; ed. Eton.
XIV.1.5 Sarra Maryam, b. Oxford 10 Mar 1973; ed. St Mary's, Ascot, and Edinburgh University (MA); director of Rainier PR; m. at Owlpen 13 July 2002 Stephen, son of Raymond EARL.

Issue of Francis and Georgina MANDER, of Heath Barn, Donnington, Glos (XIV.1.2):
XV.2.1 Luke Edward Charles MANDER, b. 27 April 1994.
XV.2.2 Frederick George MANDER, b. 12 May 1996.

Issue of Patrick Oliver and Gabrielle MANDER (XIV.2.1):
XV.3.1 Hannah Rachel, b. 1982; ed. Bryanston.

Issue of Mervyn Nicholas and Maria Prudencia MANDER (XIV.3.1):
XV.4.1 Sophia Vivien, b. 12 June 1990.

Issue of Richard C. MANDER (XIV.4.1):
XV.5.1 Theodore MANDER.

Issue of Simon Vivian MANDER (XIV.6.1):
XV.6.1 A son.

Compiled from: 'original sources of genealogical evidence' by C.H. Athill, FSA, Richmond Herald, College of Arms, London (from Robert Mander of Lapworth to 6 April 1904) for C.T. Mander; published sources in various editions of Burke's *Peerage, Baronetage, etc.* and *Landed Gentry*, Debrett's *Peerage* and *Distinguished People of Today* and other genealogical reference books; *The History of Mander Brothers* (1955); The Mander Family Bible (1742) and other family records; genealogical research of Gerald P. Mander FSA, Mark Weaver (late archivist at Wightwick Manor), John F. Osborne MBE and Monica Carolan (for early Manders), and others.

APPENDIX IV

Mander Family Chronology

1291	John Maundwer recorded as a villein with half a virgate of land in Tredington, co. Worcester.
1494/5	Marriage of John and Matilda Maunder of Armscote, Tredington.
1636	Henry Mander marries Anne Wheigham and settles at Aston Cantlow.
1675	Samuel Mander, son of Henry, marries Mary Shakespeare and settles at Ireland's Farm (formerly Lapworth Hall), Lapworth, Warwickshire.
1715	John Street property of the Clemson family with the old meeting house looted by rioters. A government commission assesses the damages.
1742	Thomas Mander, grandson of Samuel and Mary, marries Elizabeth Clemson and shortly after settles at her family house at 48 John's Street, Wolverhampton, as a baker and maltster.
1752	Birth of Benjamin Mander, eldest son and heir of Thomas Mander.
1753	Birth of John Mander, second son of Thomas.
1764	Death of Thomas Mander. His widow Elizabeth remarries Charles Hunter, a non-Conformist from Scotland.
1771	Benjamin Mander, aged 19, sets up as a baker.
1773	John Mander, aged 19, sets up as a chemist and druggist, with a chemical works in King Street.
1774	Death of Thomas Mander; his son Benjamin inherits 48 John Street.
1777	Benjamin Mander among the first Town Commissioners for borough.
1778	John Mander marries Esther Lea. John and Benjamin Mander jointly buy Cock Street property from William Tomlinson.
1779	Benjamin Mander marries Elizabeth Hanbury, of Kidderminster.
1780	Birth of Charles Mander, eldest son and heir of Benjamin Mander.
1781	Directory shows Benjamin Mander, aged 29, as 'baker, St John St.', and John Mander as the only chemist in Wolverhampton.
1785	Birth of Benjamin Parton Mander, second son of Benjamin Mander.
1790	William Bacon becomes partner of John Mander. John Mander buys Brickhouse property between Cock St. and John St.
1791	John Mander moves chemical works from King St. to Cock St. Benjamin Mander, baker, and Thomas Shepherd set up tinplate and japanning works. Benjamin defends his house with a drawn sword in the Church and the King riots.
1792	Mander & Shepherd advertise for tinmen. Directory lists John Mander as 'chemist, 34 & 35 Cock St.'
1794	Benjamin and John Mander among founders of Wolverhampton Library.
1795	Charles Mander apprenticed to his father, Benjamin, aged 15.
1799	William Cook becomes apprentice to Mander and Shepherd.
1800	John Mander buys more land next to Benjamin's in John St.
1802	Rate book shows 11 tinplate workers, including 'Mander—, 48 John St'.
1803	John Weaver joins firm of Bacon & Mander as a partner. Charles Mander begins trade of varnish making.
1805	Title deed describes Benjamin Mander as 'baker & japanner'. Joint mortgage by Benjamin and John Mander to John Best.
1812	Charles Mander marries Jemima Small, from Boston, Lincs. Benjamin Mander becomes chairman of the Union Flour Mill.

Mander Family Chronology

1814	Benjamin Mander and Committee of the Union Mill tried and acquitted for illegal combination at the Stafford assizes.
	Four Manders are Town Commissioners at the same time.
	John Mander begins his campaign against the slave trade.
1816	John Mander retires. Soon after, Charles Mander supplies carriage varnish to Queen Charlotte.
1816-39	Benjamin and Charles Mander's protracted chancery litigation for possession and endowments of the old chapel in John Street eventually leads to the Dissenters' Chapels Act of 1844.
1817	Charles Mander petitions Sidmouth to rescue two condemned men from the gallows and campaigns for the reform of the 'Blood Money' Act.
1818	William Bacon retires. Benjamin Parton Mander becomes partner in chemical works, trading as 'Mander, Weaver & Mander'.
	Charles Mander suspends payment, offering creditors 13*s.* in the pound.
1819	Benjamin Mander dies, aged 67, worth just £50.
	Charles Mander publishes pamphlet on the Old Meeting House.
	Charles Benjamin Mander, son of Charles Mander, born in Chapel Ash.
1820	John and Benjamin Parton Mander among subscribers to Wolverhampton Gas Light Company.
1822	Birth of Samuel Small Mander, second son of Charles Mander.
1827	John Mander dies, aged 73, worth £16,000, having established 'one of the largest chemical elaboratories in the kingdom'. Directory gives: 'Charles Mander, japanner & varnish maker, manufactory in John St.' and 'Mander, Weaver & Mander, wholesale chemists, Cock St.'
1830	Charles Mander repays his creditors' outstanding debts in full.
1833	Benjamin Parton Mander retires.
1834	Jemima Mander dies; Charles Mander later marries her sister, Elizabeth.
	Samuel Small Mander, aged 12, apprenticed to his father, Charles.
	William Wiley becomes partner of C. Mander to run japanning dept.
1835	Charles Mander dissolves partnership with William Wiley.
1838	Benjamin Parton Mander dies.
1840	Charles Mander sells his japanning business to William Shoolbred & Sons in order to concentrate on varnish making.
	Charles Benjamin Mander joins his father Charles in business, aged 21.
1845	Charles Benjamin Mander and Samuel Small Mander form the partnership of 'Mander Brothers'. Charles Mander retires.
1848	Shoolbred, Loveridge & Shoolbred move the japanning works they acquired from Charles Mander in 1840 from John Street to their new Merridale Road works.
1849	John Weaver dies; succeeded at Mander, Weaver & Co. by son Frederick.
1852	Birth of Charles Tertius Mander. CBM helps found first School of Art.
1853	Death of Charles Mander in Croydon, aged 73.
1861	Mander Brothers open their first London branch at 363 Oxford St.
1862	Charles Benjamin Mander purchases The Mount, Tettenhall Wood, which remains the family house until 1952.
1864	Mander Brothers open department for paint and colour manufacture.
1873	Mander Brothers acquire premises of Mander, Weaver & Co.
1875	Henry Harper appointed senior partner. CBM retires.
1878	Death of Charles Benjamin Mander, aged 59.

1879 Entrance of Charles T. Mander and S. Theodore Mander into the firm.
1880 Printing ink department opened. 1894 New works in Well Lane.
1882 Birth of Geoffrey Le Mesurier Mander.
1884 Birth of Charles Arthur Mander at Newbridge.
1889-93 Theodore Mander builds Wightwick Manor to designs of Liverpool architect, Edward Ould.
1892-6 Charles Tertius Mander four times mayor of Wolverhampton.
1900 Theodore Mander dies in office as mayor of Wolverhampton.
1903 Charles Tertius Mander serves as High Sheriff of Staffordshire, the first Mander to so serve. Centenary of the business is celebrated.
1909 Charles Tertius Mander extends The Mount to the designs of Ed. Ould.
1910 George V awards Warrant as 'Manufacturers of Varnishes and Colours'.
1911 Baronetcy granted to Charles Tertius Mander in Coronation Honours.
1917 Charles Arthur Mander wounded at Beersheba with the Staffs Yeomanry.
1919 Lloyd George announces 'coupon' election while guest at The Mount.
1921 Birth of Charles Marcus Mander at Kilsall Hall.
1924 Mander Brothers incorporated as a private limited company.
1926 Heath Town works acquired.
1929 Death of Charles T. Mander, first chairman and first baronet, aged 76. Geoffrey Mander MP (Liberal) for Wolverhampton East (to 1945).
1932 40-hour week introduced in an historic agreement with Ernest Bevin.
1933 and 1937 Sir Charles Arthur Mander mayor of Wolverhampton.
1937 Geoffrey Mander donates Wightwick Manor to the National Trust. Mander Bros Ltd. formed as a public company: 'Manders Holdings Ltd'.
1943 Charles M. Mander wounded Monte Camino with Coldstream Guards.
1945 Geoffrey Le Mesurier Mander loses his seat in Labour landslide election and declares his support for the Labour Party. Awarded K.B.
1946 Charles Marcus Mander joins Mander Bros.
1950 Birth of Charles Nicholas (Sixtus) Mander.
1950-1 Deaths of Vivian Mander, Charles Arthur Mander, Gerald Poynton Mander and Mary le Mesurier Mander (aged 92).
1952 Sale of The Mount, contents, and part of estate.
1955 Publication of *A History of Mander Brothers* by Geoffrey Mander.
1962 Death of Sir Geoffrey Le Mesurier Mander.
1963 Charles Marcus Mander High Sheriff of Staffordshire.
1964-73 Development of the Mander Centre, Wolverhampton, 4.5 acres on the historic family property (opened 1968).
1972 Development of family's Perton and Wrottesley estates by Charles Marcus Mander for housing, known as 'Perton Village'. Death of Philip Mander, aged 56, in office as the last family chairman of Manders Holdings Ltd.
1975 Birth of Charles Marcus Septimus Mander, the first of the fifteenth generation from John and Margery Mander of Tredington.
1994 The Mander Centre and the decorative paints division are sold. Premier Inks of the Netherlands is acquired and the Company starts trading under the 'Manders Premier' brand.
1998 Manders PLC bought by Flint Ink Corporation of Detroit, USA.

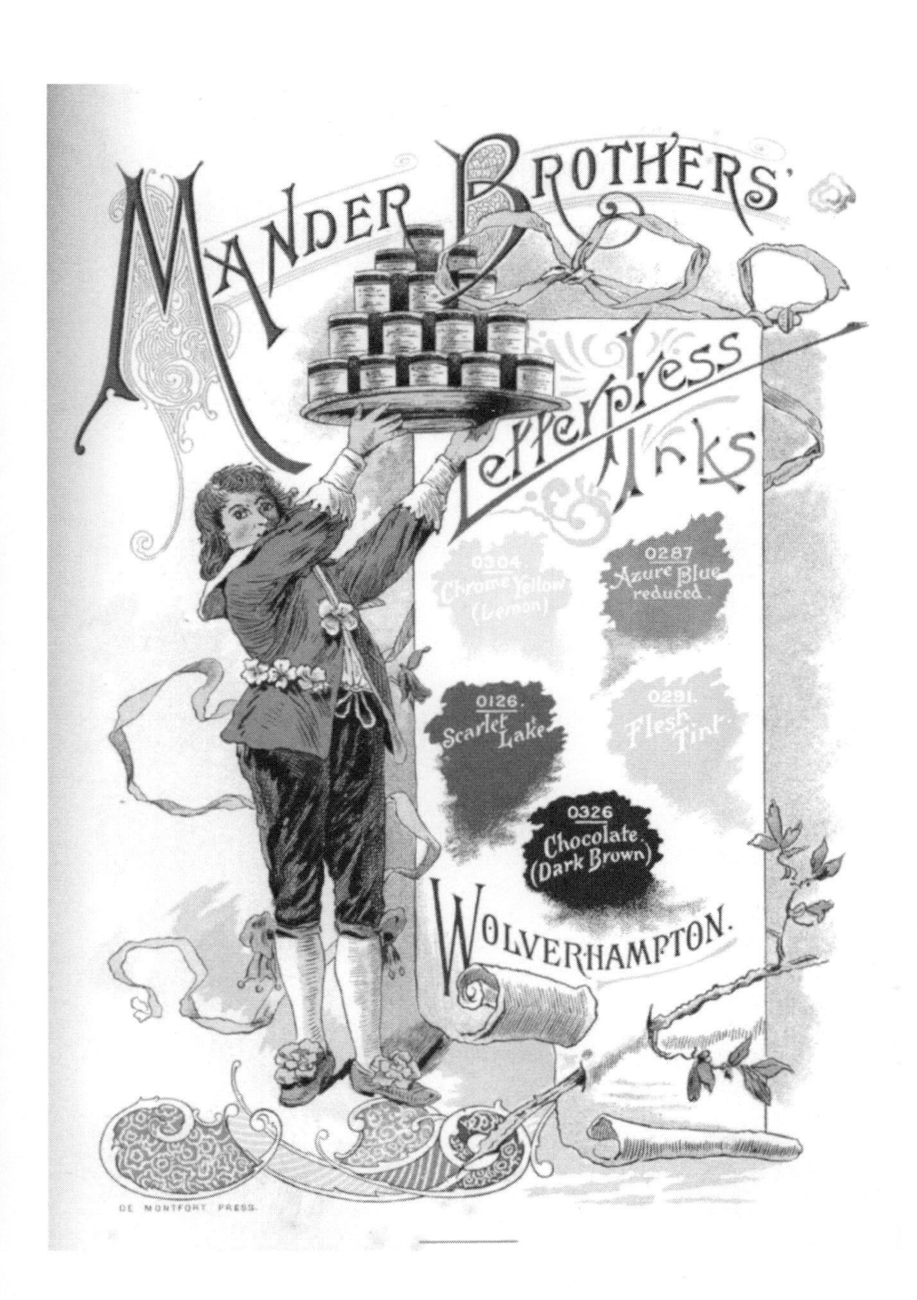
Mander Brothers'
Letterpress Inks
0304. Chrome Yellow (Lemon)
0287 Azure Blue reduced.
0126. Scarlet Lake
0291. Flesh Tint.
0326 Chocolate. (Dark Brown)
Wolverhampton.
De Montfort Press.

ESTABLISHED IN 1803 BY CHARLES MANDER.
HONI SOIT QUI MAL Y PENSE.
MANUFACTURER TO HER MAJESTY
THE LATE QUEEN CHARLOTTE.

FINIS